Unserem geliebten Groß-Glienicke herzlichst zugeeignet
Hermann Krome, Hans Pflanzer, Will Meisel u. Georg von Wysocki.

Groß-Glienicke
du meine alte Liebe
Lied

Musik:
Hermann Krome
Worte:
Hans Pflanzer

EDITION MEISEL u. CO G·M·B·H

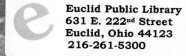

THE HOUSE BY THE LAKE

Also by Thomas Harding

Hanns and Rudolf
Kadian Journal

THE HOUSE BY THE LAKE

One House, Five Families, and a
Hundred Years of German History

Thomas Harding

Picador / New York

picadorusa.com • picadorbookroom.tumblr.com
twitter.com/picadorusa • facebook.com/picadorusa

Picador® is a U.S. registered trademark and is used by St. Martin's Press under license from Pan Books Limited.

For book club information, please visit facebook.com/picadorbookclub or e-mail marketing@picadorusa.com.

"Berlin is Still Berlin." Music: Will Meisel. Lyrics: Bruno Balz © 1949 by Edition Meisel GmbH

"Groß Glienicke, du meine alte Liebe." Music: Hermann Krome Lyrics: Hans Pflanzer © 1951 by Edition Meisel GmbH

Library of Congress Cataloging-in-Publication Data

Names: Harding, Thomas, 1968– author.
Title: The house by the lake : one house, five families, and a hundred years of German history / Thomas Harding.
Description: First U.S. edition. | New York : Picador, [2016] | Includes bibliographical references and index.
Identifiers: LCCN 2015044339 | ISBN 9781250065063 (hardcover) | ISBN 9781250065087 (e-book)
Subjects: LCSH: Harding, Thomas, 1968– —Family. | Potsdam (Germany)—History, Local. | Historic houses—Germany—Potsdam Region. | Alexander family. | Meisel family. | Jews—Germany—Potsdam—Biography. | Vacation houses—Germany—Berlin Suburban Area. | Historic houses—Germany—Berlin Suburban Area. | Potsdam (Germany)—Buildings, structures, etc.—History. | Potsdam (Germany)—Biography.
Classification: LCC DD901.P8 H37 2016 | DDC 943'.1546—dc23
LC record available at http://lccn.loc.gov/2015044339

Our books may be purchased in bulk for promotional, educational, or business use. Please contact your local bookseller or the Macmillan Corporate and Premium Sales Department at 1-800-221-7945, extension 5442, or by e-mail at MacmillanSpecialMarkets@macmillan.com.

Originally published in Great Britain by William Heinemann, a part of the Penguin Random House group of companies

First U.S. Edition: July 2016

10   9   8   7   6   5   4   3   2   1

For Elsie

CONTENTS

CONTENTS

LIST OF ILLUSTRATIONS

LIST OF ILLUSTRATIONS

LIST OF ILLUSTRATIONS

FAMILY TREES

WOLLANK

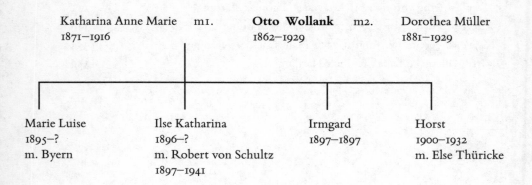

Katharina Anne Marie   m1.   **Otto Wollank**   m2.   Dorothea Müller
1871–1916   1862–1929   1881–1929

Marie Luise   Ilse Katharina   Irmgard   Horst
1895–?   1896–?   1897–1897   1900–1932
m. Byern   m. Robert von Schultz   m. Else Thüricke
           1897–1941

ALEXANDER

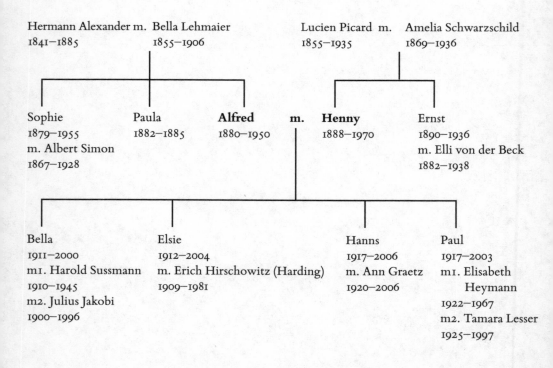

Hermann Alexander m.   Bella Lehmaier   Lucien Picard   m.   Amelia Schwarzschild
1841–1885   1855–1906   1855–1935   1869–1936

Sophie   Paula   **Alfred**   **m.**   **Henny**   Ernst
1879–1955   1882–1885   1880–1950   1888–1970   1890–1936
m. Albert Simon   m. Elli von der Beck
1867–1928   1882–1938

Bella   Elsie   Hanns   Paul
1911–2000   1912–2004   1917–2006   1917–2003
m1. Harold Sussmann   m. Erich Hirschowitz (Harding)   m. Ann Graetz   m1. Elisabeth
1910–1945   1909–1981   1920–2006   Heymann
m2. Julius Jakobi   1922–1967
1900–1996   m2. Tamara Lesser
                                             1925–1997

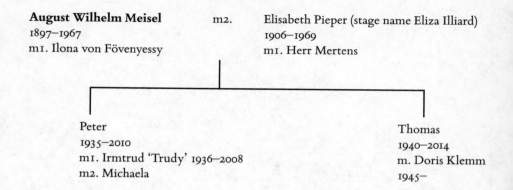

MEISEL

August Wilhelm Meisel
1897–1967
m1. Ilona von Fövenyessy

m2.

Elisabeth Pieper (stage name Eliza Illiard)
1906–1969
m1. Herr Mertens

Peter
1935–2010
m1. Irmtrud 'Trudy' 1936–2008
m2. Michaela

Thomas
1940–2014
m. Doris Klemm
1945–

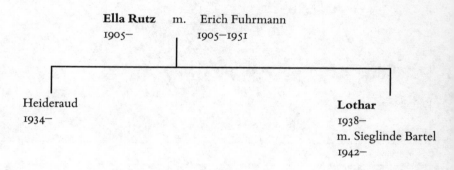

FUHRMANN

Ella Rutz   m.   Erich Fuhrmann
1905–   1905–1951

Heideraud
1934–

Lothar
1938–
m. Sieglinde Bartel
1942–

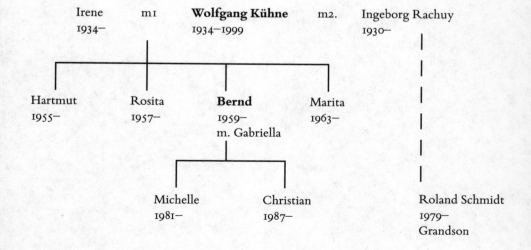

KÜHNE

Irene   m1   **Wolfgang Kühne**   m2   Ingeborg Rachuy
1934–   1934–1999   1930–

Hartmut   Rosita   **Bernd**   Marita
1955–   1957–   1959–   1963–
                         m. Gabriella

Michelle   Christian
1981–   1987–

Roland Schmidt
1979–
Grandson

GERMANY

SWEDEN

DENMARK

SWEDEN

Baltic Sea

N

North Sea

• Rügen

• Hamburg

Sachsenhausen •
• Berlin
Groß Glienicke •
• Potsdam

POLAND

GERMANY

Dortmund •
Essen •
• Hagen
• Düsseldorf
Cologne •

BELGIUM
• Brussells

Weimar •

• Leipzig

Dresden •

Tanna •
• Chemnitz

Theresienstadt •

• Prague

Auschwitz •

• Frankfurt

CZECH REPUBLIC

LUXEMBOURG

• Heidelberg

• Ketschendorf

• Nuremberg

Paris •

SLOVAKIA

FRANCE

• Stuttgart

Müllheim •

• Munich

Vienna •

AUSTRIA

HUNGARY

Basel •

LIECHTENSTEIN

0	50	100 mi
0	100	200 km

SWITZERLAND

ITALY

GERMANY 1945

French
British
Soviet
American

North Sea

Bremerhaven (US) •

• Bremen (US)

BRITISH ZONE

POLISH ADMINISTRATION

NETHERLANDS

Berlin •
Groß
Glienicke •

SOVIET ZONE

G E R M A N Y

CZECHO-
SLOVAKIA

FRENCH

LUX.

SAARLAND

AMERICAN ZONE

FRANCE

ZONE

AUSTRIA

LIECHT.

SWITZERLAND

ITALY

GERMANY 1949

East
Berlin

West
Berlin

North Sea

NETHERLANDS

POLAND

Berlin •
Groß
Glienicke •

WEST

D D R
(EAST
GERMANY)

GERMANY

CZECHO-
SLOVAKIA

LUX.

SAARLAND

FRANCE

AUSTRIA

LIECHT.

SWITZERLAND

ITALY

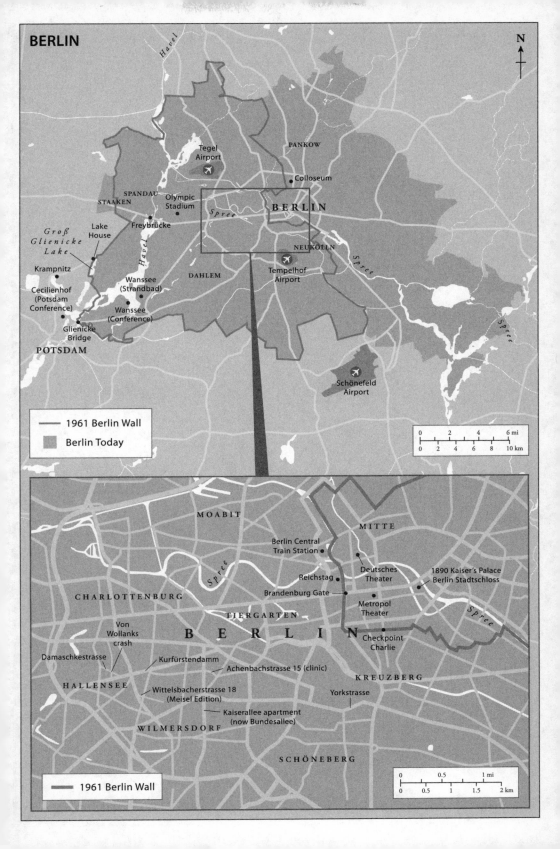

BERLIN

N

- —— 1961 Berlin Wall
- ▪ Berlin Today

Havel

Spree

Tegel
Airport

PANKOW

Colloseum

SPANDAU
STAAKEN

Olympic
Stadium

BERLIN

Freybrücke

Spree

*Groß
Glienicke
Lake*

Lake
House

NEUKÖLLN

Krampnitz

Havel

DAHLEM

Tempelhof
Airport

Spree

Cecilienhof
(Potsdam
Conference)

Wannsee
(Strandbad)

Wannsee
(Conference)

Glienicke
Bridge

Schönefeld
Airport

POTSDAM

| 0 | 2 | 4 | 6 mi |
| 0 | 2 | 4 | 6 | 8 | 10 km |

MOABIT

MITTE

Spree

Berlin Central
Train Station

CHARLOTTENBURG

Reichstag

Deutsches
Theater

1890 Kaiser's Palace
Berlin Stadtschloss

TIERGARTEN

Brandenburg Gate

Metropol
Theater

Spree

Von
Wollanks
crash

B E R L I N

Checkpoint
Charlie

Damaschkestrasse

Kurfürstendamm

Achenbachstrasse 15 (clinic)

KREUZBERG

HALLENSEE

Wittelsbacherstrasse 18
(Meisel Edition)

Yorkstrasse

Kaiserallee apartment
(now Bundesallee)

WILMERSDORF

SCHÖNEBERG

- —— 1961 Berlin Wall

| 0 | 0.5 | 1 mi |
| 0 | 0.5 | 1 | 1.5 | 2 km |

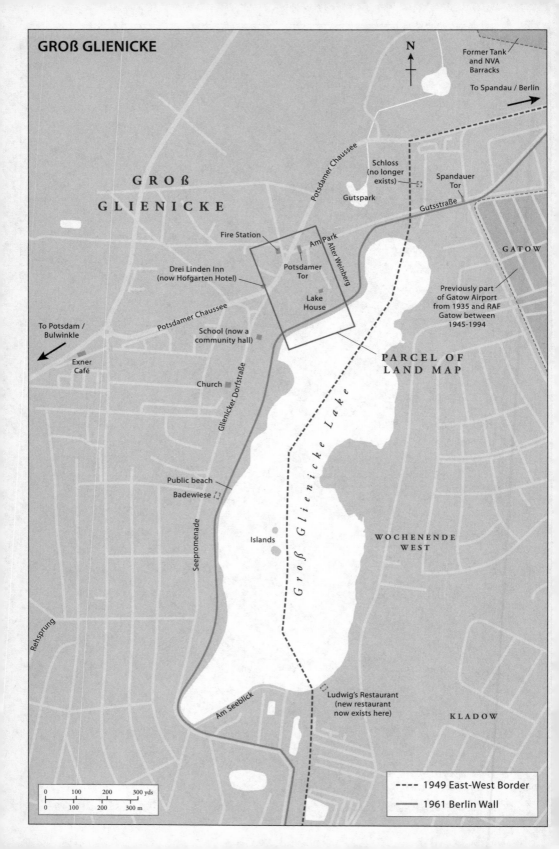

GROß GLIENICKE

N

Former Tank
and NVA
Barracks

To Spandau / Berlin

Potsdamer Chaussee

G R O ß
G L I E N I C K E

Schloss
(no longer
exists)

Gutspark

Spandauer
Tor

Gutsstraße

GATOW

Fire Station

Am Park

Alter Weinberg

Drei Linden Inn
(now Hofgarten Hotel)

Potsdamer
Tor

Previously part
of Gatow Airport
from 1935 and RAF
Gatow between
1945-1994

Lake
House

Potsdamer Chaussee

To Potsdam /
Bulwinkle

School (now a
community hall)

PARCEL OF
LAND MAP

Exner
Café

Church

Glienicker Dorfstraße

Groß Glienicke Lake

Public beach

Badewiese

Seepromenade

Islands

WOCHENENDE
WEST

Rehsprung

Am Seeblick

Ludwig's Restaurant
(new restaurant
now exists here)

KLADOW

| 0 | 100 | 200 | 300 yds |
| 0 | 100 | 200 | 300 m |

- - - 1949 East-West Border

——— 1961 Berlin Wall

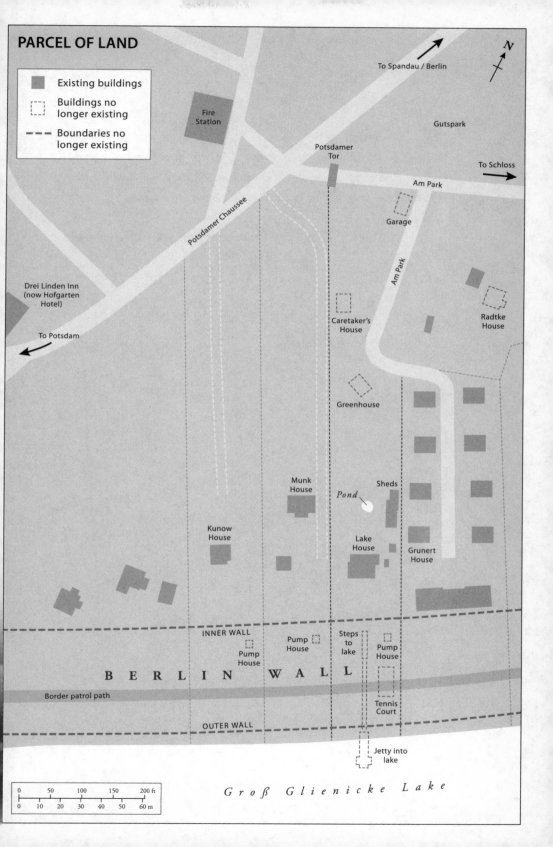

PARCEL OF LAND

Legend:
- Existing buildings
- Buildings no longer existing
- Boundaries no longer existing

To Spandau / Berlin

N

Gutspark

Fire Station

Potsdamer Tor

Am Park

To Schloss

Garage

Am Park

Potsdamer Chaussee

Caretaker's House

Radtke House

Drei Linden Inn (now Hofgarten Hotel)

Greenhouse

To Potsdam

Munk House

Pond

Sheds

Kunow House

Lake House

Grunert House

INNER WALL

Pump House

Pump House

Steps to lake

Pump House

B E R L I N   W A L L

Border patrol path

Tennis Court

OUTER WALL

Jetty into lake

Groß Glienicke Lake

0	50	100	150	200 ft
0	10 20 30 40 50	60 m		

In the sand of Brandenburg the springs of life have flowed and still flow everywhere, and every square foot of ground has its story and is telling it, too — but one has to be willing to listen to these often quiet voices.

Theodor Fontane, 18 January 1864

AUTHOR'S NOTE

To tell the story of the house by the lake, I have relied primarily on the accounts of *Zeitzeugen*, or time witnesses – people with a knowledge of the house and its history, as well as *Augenzeugen*, or eyewitnesses – those who personally experienced the events described. Every effort has been made to corroborate and confirm each statement.

Throughout I have used the place names and spellings that would be most familiar to an English-speaking audience. This is, however, a story of Germany, and so I have made a few important exceptions to this rule – most notably 'DDR' and not the anglicised 'GDR' to describe East Germany, and 'Groß Glienicke' rather than 'Gross Glienicke' to describe the village at the heart of the book.

PROLOGUE

In July 2013, I travelled from London to Berlin to visit the weekend house my great-grandfather had built.

Picking up a rental car at Schönefeld Airport on the city's southern edge, I set off round the ring road, taking an exit next to a radio mast that looked a little like the Eiffel Tower. I continued on, past signs pointing towards the old Olympic stadium and the suburb of Spandau, and then left by a sprawling petrol station, and into the countryside. My route took me through a thick birch forest. Occasionally the trees broke to reveal flat, open farmland. Somewhere to my left I knew the River Havel flowed parallel to the road, but it was hidden behind the trees. It had been twenty years since I had last visited this place and nothing looked familiar.

Fifteen minutes later, I turned right at a traffic light and saw a sign welcoming me to the village of Groß Glienicke. A few metres beyond, another sign marked what had once been a border crossing between West Berlin and East Germany. I slowed to a crawl. Half a kilometre further, I spotted the landmark I had been looking for, the Potsdamer Tor, a cream-coloured stone arch standing opposite a small fire station. I drove under the arch, and parked.

From here I wasn't sure where to go. I didn't have a map of the area, and there was nobody around to ask for help. I locked the car door, and walked a few paces down a narrow lane, overgrown with weeds and brambles, until I saw a green street sign for Am Park. Was this it? Hadn't the lane been sandy? I vaguely remembered a vegetable patch and a kennel, a neatly ordered garden and tidy flower beds. Fifty metres on, the lane suddenly stopped at a wide metal gate marked 'Private'. Although wary of trespassing, I ducked under a strand of barbed wire and pushed my way through a field of shoulder-high grass, heading in the direction of what I guessed was the lake.

To my left stood a row of modern brick houses. To my right stretched an unkempt hedge. And then, there it was, my family's house. It was smaller than I remembered, not much larger than a sports pavilion or double garage, hidden by bushes, vines and trees. Its windows were patched with plywood. The almost flat black roof was cracked and covered with fallen branches. The brick chimneys seemed to be crumbling, close to collapse.

The lake house, July 2013

I picked my way round it slowly, touching flaking paintwork and boarded-up doorways, until I found a broken window. Climbing through, my way illuminated by my iPhone, I was confronted by mounds of dirty clothes and soiled cushions, walls covered in graffiti and crawling with mould, smashed appliances and fragments of furniture, rotting floorboards and empty beer bottles. One room looked as if it had been used as a drug den, littered with broken lighters and soot-stained spoons. There was a sadness to the place, the melancholy of a building abandoned.

After a few minutes, I clambered back out of the window and walked towards the house next door, hoping to find someone to speak with. I was lucky, for a woman was working in the garden. I hesitantly introduced myself in broken German, and she responded in English. I explained that I was a member of a family who used to live at the house. Did she know, I asked, what had happened to it? Who owned it now? 'It has been empty for over a decade,' she told me and then pointed towards the shore. 'The Berlin Wall was built there, between the house and the lake,' she said. 'It's seen a lot, but it's an eyesore now.' Confusingly, I appeared to be the focus of her anger. I only nodded, staring back to the house.

I had been told about the lake house, or 'Glienicke', all my life. It had been an obsession for my grandmother, Elsie, who spoke about it with wonder, evoking a time when life had been easy, fun and simple. It had been, she said, her soul place.

My family, the Alexanders, had flourished in the liberal years of 1920s Berlin. Affluent, cosmopolitan Jews, theirs had been the values of Germany: they worked hard and enjoyed themselves, attending the latest exhibitions, plays, concerts, and taking long walks in the surrounding countryside. As soon as they could afford it, they had built themselves a little wooden lake house, a symbol of their success. They had spent every summer at Glienicke, enjoying a rustic, simple life, gardening, swimming in the lake, hosting parties on the terrace. In my mind, I kept an image of the house, compiled from the sepia-tinted photographs I had been shown since childhood: a glistening lake, a wood-panelled room with a fireplace and rocking chair, a manicured lawn, a tennis court.

But with the rise of the Nazis, they had been forced to flee, moving to London where they had struggled to establish a new life. They had escaped when so many had not, but they left with next to nothing. In my family, this was Glienicke's story: a place once cherished, then stolen, located in a country now reviled.

For as long as I can remember, my family had eschewed all things German. We didn't purchase German cars, washing machines or fridges. We holidayed across Europe – in France, Switzerland, Spain, Italy – but never in Germany. I learned Spanish and French at school, even Latin, anything but German. The elder generation – my grandmother and grandfather, my great-uncles and -aunts – did not speak of their life in Berlin, of the years before the war. It was a closed chapter. Any emotional connection to their lives in the 1920s had been severed. Reluctant to explore the past, they chose instead to focus on their new country, becoming more British than the British, sending their children to the best schools, encouraging them to become doctors, lawyers and accountants.

As I became older, I realised that our relationship with Germany was not as black and white as I had been led to believe. My grandfather refused to speak another word of German from the day he arrived in England, but my grandmother kept up her German, regularly chaperoning coachloads of German tourists around the country, pointedly eulogising Shakespeare, the Magna Carta, and what she called 'British fair play'. From her memories, her comments, jokes occasionally, I caught traces of a life now lost.

It was in 1993, four years after the fall of the Berlin Wall, that I had last seen the house. I was twenty-five years old, on a weekend trip to Germany with Elsie and my cousins. She was ready, at last, to show us her childhood city. For us, the younger generation, it was a fun family excursion, a walk down memory lane with our grandmother. It was only on the aeroplane to Berlin that I began to see what the trip really meant – what this other life was. Halfway through the flight, my grandmother walked down the aisle and sat on my armrest. 'Darling,' she said in her thick German accent, 'I want you to see this,' and handed me a brown envelope. Inside were two olive-green Nazi-era passports belonging to her husband and father-in-law, and a piece of yellow fabric emblazoned with a black J. I knew that the Nazis had forced the Jews to wear such marks. The message was clear: this is my history, and this is your history. Do not forget.

And I didn't forget. Upon returning to London, I began asking questions, seeking information about our family's past, and why it had been so carefully covered up. It was an interest that never abated. Which is why, two decades later, I had booked a flight to Berlin and was now back at the house, to find out what had happened to my grandmother's 'soul place'.

The next day, I drove from Groß Glienicke to the local government offices in Potsdam, twenty minutes south of the village. There, in the basement of the courthouse, I found an information desk staffed by an elderly woman busy at her computer. Pulling out my phrase book, I haltingly asked for a copy of the house's official land records. The woman informed me that I needed permission from the property owner to view the documents. When I explained that my great-grandfather had died in 1950 she only shrugged. I attempted to plead, and after I had produced my passport and credit cards, and sketched out a rough family tree, the woman finally relented and disappeared into a back room. Eventually she reappeared with a sheaf of papers. Jabbing her finger at the top page, she explained that the house and the land on which it stood were now owned by the city of Potsdam. I asked what that meant – what was to become of the house? She turned back to her computer, typed in the lot and parcel number, then swivelled the monitor to face me. '*Es wird abgerissen*,' she said. It will be demolished. After a twenty-year absence, it looked like I had returned just in time to see the house be torn down.

Leaving her office, I looked at the list of government departments hanging on the lobby wall. One caught my eye: Einsichtnahme in historische Bauakten und Baupläne. I knew enough German to understand that *Bau* meant building and *historische* had something to do with history. I headed upstairs, entered a long corridor filled with similar-looking white doors, chose one and knocked. Inside, I found two architectural preservationists, a tall, thin woman in her forties, and a short, bearded man of the same age. Asking first if they spoke English, I told them the little I knew about the house, and the city's plans to tear it down. Despite my sudden appearance, and my garbled explanation, they were polite and eager to help. The man grabbed a statute book from the shelf and leafed through the pages until he found the section that he was looking for. The 'Castle Clause', he said, holding the book out to me. If I didn't want the house to be knocked down, he continued, I would have to prove that it was culturally and historically significant.

Before I left Berlin, I returned to the house. Could it really be saved? I wondered. It would be an enormous task, not to say expensive. I spotted new details – broken shutters on the ground, rusted gutters, trees growing through its brick terrace. I lived hundreds of miles away, and spoke little German. My life was busy enough. I had no time to take on another project and, in any case, it looked like I might be too late.

But more than this, should it be saved? Standing before me it seemed so unimpressive, a fragment from some half-forgotten memory. It was nothing really, barely more than a shell. Yet, there was something about the house, something intangible, something compelling. Most of all, it had been the focus of my grandmother's attention for as long as I had known her. It had meant a huge amount to her, and she had made clear that it should mean a lot to us, her grandchildren, too. It would have been so easy to walk away.

This is the story of a wooden house built on the shore of a lake near Berlin. A story of nine rooms, a small garage, a long lawn and a vegetable patch. It is a story of how it came to be, how it was transformed by its inhabitants, and how it transformed them in turn.

It is the story of a building that was loved and lost by five families. A story of the everyday moments that make a house a home – of morning chores, family meals around the kitchen table, summer-afternoon snoozes and gossip over coffee and cake. It is a story of domestic triumphs and tragedies – of weddings and births, secret trysts and betrayals, illnesses, intimidation and murder.

It is also the story of Germany over a turbulent century. A story of a building that withstood the seismic changes that shook the world. For, in its own quiet and forgotten way, the house was on the front line of history – the lives of its inhabitants ripped up and remade again and again, simply because of where they lived.

Above all, it is a story of survival, one that has been pieced together from archival material and building plans, recently declassified documents, letters, diaries, photographs, and conversations with historians, architects, botanists, police chiefs and politicians, villagers, neighbours and, most importantly, its occupants.

This is the story of the house by the lake.

PART I

GLIENICKE

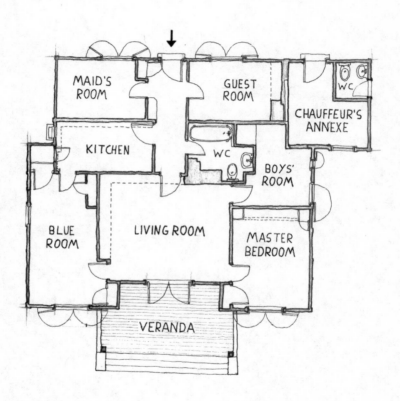

MAID'S ROOM

GUEST ROOM

WC

CHAUFFEUR'S ANNEXE

KITCHEN

WC

BOYS' ROOM

BLUE ROOM

LIVING ROOM

MASTER BEDROOM

VERANDA

I

WOLLANK
1890

Sitting astride his horse, Otto Wollank made his way slowly through a narrow avenue of ripening vines, towards a lake, shimmering in the early-morning light. The way was sandy and treacherous, he had to be careful that his mare did not slip on one of the many stones, or brush up against the gnarly, twisted branches that marked his path. But there was no rush, for Otto was in a contemplative mood, considering whether he should acquire the estate through which he rode.

Of average height, and with a round chin and unimposing physique, the twenty-seven-year-old would have made scant impression, were it not for the enormous moustache which he sported below a white fedora, tilted gamely to one side.

From a bluff at the vineyard's edge, he looked out at the land around him. At the estate's centre lay the beautiful Groß Glienicke Lake. Two and a half kilometres long and five hundred metres wide, the lake was large enough to sail a dinghy, but smaller than most of the other waterways which dotted the Brandenburg countryside. There was good fishing here, Otto had been told: one could catch carp and eel, or – with some skill – a pike, up to one and a half metres in length, which swam through the lake's deepest sections.

Otto Wollank

To the east and west of the lake a thick forest hugged the shore: a mixture of black alder, towering trees, with thin dark trunks, whose green triangular crowns blotted out the sky, and willows, whose branches reached out over the lake's edge. Below, growing in the sandy soil, spread a sweet-smelling blanket of ground elder, lilac and irises. In the lake's shallows, tall grasses swayed, alternating with a patchwork of lilies from whose pads pink, white and yellow flowers erupted.

To the north of the lake lay marsh, and then an ancient woodland filled with oak and Scots pine. These woods contained a rich variety of wildlife – deer, wild boar and red fox – each an attractive target to a hunter. Beyond these woods, to the west, stretched out the Döberitzer Heide, a wide-open heath that had been used by Prussian soldiers as a training ground for over a hundred years.

The lake's margins went undeveloped, without a single house, jetty or dock along its shore. Unsurprisingly, the area was a haven for birds: giant white cranes, who passed through from Siberia and Scandinavia on their way to Spain; bitterns with their loud calls booming out from the dense reeds; swans swimming in pairs on the water; and woodpeckers, drilling the trees nearby.

Advertised as one of the largest parcels in the state of Brandenburg, the estate contained some of its prettiest and most productive land. And while decidedly rural in nature, it was only a morning's ride to two major cities, Berlin and Potsdam. The property itself had many names. To some, it was known as the 'Ribbeck Estate' after the renowned Ribbeck family who had owned it from 1572 to 1788. But the Ribbecks had not lived at the property for more than a century and, it having changed hands so many times since, most of the locals now called it the 'Groß Glienicke Nobleman's Estate', or more simply the 'estate'. For the past sixty years the land had been owned by the Landefeldts, a local family with farming in their blood. But after years of mismanagement and falling profits they had been forced to sell.

On offer was four thousand *Morgen* of land, a *Morgen* being equal to that area which one man and one ox might till in a morning, roughly equivalent to two-thirds of an acre. In all, the estate was two and a half kilometres long and four kilometres wide. In addition, the sale included an array of farm buildings, plus the cattle, pigs, goats, geese and horses that populated the fields and barns, the farm machinery, and that year's harvest.

Otto turned his horse round and retraced his steps back towards the village of Groß Glienicke, on the northern end of the western shore. It was an ancient settlement, one of the oldest in the region, dating back to 1267, and an insular place, populated by families who had lived here for generations, who knew each other's business, who feared strangers. With the exception of one Catholic couple, all of Glienicke's three hundred or so villagers were Protestant. The little stone houses were built along the Dorfstraße, or village street, a road that ran along the lake's western side, constructed a hundred metres from the water's edge. There was a grocery and a baker's, a small stone-faced school, and a windmill. At the village's centre was the Drei Linden Gasthof, a two-storey inn that for centuries had served as a local watering hole, and which was fronted by three lime trees. In Germany, as in other European countries, the lime was a sacred tree, whose presence protected against ill luck.

At the lake's northern tip, two hundred metres from the lake shore, stood the schloss, or manor house. Three storeys high, the schloss was built of white brick, with a shallow-pitched roof and tower, and contained more than twenty bedrooms and sixteen fireplaces. Inside, the living and dining rooms had floors of wide oak planks, the stairs rose in steps of polished marble and the walls were covered with the finest plaster. Its front hallway ceilings were adorned with colourful frescos: one showed a scantily clothed man firing an arrow at a flock of flying cranes; another depicted a bare-breasted woman looking coyly aside, as angels showered her with petals and serenaded her with a golden harp.

As he continued on around the estate, Otto saw the workers busy with their labours. White-scarfed women, in clogs and long grey dresses, pulled large square-shaped tins from the oven, providing endless loaves of bread for the village. A line of labourers knelt in a wide muddy field next to round-bottomed wooden baskets, placing small potatoes in long rutted rows. Grey-capped men, in shirts and vests, walked behind horses, encouraging their charges with long whips, as they ploughed one of the many fields. Meanwhile, others bound giant bushels of wheat with twine, the windmill behind them, its four sails beating the air. Each of their faces appeared old, weather-beaten, unsmiling.

This land appealed to Otto. It was a gentle place, full of potential, yet uncrowded, unhurried and steeped in tradition.

Groß Glienicke lay fifteen kilometres west of Berlin's city boundary. While life had changed little for this small Brandenburg village, the same could not be said of Berlin, for, by 1890, it had established itself as the most important city in Germany.

Nineteen years earlier, Berlin had been declared the capital of a new German empire. Until that time, Germany had been a fragmented country, without an effective central economic, military or political structure. Since 1871, Germany and its twenty-five kingdoms, principalities, grand duchies and cities, had been joined together as a single empire, overseen by Kaiser Wilhelm I.

It was also in 1871 that Berlin had been chosen to host the empire's Reichstag, or parliament. The members of this Reichstag were directly elected by men over the age of twenty-five and it was led by a chancellor appointed by the Kaiser. As the seat of government, the city attracted powerful interests, supported by legions of professionals, each with their own retinues, families and domestic staff. Then there was the military, with its influential officer class, whose presence was felt everywhere in Berlin. Almost every day a troop of soldiers was seen parading or marching through the city streets. Military uniforms were worn both on and off duty, and they had become a statement both of fashion and social standing. With barracks located in Berlin and the nearby city of Potsdam, tens of thousands of soldiers lived in or around the city.

Meanwhile, Berlin had established itself as one of Europe's centres of intellectual and cultural excellence. Its Friedrich Wilhelm University boasted an impressive list of former students and academics, including Arthur Schopenhauer, Georg Hegel, Karl Marx and Friedrich Engels. Similarly, Berlin's Kaiser Friedrich Museum was one of Europe's finest, exhibiting extraordinary Byzantine and Egyptian antiquities, as well as paintings from the masters: Raphael and Giotto, Rembrandt and Holbein.

In 1888, Kaiser Wilhelm was succeeded by his son, Friedrich III, who died of cancer of the larynx after ruling for only ninety-nine days. Friedrich's son Wilhelm II then took the throne, aged only twenty-nine. Since that time, Wilhelm II had ruled from an enormous white-stoned baroque palace on the banks of Berlin's River Spree. Forming the hub of royal patronage and command, the palace was serviced by thousands of courtiers and bureaucrats, accountants and engineers, artists and bankers.

Following these momentous changes, the imperial city was transformed in a few short years from a sleepy provincial town into one of Europe's leading metropolises. Attracted by the rapidly expanding economy, and the opportunities that it provided, a rush of newcomers entered the city. Berlin's population doubled, from 800,000 in 1871, to over 1.6 million by 1890.

As part of this expansion, large tracts of land on the city outskirts were developed. The vast majority of these new buildings were apartment blocks, often hastily and inexpensively built, and before long, two-thirds of the city's residents were tenants. Many of the developers came from the middle classes, and were soon amassing vast fortunes. One of these developers was Otto Wollank.

★

Born on 18 September 1862, in Pankow, a northern suburb of Berlin, Otto was the eldest son of five children. Tragedy struck early when his thirty-four-year-old father, Adolf Friedrich Wollank, died when Otto was only five years old. Luckily for the family, Adolf left a large inheritance, having purchased hundreds of acres of land in Pankow during the middle of the nineteenth century, before Berlin's massive population explosion, when prices were still cheap.

After graduating from school in 1881, Otto enrolled in agricultural college in Berlin, undertaking work experience on various farms in northern Germany. He also travelled to France, Italy, North Africa, Greece and Turkey during this period. At the age of twenty, Otto began his military service, enlisting with the 2nd Dragoon Guards regiment, with whom he perfected his riding skills and practised basic military techniques. He then joined the Danzig Death's Head hussars, known to include some of Germany's best horsemen and to produce military advisers to Kaiser Wilhelm.

After leaving the cavalry, Otto took over his father's property business, growing it rapidly over the next few years. It was relatively easy to make money. All Otto had to do was find willing buyers, a simple matter given the city's shortage of new homes. Within a short while, he was turning a massive profit. The question was: how to invest it?

Otto was an ambitious man. He wished to progress beyond his father's status as a tradesman. During his time as an officer in the army, and while selling property in Berlin, Otto had learned that the corridors of power were controlled by the aristocracy. No matter how much wealth was accumulated, it was close to impossible to find political favour unless one was a member of the nobility. To fix this problem, he would have to purchase a rural estate, with the hope that this would make him suitable to marry into a noble family. Which is why Otto Wollank had ended up surveying the estate in Groß Glienicke.

On 18 February 1890, apparently satisfied by what he found, Otto Wollank made an offer to purchase the estate, which was accepted. So it was that four days later, on 22 February, the landowner, Johann Landefeldt, and the purchaser, Otto Wollank, met at the Spandau courthouse located ten kilometres north of Groß Glienicke. There, at quarter past eleven in the morning, they signed their names to the purchase contract: in exchange for 900,000 marks, Otto Wollank was now the *Rittergutsbesitzer*, or landlord, of Groß Glienicke.

Over the next few years, Otto worked tirelessly, throwing himself into modernising the estate. Keen to apply the scientific methods he had learned at college, he reorganised the manor farm. Using fertilisers and pesticides he increased crop yields. He built a new steam-powered mill to grind the wheat more efficiently. He introduced pasteurisation to milk production, extending its shelf life, and then developed a chain of shops in Berlin in order to sell the milk. Next, he built a brickworks, diversifying the estate's income beyond those of a traditional farm, providing bricks for houses on his estate, as well as the village beyond.

Along the lake's sandy northern shore, he planted a vineyard. Young vines were laid out in long rows, held up by trellises that stretched from the estate's entrance, at the Potsdamer Tor, down to a bluff overlooking the lake. Once the vineyard was established, labourers picked the grapes, which were then crushed and juiced, before being fermented in large metal vats that Otto had installed in one of his barns.

Concerned for the welfare of his workers, Otto converted an old farm building into a nursery. As the labourers' children grew up, the nursery added on a kindergarten and then a school. Initially, the local landlords remained unsure of this Berlin interloper, who had purchased his way into their rarefied circle, but the villagers warmed to their new landlord. In an unpublished family history, a member of the Wollank clan later recalled that Otto was a good landlord who cared for the workers. More than this, he was viewed as '*gütig und mitfühlend*,' or 'kindly and compassionate'.

On 15 June 1894, four years after arriving in the village, and now aged thirty-one, Otto married Katharina Anne Marie, a twenty-three-year-old local girl from an established Brandenburg family. A year later, they had their first child, Marie Luise, and then, eleven months later another, Ilse Katharina. A third daughter, Irmgard, was born almost exactly a year after that, but she died when only two days old. Finally, they had a son, who was born on the twenty-third day of the first month of the new century. He was baptised at the schloss, and given the name Horst Otto Adolf. Otto was thankful that at last he had a male heir.

The schloss was a wonderful place to grow up. Educated at home, Marie, Ilse and Horst had plenty of time to play in the fields and woods. Their father built a wooden playhouse for them, an ornately carved structure that was tall enough for an adult to stand, and wide enough to host a tea party for their friends.

As soon as they were old enough, the children were allowed to swim and sail on the lake, exploring its islands, hidden beaches and coves. Although Horst was often unable to participate in the more arduous recreational activities due to his persistent ill health, he was taught to ride a horse, and to shoot with an air pistol, and later with a hunting rifle. The girls, meanwhile, contented themselves with singing lessons in the front parlour.

Every October, the villagers and the Wollanks came together for the *Erntedankfest*, or Thanksgiving festival, to celebrate the gathering of the harvest and the good fortune of the village. Assembled in the schloss' courtyard, the villagers awaited the landlord's arrival. The men were dressed in their Sunday-best suits;

the more affluent wore fedoras and ties, others sported peaked caps. The women wore formal dresses and were accompanied by boys in lederhosen and girls in frocks. Also present were the men of the fire brigade, their belts and buckles gleaming, the village pastor, and the nightwatchman, who lived in a house next to the Drei Linden and who provided security to the village in the absence of a police force.

After some time, the landlord's family joined the crowd on the front steps of the schloss, greeted by the villagers. A few moments later, children were pushed forward carrying the *Erntekrone*, large wreaths of wheat and flowers tied to long poles from which hung multicoloured ribbons. After the landlord had thanked everyone for coming, he led them away from the schloss, with his family at the head, marching along the sandy lane which ran around the northern tip of the lake, past farm buildings and the new vineyard. At the end of the lane they walked under the Potsdamer Tor, the stone arch that marked the entrance to the schloss and its manor park, and upon which was carved the Wollank family crest: the head of a black wolf and a crown painted in the red and white colours of Groß Glienicke. Now on the Potsdamer Chaussee, the procession turned left at the fire station, and down to the fourteenth-century stone church.

While the rest of the party entered the church through the large wooden doors on the nave's northern face, the Wollanks arrived via the landlord's personal door, on the eastern side of the building. Inside, the church gleamed following the renovation recently paid for by Wollank: a crown of gold-fringed alabaster hung above the colourfully decorated pulpit – painted in rich greens, blues and reds; an enormous oil painting of Christ was placed behind the altar, on which were inscribed the words *Ecce Homo*; an oil painting portraying the Last Supper featured a former owner of the estate, Hans Georg Ribbeck, as one of the disciples; and at the ceiling's centre, the sun appeared through a hole in the painted clouds, on which was written the Hebrew word for God, יהוה.

As to Otto Wollank himself, his situation appeared stable and secure. The estate was developing nicely. The harvest had been good. His villagers were well fed and his wife and three children were healthy and happy. Sitting in the lord of the manor's box, located to the left of the altar and above and in front of the rest of the pews, its side emblazoned with the family crest, and singing the harvest festival songs, Otto's life had never seemed better.

2

WOLLANK
1913

By 1913, the estate had become a place of note, a model farm that was finally making money.

Impressed by Otto's tireless efforts, the acres of productive land, his fine-looking herds of cattle and the beauty of the estate itself, the regional landowners now paid Otto grudging respect. He and his family began to be invited to dinner parties and other social events. His teenage daughters were courted by the local gentry. His son was educated at the gymnasium in Potsdam, destined to join the officer corps and, perhaps later, the civil service.

Before long, word of Groß Glienicke's transformation, and the achievements of its landlord, had filtered through to Berlin. Otto Wollank's farm, it was said, had become a '*Mustergut*', an exemplary estate. On 16 April 1913, Otto Wollank wrote a direct petition to Kaiser Wilhelm II requesting that he be given a knighthood. This was typical of the time, in which up-and-coming young estate owners promoted themselves to the royal court. As part of his application, Otto provided a summary of his biography and then, under the heading of 'Political Views', explained that he was 'raised in a thoroughly conservative family' and was loyal to the Kaiser, 'to the deepest inner conviction'. He went on to say that 'despite the incitement of local workers by agitators from Spandau', he believed that he had 'successfully served the [Kaiser's] cause in my vicinity'.

The knighthood petition was first processed by the office of the president of the state of Brandenburg, based in Potsdam. In their report, they confirmed that Otto had been truthful in his application. They also listed his assets, which included the thousand-hectare Groß Glienicke Estate (1.5 million marks), three houses in Berlin (418,638 marks), various property holdings in the Berlin suburb of Pankow (645,667 marks), and other capital assets (2,127,250 marks).

Four months later, on 19 April, Kaiser Wilhelm instructed his officials to ennoble Otto Wollank, the one condition being that he pay 4,800 marks for his knighthood. Twelve days later, on 1 September, Otto received confirmation of his ennoblement through the issue of a diploma by the Heraldry Office. The official announcement was made in the state publication, the *Staatsanzeiger*, as well as the *Gothaer*, a periodical on the German nobility. Though no ceremony was held with the Kaiser himself, Otto celebrated the occasion with friends and family at home in the schloss.

From this point forward he would be known as Otto *von* Wollank. Not only did this bring him respect and status, it brought responsibilities. For, as a member of the local nobility, Otto was now expected to show leadership to the citizens of Groß Glienicke. He didn't have to wait long.

On the morning of 30 June 1914, Otto von Wollank sat in his dining room, reading the cream-coloured broadsheet that had been delivered earlier that day. Unlike the more liberal *Berliner Tageblatt* and *Vossische*

Zeitung, Otto's *Norddeutsche Allgemeine Zeitung* was a conservative newspaper, a staunch supporter of the Kaiser.

Otto was stunned. According to the front page, the Austrian Archduke Franz Ferdinand and his wife had been shot the previous day by a Serbian nationalist in the Bosnian capital of Sarajevo. Austria–Hungary was considered one of the Kaiser's most important allies; many would view an attack on the Austro-Hungarian royal family as an attack on Germany. The *Norddeutsche Allgemeine Zeitung* reported that 'the Archduke Franz Ferdinand has been associated with our emperor in mutual affection' and that the Duchess was 'well known to the Berlin court . . . so our imperial house is hit by the painful passing of the Archduke and his wife'. The article concluded that 'the warmest compassion turns to the three children who are orphaned' by the killing, reporting that Kaiser Wilhelm would be attending the funeral in Vienna.

Over the next days and weeks, Otto read the news with increasing trepidation: journalists demanding the assassins' arrest, governments threatening ultimatums, troops being mobilised. On 28 July, Austria–Hungary declared war on Serbia; on 1 August, Germany declared war on Russia. By 5 August 1914, Otto's newspapers carried ominous headlines: 'Britain Declares War on Germany' and 'Now Against the Russians, the French and English!' The First World War had begun.

According to the newspaper reports, Germany would likely soon be victorious. With an overwhelming number of troops, unsurpassed military training, and modern techniques, it was hard, wrote the editorials, to imagine a prolonged conflict. To a firm patriot and supporter of the Kaiser like Otto, such arguments would surely have been convincing. Though even Otto, the trained cavalry officer, must have wondered about the certainty, given war's unpredictability, the number of countries involved and their, as yet, unknown military strengths.

By the middle of August, the German Army had expanded from 800,000 to more than three and a half million soldiers. This surge mostly comprised army reservists, but also included 185,000 volunteers. At this time, there were a little over 120 men living in Groß Glienicke of working age. Of these, eighty were enlisted, thereby reducing the male working population by two-thirds. Soon, the estate was suffering a labour shortfall. The women were forced to fulfil the roles of their husbands, brothers, fathers and sons, and gathered the bulk of the harvest that summer. The decline in the village's male population became still more apparent at the Thanksgiving celebration that took place in October, two months after the war's start, with row upon row of empty pews.

At fifty-two, Wollank was too old to fight. Eager to serve his country, however, he volunteered for the Third Central Horse Depot in Potsdam, taking the rank of captain. Later, he was transferred to the High Command in Berlin, where he was responsible for the distribution of food and provisions to hospitals.

Given Otto's military background and loyalty to the Kaiser, it was assumed that his fourteen-year-old son, Horst, would enlist as soon as he was able. Horst had already seen two of the classes above him graduate and be conscripted directly into the army. A few classmates, some as young as fourteen and fifteen, had volunteered. But, despite all this, Horst, continued with his education.

From the newspapers, and through his contacts in Berlin, Otto kept up to date with the war's progress. Since December 1914, a major front had developed in France, with Germany's Fifth Army, made up of hundreds of thousands of soldiers, facing off against French forces. Intending to break the deadlock, the German Army initiated a major assault near the city of Verdun in February 1916. After early gains, the battle ground to a bloody stalemate, resulting in over 300,000 casualties on the Kaiser's side. It had become clear to Otto that the war was unlikely to end any time soon.

Conservative in nature, Otto von Wollank did not send his daughters to school, nor did he involve them in the estate's management. Instead, the young women sat at home with their mother, practising their needlework, reading and entertaining guests. While Horst would, health permitting, attend agricultural college and then serve an apprenticeship on the farm, the only plan for the girls was to find them suitable husbands.

Although social engagements were less frequent, the occasional afternoon tea or Sunday lunch still took place, attended by elderly neighbours and their younger female charges. The problem, as far as arranging a wedding for Marie Luise and Ilse was concerned, was that most of the eligible young men were away, either being trained at the military academies or already serving at the front. Such thoughts were thrown into disarray when, on 11 November 1916, Otto's wife suddenly died. She was only forty-five years old. The cause of death is unrecorded. After a short service that was held at the church, and which was attended by much of the village, Katharina was buried in the park next to the schloss.

Otto spent the remainder of the war trying to run the estate as best he could. Then, on 29 January 1918, he married Dorothea Müller, a noblewoman from Berlin nineteen years his junior. All of Otto's children attended the wedding, including Horst, who, though now graduated, had avoided conscription due to his general ill health.

After his bride moved to the schloss, to help manage the domestic staff and to care for the three children, Otto's mood lifted. According to villagers who remembered her, Dorothea was a friendly woman, with a warm personality, who quickly became beloved. Her arrival brought with it a hope that things were about to take a turn for the better.

Finally, on 11 November, word arrived in the village that the war had ended. A German delegation made up of two military officers and two politicians had met their counterparts from England and France, and signed an armistice. Otto's relief soon turned to anxiety when he learned that, following a series of worker and soldier revolts that had erupted around the country, the Kaiser had been forced to abdicate and fled to the Netherlands with his family. With his patron now gone, Otto worried what this would mean, not only for the estate, but for his standing within the community.

Dorothea von Wollank

In November and December 1918, politicians from the Social Democrat Party (SPD) worked together with members of the armed forces to fill the political vacuum. But the provisional government was unable to maintain order for long. The push for parliamentary democracy was countered by left-wing groups inspired by the Soviet revolution of the previous year. The protests culminated in the so-called Spartakus uprising, starting on 4 January 1919, in which protesters erected barricades in the streets of Berlin and seized several newspaper offices, including the organ of the SPD. To support the action, the German Communist Party called a general strike. Over half a million protesters surged into Berlin. One of the radicals' key demands was the redistribution of land, particularly of the estates owned by those recently ennobled, such as Otto's. Over the next few days, the protesters brutally clashed with bands of former veterans on the city streets, and hundreds were killed. It was the veterans who emerged triumphant, however – recapturing the city centre with support from government forces. A shaky equilibrium was established.

Otto's fear abated somewhat when, following elections held on 19 January 1919, a national assembly was convened in the small town of Weimar, three hundred kilometres south-west of Berlin, intent on stabilising the country. Out of this assembly, a new constitution was approved, including significant changes to Germany's power structures. Women could now vote, as could all men over the age of twenty (the minimum age had been twenty-five). Also for the first time, the country would have a president, who would serve as the new head of state. Critically, the president would be able to appoint, or dismiss, the chancellor – who would run the government – and, under Article 48, would have the power to suspend civil liberties, including habeas corpus. In another broad change, a supreme court was established and the imperial flag of black, white and red was replaced by a tricoloured black, red and gold. Finally, the constitution laid out a set of 'basic rights' for its citizens; for instance, Article 115 declared that 'a German's home is an asylum and is inviolable'.

With a new constitution, flag and parliament, the politicians announced a new era: a German republic. Later this period would become known as the 'Weimar Republic'. The *Kaiser Reich*, which had commenced with the unification of Germany in 1871, with its system of royal patronage, was officially over. Gone with it were the nobility. From this point forward, Otto was informed, he could no longer call himself a knight. Nonetheless, he could use the 'von' before his surname, and keep his estate.

The politicians' efforts to maintain order were undermined by the agreement they signed with the Allied powers on 28 June 1919, which became known as the Treaty of Versailles. Right-wing and nationalist groups were outraged by the treaty's terms which they considered both treacherous and humiliating. Germany would now have to pay the Allies substantial reparations in return for war damages, and were forced to give up large areas of land, including ceding Alsace-Lorraine to France and parts of Upper Silesia to Poland. Perhaps most upsetting, at least to the soldiers and officers who had fought in the war, Germany was forced to reduce its army to 100,000 men, its General Staff was dissolved and it was allowed only two military schools, one each for the army and navy.

Berlin became gripped by street fighting. Other rebellions broke out in Hamburg and Frankfurt. A Soviet-style republic was declared in Munich, before being brutally quashed by right-wing paramilitary groups. Thousands died in the violence. Then, on the evening of 12 March 1920, an army brigade marched into Berlin's city centre in an attempt to take over the government. This *coup d'état* became known as the Kapp Putsch, after one of its leaders, Wolfgang Kapp. In response, the National Assembly fled to Dresden and then to Stuttgart. To demonstrate that they still had the people's support, the politicians called a general strike, and were rewarded on 14 and 15 March when over 12 million people refused to go work. The economic impact was immediate, with transportation grinding to a halt, and utility suppliers such as gas, water and electricity unable to provide services. A few days later the putsch was seen as having failed and the government returned to Berlin. Despite this success, the events revealed a country deeply divided between right- and left-wing factions.

Though the politicians were back in control they soon faced another critical problem: the country was running out of money. The nation's reserves had been bled dry by the war and the weak economic situation and political instability exacerbated the problem. This situation was made worse as Germany began paying the enormous financial reparations to the Allies, draining the country of much-needed foreign currency. The political and economic instability did little to improve the Groß Glienicke Estate, which was still recovering from the hardships sustained during the war. More than twenty men had died in the conflict and, with many others badly injured, the working male population had been reduced by more than 30 per cent.

Then, in 1923, following repeated attempts to liberalise the economy, the country was gripped by rampant inflation. In late 1921 one gold mark had been worth ten paper marks; a year later a gold mark was worth 10,000 paper marks; and by 1923 the rate was one to 100 million. This hyperinflation had a direct impact on the Groß Glienicke Estate. The price of agricultural products collapsed while those of fertiliser, fodder and wages sky-rocketed. Otto now found it impossible to pay his workers, given the exponential fluctuations in currency. Without reward, the labourers became demoralised, many refusing to turn up for work. The estate faced ruin.

Otto's one small happiness was his family. In the space of four years, starting in 1920, all his children were married. His eldest daughter, Marie Luise, married a landowner from Bavaria, and a year later, Horst, married a twenty-two-year-old from Oranienburg, a small town north of Berlin. Yet of all the matches, Otto was most pleased with Ilse Katharina's groom, Robert von Schultz.

*

Born in 1895 into a landowning family of aristocrats on the island of Rügen, off Germany's Baltic coast, Robert von Schultz was a man steeped in conservative traditions. At the age of nineteen he had volunteered to fight in the First World War, suffering three serious wounds, and receiving the Iron Cross First Class and Austrian Military Cross of Merit Third Class for his bravery. After the war's end, and like many of his former comrades, he had become embroiled in the street fighting between communists and right-wing veteran groups that had seized Berlin. Then, looking for a means to earn a living, he took up agriculture studies. A short, rotund man, with a high forehead and double chin, he exuded confidence and bravado.

Otto was pleased with his new son-in-law. They were both fervent supporters of the monarchy, had both served in the military and both had a passion for agriculture. Following the marriage to his daughter, Otto invited Robert to work with him alongside Horst. One day, one of these two young men would be chosen to manage the estate. For now, Otto let it be known that he had not yet made up his mind whether it would be the son or the son-in-law.

Within a short time, the estate filled with prams and nurses. Otto liked nothing better than to sit on his terrace, watching his small grandchildren toddling around the front lawn or chasing the geese and ducks that gathered by the lake shore. And gradually, as the hardships of war receded, the ancient rhythms returned to the estate and the village. Thanksgiving celebrations were better attended, as were the Easter celebrations and the church service on Christmas Eve. One of the women from the estate's dairy, a certain Frau Mond, opened a shop in the village opposite the Drei Linden, selling milk, cheese and butter. Then a butcher from Kladow, a village located on the eastern shore of the lake, opened a branch shop in Groß Glienicke, supplying high-quality cuts of steak, pork chops and sausages. Better times seemed to be coming to the village.

Despite the improvements in the general economy, the Groß Glienicke Estate's finances never fully recovered, crippled as it was by the preceding year's losses. By 1926, now well into his seventh decade and weakened by a series of illnesses, Otto realised that he must narrow the shortfall in the accounts. With the support of his children and their spouses – who understood the dire financial situation – Otto devised a plan. He would reduce his outgoings by cutting back on some of the household expenses and he would ask the estate manager to increase the yield of that year's harvest.

But such measures alone, Otto knew, would prove insufficient. They had been tried before and would result in modest gains. To ensure more dramatic results, Otto decided that he must lease out a portion of the estate's land. From his friends in Berlin, he had noticed that there was a growing appetite for second homes in the country. Why not attract some of these wealthy Berliners to Groß Glienicke? After all, it was a beautiful spot, and only a short drive from the city centre.

3

ALEXANDER
1927

One spring morning in March 1927, Dr Alfred Alexander and his family climbed into their dark blue open-topped S-model Mercedes-Benz, outside their apartment in western Berlin, and headed out to Groß Glienicke.

Alfred and his wife Henny, dressed in a warm winter jacket and mink coat, hats and gloves, sat in the front while their four children – Bella, Elsie, Hanns and Paul – were crammed in the back. Alfred liked to drive, so the chauffeur had been given the day off. Their route took them through the crowded city streets, along the Heerstrasse – the main thoroughfare heading west out of the city – across the narrow Freybrücke, the iron bridge that spanned the River Havel, and then left onto Potsdamer Chaussee which, after a long straight drive through woods, brought them to Groß Glienicke. The journey took just forty minutes.

The village seemed small to Alfred, a place from another time with its modest houses, stone barns and medieval church, so different from the tall apartment buildings, busy streets and sophisticated shops of western Berlin. From the village's centre, he turned left at the fire station, went under the Potsdamer Tor, and parked a few metres down a dirt road. There they were met by an estate manager.

The parcel of land that the manager showed them was rectangular in shape, thirty metres wide, running for two hundred metres from the outer wall of the Potsdamer Tor downhill to the shore of the Groß Glienicke Lake. It was a long narrow strip that was big enough to provide privacy, but small enough to be manageable. In all, there were three sections: a high flat area that had been part of the old vineyard, filled with twisted vines and bent trellises, which ran for about 150 metres and ended on a bluff overlooking the lake; a slope which dropped almost vertically, covered with stones and wild trees; and finally a flat sandy area at the bottom, twenty-five metres in length, where black alder and willow trees grew. Best of all was the lake, at the foot of the lot.

Having stopped for a while to enjoy the view from the top of the bluff overlooking the lake, the Alexanders clambered down to the

Groß Glienicke Lake

water. The lake was small, but it would be a wonderful place to swim in the summer. To the left, they could see the schloss, barely visible through the trees. To the right, at the lake's centre, were two small islands covered with trees. If they had a boat, they could paddle out to them, and perhaps even camp.

Alfred John Alexander had started well enough. On 7 March 1880, he was born in Bamberg, a picturesque Bavarian town located on the banks of the Regnitz River in central Germany. His family was middle class, made up of doctors and lawyers. They were well regarded in the community, honest, hard-working, and were frequent attendees at the town's synagogue.

Despite this, Alfred's early years marked him with a melancholia that he was never quite able to shake. When he was five years old his sister Paula had died of pneumonia. A few months later, shortly before Christmas 1885, he learned that his forty-four-year-old father, Hermann, had died of leukaemia. The next day Alfred was taken to see his mother, Bella. Her chestnut-coloured hair had turned white even though she was only thirty years old.

Alfred was a kind but serious boy without a sense of humour. He worked hard at school, frequently gaining marks that put him top of the class. He was also sensitive, prone to crying at the smallest provocation, whether it was another child hurting him or a particularly beautiful piece of music. Above all else, he was desperate for his mother's approval, and when she displayed her pride in the boy he was at his happiest.

At the age of fifteen Alfred announced to his mother that he intended to become a doctor and find a cure for his father's disease, leukaemia. Laudable as this was, his mother was disappointed. It was her intention that he would study to become a lawyer, like his father.

When Alfred persisted, his mother asked her father and brothers to persuade him, but they were unable to change the boy's mind. Reluctantly, she finally gave Alfred her blessing when he was seventeen, but, he later recalled, with one condition: 'Promise me that you will be a good doctor!' she said. By good doctor she had meant someone at the top of his profession, who works in general practice rather than research, and who helps all patients, no matter their financial status.

So it was that, upon graduating from school, Alfred went on to study medicine at the Friedrich Wilhelm University in Berlin and then at the Ludwig Maximilian University in Munich. Of medium height, with wide shoulders, thick lips, dark curly hair and a narrow moustache, Alfred was not unpleasant to look at, though his intense gaze and serious demeanour proved to be a deterrent for most women.

He worked hard and passed the first *Physicum* exam with top marks and completed his final *Staatsexamen* within three years. Bella was delighted with her 'wunderkind' son, and at 10.45 in the morning on 19 June 1903 a telegram arrived for Alfred at the Munich telegraph office:

CONGRATULATIONS ON THIS JOYFUL SURPRISE, WARMEST GREETINGS – MAMA.

Once qualified, Alfred took a job in Odelzhausen, a small town located fifty kilometres north-west of Munich, where he began his scientific research which he hoped might lead to the cure for leukaemia. As soon as he received his first pay cheque he handed his earnings over to his mother. Two years later, in 1905, the young Dr Alfred Alexander was offered the prestigious job as first assistant to the director of the Freiburg University Hospital. There was one stipulation: in order to accept the position Alfred was told that he must convert to Christianity. His only alternative was to take an inferior position with a far lower salary in Berlin. He took the Berlin job.

The following year, Bella was struck down by severe heart and asthma attacks. She was fifty-one years old, and when Alfred heard the news he asked his supervisor for compassionate leave and hurried to his mother's side. He was shocked by her condition: her breaths came in short gulps, her chest was gripped by pain, and she was profoundly weak. Having seen his mother, he went in search of her physicians, Dr Guntzberg, who he did not know well, and Dr Julius Kahn, who he had known for some time and trusted. Asking about his mother's prognosis he was told that she was beyond hope. A few days later, his mother begged him for help. In his private memoirs Alfred later wrote:

> I put it to her medical advisers whether there was a chance of prolonging her life, which to me was the most precious thing on earth; but they merely shrugged their shoulders. Then I knew what I had to do. The love and gratitude which I felt for this wonderful woman and mother prompted me to beg my friend Julius Kahn to administer morphine, which I knew, on the basis of medical opinion of the time, would not only ease her pain but also end her life.
>
> Dr Guntzberg was outraged by this 'damaging' suggestion, but Julius Kahn gave her the injection which calmed her down very quickly and before long she went to sleep without suffering pain any longer. She looked at me in a way I shall never forget and said: 'Thank you, dear boy.' These were her last words, and though her death was a heavy blow for me, I have never regretted having made that decision and I am today even more grateful to my dear friend Julius Kahn. There was no possible way to save her, but I was able to tell myself that she died painlessly through an act of euthanasia. With her passing a most wonderful woman left this world.

After his mother's death, Alfred resolved to give up his scientific research, and become the 'good doctor' his mother had wished. He returned to Berlin and began building a general practice. Three years later, in 1909, Alfred met Henny Picard during a visit to Frankfurt. Henny was a buxom woman with a round face and strong arms, who, though never slim or fashionable, cast an attractive figure with her sharp sense of humour and a sparkle in her eye. Where Alfred came from a middle-class family of doctors and lawyers, Henny was descended from two of Europe's most successful Jewish families: her father, Lucien Picard, was a highly respected banker, a director for Commerz Bank, and the Swiss Consul in Frankfurt; her mother, Amelia, was a Schwarzschild, one of the most powerful Jewish families in Frankfurt, second only to the Rothschilds.

Alfred and Henny fell immediately in love and, despite her concerns about his dark moods, they were married just months after meeting, after which Henny moved into Alfred's small bachelor pad on the busy shopping street of Kurfürstendamm. A year later, she became pregnant, and the Alexanders moved round the corner to a large apartment which took up the entire first floor of 219/220 Kaiserallee, today called Bundesallee, one of the smartest addresses in western Berlin. The apartment had twenty-two rooms, including five bedrooms, three living rooms, one bathroom, two rooms for the maids and a large kitchen. The front room was the width of the whole apartment, large enough to comfortably seat forty people for dinner, and had two balconies overlooking the Kaiserallee.

Then, on 18 March 1911, they had their first child, whom they named Bella after Alfred's much-loved mother. Some twenty months later, on 3 December 1912, a second child was born, whom they called Elsie. With Alfred working hard tending his patients and building his practice, Henny spent time with the children, establishing a home for the growing family. Soon she was managing a large staff, including a maid, a cook, a cleaner, a chauffeur, and even a man who came once a week to wind up the clocks.

Despite her affluent upbringing, Henny remained an unspoilt, modest and self-possessed woman who exerted a calming influence on her more tempestuous husband. As Alfred wrote in his memoirs:

My dear mother would have certainly approved of you and would, had she known you, given us her blessing. You are so very much like her in many ways, in your lovely eyes, your smile and in your whole being – that kindly understanding, this readiness to be of help not only to your family but to all who turn to you for assistance. You have such understanding for everything, so much patience, and I must confess that, although I do love you with all my heart, I have not always made it easy for you in view of my excitable and often short-tempered behaviour.

Five years after their marriage, and following the outbreak of war in 1914, Alfred was conscripted into the medical corps of the German Army and deployed to the Alsace where he ran a field hospital for victims of gas attacks. Whenever he could, he took a train back to Berlin to see Henny and the children. During one of these brief wartime visits Henny again became pregnant and, on 6 May 1917, she gave birth to identical twins, Hanns and Paul – with Hanns fifteen minutes older than his brother. When Elsie and Bella saw the boys for the first time they mistook them for little red dolls, running up to their mother and grabbing the two babies as if they were toys. Elsie chose Paul and Bella chose Hanns and this sense of divided responsibility for the boys persisted for the remainder of their lives.

Acknowledging his efforts during the First World War, the army awarded Alfred the Iron Cross First Class, one of the few Jews to receive such an honour. With the war over in November 1918, Alfred returned to Berlin and set about rebuilding his business. Within a few years, he had established a thriving medical practice, becoming one of Berlin's most prominent doctors. In 1922, he built a clinic at Achenbachstrasse 15, a four-storey building in western Berlin. Furnished with the very latest equipment, including X-ray machines, a laboratory and a roof terrace where clients could recuperate in the open air, the sanatorium's beds were soon full. Alfred also had private consultancy rooms within the family apartment on the Kaiserallee, and his patients now included Albert Einstein, Marlene Dietrich and Max Reinhardt, the director of Berlin's Deutsches Theater.

By 1927, having navigated the turbulent years of the decade, with all of its hyperinflation and economic uncertainties, Alfred was exhausted. Still burdened by his childhood wounds, he longed for a place to rest.

One day, in the spring of 1927, Dorothea von Wollank had come to see Dr Alexander at his consulting rooms in Berlin. After the medical examination was complete, Dorothea mentioned that her husband was leasing parcels of land along the shore of the Groß Glienicke Lake. She wondered whether the doctor might know of anybody who would be interested.

That night at dinner, Alfred announced that he would like to build a lake house to the west of the city. It would be somewhere to visit at weekends, he told his wife and children, perhaps even over the summer. Alfred was not alone in his desire for a *Weekend-Haus* – many of his friends and associates already had country homes. The painter Max Liebermann had a massive stone villa next to the Wannsee, and the architect Erich Mendelsohn had a magnificent lakeside house a few kilometres to the north. What made Alfred's choice special was that he wanted to build a small wooden cottage, rather than an enormous villa or chalet.

Elsie and her siblings were familiar with the lakes near Berlin. In the summertime, when the temperature could reach thirty-five degrees Celsius, their parents would take them to the Wannsee Strandbad, the largest open-air lido in Europe. There, a sandy shoreline had been transformed into a family beach over a kilometre long and eighty metres wide – a *Strand* which played host to more than 900,000 Berliners each year: men in suits and women in long dresses taking tea in thatched shelters; children building sandcastles with their parents; short-skirted women bathing, scandalously, with topless men in the shallow waters.

Alfred was looking for solitude, however, away from the colourful crowds of the Wannsee, as a respite from his hectic, noisy Berlin life. Elsie, now fourteen years old, was worried that this meant long, lonely weekends stuck with her parents – or worse, their stuffy friends – in some tiny cottage in the woods, far from city excitement.

On 30 March 1927, a few days after the family's first visit to Groß Glienicke, Alfred travelled to the village and struck a deal with Otto von Wollank: the Alexanders would lease the parcel of land for fifteen years. They would be allowed to build a house, use the lake and, it was understood, the Alexanders would have the first option to buy the land if and when Wollank decided to sell.

At the lake that day, Alfred Alexander also met Professor Fritz Munk, who had leased the adjacent parcel. Like the Alexanders, the Munks had chosen their lot for the lake view, but also for the magnificent oak tree that stood at the edge of the bluff. Similar in age to Alfred, Fritz was also a renowned doctor. The director of the Martin Luther Hospital in Berlin, Fritz's private patients included Otto von Wollank, himself as well as the politician Franz von Papen and the deposed Kaiser's son, Prince Wilhelm. Of medium height, with a round doughy face, bushy moustache and thin wire glasses, Fritz Munk was a man of great formality, accustomed to wearing suits at all times, even in the country. The doctors knew of each other, but had never met.

Now, together in Groß Glienicke, the two men talked. They quickly realised that they shared a vision. They both wanted to build a weekend house, something that was different from the high-ceilinged opulence of their Berlin homes – a simple one-level structure, built of natural materials on the bluff, maximising the lake view.

The two doctors agreed to attend the *Wochenende* exhibition that was then taking place in the fair grounds of Berlin. As part of the event, an array of wooden cottages had been built in neat rows. Designed by some of Germany's most renowned architects and made from high-quality materials, these country homes had been priced to make them affordable to Berlin's growing upper-middle class. Walking around the models, Alfred and Fritz discussed the various blueprints: Which model suited them best? How many bedrooms did they need? How would they heat their properties? What alterations should they make to the basic model?

Having selected their preferred designs, they hired Otto Lenz, a Berlin-based builder who had established a reputation for the construction of attractive wooden cottages. On 28 May 1927, Fritz Munk's application to build was approved by the county administration, which was located in Nauen, thirty-eight kilometres west of Berlin. The Alexanders' planning application was approved a day later.

In early summer 1927, a group of men arrived on the Groß Glienicke Estate. It was early, just after daybreak, and they wanted to put in a good start before the temperature climbed above thirty degrees, which it often did at this time of year. As was typical for members of the

Brandenburg carpenters' guild, the men wore black corduroy trousers, thick and tough to withstand hard labour; white hemp shirts, open at the collar; black woollen vests with white buttons; black-leather shoes; and wide-brimmed black felt hats to keep the sun's rays off their faces and necks.

They were soon joined by Otto Lenz, the builder. Though Lenz was the overall supervisor, the day-to-day construction would be overseen by the master carpenter. While the men unloaded the tools from the horse and cart, Lenz and the master carpenter walked the property, discussing the peculiarities of the land and the Alexanders' specific requirements. Once satisfied that his employee understood what was necessary, Lenz handed over the plans, wished the team good luck and returned to his office at Yorkstrasse 40 in Berlin.

The builders' first task was to clear the land, particularly the old vines that stretched in long rows down the spine of the property. This was back-breaking work. The roots of the vines were more than a metre deep and, after years of growth, had become thick and entangled. With pickaxes, shovels and long metal bars, the men strained to prise the fibrous roots from the sandy soil, then worked the land until it was smooth and free of large stones. It took a week to clear. Only the most mature trees on the lower section of the property near the lake were left standing: an oak, two pines and a willow.

As with all such houses, the construction followed a predictable pattern. First the men laid out the house's perimeter. Using a long coil of string tied to wooden pegs they marked out a rectangle nine metres wide and eleven metres long. Then they dug a trench with the help of pickaxes and shovels. Into this they poured a mortar mixture, made of sand mined from the shore, limestone which the workers had transported in sacks from Berlin, and water carried up in buckets from the lake. As one team of men poured the foundations, another excavated the cellar. Next, the men dug a large hole away from the north-east corner of the house, at least three metres deep and one metre across, which would serve as the house's cesspit.

Once the concrete of the house, cellar and cesspit had set, the men began laying the first course of pinkish-red bricks. These had been produced on the Estate and were waiting in neatly stacked piles to one side. After a few days of slow, methodical work, the foundations were in place, and along these were then laid horizontal pine beams and vertical posts. The builders next added the trusses, large triangular-shaped wooden wedges that would hold up the roof. They then framed out the internal walls, hammering in the openings for the doors and windows, and erected the joists that would support the ceilings. They also framed out the built-in cupboards, recessed bookshelves, and alcoves for the pull-down tables and beds, all of which had been specifically requested by the Alexanders.

Two weeks after construction had started, the house was fully framed, its interior now taking shape. Nine rooms had been squeezed into the house's small footprint, including five bedrooms, a living room, a bathroom, a kitchen, along with an annexe for the family's chauffeur, comprising one room and a toilet.

With the beams holding the roof now in place, it was time to celebrate the *Richtfest*, or 'topping out' ceremony. Though the house was far from being complete – the other side of the lake was still visible through the robust framework – it was traditional for the builders to gather in front of the house with members of the family to mark this stage of construction. Tables were set out and laden with apple schnapps and beer, cold meats, bread, cheese and cakes.

At a certain point in the ritual, one of the workers climbed a ladder to the top of the roof and attached a *Richtkrone*, a large wreath of evergreen leaves and flowers, from which hung colourful ribbons. As was the custom, the master builder raised his glass to the sky, wishing the house and its owners good fortune. Then drinking the remaining schnapps, he threw the glass on the ground, and the group cheered as the glass broke.

Since the Alexanders never intended to live at the house year-round, Otto Lenz had not included insulation within the walls, ceiling or cellar, and there had been no talk of a proper heating system. Indeed, the word '*Sommerhaus*' had been written at the top of the sketch submitted to the local planning department. However, the family still needed a minimal heating system, to warm the water for their baths, and for the few chilly weeks in spring and autumn.

Following Otto Lenz's design the workmen erected two brick chimneys, one for the kitchen and one for the living room. They then built a network of firebrick-clad horizontal pipes that would run from an enclosed metal woodstove in the cellar and then under the floors of the house, carrying hot air into the living room and bedrooms. Once the plumbers and electricians had completed their work, the carpenters set about finishing the interior of the building, using wood almost exclusively, in line with the architect's instructions to use natural, simple materials. As a result, the workmen laid the floors in narrow lengths of pine plank running east to west, the only exception being the concrete bathroom floor. The walls were tongue-and-groove pine, behind which the builders stuck sheets of newspaper, marking the construction date and providing some limited insulation. Most of the ceilings were also covered with tongue-and-groove pine, apart from the large room at the centre of the house and the master bedroom, whose walls and ceiling were clad with more expensive sheets of wood panelling.

Outside, the cottage was sheathed with darkly stained horizontal wooden planks, overlapped to keep out the rain. Large single-pane windows were inserted into the holes left in the walls, equipped with thick metal handles and fasteners. Two heavy black-painted entrance doors were added on the northern front of the house; one, in the centre, led to the main living quarters, the other, to the left, to the chauffeur's annexe, and each contained a diamond-shaped window that had been cut in at eye level. The windows had wooden shutters, painted in cobalt blue, emblazoned with a large white diamond, matching the entrance doors' motif.

The roof came next. Metal gutters and downspouts were added, their jagged circular ends pointing away from the house to keep the moisture from the foundation. A veranda was built at the rear of the house, sheltered by a plain wooden roof resting on two white columns. From here the family would be able to sit on the edge of the bluff, overlooking the lake.

At the foot of the slope, the builders constructed a concrete pump house to enable the Alexanders to water the garden. This pump house would also serve as a storage shed – for garden chairs, boat equipment, bicycles – and was roofed with a terrace, where the family could sit out for an evening drink.

There was still considerable work to be completed on the outside: the landscaping of the garden, the building of a tennis court on the flat land next to the lake, the terracing of the slope below the house, as well as a two-metre-wide stone path which would run from the parking area at the top of the property down to the house. The Alexanders had also called for the construction of various outbuildings – a wooden house for the caretaker to live in, a large greenhouse and a garage. Yet, despite the long list of to-dos, and a little over two months since the start of their labours, the house was now ready for occupancy.

Before entering the house for the first time, the Alexanders gathered by their front door. In one hand, Alfred held a hammer and some nails he had brought from Berlin. In the other was a *mezuzah*, a metal cylinder which held a tiny scroll containing the ancient Hebrew words: 'Hear O Israel, the Lord our God, the Lord is one.' After saying a short prayer, he tacked the *mezuzah* onto the right-hand side of the main entrance.

Then, opening the black-painted wooden door, Alfred invited his children to explore the house. Delighted, Bella, Elsie, Hanns and Paul ran ahead. Immediately upon entering was a corridor, with two doors on each side. On the right they found the maid's room and kitchen. On the left, the guest room and bathroom. With doors crashing open and shut, and much scurrying of feet, they discovered the room at the end of the corridor, the living room, the largest room in the house and the heart of the building. Its walls were covered with polished wood panelling, edged with mint-green painted strips. The ceiling was salmon-coloured and had been split into small squares by more strips of wood. The overall effect was simple and chic. In the right-hand corner, the carpenters had built an L-shaped bench around a large glossy red wooden table, large enough for the family to eat dinner. In the left-hand corner was an open fireplace framed by an arch of bricks and shielded by a hearth of yet more bricks.

From the living room, the children found they could enter three other rooms. One door led to the 'Blue Room', where the girls would sleep. While Elsie wasn't happy to be sharing with her sister, she was thrilled with the room. Its ceiling had been painted sky blue, its two built-in cupboards – one for each of the girls – were cobalt blue, while its wood-panelled walls were left bare. Two pull-down beds, covered with cream-coloured quilts, stood equidistant between the windows and the door. Best of all was the view from the double windows of the lake.

Through a door next to the living-room fireplace, the boys found their bedroom. It was the smallest bedroom in the house, just large enough for a chair, a table and a bunk bed. It was also the darkest room, with two small rectangular windows. The Alexanders clearly did not expect the boys to spend much time inside.

The final living-room door led to the master bedroom, which was where the parents would sleep. It contained a large chestnut wooden bed which had been installed permanently into a recessed wall at the rear of the room. There were built-in cupboards above and to the side of the bed. Two large windows, matching those of the Blue Room, opened in front of the bed, affording a glorious lake view.

On the far wall of the living room a set of French windows had been installed, leading out to the rear veranda. From there, wide steps led precipitously down to the as-yet-unseeded lawn, and the lake rippling fifty metres beyond.

The house contained two additional rooms, but the children could only reach them by running outside and entering through another door to the left of the main entrance. This 'chauffeur's annexe' took up a corner of the square house and was big enough for a bed, a chair and a table on which to lay his clothes. Attached was a small toilet, which was accessed by going outside and entering from yet another door, this time on the eastern side of the house.

From the outside it appeared compact, yet, on entering, there was an unexpected amount of space. Otto Lenz had somehow built a home that conveyed modesty and that blended into its natural

Rear view of the lake house, photograph by Lotte Jacobi, 1928

surroundings, but was large enough to take care of the entire Alexander clan, their staff and guests. The effect was magical.

With the Alexander house now complete, Otto Lenz's crew moved on to the Munk house next door. It was of a similar design, one level, wooden, with a terrace overlooking the lake, a pump house and garden. It even had the same diamond-shaped motif on the doors and windows.

The Alexander and Munk houses were the first weekend retreats to be built in Groß Glienicke. Next came a house for Dr Martin Wall, a judge whose chambers were located on Kurfürstendamm near the Alexanders' apartment in Berlin. Ewald Kunow, a pharmacist from Berlin's suburbs, built a small wooden cottage on the other side of the Munks'. Then came Otto von Wollank's own lawyer, Erwin Koch. Over the next few months there would be more homes constructed on land leased to the Wollanks' other acquaintances.

Otto and Dorothea soon began advertising the land in magazines and newspapers. Deals were struck with strangers, all of them city folk seeking refuge from their busy urban lives. Then, inspired by his success with the old vineyard, Otto instructed his agents to sell an entire section of the estate to developers, this time along the lake's eastern shore. Known as *Wochenend West* – from a Berliner's perspective it was considered to be located in the west – the parcel was soon subdivided, and the lots advertised in flyers circulated in the nation's capital.

Observing the Wollanks' success in selling land, a few local farmers placed their own properties on the market. Before long, new homes were springing up along the southern shore of the Groß Glienicke Lake. Now it was not only weekend houses that were being built, but full-time residences, two storeys high, constructed from brick and covered with stucco, and complete with central heating to furnish year-round living. Such homes were closer to villas and mansions than weekend cottages.

For the residents of Groß Glienicke, these newcomers – doctors and lawyers, film stars and bank directors, actors and composers – were *Ortsfremde*, or outsiders. They seemed foreign, with their big cars and expensive suits, their quick-talking and Berlin accents. They were unused to women and men swimming together at the village's public beach, clothed in skimpy shorts and bathing suits.

Groß Glienicke was now split into three sections: the Groß Glienicke Estate, where the Wollanks lived with their workers; the village itself, with its family-run shops, small stone houses, school and church; and now, the quickly growing settlers' community, with fancy houses, chauffeurs and weekend parties.

In time, the villagers grew accustomed to their new neighbours, with many of the locals finding work as builders and labourers, and later as gardeners, cleaners, cooks, nannies and security guards. Slowly the worlds of the city and the country began to merge.

4

ALEXANDER
1928

At fifteen years old, Elsie Alexander had developed a strong personality. Quick-witted and confident in her beliefs, she was never afraid of voicing an opinion. Yet she was also charming, her sharp tongue softened by a smile. With cornflower blue eyes, an oval face, and long brown hair braided into two plaits that fell below her waist, many thought her attractive. Yet she considered herself to be plain-looking, even ugly.

While on the surface friends, Elsie and her elder sister, Bella, could not have been more different. Where Elsie was blunt and assertive, Bella was diplomatic and cautious. Where Elsie was ambitious, dreaming of becoming a doctor like her father, Bella spoke of marrying some nice, rich businessman, of becoming a homemaker like her mother. From an early age there had been competition between the girls – for their parents' attention, for the best gifts, for the most handsome boyfriend. Elsie later recalled that Bella was the more beautiful of the pair and would therefore arrive late to a party, so everyone would see her, while she, Elsie, would go straight to the corner, so that she could avoid attention.

Life at the weekend house was a simple affair, made up of sleeping, eating and spending time by the lake. The family rarely left the property, and when they did, it was usually to shop for food. While the sisters read magazines, wrote letters or chatted with friends they had invited along, their eleven-year-old brothers, spent as much time as they could outside: roughhousing on the terrace, climbing trees and honing their football skills on the front lawn.

If they had been observant Jews, the Alexanders would have remained in the city to attend Friday-evening and Saturday-morning services at their local synagogue on Fasanenstrasse. Instead, they called themselves 'Three-Days-a-Year Jews', attending synagogue on the two days of Rosh Hashanah and the one day of Yom Kippur. As a result, the Alexanders typically drove out to the house on Friday evening and remained till Monday morning.

In early summer, if the temperature was high and the pollution in the city unbearable, the family lived full-time at the house. On schooldays, the four Alexander children woke at six to swim in the lake. Careful not to disturb their parents, they padded through the living room and onto the veranda, down the rough wooden steps, and across the dew-slicked lawn to the end of the jetty, where they shucked off their robes and dived into the water. Afterwards, as they were drying, they watched swans gliding through the reeds or a flock of geese flying in a V-formation overhead. The children loved this time of day.

Once they were dressed, the chauffeur drove them to school in western Berlin, a short forty-minute journey away. His instructions were to park a distance from the school's entrance, for the children were anxious not to be teased about their wealth.

If it was a weekend, or the summer holidays, the children slept until eight. When they were woken, by the morning light or by one of their father's cockerels, they made their own breakfast, as their cook and maids remained at the Berlin apartment, and their mother liked to sleep in. The simple country food was stored in the kitchen pantry: heavy dark bread from the village, soft cheese from the local farm, and cherry compote made with cherries from the garden.

When not at school, the children were expected to take care of themselves. A favourite pastime was the cherry game, in which the four children raced over to the orchard that grew on the flat ground between the Potsdamer Tor and the house, competing to see who could stuff the most cherries into their mouth. Bella usually won. On one occasion, she managed to hold thirty-four cherries in her mouth, so many that her cheeks felt sore for days afterwards.

The twins would set off to explore the woods or go on bike rides once their sisters tired of them. They roamed freely along the shore or in the forest behind the schloss. It was the perfect place for two troublesome boys, for there were few neighbours to disturb and little chance that complaints would be made.

With their brothers gone, the girls often played tennis. Dressed in whites – white blouses, long white trousers, white socks and shoes – the girls spent hours on the court. Neither struck the ball very hard. Their serves were soft and their ground strokes fell short. This was partly due to a lack of skill, but also because whoever hit a ball into the lake had to retrieve it. Nevertheless, the games were fiercely competitive and the girls well matched.

Alfred, meanwhile, busied himself in the vegetable garden. He had dug, raked and tilled a long stretch of soft soil – the earth here was mostly clay and sand – into which he planted row upon row of seeds: lettuces, tomatoes, cucumbers, and beans. Next to these beds he cultivated a long asparagus patch. Here, among his asparagus and runner beans, his buckets and hoes, and wearing lederhosen and a loose shirt, Alfred whiled away his mornings, digging the dirt and watering his vegetables. Not content with just a vegetable garden, Alfred also built himself an enormous greenhouse which he named his 'orangerie', a reference to the ornate construction dominating the royal palace gardens of Sanssouci, Potsdam, a few kilometres to the south. With a concrete foundation, fireplace, chimney, retractable windows and stretching twelve metres in length, this greenhouse was wider than the *Weekend-Haus* itself.

Alfred Alexander

Henny Alexander

Henny usually woke late, in time to prepare lunch, calling the family in by ringing a bell that dangled from the porch ceiling. If the weather was good they ate outside, on a long table covered with a white cloth that stood on the terrace overlooking the lake. Far from the decorum of Berlin, the boys were shirtless and shoeless. These lunches were generally simple affairs of cold meats and cheeses, salads from the garden, boiled eggs and pickled herring.

After lunch, Henny liked to head into the local villages in search of items to decorate the cottage. Uncomfortable with the stuffy formality that she had to suffer in the city, Henny wanted the interior to be cosy and unpretentious. For the living room she acquired a rocking chair and two simple high-backed wooden chairs. On the wall she hung a rack upon which stood eight pewter plates. A brass clock was attached to the wall in the corner next to the fireplace, regulated by two tubular weights that hung from its base. A carpet covered most of the floor, patterned in a series of ever-decreasing squares. A guest book lay open on a stand, ready for visitors. The house's wooden interior was left unpainted.

In pride of place were the old Delft tiles that Alfred had collected while on a tour of Holland and Belgium and which Henny had installed above the living-room fireplace. In all there were thirty blue-and-white tiles, set in five rows of six, featuring old romantic scenes from the Low Countries — a child on a rocking horse, a man watering his plants, a windmill on a hill overlooking a lake, a carpenter making a casket, a woman in a large hat walking in her garden — echoing the pastoral idyll to which the Alexanders aspired.

With Henny occupied by domestic chores, and Alfred asleep in a chair under a lime tree, the children would typically spend the afternoon in the lake. Having changed into their bathing suits in a red-and-white-striped tent by the shore, they ran down the jetty, shouting and yelping, and jumped into the lake's cool water.

After the day's activities, Elsie returned to the Blue Room to change into evening clothes. She loved this room, which she and her sister had so carefully decorated. On the wall hung a large mirror, where they could check their hair and make-up. Next to each bed was a small pink side table, and a chair, often draped with clothes. As well as the two pull-down beds, there was an upholstered bench on which they read books, and a collapsible table where they wrote their letters.

Sitting on her bed, Elsie worked on the family photo album. Made of thick card and with a hessian-bound cover, there were pictures of waves lapping against the jetty, the family car parked on the rutted drive, her mother eating at the table, the chickens and geese on the lawn, the reeds in the water. At the front of this book Elsie wrote a few lines:

At the little house, life is happy
Time passes pleasantly by,
With sport and games and much laughter.
You can swim in the lake's cooling waters,
So perfect after the heat of the day.
And when the bell sounds for supper
One feels refreshed, young and beautiful.
Enjoying life at Glienicke.

The house also provided the Alexander children with an attractive setting for birthday parties. Bella was the first to take advantage of this by inviting a select group of friends to celebrate her seventeenth birthday in March. Two months later, Hanns and Paul held their own party, with a crowd of boys arriving from Berlin. Theirs was a more rambunctious affair, with running races, swimming in the lake and games of cowboys and indians. As her birthday fell in December, Elsie would be the only sibling unable to hold a party at the lake house. Though she invited her friends to the family apartment, a more sophisticated venue, she wished she too could have celebrated her birthday in Groß Glienicke.

As the decade drew to a close, Alfred was appointed the head of the Berlin Chamber of Physicians, a great honour for the Jewish doctor from Bamberg. His reputation grew, and so did the number and notoriety of his patients. Elsie and her siblings now saw a dazzling line of people entering and leaving their father's consultancy room located off the front hall of the family's apartment in Berlin. The Nobel Prize-winning physicist James Franck came to see the doctor, as did the actors Paul Wegener, Max Pallenberg and Sybille Binder. Sometimes they saw the singer Sabine Kalter, or the poet Walter Hasenclever.

Such luminaries also visited the apartment for social occasions. On one evening, for instance, Albert Einstein and his wife came for dinner. Through the dining-room door, Elsie and her siblings could see that the professor was wearing his house slippers. The stories about him being an absent-minded professor appeared to be true. After dinner the men took coffee in the salon, where Alfred hoped to ask Einstein about the theory of relativity. When Alfred returned to his wife later that evening, he recounted that the two had become so engrossed in discussing the latest detective novels, a passion they shared, that he had forgotten to ask.

Many of Alfred's patients and friends were also invited out to Groß Glienicke, to spend the day by the lake, and later dine on the terrace. Some, like Einstein, had weekend houses of their own nearby. Others, with names like Leon and Ritscher, Mendelboom and Bergmann, Strauss and Levi, came by car from Berlin.

One visitor was the photographer Lotte Jacobi, who had made a name for herself by taking pictures of famous actors and scientists. Like Alfred, she sometimes worked at the Deutsches Theater – he as a doctor, she as a photographer – which is where they probably met. On 12 June 1928, Jacobi took a series of pictures. In one of these, Henny's father, Lucien Picard, is caught holding the *Vossische Zeitung*, the morning's headlines declaring that a new cabinet had been formed. She took another picture of the lake, a serene waterscape in which not a house can be seen along the lake's shoreline, only the village church, its steeple poking through the canopy of trees. The other photographs are of the house itself: inside the living room, a close-up of the house from the rear, and another from the shoreline, looking up the garden steps to the terrace. In her images, Jacobi captures a charming place, well-lived-in, relaxing, somewhere you would want to spend the weekend.

★

While the Alexanders prospered, so too did Berlin. By the mid 1920s, with the peace and security provided by price controls, currency exchanges and foreign loans, Germany's economy had stabilised, and was beginning to boom. Nowhere was this more apparent than in the capital. Where Berlin had been a city of 1.6 million at the war's end, by 1928 it was home to over four million. The expansion was partly due to a major annexation which had taken place in 1920, with the city absorbing suburbs such as Spandau, Charlottenburg and Neukölln. Indeed, the urban growth had been so rapid that the capital's boundary now ran only one kilometre east of the Groß Glienicke Lake.

Berlin's expansion reflected the city's new-found economic wealth. Siemens had electrified the city's railways lines, and in November 1928, the Berlin Transport Company was established, making it the world's largest urban transport company. New canals were built, as were roads and factories, schools and parks. Out of this economic transformation blossomed a cultural renaissance. This was the period of dancing girls and jazz clubs, featured so colourfully in Christopher Isherwood's *Goodbye to Berlin*. It saw the emergence of a new wave of film directors, such as Fritz Lang and his *Metropolis*, warning of the dangers of automation and modern cities. It was also the start of the Bauhaus movement, which promoted an unfussy, elegant and functional design over the ornate and opulent. Millions of marks were invested in cultural centres, such as the Deutsche Oper. The capital's theatres became renowned worldwide for their experimen-tation, providing venues for both expressionism and works more grounded in reality, such as the plays of Bertholt Brecht. Berliners had their own dialect, spoken in clipped, abbreviated tones, and often with a heavy dose of irony. Some people even spoke of there being a 'Berlin air'. These were the so-called 'golden years' of the Weimar Republic. Soon the capital's streets were heaving with pedestrians and vehicles. The city's main square, the Potsdamer Platz, was now the busiest traffic intersection in Europe.

As the economy continued to improve so did Alfred's practice. The number of patients increased as did their willingness to pay on time. Yet, while he appreciated his good fortune, and enjoyed attending the theatre and the opera, Alfred found the city's congestion and noise tiresome. Soon the Alexanders were spending entire summers in Groß Glienicke, away from the frenzy and suffocating heat of Berlin. As late autumn turned to winter, and winter turned to early spring, they counted off the days until they could pack their bags and drive west.

For the Alexanders, their *Sommerhaus* had become a refuge, a haven.

Alfred (front centre), Elsie and Bella (back row left) and friends at the lake, 1928

5

WOLLANK
1929

Following on from Otto von Wollank's parcelling off of land, the Groß Glienicke Estate finances had now stabilised. The same could not be said for the landlord's health. In the early months of 1929, Otto suffered a stroke. Unable to manage the estate he asked his son-in-law, Robert, to supervise the day-to-day operations.

That autumn Otto's wife, Dorothea, also fell ill. A doctor's appointment was arranged and, on 23 September 1929, they were driven by their chauffeur, Alfred Pohl, into the city, where Dorothea was dropped off at a clinic in Halensee. According to later newspaper reports, Otto collected his wife and a nurse, Augusta Riesel, at a little after three in the afternoon, and they then drove along the busy Kurfürstendamm towards the city centre.

The car then turned left onto Nestorstraße, a quieter street, taking them north into Charlottenburg and towards home. One block from Kurfürstendamm, and driving with extreme care, the car crossed into Küstrinerstraße (today known as Damaschkestrasse), a road that joined at an acute angle. Halfway across the intersection the Wollank vehicle was struck by another car coming at speed towards them from the east. They were hit with such force that the car rolled over twice before crashing into a truck parked at the kerb.

With the Wollank car now stationary, all four occupants were buried under the debris. The nurse died at the scene, but the driver somehow crawled out unscathed, as firemen pulled Otto and Dorothea from the wreck, alive but terribly injured. Dorothea was taken to Dr Alexander's clinic nearby, on Achenbachstrasse, but died at 8 p.m. For a while the doctors thought they could save Otto, who had sustained skull fractures, but his injuries were too severe to operate and, early in the morning of 24 September, he too was declared dead. Otto was sixty-seven, Dorothea only forty-eight.

According to Herr Miltmann, the police officer in charge of the investigation, there was no evidence that either car had tried to brake before impact. The driver of the second car was Otto Grojel, a charcoal company sales representative. When he had seen the other vehicle, Grojel had misjudged the distance between the cars and failed to brake. He was not taken into custody because the police did not believe he would flee. Both cars were transported to the police station for later examination. Somehow both drivers had survived and both were later charged with reckless driving, convicted and imprisoned.

Given that it involved nobility, the crash attracted wide publicity. The *Vossische Zeitung* ran a story under the headline 'CAR CRASH IN CHARLOTTENBURG', and another the next morning, 'ESTATE OWNER WOLLANK DIES IN CAR CRASH'. Taking an editorial position, the newspaper pointed out that the corner of Küstrinerstraße and Droysenstraße had long been known as dangerous and they called for the government to solve the problem so that a similar accident would not reoccur. The article concluded by saying that Otto von Wollank lived in Groß Glienicke, where he had planted a vineyard along the north shore, and that his land was 'one of the most beautiful properties located near Berlin'.

The Wollanks' funeral procession, with Potsdamer Tor visible in the distance

A few days after the accident, on 26 September 1929, the coffins of Otto and Dorothea von Wollank were carried in two horse-drawn black coaches through the streets of Groß Glienicke. A large crowd watched as the funeral procession made its way, accompanied by a brass band. Among the mourners were Dr Alfred Alexander and Professor Fritz Munk. The men wore top hats and tails, the women long black dresses and veils. The lord of the manor and his wife were transported along Potsdamer Chaussee, under the Potsdamer Tor, to a burial ground in the woods next to the schloss. Later, a monument would be built to mark the loss of the Wollanks, with the engraved words: 'We know not the place where our loved ones are – we know the place where they are not.'

On 1 October, five days after the funeral, Otto's three children gathered at Alexanderstraße 16, Berlin, at the offices of Dr Koch, the family's lawyer, to hear their father's last will and testament. Also present were Ilse Katharina's husband Robert von Schultz and Horst's wife Else; Marie Luise, having divorced three years earlier, had come alone. Each of the children brought with them a lawyer. The reading of the will would prove a tense affair; much was at stake, for their father had owned a significant amount of Berlin property in addition to the land in Groß Glienicke.

With the children seated in front of him, Dr Koch handed out copies of the death certificates. Once these had been read each child was handed a sealed copy of their father's will, dated 30 June 1925. This was a lengthy and complicated document, dealing with numerous beneficiaries. A key point was that if Otto von Wollank died before his wife, which given that she was nineteen years his junior had been considered likely, then the vast majority of his wealth flowed to her. As Dr Koch explained, however, according to the times of death recorded on the death certificates, this was not the case. Otto had died a few hours after his wife. As a result, following the serpentine logic of the will, the inheritance would be split three ways: $\frac{2}{12}$ to the child who lived in and managed the estate and $\frac{5}{12}$ to each of the others.

Strangely, the will did not suggest which child should inherit the $\frac{2}{12}$ share and the estate. Perhaps, Otto wanted his offspring to decide. After some discussion, it was agreed that Horst and Marie Luise would inherit the greater shares, while Ilse Katharina would live at the schloss. It is likely that Marie Luise was not interested in the estate given that she was not married and had no experience in running a farm. Why Horst chose not to take over the estate isn't so clear. Maybe, concerned about his poor health, he worried that he might not be able to take on the estate management. Whatever the reason, the three children appeared satisfied with the will's outcome.

Ilse now owned the Groß Glienicke Estate. In practice this meant that the day-to-day operations, including the farmland, the forests and the heath to the west of the lake, as well as the lakeside parcels that had been rented to the settlers from Berlin, were now under the control of her husband, Robert von Schultz. And Robert von Schultz was a very different character from the kind-hearted, well-loved, if slightly disorganised businessman Otto von Wollank.

Where Otto had been steeped in the values of the *Kaiser Reich* – committed to the military, the royal family and tradition – Robert was a product of the street battles of the 1920s, believing in the violent overthrow of the government, the supremacy of the German people and the importance of race. Above all else, the Alexanders' new landlord fostered a searing hatred for one group of people whom he blamed for all that was going wrong in his country: the Jews.

Robert von Schultz

At the time that he became landlord of the Groß Glienicke Estate, Robert von Schultz was a regional leader of the Stahlhelm Bund der Frontsoldaten, one of the many right-wing organisations then active in Germany. Meaning 'steel helmet', the Stahlhelm had been established in 1918 by Franz Seldte, a German officer who had lost his arm while fighting in the First World War and who demanded that his country be allowed to rebuild its military strength. Deeply conservative and a supporter of the monarchy, Seldte wished to see Kaiser Wilhelm II return from his exile in the Netherlands and regain his throne. By 1930, the Stahlhelm had over 500,000 members and was the largest paramilitary group in Germany.

Robert von Schultz had joined the Stahlhelm in 1926. As a member of a prominent local family, he had then been quickly promoted to the position of regional leader and placed in charge of recruitment and training of the young men in Groß Glienicke and the surrounding areas. As with all members of the Stahlhelm, his uniform included a grey woollen cap with a black peak, emblazoned with a 'Der Stahlhelm' badge; a grey jacket crossed by a leather strap which sported a buckle stamped with a miniature steel helmet; grey woollen trousers and black boots.

At the core of Robert's ideology was a pride in the fatherland and its people. Critically, he wished to keep his country free of the Jews and communists whom he believed had forced the Kaiser to abdicate in November 1918, and had caused the hyperinflation and high unemployment of the Weimar Republic. One of those he particularly despised was Ernst Thälmann, the thirty-nine-year-old head of the Communist Party who, in 1925, had run as a candidate for the German presidency and then thankfully, as far as Robert was concerned, lost to the former Army Chief of Staff, Paul von Hindenburg. In their meetings and publications the Stahlhelm frequently conflated left-wing activism with being Jewish, often using the words interchangeably. An article published in the *Der Stahlhelm* newsletter in 1925, for instance, declared that 'we tell our aims with an honest and brutal frankness, and these aims are highly dangerous for the Jewish-Marxist rabble. We want nothing more than they already possess, that is to say the power in the state.'

Since becoming the Stahlhelm regional leader, it was quite common to see Robert von Schultz riding through Groß Glienicke in the back of a farm truck, standing alongside other volunteers, dressed in their paramilitary uniforms. Starting at the schloss, they would roll along the sandy road on the lake's north shore, past the gates to the Alexander property, through the Potsdamer Tor and down the Potsdamer Chaussee, shouting slogans and waving their guns in the air. There were rumours of abductions, midnight interrogations and even torture. Most of the villagers didn't want to have anything to do with Robert's mob. The violence scared them. Yet there were some local young men who were attracted by the uniforms and the ideology, not to mention the drinking and the brawling, and as a result, the size of the Groß Glienicke Stahlhelm brigade continued to grow.

In their spare moments, Robert von Schultz and his Stahlhelm comrades crowded into the local pubs, particularly the Drei Linden, the imposing two-storey stone-faced inn that stood two hundred metres south of the Potsdamer Tor and the entrance to the Alexander property. For centuries the Drei Linden had served as the village's watering hole, providing rooms for travellers, and a large courtyard in front for their carriages. It was here, in the wood-panelled bar, that Robert's men banged out a tune on the piano while others half shouted, half sung the old street-fighting songs. Later, holding aloft oversized glasses of beer, they cried 'Kick out the philistines!' and 'Sharpen the knife!', referring to the politicians then in power, as well as various anti-Semitic slogans, such as 'Germany for the Germans' and 'Foreigners and Jews have only guest rights'.

Robert was often at the centre of these delinquencies. Sometimes, such gatherings moved from the Drei Linden to the schloss. Labourers who lived close to the estate spoke of hearing '*Prunk-und Zechgelage, rauschende Feste,*' or drinking and rough feasts, taking place at Robert's house. There were also reports of firearms being let off and late-night excesses which disturbed the calm country environs.

The virulent nationalism and anti-Semitism professed by Robert von Schultz and his comrades was a rarity in the Germany of 1929. Though pogroms against Jews had taken place in the early nineteenth century, such attacks had mostly died down by this time. The improved status of the Jewish population was symbolised by laws that guaranteed their rights and privileges. In 1812, Prussia had passed an emancipation law, followed by Hanover in 1842. Then, in 1871, full emancipation for the Jewish population was enshrined with the introduction of the first ever German constitution. Nevertheless, anti-Semitism did still exist in Germany. Jews could not become officers in the German Army and it was difficult to become a university professor, or hold other state positions, without first converting to Christianity. Notoriously, in 1916 the German military had conducted a count of the Jews in their ranks (the *Judenzählung*, or Jewish census), after persistent accusations that Jews were not pulling their weight and that Jewish soldiers were avoiding front-line service. Yet, such instances of anti-Semitism were the exceptions rather than the rule. After all, over 100,000 Jewish soldiers had served in the German Army during the First World War, and more than 30,000 – including Alfred Alexander – had been decorated for their bravery. Which is why, for the first two decades of the twentieth century, most Jewish families who lived in Germany, such as the Alexanders, considered themselves to be Germans by nationality, and Jewish by religion; their daily lives unhindered by ethnicity or prejudice.

This would soon change, however. On 24 October 1929, three weeks after the reading of Otto's will in the lawyer's office, the New

York Stock Exchange fell by a massive 11 per cent in one day. After years of excessive speculation, the market had received a string of bad news – disappointing corporate results, a worsening agricultural recession, falling consumer purchasing – which had derailed the market confidence. Four days later, on 28 October, the NYSE lost another 13 per cent, and another 12 per cent the following day. This marked the start of a three-year collapse of the NYSE, which resulted in an 89 per cent loss in the market's overall value by July 1932.

The Wall Street Crash, as the market rout became known, had profound consequences for the German economy, as well as its politics. When the American banks, which only a few years before had eagerly lent money to the Weimar Republic, now called in their loans, the German debtors were unable to pay. Almost overnight, Germany had lost one of its major sources of investment. German international trade fell to 50 per cent of its level the year before, crop prices fell 60 per cent and the rate of unemployment rose to 14 per cent of the working age population, amounting to some 3.2 million people.

In the midst of this crisis many turned to the now vocal far-right political groups who blamed the betrayal at Versailles, war profiteers, communists and, most of all, the Jews, for Germany's economic collapse. One such group was the National Socialist German Workers Party (NSDAP), or the Nazi Party. Originally founded as the German Workers Party (DAP) in January 1919, the Munich-based party was one of dozens of *volkisch* or 'folk' organisations – ostensibly far-right groups – now operating in post-war Germany. These groups attracted considerable support by promoting the ideas of national supremacy and ethnic purity, and by extension being anti-Slav and anti-Semitic. In September 1919, when Adolf Hitler had participated in his first DAP meeting, only forty other people had been present. By July 1921, Hitler had taken over as party leader and, within two years, membership had climbed to more than 20,000 people. Since then, the Nazi Party had spread across the country, and was now a significant political force.

So it was that, in the September 1930 elections, the Nazi Party surprised everyone when it received over six million votes, 18 per cent of the ballot, making Hitler's party the second largest in the Reichstag. For the first time, anti-Semitism became an ideology upon which it was possible to win elections. The extreme, and up till now minority, views of Robert von Schultz had suddenly become mainstream.

A few weeks after the 1930 elections, and not long after he took control of the Groß Glienicke Estate, Robert was approached by a senior member of the Sturmabteilung (SA), or Brownshirts – the paramilitary wing of the Nazi Party – to see if they could use his Groß Glienicke Estate for training. Though not a member of the party, Robert consented, and soon brown-shirted thugs could be seen taking part in rifle practice, drills and hand-to-hand fighting in the grounds of the estate, a few hundred metres from the Alexanders' weekend house.

6

ALEXANDER

1930

It was the autumn of 1930, and Elsie arrived at her first day of lectures at Berlin's Friedrich Wilhelm University. She had the grades to study where she liked, but had elected to remain in Berlin, partly because it allowed her to live with her parents, and partly because this was where her father had studied medicine.

Pushing open the wide double doors, Elsie found herself in an enormous lecture hall. In front of her, long rows of wooden benches descended to a large wooden desk, lectern and blackboard. All she could see were the backs of hundreds of her fellow students' heads, young Germans who, like herself, were studying medicine. To Elsie, the 7 a.m. lecture was already a hardship given her propensity for sleep. Worse still, with all the seats occupied, Elsie was forced to stand at the back of the hall with the other latecomers, straining to hear the mumbling professor explain the basics of human anatomy.

Over the next few days, Elsie woke earlier and earlier, hoping to secure a seat. Eventually, she found that the only way to guarantee a spot near the front of the hall was if she got up at six. Now that she was able to actually hear the lecture, she realised that she wasn't particularly interested. Much of the course involved rote learning

– the Latin names of parts of the body, the various elements of the circulatory system, cellular and sub-cellular structures – which was tiresome. Having grown up surrounded by artists and actors, theatre directors and photographers, Elsie discovered that she was keener to study the philosophy of Kant and the novels of Goethe than how to cure syphilis or when to remove an optic nerve.

Always a curious person, and inspired by the work of the many Jewish correspondents she had either met through her father or whose articles she had read in the newspaper, she now decided to study journalism. Many of the country's leading newspapers were owned and managed by Jews, and while the vast majority of their journalists were male, there were some notable exceptions. These were Elsie's heroines: journalists such as Bella Fromm, for instance, who worked as the diplomatic correspondent for the Ullstein papers, and Elisabeth Castonier, a satirist who wrote for a weekly paper named *Die Ente*.

Towards the end of the academic year Elsie approached her supervisor to see if she could switch course. When he told her that she could – it was quite common for students to move from one course to the next, from one university to another – Elsie informed her parents that she no longer wanted to become a doctor, and instead wished to move to Heidelberg to study journalism. Heidelberg was Germany's oldest university, situated in south-west of the country, an hour's drive from the French border and a ten-hour train journey from Berlin.

In the first week of October 1931, Elsie and her family gathered at Anhalter Bahnhof, one of Berlin's main railway stations and known as the 'gateway to the south'. While her parents would clearly miss her, the same was probably not true for her sister. Over the past few months, Bella had become preoccupied with her new boyfriend, Harold, a handsome young Englishman, who was in Berlin to study German banking. With her black Olympia Erika typewriter in one hand and a suitcase in another, Elsie boarded the train and waved goodbye to her family.

Elsie had chosen her university not only for its journalism course, but also because of its liberal reputation, led as it was by professors such as the philosopher Karl Jaspers and the economist Alfred Weber. It was a town noted for the beauty of its landscape, nestled as it was between the Neckar River and the Königstuhl Mountains, as well as for its picturesque town centre, featuring a romantic castle, ancient red stone bridge and a medieval marketplace. It wasn't Berlin, but she was ready for something different.

Now nineteen, and living away from home for the first time, Elsie started a diary. It was a simple notebook, bound in black leather, its pages thinly lined in blue. Many of her concerns were typical of a girl her age. She wondered if she had friends and why she felt so lonely despite her parents' love. She said that her father was a 'mensch, full of love, kindness, a sense of duty', and asked why there were 'so few persons of this quality'. She claimed that he loved her most of all his children, but noted that his melancholia put distance between them. 'He is also very proud of me, why? Because I'm intelligent? I can't help that, it is really only that duty calls me to be doing something.'

In her diary, Elsie documented her growing unease.

Why then am I here? I didn't will it at all, now I must abide, 'live'. And I have such a dread of life. So many individuals live not really as they would like. They eat and sleep and for income they must earn money, labour on. This labour becomes the content of their life, it becomes a circular thing, to eat in order to work, to work in order to eat. I call that existing. And life? Pappi lives, as did Goethe, Mozart, Rilke, Beethoven. Whether they were happy? What does being happy really mean. Am I happy? Have I never been?

Gradually, Elsie began to adjust to being away from home and adapted to her new life in Heidelberg. In July 1932, nine months after Elsie's arrival at the university, Germany held a national election. It was the first time that Elsie was eligible to vote and she was excited by the prospect. Appalled by the Nazi Party, and put off like so many of her class by the radical rhetoric of the Communist Party and its leader Ernst Thälmann, Elsie cast her ballot for the Social Democrats. She was disappointed by the result. For the first time, the Nazi Party won the most seats, with 37 per cent of the vote. In the days that followed, however, neither Adolf Hitler nor any other party was able to attract enough support to form a government.

With such an unclear result, Paul von Hindenburg – who had remained in office as president since 1925 – declared that another election would need to be held, later that year, on 6 November 1932. While Elsie kept herself busy with studies, all around her fierce political campaigning was taking place. Between 11 October and election day, Adolf Hitler gave more than fifty speeches, sometimes as many as three a day. On 1 November, for instance, he spoke to over 40,000 people in Karlsruhe, a town less than an hour's drive from Heidelberg. Many of the students from Elsie's class attended the event.

On 6 November, Elsie voted again, along with 36 million other German citizens. Despite the Nazi Party share of the vote decreasing to 33 per cent, they were again the leading party and once again unable to attract sufficient support from other parties to form a government. Over that Christmas and into the new year, President Hindenburg worked hard to build a coalition.

Meanwhile, Elsie's diary entries remained focused on her family, particularly the news that Bella had become engaged to Harold.

5 January 1933

1933: What will it bring? I do not know. But what it will take from me, that I know: my sister. Bella is engaged and is to be wed this summer. Off to London. That means an end not only to her childhood, but to mine. Even though I have never admitted it to anyone, I am so closely bound to her that I cannot imagine a home without Bella.

But Bella deserves to be happy. We had a splendid childhood. And this memory she should take with her and think about it whenever clouds appear. And if she is terribly happy, she should consider that the foundation of her good fortune was the sunshine in Glienicke, the childhood at home. And what will I do? I am afraid of this year.

Elsie kept in touch with her family by telephone and mail, and closely followed political events by reading the newspapers. During the first few weeks of 1933, President Hindenburg continued his efforts to form a government that did not include Hitler. It soon became clear that his attempts were in vain, however, for no stable coalition could be formed without including the Nazi Party.

Over the next few days Franz von Papen and Hitler engaged in a series of tough negotiations to resolve who would head the next government. It was now that the founder of the Stahlhelm, Franz Seldte, agreed not only to support the Nazi Party, but also that his troops would be folded into the Sturmabteilung (SA). With the hundreds of thousands of Stahlhelm members now behind the Nazi Party, Papen encouraged Hindenburg to appoint Hitler as chancellor. As part of the deal, Seldte would join the cabinet as minister for labour. After further consideration, Hindenburg concluded that he had no choice and, on 30 January 1933, reluctantly appointed Adolf Hitler as chancellor.

In the days following his appointment, and unhappy with leading a minority government, Hitler called for yet another round of national elections, this time on 5 March. Nazi paramilitary groups launched a series of violent attacks on the other parties. Newspapers that were critical of the government were raided and closed down. Brownshirts broke up meetings of the Social Democrats and the Catholic Centre Party, beating up their speakers and members of the audience. The leader of the Communist Party, Ernst Thälmann, was arrested and placed in jail, accused of fomenting the violent overthrow of the government.

Dismayed and infuriated by the Nazi Party's growing power, and hoping to gain an audience for her views, Elsie submitted articles and opinion columns to the Berlin newspapers in early February 1933. These pieces were only obliquely critical of the regime, for Elsie worried that she would attract too much attention to herself. To her surprise, some of her articles were published, including one about the Winterhilfswerk, a Nazi Party charity that encouraged people to eat less meat and the money saved would be donated to the poor during winter. In her article, Elsie called the campaign hypocritical, pointing out that most affluent people were able to give money while continuing to eat fine food.

Elsie's burgeoning career soon came to a rapid end, however. On 27 February 1933, a fire erupted at the Reichstag. The police were called and found a young Dutch communist by the name of Marinus van der Lubbe at the scene of the crime. Van der Lubbe admitted starting the fire and was arrested. Within a few hours, Adolf Hitler contacted President Hindenburg, encouraging him to suspend civil liberties and so protect Germany from the Communist Party. Though the true identity of the arsonists was hotly contested then, and has been ever since, the following day, on 28 February, the president signed the Reichstag Fire Decree, suspending civil liberties, including habeas corpus, the right of free association, the secrecy of the post and freedom of the press. Elsie's future profession had been curtailed before she had even graduated. Germany was now being governed as a dictatorship.

The 5 March election was held only six days after the Reichstag fire. In the preceding days, more than four thousand communists were arrested and placed in jail, considerably suppressing the anti-Nazi vote. On election day itself, over 50,000 'monitors', belonging to the SA, stood guard at polling stations, intimidating those who were about to vote. When the votes were counted, the Nazi Party had raised their share from 33 to 44 per cent, with over 17 million Germans now voting for the Nazi Party. Quickly gaining the support of the German Nationalist People's Party (DNVP), who had won 8 per cent of the vote, Adolf Hitler now commanded a majority.

Hoping to unite the country and demonstrate a link between the Nazis and their imperial antecedents, Hitler declared that a mass rally would be held in Potsdam on 21 March. He understood that even though the Kaiser had been forced out of power fifteen years earlier, a large proportion of the population held the royal family, and the traditions they stood for, in high regard. Indeed, many longed for the stability and military power epitomised by the emperor. Potsdam was the royal family's summer residence, and was considered by many to be the spiritual centre of the German Empire.

The so-called 'Day of Potsdam' was covered in great detail by both German and foreign correspondents. When Hitler arrived that morning in his open-air car, the city was decorated with thousands of banners, both the swastika-emblazoned flag of the Nazi Party, as well as the black, white and red tricolour of imperial Germany. Tens of thousands of citizens lined the streets twenty-deep to see the new chancellor drive slowly by, followed by vast columns of SA and Stahlhelm troops, marching in perfect unison.

Later that day, Hitler visited the former Crown Prince Wilhelm – the deposed Kaiser's son – at Cecilienhof, the prince's home in Potsdam. With his father still exiled in the Netherlands, Wilhelm was the most senior member of the royal family remaining in Germany. Already a member of the Stahlhelm and a supporter of the Nazi Party, through this meeting the prince declared his public endorsement of Hitler and his party, thus merging the royalist and Nazi Party causes.

Finally, in a carefully choreographed moment, Hitler and Hindenburg met in the street, surrounded by cheering crowds. The chancellor wearing a dark conservative suit, the president, his full military attire, including a pike helmet and a jacket bedecked with medals, they shook hands; Hitler's hands were bare, Hindenburg's gloved. Their palms still gripped, Hitler gave a slight bow, appearing to humble himself before Germany's president. It was a highly symbolic day, an effort by the chancellor to wrap himself in Germany's Prussian and military past.

Two days later, parliament met at the Kroll Opera House in Berlin, where the legislature had re-established itself since the Reichstag fire, and passed the 'Enabling Act', effectively giving the chancellor the power to pass laws without consulting parliament. Hitler had assumed absolute control of the political process.

On 1 April, less than two weeks after the Day of Potsdam, Elsie was back in Berlin for the Easter holidays. With the Jewish festival of Passover due to begin a few days later, she had hoped for a period of peace and enjoyment at the family's apartment on the Kaiserallee.

On the radio, the Alexanders heard Joseph Goebbels, the minister of propaganda, calling for a national boycott of Jewish businesses. Not knowing what to expect, they had remained at the apartment. Early that morning, the family became aware of a commotion outside their building. They saw a small group of people gathering on the pavement, next to the bronze sign that announced that this was where Dr Alexander had his consultancy rooms. It had been easy to find him. The general telephone book listed the details, as did the Jewish telephone directory, which not only gave Alfred's street address, but announced at the front of the book that he was head of the Berlin Chamber of Physicians.

An hour later, the crowd had grown. People were pointing at the Alexanders' apartment and exclaiming that Jews worked and lived there. The family peered anxiously out of the window where they could see the mob. Many wore the brown-shirted uniforms of the SA, others wore swastika-decorated armbands on their arms. If they

Joseph Goebbels calls for boycott of Jewish business, Berlin, 1 April 1933

remained in place, it would be impossible for Alfred's patients to visit him that day.

Shouting 'Dirty Jews' and 'Don't buy from Jews', the crowd surged forward, threatening to break into the building. It was then that Otto Meyer, a family friend and an old army colleague of Alfred's, stepped in front of the crowd, calmly and forcefully telling them to disperse, that they were attacking a man who had received an Iron Cross First Class. The mob, with much muttering, moved on to an easier target.

The Alexanders had been lucky. By the end of the day, Jewish businesses and business owners had been targeted across Germany. Thousands of shops were daubed with yellow-painted Stars of David and graffiti declaring 'Jews are our misfortune'. In his diary that night, Goebbels wrote: 'There is indescribable excitement in the air. The press is now working in total unanimity. The boycott is a great moral victory for Germany. We have shown the rest of the world that we can call up the entire nation without provoking turbulence. The Führer once again has struck just the right note.' The following day, the Berlin newspapers celebrated the patriotism of those who participated in the boycott and attacked the international Jewish organisations who threatened the nation. Not one article or opinion was published criticising what had been a government-sanctioned pogrom.

Shocked by the sudden turn of events, Elsie noted in her diary:

5 April 1933

A quarter of a year ago the individual path of life was foremost in my thoughts. And now? Now it is no longer about me or about my family, but about everybody. The great political changes that began on 30 January have influenced the entire world. Half a million people, 556,000 Jews in Germany, were the cause for great debates in the Reichstag – in the world. Concern for the fate of these people suddenly worked a miracle. All the Jews in the whole world became conscious of their Jewishness and – became proud of it. International Jewry is really the one *international* power. All that is lacking is a great head that recognises and capitalises on the fortunate aspects arising from this fact. I believe that no country, including Germany, can manage without the aid of this International. Who, for example, is in a position to obtain large foreign financial credits? The internationally respected Jew as head of a large bank, with his extensive connections abroad. So long as the heads of the largest banking houses all over the world are Jews, Germany cannot dispense with the Jew.

But all these considerations do not alter the fact that thousands of Jewish employees, doctors, lawyers have been impoverished in the space of a few hours. From what will these people live? People who during the war fought and bled for their German fatherland, who lost all their money in Germany's inflation, and who have at last through hard labour found their life's work – now they stand on the brink of the abyss. 1933. Freedom, equality, brotherhood, human rights, love for one's fellow man. Empty words, so true in every schoolbook reader, but harder to believe in real life. I have always been proud of my Jewishness. Today I would be ashamed to be a German Christian.

Then, on 7 April 1933, the Nazi government passed the Law for the Restoration of the Professional Civil Service. From this point, Jewish professionals were banned from working for the government. This included bureaucrats and office workers, but also teachers, judges and professors. An exception was made, at least for now, for First World War veterans. Nevertheless, this was the first major law to restrict the rights of the Jewish population, and tens of thousands were affected.

Two weeks later, on 25 April, the German government passed a law limiting the number of Jewish students who could attend schools and universities. This legislation, the authorities declared, would solve the overcrowding in the country's educational establishments. From this date, Jewish students would be restricted to 1.5 per cent of the university population.

Unlike many of her friends, however, Elsie was permitted to remain in Heidelberg. For although Jewish, her father's war record again proved vital, allowing Elsie to receive special treatment. Yet she was not unaffected. On 17 May, members of the Heidelberg faculty and students removed books from the library that had been written by communist, Jewish or other authors deemed unacceptable to the Nazi Party, piled them up at the centre of the Universitätsplatz, and set them on fire. The university's motto was changed from 'The Living Spirit' to 'The German Spirit'. And then, to ensure that everyone knew what Elsie was, the spines of her books were marked with yellow stripes.

It was around this time that Elsie made her last diary entry.

We Jews exert ourselves to the extreme to be regarded as Germans. In 1914 we were viewed as Germans, again during the inflation. But today? A people, who have demonstrated on 1 April 1933 [boycott of Jewish shops] upon which rung of civilisation they stand, need not reject me. To this people I do not *want* to belong. But what then? Stateless? Outside the law? And what about my future children? To whom will they belong? And still I love this land, love this world, but hate the people. No I despise them, and all those who allow this blot on civilisation. They want to make me ashamed to be a Jew. No, I am proud of my Jewishness but I am ashamed of my Germanness. At this time foreign lands view us with pity: A German Jew! [the three preceding words were in English]. But later on? Then I shall again be the German, a citizen of the people among whom 1 April 1933 was celebrated. Fate! But can one bring children into the world, can one take on a responsibility of such proportions?

A few weeks later, on 4 June 1933, the family gathered at Berlin's Friedenstempel synagogue for the wedding of Bella and Harold. Four hundred people were in attendance.

Downstairs, the men sat in rows of wooden pews; they wore top hats and long tails. Upstairs, in the balcony section, also seated in pews, the women were attired in formal dresses and hats. In front of the Ark, the ornamental chamber that contained the Torahs, the bride and groom stood under a chuppah, a cream-and-blue fabric canopy held up by four wooden posts that had been garlanded with flowers. The bride was dressed in a stunning ivory bridal gown, her face covered with a veil; the groom was in tails like the other men. Beside them stood the four parents – Harold's family had travelled from London – along with Rabbi Joachim Prinz, who officiated over the ceremony. Once the vows had been exchanged, Harold stamped on a glass that had been wrapped in a cloth. With the sound of it breaking, the congregation called out *mazel tov*.

Later, the guests were invited to a reception held at the Adlon Hotel, a massive yellow-stoned five-storey building on the Unter den Linden, known for its luxurious interior and superior service. As the coffee was served, and after the groom had made a speech – rather long as was the English tradition, but which was a bit of a surprise to the assembled Germans – Elsie stood to congratulate the married couple, before reading a poem she had written in their honour, and which captured the bitter-sweet texture of the moment.

> Four words I'd like to say to you two
> A mere four words, I wish you luck,
> For this celebration here today,
> For all the days yet to come,
> I wish you luck, I wish you luck!
>
> Just three words must the two of you retain,
> Just three words: Love one another
> Despite all external forces,
> Love one another, love one another!
>
> Lastly I say two words most heartily to you
> *Auf Wiedersehen.*
> We should look forward to the days
> When we happily meet again!

At the end of the evening, the wedding crowd gathered outside the golden doors of the hotel's main entrance to wave goodbye to Bella and Harold as they set off for their honeymoon in Venice. For now, a semblance of ordinary life could be maintained, but for how long, nobody knew.

★

After a summer break in Glienicke, of swims in the lake, sleeping in and sunbathing on the lawn, Elsie returned to Heidelberg for the autumn term of her third year. She had barely settled in, however, when her studies were interrupted, on 4 October, with news of the latest law that had been announced in Berlin: from this point forward, Jews could not work as journalists, nor could they work as newspaper editors. Anyone found guilty of breaking this law could be jailed for up to a year. It was hard for Elsie to motivate herself to study for a career from which she was barred. Then, at the end of the academic year in July 1934, despite achieving excellent results, Elsie was informed that she would not be welcome back at the university. Bitterly disappointed, she packed her belongings and returned to Berlin, joining her family in Glienicke.

One of Elsie's least pleasant chores now was collecting milk from the estate's dairy. Fully aware that the master of the schloss, Robert von Schultz, was a member of the Nazi Party (he had joined on 28 April 1933), as were many of his workers, Elsie tried to avoid contact. But the dairy was the closest place to purchase milk and so, with a sinking heart, and with an empty metal container in her hand, she travelled back and forth to the dairy every evening. One day, just as dusk was falling, she walked past the schloss and saw a number of military vehicles parked in the courtyard. Seeing the men dressed in SA uniforms, she averted her eyes and hurried on to the dairy. Once the pail was filled, she took an alternative route home, walking back along the shoreline.

Though they had been coming out to Groß Glienicke for more than seven years, the Alexanders were still treated as outsiders by the village. Sometimes, Henny would come in to contact with the locals, when ordering supplies from Frau Mond, the owner of the dairy shop, sides of meat from the butcher or, if they were hosting a large social gathering, a special cake from the baker. Other than that, the villagers and the Alexanders did not interact. Given the worsening anti-Semitic climate, they now thought it best to keep an even lower profile.

By this time, the village of Groß Glienicke had grown to a little over seven hundred people. The majority lived in the village, either running their own business or working in Potsdam; 28 per cent of the population worked on the estate, and the remainder, 20 per cent were 'settlers', professionals from Berlin who spent their weekends by the lake. In a note on the history of the village, the Wollanks' lawyer, Erwin Koch, wrote that 'there are a lot of different opinions on the settlers in the village'.

It was around this time that Robert von Schultz offered Professor Munk the opportunity to purchase the land under his weekend house. Like the Alexanders, Professor Munk had leased his parcel back in 1927, but the Alexanders were not invited to purchase their land. This was almost certainly because of the political inclinations of von Schultz, who was openly anti-Semitic. Otherwise, he would have been only too pleased to sell the land to Dr Alexander, given the estate's desperate need for cash.

Meanwhile, Elsie told her parents that even if she could not study she would work as a journalist. Having forged a set of press credentials on her typewriter, she set off in search of stories. At first, she walked around the village, taking pictures of the lake, the houses and the shops. Then, feeling bolder, and in the teeth of her mother's pleas, the twenty-one-year-old ventured into Berlin's city centre. On one occasion, she climbed a tree and photographed Hitler's SA marching along the Unter den Linden. When she found out, Henny was furious, and told her not to take such risks. But her mother's advice had little effect on Elsie, and before long she was out on the streets again taking photographs.

With the political situation increasingly dangerous, dinner conversations became fraught. Newly married and back from her honeymoon, Bella said that she was ready to leave Germany, as did Elsie. Their father disagreed, believing that the German people would come to their senses. They would stay, he said, but should keep a low profile.

Fritz Munk with Alfred and Henny Alexander, Groß Glienicke

Professor Munk concurred with the sisters. One hot summer evening in July, Munk walked up to the garden fence and called out to Alfred Alexander. The doctor stopped what he was doing and, hearing the urgency in Munk's voice, fetched Henny to join them. After swapping pleasantries, Professor Munk spoke frankly about the political situation. In his capacity as director of the Martin Luther Hospital in Berlin, he said, he rubbed shoulders with many senior government officials. They had told him that Jewish Germans would find life increasingly precarious. A well-known physician such as Dr Alexander would be in the Nazis' cross hairs.

'Dr Alexander, there are difficult times ahead of us,' said Fritz Munk. 'I recommend that you leave Germany immediately.'

'Why should I?' responded Alfred Alexander. 'I was a soldier and an officer in the war and I received the Iron Cross. Nothing will happen to me.'

'Don't rely on that,' the professor replied. 'It can't help you much any more.'

Unconvinced, but grateful for his neighbour's concern, Alfred thanked Professor Munk and told him that he believed the troubles would soon blow over. After a few more words, the neighbours said their goodbyes and returned to their families on either side of the fence.

7

SCHULTZ
1934

Late in the evening of 30 June 1934, a convoy of vehicles drove up the long gravel driveway to the Groß Glienicke Estate. Out of them jumped a troop of black-shirted men who pushed open the large oak front door and rushed in to the schloss. They were members of Hitler's elite security force, the Schutzstaffel, or SS.

A few minutes later, the men marched out of the white-stoned building. Two of them held a short, beefy man with a ruddy scowling face whose hands were manacled behind his back. It was Robert von Schultz. After bundling him into a truck, they drove to the SS barracks in Potsdam ten kilometres away.

Robert's arrest was one of thousands taking place across Germany that week as part of a clandestine nationwide campaign organized by Hitler to eliminate opposition to his new regime. The Night of the Long Knives, as it came to be known, was primarily aimed at quashing the independent SA, seen by Hitler as a potential threat, given its history of street violence, and the ambitions of its leader, Ernst Röhm. Approximately eighty-five SA leaders were executed in the purge, including Ernst Röhm himself, who was shot three times in his prison cell. Many more SA members were imprisoned and interrogated –

including Robert, who was roughly questioned, and charged with treason against the state, and, perhaps even worse, against the Führer.

While her husband was being held, Ilse von Schultz was approached by a civil servant from Berlin. He represented the Reich aviation minister, Hermann Göring, and brought with him a request that she sell a large area of her family's land to the east of the Groß Glienicke Lake.

As far as Ilse was concerned this was a lucky break. With her husband in jail, the estate's finances had gone from bad to worse. Since the early 1930s, Robert's primary crop had been wheat. Some of this harvest he sent to the village windmill where it was ground into flour; the rest he fermented in enormous vats, and then distilled to produce *Korn*, a grain-based spirit. However, the family's fortunes had experienced a dramatic decline earlier that year when Hitler's regime placed price restrictions on private alcohol production. That is not to say that the manor was without worth. According to the tax records at this time, the estate had 49 horses, 132 cows, 140 pigs, 147 rabbits, 230 ducks and geese, 1,714 hens, 29 turkeys and 16 beehives. The Schultzes, however, could not survive on the sale of duck and hen eggs, rabbits and honey.

Ilse realised that the aviation minister's offer could save the estate from ruin. For the ministry, the deal was a crucial part of their secret rearmament programme. Ever since the signing of the Treaty of Versailles in 1919, Germany had not been allowed an air force. But Göring, had every intention of building up the country's Luftwaffe, and he had chosen Groß Glienicke and its environs as a key location. It was near Berlin, it was flat and free of nearby tall buildings, and therefore suitable for aircraft landings and take-offs.

After being held in captivity for more than sixty days, Robert von

Schultz finally stood trial. If he was to avoid prosecution, he would have to demonstrate that he was a 'good Nazi'. The first witness was the owner of the Drei Linden, Herr Krause, who said, 'I think Schulz is trying to convince the people to think badly of the Führer.' Next, a member of Robert's Stahlhelm brigade, a certain Alfred Eichel, said that he heard Robert comment in Potsdam, on 1 May 1933, that 'the Führer isn't going to last long'.

A third witness accused Robert von Schultz and his men of holding 'wild parties' at the schloss and of firing guns in local pubs. Another accused him of having too close a relationship with Karl Ernst – the leader of the SA in Berlin who like Robert had been arrested on 30 June, before being executed by a firing squad – and of benefiting financially from that relationship. Then came yet another witness, Fritz Müller, a member of the SA, who said that Robert and his gang had once beaten him until he was unconscious. Finally, Herr Steek, a well-known local communist, accused Robert of turning up at his house one night, punching him in the face and, with two SA leaders, hitting him with a bullwhip until he lost consciousness.

Robert denied the charges. In a statement, given on 29 September 1934, he said that he had never 'made fun' of the Führer, arguing that it was 'not part of my personality to dirty the nest that I come from'. He acknowledged that he and his men frequently visited the area's pubs, but said that he had never personally witnessed any guns being let off, though he confessed hearing that his butler had fired one shot, for which he had been later punished, 'according to the rules of the Stahlhelm'. Yes, he conceded, he had often met with the former group leader Karl Ernst, but he had never profited from this relationship.

Robert admitted that Fritz Müller had been beaten but added that he had not even been in the room when the beatings had taken place. As to the communist Herr Steek, Robert remembered that the prisoner had been 'very rude' during his questioning and had to be 'restrained'. 'I admit without hesitation,' he testified, 'that in some cases when dealing with bad boys I have punished them, but I don't agree that any of these were disproportionate to the situation.'

To prove that he was a loyal supporter, Robert passed the court paperwork showing that he had joined the Nazi Party on 28 April 1933 and to demonstrate that that he was an adherent to the cause of National Socialism, he provided witness statements from friends and associates. What more evidence was required, he asked, of his loyalty to Adolf Hitler?

With Robert von Schultz's testimony concluded, the trial came to an end. Shortly afterwards, he was found not guilty, although dismissed from the SA and on 27 October he was released from prison. Upon his return to Groß Glienicke, he learned that his wife had accepted the offer from the Ministry of Aviation. Almost a quarter of the estate had been sold to the military.

By the start of 1935, work commenced on the new airfield, just a few hundred metres from the north-eastern corner of the Groß Glienicke Lake. Known as Berlin-Gatow, the facility was slated to become one of only four training schools for Göring's quickly expanding air force, but as the closest to the nation's capital, it would become the most high profile. The brief was to build a training school for technicians and an academy for pilots. The plans for the buildings were laid out by Ernst Sagebiel, the same architect who had designed the Ministry of Aviation in Berlin, and later the airport at Tempelhof near the city's southern boundary. Over four thousand labourers, many from Groß Glienicke and nearby villages, set to work, first constructing the airfield and then the school buildings themselves.

On 2 November 1935, Adolf Hitler attended the official opening of Berlin-Gatow. From this time forward, he would often choose to use this airfield for his personal journeys, including to his mountain retreat in Berchtesgaden, providing a degree of privacy that he could not find at Berlin's other airfields. A few months later, on 21 April 1936, Göring took part in the Luftwaffe Day ceremonies at Gatow, during which he invited military officers from around the world to visit the airfield, proudly displaying what was a flagrant contravention of the Treaty of Versailles.

Meanwhile, Robert returned to his schloss, broken, paranoid and overwhelmed by mounting debts. Realising that selling parcels of land was not going to stave off their financial problems, and fearing that that he might be rearrested, Robert and Ilse loaded their four children into a car, and drove away from Groß Glienicke. This was the end of an era, for no member of the Wollank family would ever live at the schloss again. The estate's management would now rest with a supervisor.

Having left the estate, the Schultzes drove three hundred kilometres north, up to the Baltic Coast, and over the Stralsund Crossing to the island of Rügen. Here, Robert moved his family into his father's old manor house, away from the political and economic turmoil gripping the rest of Germany.

8

ALEXANDER
1934

Intent on enjoying their summer, the Alexanders organised a birthday party for Lucien Picard, Elsie's grandfather. To memorialise the day in crisp 16mm black and white, Alfred walked around filming the occasion on his movie camera.

In the morning, long tables and folding chairs were set up on the lawn below the house. The tables were covered with white linen and laid with the family's best silverware, transported from their home in the city. Soon after, the musicians arrived: five men dressed in tails, starched shirts and patent leather shoes, carrying violins, oboes and a small drum. They set up on the terrace above the pump house.

Lucien wore a well-tailored pinstriped suit, a white shirt with the collar turned up, a striped tie and a waistcoat, a similar outfit to the one he had worn every day of his forty-year banking career. Elsie and Bella were dressed very differently. Keen to follow the latest fashion, Bella had cropped her hair short, parted to one side, and was wearing a short-sleeved white shirt tucked into her trousers. In contrast, Elsie still wore her hair in two long plaits, and was dressed in a conservative white skirt and plain white shoes.

The guests soon arrived and, with the musicians playing tunes from Berlin's hottest cabaret venues, were served aperitifs on the veranda. Next came lunch; men and women were seated alternately and couples split so that they were forced to speak with someone they didn't know.

Before coffee, Alfred gave a speech celebrating his father-in-law's long life and then raised a toast in his honour. 'To Lucien Picard,' he called. The rest of the guests stood and echoed the words, leaving the elderly man the only person still seated. Then, as was the family tradition, Elsie and her brothers and sister gathered at one end of the table and sang a song, using a popular melody but changing the words to tease their grandfather. Bella had the better voice but Elsie had penned the words. People commented on the charm and talent of the Alexander children.

Throughout the day, Alfred walked around the party, his camera spooling away, capturing the mood: a large group of young and old Jews, well educated, doctors, lawyers, artists, singers and actors, mothers and fathers, sons and daughters, happy, smiling, laughing, relaxed and unworried, at least at that moment, about the future.

A few weeks later, Elsie invited a group of friends from university out to Glienicke. With them was Rolf Gerber, a handsome and large-framed young man from South Africa, who was visiting Berlin for year to study German. Elsie and Rolf took an instant liking to each other, playing long games of tennis and walking along the lakeshore. Their friendship blossomed back in Berlin, where they often attended dances and parties together, with Bella, as chaperone, in tow.

By this time, Alfred's medical business was under threat. With the newspapers, radio and streets filled with Nazi propaganda, many of his non-Jewish patients had stopped visiting. On 17 May 1934, in a bid to tighten the screws, the government outlawed the reimbursement of Jewish doctors through the public health insurance funds, dramatically reducing his fees. Then, the mayor of Munich banned Jewish doctors from treating non-Jewish patients, and it seemed only a matter of time before Berlin followed suit.

Over breakfast, lunch and dinner the Alexanders discussed the worsening situation. Henny thought it was time they left the country. Many of their friends had already departed, or were making plans to do so. Of the more than 500,000 Jews living in Germany when the Nazis had taken power, over 37,000 had already fled.

While the children agreed with their mother, Alfred persisted in believing that the political situation would improve, clinging on to the belief that the country of his birth – moreover the country that he had fought for – would see reason and throw the Nazis out of power. Even if they decided to leave, how would they manage their departure? What would they do with the business? Where would they go? In the face of Alfred's position, all the family could do was monitor events.

As Germany's political atmosphere darkened, and as their romance grew, Elsie and Rolf began discussing where they should live. Elsie suggested London, given that Bella and Harold were already in England and Rolf had an automatic right to live there as a South Africa citizen. Rolf, however, said that he wanted to return to Cape Town, so that he could be close to his family. Either solution would require them to marry, for Elsie to gain an entry visa, but Rolf made it clear that he was not ready for such a commitment.

Upset by Rolf's rejection, Elsie tried to change his mind, but she was unsuccessful. A short while later, Rolf returned to South Africa. 'I wasn't angry,' Elsie later recalled. 'I was in love. What can you do?' She was heartbroken.

★

Elsie spent the rest of that languid summer at the lake house. Often she would sleep in, and then, if she had the energy, she took walks around the lake and into the woods. In the afternoons, she kept an eye on her grandfather who suffered from digestive problems and needed frequent medical attention. Then, in the evenings, she had dinner with her parents and their guests, after which they played card games such as 'oh hell' or bridge, often for money.

Then, towards the end of the summer, Elsie's boredom was interrupted by the arrival of Bella from London. Now five months pregnant, and despite the precariousness of the political situation, Bella had returned to Glienicke. As Mrs Harold Sussmann she had a British passport and was therefore able to travel in and out of Germany without trouble. Elsie found herself becoming jealous of both the baby and her sister's marriage. This was not helped by Bella sitting each evening on the terrace, the table shaking as she typed and read aloud long letters to her husband in England. In these letters, Bella complained that she felt 'ten months pregnant', and addressed Harold in adoring terms – 'my darling hubby', 'my darling schnucke', 'my darling schnuckeltier' – gloating about the baby, whom she already called 'Sigi', and talking endlessly about how glorious England was and all the wonderful times they would have together there.

One morning the family heard on the radio that Paul von Hindenburg had died. To the Alexanders this was worrying news, for they considered Hindenburg to be one of the few restraining hands on Hitler's shoulder. Yet Bella appeared unconcerned by the president's death, which warranted only the briefest of mentions in her next letter to Harold. She believed that 'everything will go its way', and spent the morning in the city having a dress fitted and purchasing a pair of blue shoes.

★

In December 1934, word arrived back from London that Bella had given birth to a boy, called Peter. The following spring, thrilled now to be a grandfather, Alfred sat down at a table at the lake house and wrote a letter to Harold and Peter. He wrote in English, a language of which he was not confident.

> My Dear Grandchild
>
> I have been much pleased, my dear Harold, in receiving your letter and to learn that you and the sweet Peter are well. I am anxious to make soon the acquaintance of the latter and I promise you that I shall treat him very well. As a surprise for the welcome I shall write to you in English, as Peter would not understand another language.
>
> You will be glad to receive an English letter from me, I had intended to buy an English dictionary but Elsie had forgotten to send it to me, therefore I was compelled to write this without help and you must excuse this rather 'German' style.
>
> Here everything is as nice and beautiful as the preceding years and you will admire not only my language but also the fine surroundings.
>
> With my sincerest love for you and the first grandchild and best greetings to all the family.
>
> I remain, yours truly,
>
> Grandfather

With Bella settling down in England, and motivated in part by boredom, Elsie volunteered full-time for the Cultural Association of German Jews. Since April 1933, when the Nazi Party had passed the Law for the Restoration of the Professional Civil Service, Jewish singers, dancers, writers and musicians had been banned from performing in the city's main cultural venues. The Association had been established in response, to allow Jewish artists to play for Jewish audiences. Though unpaid, Elsie helped out in the office, typing up letters and assisting with the administrative tasks. In return, she was able to attend the concerts, plays and operas for free.

At one evening concert, Elsie met a young Jewish leather merchant, named Erich Hirschowitz. He had a nice smile, thick greased-back brown hair and a high forehead. Later, Elsie discovered that one of her co-workers had played matchmaker, arranging for them to sit next to each other. Talking to Erich, she learned that he played the violin and shared her enjoyment of music and culture. He asked her out and soon they were attending concerts together. She was not as besotted as she had been with Rolf, but Erich was funny and had a kind face.

In due course, Elsie invited Erich out to Groß Glienicke, to see the house and to meet the family. At the lake one day, Erich explained that he was spending much of his time travelling back and forth from Berlin to London where he was setting up a leather company for his father. He invited Elsie to join him in England. Bella of course was now living there, and Elsie thought that Erich's British entry permit and contacts might be helpful if she had to flee Germany. Not long after, on 1 April, Elsie and Erich announced their engagement.

Hearing the news, Rolf now wrote from South Africa, begging Elsie to reconsider. But Elsie had made her decision and, on 28 July 1935, she and Erich were married in Berlin. The large wedding they had planned was cancelled given the government's restrictions on Jewish gatherings, and instead, a small reception was held for a dozen family members at the apartment on the Kaiserallee.

After the lunch had been served, and over coffee, it was customary to read aloud the telegrams sent by well-wishers to the bride and groom. Since so few people had been able to attend, Elsie and Erich received over two hundred telegrams. A few were read, including one from Cape Town:

WARMEST CONGRATULATIONS ALL THE BEST = ROLF GERBER

97

The next day, driving a black Austin 7, Elsie and Erich left Berlin for their honeymoon. They headed south-west for Switzerland, along the main highways, via Leipzig and Nuremberg. Choosing to take a more scenic route, they left the main road and drove towards the Black Forest. Arriving at a small village in Bavaria, they came across a wooden sign that had been posted on the outskirts of the village. The sign read '*Juden verboten*': Jews forbidden. Shocked by the naked anti-Semitism, Elsie and Erich found a way around the village, only to encounter similar signs posted nearby. Upset, they continued on their journey to Switzerland, where they had a few quiet days in Basel, before travelling on to Italy.

Returning to Berlin at the end of August, they moved into an apartment which had been furbished for them by their families. Located at Kurfürstendamm 103, it was only a short walk to Elsie's parents on the Kaiserallee. For now at least, they agreed, they would remain in Germany.

On 15 September, further discriminating measures were announced at the annual Nazi Party rally in Nuremberg. The Reich Citizenship Law concerned those deemed not to have German blood – so called 'non-Aryans' – a definition which included the Jews. These 'non-Aryans' were now considered *Staatsangehörige*, or state subjects, while those of German blood, the 'Aryans', were *Reichsbürger*, or German citizens. Another measure, the Law for the Protection of German Blood and German Honour, declared that Jews and non-Jews could no longer marry, nor have extramarital intercourse. One person immediately affected was a good friend of Elsie's who worked as her father's assistant. This man was in love with a girl from a non-Jewish aristocratic family and now faced real dangers if they continued the relationship. Wanting to help, Elsie invited the couple to discreetly

Wannsee beach, 1935

make use of her and Erich's new apartment. By doing so, Elsie took a big risk; the penalties for breaking these laws ranged from hard labour to imprisonment.

In the following weeks, the rise of anti-Semitism crept closer and closer to Elsie and her family. Her brothers were forced to leave their school because they were Jewish, and both were called 'dirty Jew' in the streets of Berlin. Then, at Wannsee Strandbad, the massive lido near Groß Glienicke, which the family still sometimes visited, a sign had been placed in front of the entrance declaring '*Juden ist der Zutritt untersagt*': Jewish entry is prohibited.

Eight years earlier, in 1927, the Alexanders had been the first Jewish family to live in the village. Before long they had been joined by others, so that by 1935 there were twenty-five Jewish families registered as living full- and part-time around the lake, making up

99

nearly a quarter of the village's total population. These were Berliners with varied professions: doctors, accountants, lawyers, dentists, company directors, actors and singers. There was even a Jewish ice-hockey player. Following the announcement of the Nuremberg Laws, however, most of these families stopped coming, more intent on planning their escape from Germany than spending weekends by the lake. Still Alfred clung on to the belief that his countrymen would see sense, that they would finally understand the madness of Hitler and his cronies.

In early 1936, Alfred travelled to London to see Bella and her newborn son. While he was away, Henny received a phone call from Otto Meyer, the old German Army colleague who had protected their home during the 1933 Jewish boycott. He said he had urgent news about Alfred. 'They will be coming for him, and you must see that he goes into hiding at once.' Apparently, the Gestapo had compiled a list of Berlin's most prominent Jews whom they planned to arrest, and Alfred's name was high on that list. Thanking Meyer for his concern, Henny immediately sent word to Alfred that he must stay in London. She then discussed the situation with Elsie, Hanns and Paul, and they quickly agreed that they had to leave as soon as possible.

At this time, the Nazi government was encouraging Jewish families to emigrate. Obtaining exit documents was relatively easy. Far more difficult was securing an entry visa from the country to which the refugee hoped to travel. First to leave were Lucien and his wife Amelia. As she had been born in Basel, it was quite straightforward for them to relocate to Switzerland. Next was Paul. Through Lucien's banking contacts, he was able to secure a job and entry visa to Switzerland.

A few weeks later, in the spring of 1936, Hanns took a bus to the British Consulate in Berlin. Arriving early, he lined up with the hundreds of others, all hoping for a British entry visa. Luckily,

Harold's family had arranged a job for Hanns in a London bank and so, unlike many of the other applicants that day, Hanns walked away with his documents in order. At the end of May, having said goodbye to Henny and Elsie, Hanns climbed aboard a train in Berlin and headed for Switzerland where he would take a plane to England. A few days later, on 2 June, he arrived at Croydon airport in London, where he was greeted by his sister Bella.

Erich, meanwhile, was already in England. As he had been managing his father's leather company in London for some years, his papers were in order and he was allowed to travel in and out of the country at will. And because of her husband's position it had been simple to obtain an entry visa for Elsie from the British Embassy. But before Henny could leave Germany she would have to pay the *Reichsfluchtsteuer*. Officially a flight tax imposed on any persons with over 200,000 reichsmarks in assets who wished to leave the country, it was, in practice, a simple way of fleecing Jews of their wealth. The only way that Henny could pay for this tax was by selling Alfred's clinic on Achenbachstrasse. The sale of the clinic would not be as easy as Henny had hoped. According to the Nazi laws, she could not sell to a Jew, nor was she likely to be able to sell to a supporter of the party, who would be less than keen to take over the clinic with its Jewish staff and patients.

At the start of the summer Henny managed to find a buyer, but then the deal collapsed at the last minute when the offer was withdrawn. Elsie and Henny began to panic. They knew that the political situation would worsen in September after the Olympic Games had ended and the world's media had left Berlin. They agreed that if they couldn't find a buyer by then, Elsie would leave. She didn't want to abandon her mother, but they had little choice. For Henny, the situation looked desperate.

★

Hosting the Olympic Games was Hitler's chance not only to show-case his country's athletic superiority to the rest of the world but also to convince them that news reports that Germany was harshly treating its Jewish citizens and political critics were unfounded. In the days before the opening ceremony, and while the world's media was in town, the regime backed away from their harshest anti-Jewish measures. Most anti-Jewish signs were removed from shops and lamp posts and newspapers toned down their anti-Semitic rhetoric. Even the 'Jews prohibited' sign at Wannsee Strandbad was taken down, on the instruction of the Foreign Ministry. Many expected that this softening of anti-Semitic policies would be quickly reversed once the Games had come to an end. Some, including Henny and Elsie, believed that come September they would have their passports removed.

As part of the preparations for the Games, an Olympic Village was built in the old Prussian military grounds on Döberitzer Heath, some ten kilometres north-west of Groß Glienicke. There were 140 houses for the competitors, including the sprinter Jesse Owens. His every meal, shower and practice session would be followed by the international press, thrilled by the idea that an African American athlete might threaten the arrogance of the host nation.

The Olympics came even closer to Groß Glienicke. Great excite-ment surrounded the bicycle road race as it was to be the first that would include a mass start. The 100-kilometre route would take the cyclists from the Avus motor-racing circuit in Berlin, through the city's western suburbs, down the Potsdamer Chaussee, into the village, past the Potsdamer Tor and the entrance to the Alexanders' property, and then looping back through the Brandenburg countryside to Berlin. A few weeks before the race, the village council were ordered to widen the main road in preparation for the race, and had dutifully cut down the three lime trees that had stood for over a century outside the Drei Linden Gasthof.

In early July, hoping to soon finalise their travel arrangements,

Elsie and her mother sought refuge at the lake house. It was quiet with everyone now gone, forlorn. There was nobody to play tennis with. Nobody to swim with. The cucumbers, tomatoes and potatoes sprawled overgrown and unharvested in the vegetable plot. They ate their meals at the pull-down table in the kitchen. To have eaten at the large red table in the living room or out on the veranda would have been depressing.

Meanwhile, Henny redoubled her efforts to locate a buyer, but when another deal came and went, their situation became increasingly precarious. Finally, in early August, Henny had an offer. They were a 'mixed' couple – the husband was Jewish, the wife was not – and therefore legally permitted to purchase the property, albeit at a heavily discounted price. Henny agreed, and with these funds paid the flight tax. She next obtained her exit stamp from the German immigration authority, and having queued up all day at the British Consulate, managed to secure an entrance visa for England. They were, at last, ready to leave.

Together, Elsie and her mother closed up the cottage. First, they made an inventory of all that remained in the house, the furniture and the crockery, the paintings and kitchen appliances. Next, they pulled the boat out of the lake and took the tennis net down, storing them, along with the garden furniture, in the pump house. Having draped sheets over the furniture, and locked the windows and doors, Henny and Elsie then returned to Berlin, where they handed the house key and the inventory to the family lawyer, Dr Goldstrom. Take care of the lake house, they told him.

In late August 1936, Elsie took a train to Amsterdam, her fingers laden with gold rings and with more jewellery sewn into her mink coat. She carried her black Erika typewriter in one hand and an eiderdown in the other. There, at the ticket barrier in the main Amsterdam station, she was met by Erich. When he saw what she was carrying he asked, 'Do you always travel with your eiderdown?'

To which Elsie replied, 'I'm not travelling, I've come, I'm not going back!' This surprised Erich, who was still eager to return to Germany and to his business, and was relatively unmoved by the possible dangers he might face. But his wife had made the decision, he would not be going back. Ruefully, he told Elsie that he hadn't even said goodbye to his friends. A few days later Elsie and Erich took a ferry from the Hook of Holland to Folkestone, and then a train on to London.

Shortly afterwards, Henny arrived. She had made her own way by train and ferry, through Germany, France and the Netherlands, to London, where she was greeted by her family. Bella, who had been in the country for a few years, was living with Harold and Peter in a small flat in West Kensington. Henny and Alfred found temporary accommodation in central London while Elsie moved into a flat that Erich had found in south London. This left the boys, Hanns and Paul, who had found rooms in a boarding house in the centre of town.

The Alexander clan had reassembled in England. They were now refugees.

PART II

THE LAKE HOUSE

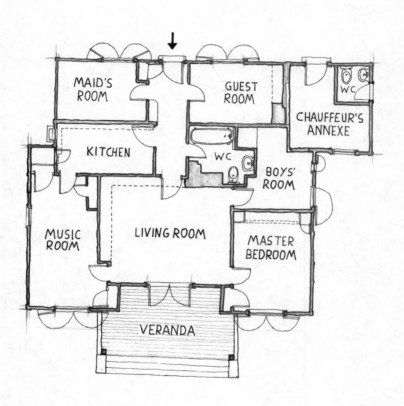

MAID'S ROOM

GUEST ROOM

WC

CHAUFFEUR'S ANNEXE

KITCHEN

WC

BOYS' ROOM

MUSIC ROOM

LIVING ROOM

MASTER BEDROOM

VERANDA

August 2013

It's dark when my wife and I pull into Groß Glienicke. We have been driving for more than fifteen hours, having left England early that morning. We are more than ready for the journey to end. Our car is loaded with suitcases, camera equipment and laptops – enough supplies to last us for the five weeks we will be staying.

It takes us less than two minutes to cruise from one end of the village to the other, down dimly lit streets, peering into the gloom for our hotel, the Hofgarten. We turn round and drive back along the main road, passing a kebab shop, a cafe, a small supermarket and a handful of houses.

Eventually we find the Hofgarten. Like the rest of Groß Glienicke it's completely dark, with no signs of life. I spot a telephone number taped to the door, and call it – but nobody responds. Desperate for a bed and a hot shower, I try Sonja, a local resident who's agreed to help me with my research. Thankfully she picks up and offers to call the owner. A few minutes later they drive up in separate cars. Having handed over our passports, I ask about the room, does it have Wi-Fi, what time is breakfast? When it becomes apparent that the hotelier doesn't speak a word of English, I try my few German phrases, and when these fail, Sonja helpfully steps in.

Once we're checked in, Sonja shoulders her bag and turns to leave, reminding me that she's set up my first meeting for eight o'clock the next morning. I thank her for all her help and say goodnight. I am feeling embarrassed, not to say a little humiliated.

The next day I sleep through my alarm. Pulling on my clothes, I grab my notebook and run outside. I turn left onto the main street, the Potsdamer Chaussee, and see Sonja and an elderly-looking man waiting a hundred metres up the road. I am half an hour late. Running up to them, and now out of breath, I hurry out an apology, which Sonja translates, before I am *introduced. 'This is Burkhard Radtke,' she says. 'He is the village's unofficial historian.'*

Looking unimpressed, Burkhard shakes my extended hand, turns and then walks off. Realising that I am to follow, I chase after him. For the next two hours, my guide takes me on a detailed tour of the village. He indicates the main historical points of interest along with the major geographical landmarks, Sonja translating as he speaks. I try and take notes, but he is throwing so much information at me that it is hard to keep up. Yet I am fascinated by what he is telling me.

Over the next few days Sonja and Burkhard introduce me to a few residents, who then direct me to still more. Each time phone calls are made, I am vouched for, my mission is explained, meeting times are agreed and thanks are given. It is a laborious process. Most people agree to meet, but not everyone – some are too busy, others are too shy. Interviews take place in the Greek restaurant, the doner kebab shop, the Exner cafe, or in the hotel courtyard, which the locals all refer to as the Drei Linden – for decades it has served as the village pub.

I am invited into people's homes and served endless rounds of Kaffee und Kuchen, *or coffee and cake. I show old photographs of the lake house and ask my hosts to share their memories, whatever they might know about the village, the house, the families who lived there.*

Strangely, I am asked the same question at almost every meeting – sometimes repeatedly. Have I made a claim for the house? I am not sure what they mean – I explain that the land is owned by the local government, that it is to be redeveloped. But they ask again – hasn't my family ever tried to get the house back, or, at the very least, received compensation for its seizure?

After a week or so, I decide to visit the the Berlin State Archive, located in a former ammunitions factory in the city's northern suburbs. Having filled out an application form, and explained the purpose of my research, I ask for any files that are associated with Alfred or Henny Alexander. Only a few minutes later I am sitting at a desk and looking at a tatty orange file with the label 'Alexander: 222/JRSO/ 51'.

According to the documents, Henny Alexander filed a petition against the

West German government in 1952, claiming compensation for the loss of their house in Groß Glienicke. A hearing was held, eight years later, on 12 December 1960, in Courtroom 149, on Karlsbader Strasse in West Berlin. My great-grandmother was represented by a Berlin lawyer. Three weeks later, on 3 January 1961, the court released its findings: the Alexanders would be paid the sum total of 90.34 marks in compensation of their lost property, about £300 pounds in today's money.

I email my father to tell him the news. He writes back to say that he thinks there was another claim made on behalf of the family by the Jewish Claims Conference (JCC) – an organisation that seeks justice for Jewish victims of Nazi persecution. He has some paperwork somewhere, he says.

Attached to his email is an Alexander family tree. Strangely, it is missing the death dates for five of my grandfather Erich's relatives: Alfred Werthan and his wife Else, along with Emil Lesser, his wife Rosa, and their son Franz. I quiz my father, but he has no idea why the information is missing – his parents, Elsie and Erich, never spoke of them, he replies.

I email other family members, but no one seems to know what happened to Erich's relatives, and I cannot find any trace of them in Berlin. They must have fled, we speculate – to South America or Israel – or perhaps they died before the war, and the records went missing. But the days pass, and I can find nothing. As a last resort, I visit the Yad Vashem website, which hosts an online database of Holocaust victims. Of the more than six million Jews killed in the Holocaust, the names of over 4.3 million people have been entered. I type in the names of Alfred and Else Werthan and, to my great surprise, a report appears.

According to the website, on 27 February 1943, SS officers from the Leibstandarte (Hitler's elite bodyguard unit) raided various Berlin factories and, armed with whips and truncheons, rounded up thousands of Jewish workers. Among those arrested were Erich's Uncle Alfred and Aunt Else, both of whom were profoundly deaf. Alfred and Else were then loaded onto a truck and deposited in one of the city's assembly camps. Two weeks later, on 12 March, they were woken early and forced to walk three kilometres through the streets of Berlin – via Jagowstrasse, Perleberger Strasse and Quitzowstrasse

— to *Putlitzstrasse station. They were then put on transports 31 and 36 (they were the thirty-first and thirty-sixth to leave Berlin for the ghettos and killing sites in Eastern Europe). When the transports arrived in Auschwitz, Alfred and Else were offloaded from the trains, and then killed in one of the camp's gas chambers.*

I put the next three names into the database. In July 1942, Erich's Uncle Emil and Aunt Rosa were deported to Theresienstadt, where they too died. Their son, Franz Lesser, Erich's first cousin, was deported on 5 September 1942 to Riga in Latvia. Upon arrival, he was taken to nearby woods and shot.

Growing up, we had been told that our close family had been 'lucky', that we had managed to escape Germany in time. And yet my grandfather's two aunts, two uncles and first cousin had been killed in the Holocaust.

My grandparents knew, but chose not to speak about it. I cannot believe that I was only finding out about these crimes seventy years after they took place. We were not so lucky after all.

9

MEISEL

1937

For eight months the lake house stood empty. Autumn, winter and spring came and went. The fireplace remained unlit. Storms rolled across the lake, slamming against the cottage's thin frame.

The asparagus plants in the garden grew tall and ragged, gone to seed. Reeds coiled up around the pillars of the lakeshore jetty. Orange, red and brown leaves piled up in the corners of the veranda, twisted and curled after the summer's heat. The grass to the front of the house was a wild meadow, uncut for an entire season. As to the house's interior, it remained dry and untouched by the elements, secured by shutters and doors bound tight against the wind, and a roof that held its own against the winter rains.

In September 1936, the Berlin Labour Court had ruled that Germans who were married to Jews, or other non-Aryans, could be dismissed from their jobs. The next month, a decree was passed forbidding Jewish teachers from tutoring Aryan children. In November the Nazis blacklisted some two thousand works written by Jewish authors. A few weeks later, the last Jewish department store in Germany was seized by the government and sold to a non-Jewish owner and in January 1937, all Jewish-owned employment agencies in Germany were forcibly closed and the Reich aviation minister, Hermann Göring, ordered Reinhard Heydrich, the head of the Reich Security Main Office (RSHA), to speed up the emigration of any Jews still living in Germany.

As so often happens in times of crisis, one person's misfortune provided an opportunity to another. When Hitler came to power in January 1933 there were around 100,000 Jewish businesses owned and registered in Germany; within five years more than two-thirds of these businesses had been transferred to non-Jews. The Nazi Party called this process 'aryanisation', and it not only affected Jewish-owned companies, but also Jewish-owned bank accounts, intellectual property, land and buildings. Typically the transactions were grossly unfair, with a property sold well below market value, given that the Jewish seller was under pressure to leave the country. Aryanisation was a policy that was officially sanctioned by the Nazi Party, who considered the transfer of assets a matter of honour, reparations for the economic chaos that the Jews had allegedly inflicted on the German people.

So it was that, on 10 February 1937, Wilhelm Meisel, composer and music publisher, walked into a lawyer's office at Kurfürstendamm 24, hoping to make a good deal. Five foot eight and of medium build, Meisel was not an imposing figure. His round pudgy face, blond hair, sparkling blue eyes and jovial demeanour generally put people at ease. He was greeted by Dr Goldstrom, representing his clients, Alfred and Henny Alexander, who was authorised to agree a lease on their behalf.

Having discussed the terms of the agreement, Meisel and Goldstrom sat at a table and signed the lease. The contract stated that Will Meisel and his wife would pay the Alexanders 2,000 reichsmarks a year, half of which the Alexanders would keep as profit, with the other half to be paid to Robert and Ilse von Schultz, the landlords. All funds would flow through Dr Goldstrom's office. The sub-lease was for three years, but thereafter would continue, if both parties agreed, until 30 March 1942, the date which marked the end of the Alexanders' original lease with the Wollank family.

August Wilhelm Meisel was born on 17 September 1897, in Neukölln, a south-east suburb of Berlin. A few years earlier, his parents, Emil and Olga Meisel, had left Marienwerder, a farming district located ninety kilometres north-east of Berlin, wishing to take advantage of the opportunities that Germany's capital city afforded.

Upon arrival, his parents had been surprised to discover that nobody in Neukölln taught ballroom dancing. Both superb dancers, Emil and Olga saw their chance, and established the Meisel School of Dance. From an early age, Will was conditioned to perform – appearing in his first show at the age of five. Surrounded by tutus and ballet shoes, tiaras and rhinestone-bedazzled gowns, braces and armbands, he grew up amid the prancing steps and personal dramas of divas and danseuses. Starting with classical ballet, he quickly mastered the tango, waltz, foxtrot and tap, spending the majority of his waking hours in the mirrored studios of his parents' dance school. As a teenager, he regularly competed in his father's dance competitions. He also learned to play a variety of instruments. At the piano, Will's father would stand next to him, and if he hit the wrong key, would slap him in the face. Will later recalled that 'this motivated me', and that his father had told him: 'Music will feed you in your life.'

Following the outbreak of the First World War, Will Meisel enlisted and was sent to Ypres in Belgium, where he suffered gas poisoning. While recovering in a hospital back in Germany, he often played the piano for the other injured soldiers. Through trial and error, he learned that the tunes with the catchiest melodies and lightest lyrics garnered the greatest response, and he endeavoured to learn as many of these as possible. At the war's end, he joined the premier dance venue in Berlin, the Royal Court, on Unter den Linden, and by his twenties he was writing his own songs and performing them around Germany. Not satisfied with being simply a composer and dancer, Will wanted to become the director of a cabaret club.

Since arriving from Paris at the turn of the century, the number of Berlin cabaret clubs had exploded, with over fifty venues concentrated in the city centre. Over the course of an evening, burlesque dances, comedy skits and musical sets were performed before an audience seated at tables, who were served food and drinks. Unlike their French cousins, Berlin's clubs also became known for their satirical shows. During Wilhelm II's reign, criticism of the government and royal family had been banned from playhouses. No longer restricted, following the rise of the Weimar Republic, and to the delight of their spectators, the lampooning of politicians and black humour now flourished at the cabaret venues.

Within a few years, Will was not only a club director, he also owned a portfolio of venues, including the Palais, the Amorsäle (Love Salons), the Eulenspiegel (Owl Mirror) and the Paprika (later given the more society name of the Jäger Casino). At the start of 1926, Will Meisel married Ilona von Fövenyessy, a fine-looking Hungarian singer whom he had known since his teenage years. Inspired by her beauty, he wrote a tango melody for her entitled 'Ilona'. The tune was catchy and proved successful. Yet despite being a hit, Will was disappointed that he earned so little money. If he was to be financially successful, he realised, it was best to control the entire recording and publishing process.

Shortly afterwards, one of Will's composer friends, Herman Schulenberg, made a recommendation:, 'Why don't you form your own publishing company?'

'I don't understand anything about it,' Will answered.

'And so what?' Schulenberg replied. 'The other publishers don't understand anything either.'

Convinced, Will founded Edition Meisel & Co. in the back room of one of his clubs, on 15 May 1926, at the age of twenty-nine. His friend Schulenberg became an early partner. While Will would have liked to have published classical music, in the tradition of the great German artists – Brahms, Strauss, Mendelssohn, Wagner and Beethoven – that market was already crowded. Instead, he focused on the light-entertainment music of operettas and movies. Though such songs were disparaged by the critics, they were loved by the German public.

Will Meisel

Within a few months, Will had signed many of the leading lyricists and composers of the day, almost all of whom were Jewish: the cabaret performers Willy Rosen and Harry Waldau, for example, and Richard Rillo who wrote the music for *Der Blaue Engel*, Germany's first major sound film. Another rising star to join his list was Kurt Schwabach, who wrote 'Das lila Lied', believed to be one of the world's first gay anthems. Its lines include 'And still most of us are proud, to be cut from different cloth! / We are just different from the others who are being loved only in lockstep of morality.' There were many whose music was popular at the time but whose mark has faded, such as Marcel Lion and Harry Hilm, Hans Lengsfelder and Friedrich Schwarz. While others only became later renowned, such as Hans May in the film industry (he wrote the music for *Brighton Rock* in 1947), or Jean Aberbach in the music industry (in the 1950s, he recorded Elvis Presley's songs, keeping 50 per cent of the rights).

At this time, the market for published music was highly competitive in Berlin. A number of companies had recently been established, all looking to take advantage of the booming cabaret scene, as well as the emerging opportunities offered by radio. The first German radio station to regularly broadcast to the public debuted in Berlin on 23 October 1923, and by the end of the following year, nine regional stations were in operation around the country. As part of an agreement between the music publishers and the broadcasters, royalties from the songs that were played on the radio were channelled to the music publishers.

Will's philosophy, as he told anyone who would listen, was that you could not leave success to chance. Keen to market his sheet music, he travelled around the city, performing the latest tunes to radio producers, cabaret directors and musicians. Whenever he could, he encouraged the critics to write stories about him, his shows or one of his artists. Unlike other publishers, he did not charge bands to purchase his scores, and to build a relationship with the bandleader – who he realised was the decision-maker in the group – he often delivered baskets of luxury foods, which he called 'Meisel's surprise parcels'. Frequently attending social functions, he ensured that he was in as many photographs as possible. He even distributed a thousand megaphones to chorus singers who performed in clubs across Berlin, each emblazoned with his slogan, *Meisel Schlager – Nie Versager*, 'Meisel's hits – never fail'.

It was around this time, in mid 1932, that his marriage fell apart.

Ilona had returned to her native Hungary and then, fearing the rise of the Nazi Party, refused to return. On 12 November 1932, when the couple split up, the story was widely covered in the media, the *Berliner Presse* running with the headline: 'WILL MEISEL SUDDENLY DIVORCED'. The break-up did little, however, to slow the expansion of Will's burgeoning music empire.

As Will's business grew, so too did his fame and reputation, and soon he was invited to write musical scores for films. Several were huge hits, including the score for his first picture, *Liebe im Ring*, which transformed the boxing champion Max Schmeling into a movie star, and *Wenn die Soldaten*, with Otto Wallburg, a Jewish actor who was also a First World War hero.

In March 1933, Joseph Goebbels was appointed Minister for People's Enlightenment and Propaganda, having declared his intent of removing all Jews from German culture. With Goebbels now in charge of the licensing of publishing houses, studio recordings, radio broadcasts and theatres, Will realised that he could be facing trouble, given that over 80 per cent of his composers were Jewish. Before long, Edition Meisel's songs were banned from the radio and theatres were refusing to perform his operettas. Then, his Jewish creative director was thrown out of the Reich Chamber of Culture, preventing him from being employed. Over the next few months, most of his talent were either organising their flight out of the country or had already left. 'I was forced to take a deep breath,' Will later said of this loss of Jewish talent. He felt he needed to find a way to demonstrate his support for the Nazi Party and he needed to do so fast.

Six weeks later, on 1 May 1933, Will attended a Labour Day rally at Berlin's Tempelhof airport. Around him stood over one million people, all waiting to hear Hitler speak. After many hours, Goebbels appeared in order to introduce the Führer, calling him the 'standard-bearer' of the German people. Hitler strode onto the stage to thunderous applause, surrounded by his personal bodyguards.

> The First of May shall convey to the German people the realisation that industry and work alone do not make up life if they are not wed to the power and will of the people. Industry and work, power and will – only if they join forces, and only when the strong fist of the nation is raised to protect and shelter the work, only then can real blessings result.

To Will, Hitler's message was clear: if you want to succeed in business, join the party. By the end of the day, Will had made his decision. He submitted his name, date of birth and address to a functionary and handed over his membership fee. A short while later, he was given his Nazi Party number: 2849490.

Within a few weeks, Will was pleased to hear that his songs were once again being played on the radio. But whenever he suspected that he or his composers had been dropped from the playlists, he wrote to the station manager, urging them to broadcast his music.

Will now found himself busy with the film industry. By the summer of 1934, he was commissioned to compose music for eight films. One of these productions took him to Johannistal Film Studios, in south-east Berlin. After a morning's effort, he and an actor friend, Hans Söhnker, walked over to the canteen to have lunch. There he saw a dark-haired young woman eating with her friends. Judging by her beauty and charisma she had to be an actress. 'Look at that,' Will said to Hans. 'Your wife is on holiday, right over there is something for you!' The actress was so infuriated by Will's comments that she refused to talk to him.

A short while later they met again on the set for *Was bin ich ohne Dich*, and Will now learned her name, Eliza Illiard. She was acting in the same film for which Will was writing music. This time Will made a better impression, sending Eliza a bunch of roses with a note praising her interpretation of his songs.

On 3 July 1934, they bumped into each other at the premiere of Eliza's latest film, *Paganini*. In this adaptation of Franz Lehár's 1925 operetta, Eliza played the Duchess Anna Elisa of Lucca who becomes infatuated with a famous composer. At the film's climax, and wearing a sparkling ankle-length dress and a black feather in her hair, she sings a passionate love song to the film's eponymous character. With the camera on an extreme close-up, revealing every glowing aspect of her twenty-eight-year-old face, Will fell in love.

Eliza Illiard in *Paganini*

Two months after the premiere, the music publisher and the movie star met again. Now more relaxed, and away from the film sets, they made love. A few weeks later, Eliza informed Will that she was pregnant and, hoping to avoid a scandal, they agreed to marry. Eliza had already experienced trouble at work resulting from her personal affairs. A year earlier she had discovered that the Nazi Party had written to her film guild enquiring about her then husband, a certain Herr Mertens. Why, they had wanted to know, was an up-and-coming film star like Eliza Illiard married to a Jew? The message had been clear: she would not succeed if she stood by her husband. Shortly afterwards she and Mertens divorced. If she was married to Will Meisel, Eliza calculated, the party would leave her alone.

On 12 March 1935, with the bride six months pregnant, Will and Eliza were married at the Wilmersdorf town hall, in western Berlin, near where they both lived. Three months later, on 22 June 1935, their first child, Peter Hans Meisel, was born. Will Meisel was then thirty-seven years old, and Eliza twenty-nine.

On the morning of 15 October 1936, a tall thirty-five-year-old man had walked into Will Meisel's office. Even more memorable than his narrow moustache and short thinning hair parted to one side was a four-inch scar diagonally carved into his forehead.

Hanns Hartmann had worked as creative director for a number of theatres, and was now looking for a job. Following Nazi Party pressure, he had been fired from his post at Chemnitz, a city located 250 kilometres south of Berlin. Will Meisel realised that a creative director with a reputation for financial control would be a huge asset to his company, and he hired Hanns on the spot. He just hoped that the party in Berlin would not catch wind of his new employee's previous troubles.

Over the next two years, and partly out of his collaboration with Hartmann, Will's output increased unabated. Between 1935 and 1937 he wrote and published fifty-eight songs and fourteen film scores. Eliza had been busy too; in addition to her numerous engagements as a music-hall singer she had starred in two movies in twelve months: *Liebeserwachen* and *Skandal um die Fledermaus*. By 1937, the Meisels were exhausted.

For a while they had talked about needing a place to relax, a house out in the country, but not too far from the city, where they could invite friends for the weekend, or have business colleagues over for long summer lunches. Their discussions grew more serious once Peter was born. There was no garden for their young son to crawl around at their city apartment in western Berlin. In addition, Eliza had put her career on hold so that she could spend more time with her son. No longer stuck on set or in rehearsal, she longed for a bolt-hole from the city, a project she could channel her energy into.

The Meisels were soon approached by a Jewish estate agent, Herbert Würzburg, who claimed to have found the perfect property for them: a small but elegant wooden house on a lake in the nearby village of Groß Glienicke, on offer at a good price. The tenants, Würzburg said, were Jewish, and had fled to London. The Meisels needn't worry about the house being reclaimed any time soon.

10

MEISEL

1937

It was early spring when the Meisels first arrived at the lake house. While the months of snow and ice were past, the garden showed little sign that winter was over. The needles of the evergreen firs and the April flowers' few leaves were the only signs of life. Yet it was certainly warmer than it had been just weeks before and there was a sense of promise in the air.

The house came fully furnished as part of the lease. It was exciting to open the door, to choose who took which room, to open the cupboards, and to see what they contained. Walking around, Eliza checked off the three-page typed inventory detailing its contents. The living room was listed as having 24 wine glasses, 8 white beer glasses, and over 100 plates – flat, fruit, deep, middle and salad – many of which were monogrammed with an 'A'. In the kitchen, there were items such as 34 cups, 17 finger bowls, 14 egg cups, 11 glasses and 12 glass plates – as well as more esoteric items including a bread machine, 5 lemonade spoons and 4 milk pots. Items in the garden were also recorded, such as an incubator, presumably for hatching chicks, 2 fruit stands and a rocking-horse swing. She was delighted that so much was available, impressed by its quality.

It didn't take long for the Meisels to make the house comfortable. Will and Eliza took over the master bedroom, filling it with new furniture, keeping the two bedside tables, as well as the large mirror hanging on the wall. A nursery was established in the small room with the bunk bed, which Peter would sleep in, to be soon joined, they hoped, by a sibling. The cook had the maid's room next to the kitchen, while the driver stayed in the chauffeur's annexe. Guests, when they had them, would be given the spare room by the front door.

This left the Blue Room, which Will converted into a music studio. Removing the pull-down beds, he put up shelves and created a library of books about operettas and films. The last few items that Elsie had left in the cupboards were bagged and put out in the rubbish. In their place, Will stored his sheet music in neat stacks. On one wall he hung a poster from a film that he had scored. Against another he positioned an upright piano and leather stool. There was also a couch, on which Will intended to read some books and, perhaps, if he was lucky, enjoy a few afternoon naps.

Liking the house's natural and unadorned informality, the Meisels left the decor pretty much as it was. The two high-backed wooden chairs, which Henny had found in a local village, still stood to attention in the living room, next to a striped oval rug. From above the fireplace the Delft blue-and-white tiles oversaw the Meisels' happy family life.

They did make some changes. Outside, they repainted the shutters a burnt Moroccan orange, covering over the diamond motifs at the front of the house. In order to make the lawn wider, they dug up, graded and then turfed over the stone footpath that had run from the garage to the front door. Instead, they laid a new path, made of black gravel, against the fence alongside the Munk property, allowing a small vehicle to make deliveries closer to the house. They also cleared the bushes and wild vegetation that had grown up around the house in the Alexanders' absence, pruning the lower branches from the remaining trees, resulting in a well-manicured garden. Finally, they removed the *mezuzah*, which Alfred Alexander had affixed next to the front door.

Will Meisel at the lake house

The family soon settled into life at the weekend house. As with the Alexanders, they had breakfast and dinner around the large red table in the living room. They took tea on the veranda at the white table to the rear of the house overlooking the lake, and drank early-evening cocktails sitting on one of the wide wicker armchairs on the terrace above the pump house. In the late spring, as the air warmed and the wind calmed, the Meisels positioned Peter in his pram in the shade under a tree, and sat back in their deckchairs, enjoying a book or a magazine. They relished the chance to shed their formal city attire: Will typically wore a collarless shirt and shorts, rumpled socks and loafers. Sometimes he would walk around without a shirt. When it was warm, Eliza also liked to wear shorts and short sleeves, with her hair up in an untidy bundle. So far away from the film studios, she didn't care how she looked.

When it was hot enough, they carried Peter into the lake, holding him tightly as he flapped his legs and arms in the cool, clean water, squealing with delight. Or, leaving Peter with the nanny, they would swim out to the middle of the lake, from where they could see other weekenders, also paddling around in the water, or relaxing close to the edge.

In the evenings, they gathered on the veranda, Will and Eliza sitting in the wicker armchairs, and Peter in a high chair, looking out at the lake, still brilliant in the late-summer sun.

For a young family, there were few places more perfect.

After an idyllic first summer at the lake house, Will returned to Berlin to resume his punishing schedule. Focused on developing his publishing house, he wrote letters to the radio stations, encouraging them to play more of his artists' music. He printed a new catalogue which he posted to theatres and bandleaders. Not forgetting his own career, he continued to write music for the film industry and penned a number of original songs for the radio.

He was also attentive to the political needs of the day, attending meetings at the national film and music societies, as well as the occasional party rally. To demonstrate his support for the Nazi cause, he volunteered at charitable events, such as the Pressefest in Pomerania in aid of Winterhilfswerk, which distributed clothing and coal to the poor during winter.

At the end of the year, and once again exhausted from his labours, Will joined Eliza and Peter at the lake house. It was extremely cold, the uninsulated walls offering scant protection from the winter chill, but it was romantic. The lake had frozen thick after a month's frigid temperatures and, wrapping Peter in many layers of clothes, hats and a blanket, they could walk safely across its surface, dusted with sparkling icy crystals, amazed by the quiet beauty of the place. Back at the house, warmed by the fire and hot drinks, they agreed that they should try to buy the property. It would make their occupancy more stable, more official and, given the Alexanders' precarious situation, they should be able to get a good price. It would be a sound investment.

So in January 1938, Will Meisel contacted the lawyer, Dr Goldstrom, and asked if the Alexanders would be willing to sell the property. Legally, this was a complex proposition, for while the Alexanders had built and owned the house and the outbuildings – the caretaker's house, the greenhouse, pump house and garage – the land underneath was still owned by Robert and Ilse von Schultz.

Believing that the Alexanders would be desperate to unload the property, the Meisels offered the below-market price of 6,000 reichsmarks, a little under half of its actual worth. Such a purchase would include the leasehold to the land, as well as the buildings and any ownership interest that the Alexanders had in the plot.

Through their lawyer, the Alexanders rejected the Meisel offer, unwilling to give up on their weekend house for such a paltry sum. The failed bid was noted in a report written by the Berlin tax office: regarding the 'land leased by the expatriated Jew Alfred John Alexander, Gross-Glienicke, vineyard parcel 3 . . . the negotiations did not reach a conclusion'.

As the little house began to change with its new occupants, so too did the village. Photographs from this time show a generation of children growing progressively more militaristic. Boys in shorts and rolled-up sleeves, smiling and with hair that fell beneath the ears, their bodies relaxed and casual, became boys wearing Hitler Youth uniforms, hair cropped short, standing stiff and erect. The same could be said of the girls, whose long hair was cut or tied up in a tight bun, their dresses falling more conservatively below the knees, their smiles now erased.

By November 1938, though many of the settler houses in Groß Glienicke continued to be owned by Jewish families, very few lived there. Most had found a way to flee Germany, begging and bribing their way out to England, America and Palestine. Those who remained were either exceptionally brave, or in hiding. One who chose to stay was Rudi Ball, the ice-hockey champion and captain of the German team. He had become too famous to persecute, as the only German Jew to compete in the 1936 Winter Olympics, which had been held in southern Germany. He had been controversially dropped from the national squad only to be reinstated after his teammates threatened to strike. Most weekends Rudi stayed at his small house on Uferpromenade 57 in Groß Glienicke.

The village's now vacant houses were easy targets for local thugs. On the evening of 9 November 1938, a group of men gathered outside the Badewiese, the lakefront restaurant on Seepromenade that had been built next to the Groß Glienicke public beach the year before. Most of these men had been members of Robert von Schultz's Stahlhelm brigade. Some wore swastika bands around their arms; others wore SA and SS uniforms. Walking across the road, they pushed their way through the gate of number 9 and set fire to the house. This was the weekend home of Dr Alfred Wolff-Eisner, a renowned physician and researcher.

The authorities and citizens of Groß Glienicke were well aware of the assault on the Jewish family's home. It could hardly have been in a more prominent position, situated as it was opposite the village's public beach. Yet nobody, not even the fire brigade, attempted to put out the fire. By the next morning the house had burned to the ground. Luckily, nobody was hurt in the attack as the Wolff-Eisner family were at their home in Berlin.

The destruction of the Wolff-Eisner house was part of a nation-wide pogrom against the Jews, in which over 250 synagogues and seven thousand shops and businesses were attacked across Germany in what became known as Kristallnacht. The following morning, two thousand Jewish men were rounded up in Berlin, and marched to Sachsenhausen, a concentration camp located to the north of the city. In the following weeks, tens of thousands of Jews fled the country, abandoning their businesses and property. From this point forward, it was extremely rare to see a Jewish family in Groß Glienicke.

Despite the loss of several key workers, Edition Meisel continued to grow. Will had, for the first time in a while, cash to invest, and began to make enquiries about Jewish-owned businesses now appropriated by the state.

On 23 November 1938, two weeks after Kristallnacht, Will wrote a letter to Hans Hinkel, the leader of the Reich Chamber of Culture, expressing his interest in purchasing businesses that had been aryanised.

With reference to my conversation with the lawyer, Dr Walch, I hereby inform you that in the course of the aryanization of Jewish publishing companies, I am interested in taking over such publishers.

I have been a publisher for 12 years and am on the advisory board of the music publishing section of the Reich Chamber of Music. Furthermore, my employees have the professional expertise to guarantee that I will fulfil all tasks demanded of a music and stage publisher covering serious music and stage literature to entertainment. I am therefore interested in all the publishing companies being considered at present, but above all Edition Peters in Leipzig and Universal Edition in Vienna. Where applicable I am willing to participate financially, within the limits of my resources. If you see a possibility of engaging me or my publishing company, please notify me accordingly.

While he was waiting to hear back from Hinkel, Will wrote to Dr Goldstrom, again expressing his desire to acquire the lake house. And again, Dr Goldstrom said that the Alexanders were unwilling to sell the property for the price offered. Frustrated, Will told his wife that they had once more been rejected.

In the spring of 1939, the family's mood lifted when Eliza announced that she was pregnant. As the weather grew warmer, the Meisels spent almost every weekend at the house, focused more on family fun than questions of property. By the time it was warm enough to swim in the lake, a bump was noticeable underneath Eliza's swimsuit.

That summer, the house's ownership position dramatically changed. On 24 July 1939, the names of Alfred, Henny, Hanns and Paul Alexander appeared in the *Reichsgesetzblatt*, as part of the *Ausbürgerungslisten*, lists of those (mostly Jews) whose German naturalisation had been revoked. Word of this filtered back to the Alexander family in London. They were now officially stateless.

Less public, and unknown to the Alexanders, was a letter which the Gestapo had sent on 22 March to the Berlin tax office. The letter contained an itemised list of the Alexanders' assets that were to be seized, including:

The rented plot of land in Groß Glienicke Weinberg parcel 13 [*sic*], with:
I. A weekend house, dimensions approx. 12m x 10m, with open veranda, seven rooms living and bedrooms with furniture
II. Small caretaker's house 3.5 x 5m, 2 rooms and kitchen
III. Greenhouse, 5 x 10m

IV. Potting shed 4 x 10m

V. Garage 3 x 9m

Quietly, almost without notice, the Gestapo had taken ownership. The Alexanders had lost the lake house.

A few months after the government's seizure of the Alexanders' property, Ilse and Robert von Schultz received their own disturbing news from the Berlin tax office.

For years now, they had struggled to manage the financial affairs of the Groß Glienicke Estate. Despite selling vast tracts of land to the airfield in Gatow, and to developers who were building weekend residences on the lake's eastern side, they had been unable to make ends meet. After numerous attempts to collect what was due, the tax authority wrote to Robert and Ilse, declaring that they were in default and that their Groß Glienicke property had been confiscated by the government in lieu of unpaid taxes.

Over the following months, the estate was carved up between various government departments. The land to the north of the schloss, for instance, was requisitioned by the German Army, who decided it would become home to the nation's 67th Tank Regiment. Soon, a team of labourers began constructing a series of two-storey grey-stoned barracks. Next to the barracks a dozen *Panzerhallen*, or tank hangars, were built, and around the facility a tall perimeter fence was erected. With the airfield to the east, the training grounds on the Döberitzer Heath to the west, and now the tank regiment to the north, Groß Glienicke was all but surrounded by military encampments.

★

On 1 September 1939, the lightweight tanks of the 67th Groß Glienicke Tank Regiment fired up their engines at the Czechoslovakian border, and, along with other German forces, rolled into south-western Poland. Pushing rapidly past the city of Krakow and on through the vast Swietokrzyski Forest, they overcame stiff but inadequate resistance, and quickly reached the foot of the Lysa Góra mountain, six hundred kilometres east of Berlin.

The Polish invasion triggered the existing mutual defence agreements between Poland, France and Britain, obliging France and Britain to declare war on Germany on 3 September. They were soon followed by other members of the British Commonwealth: Australia, South Africa, New Zealand and Canada. Within weeks, the Soviet Union had invaded eastern Poland. The Second World War had begun.

The incursion into Poland was accepted by most of the German population as a defensive measure. Guided by the Nazi Party, the press had for years demanded that its leaders stand up to the international bullies, as they saw it, who had not only imposed financial hardships on Germany but had seized its land. This near-universal support for military intervention was echoed in Groß Glienicke. The few dissenting voices – the Jews, the communists, the politically critical – had long been silenced by Hitler's terror tactics.

At the start of the Second World War, there were a little over seven hundred people living in the village. Since 1935, eighteen-year-old boys had been routinely conscripted into the military, with the result that the village lost around ten sons each year. With the conflict's start, all reservists were called up, including the children of Professor Munk, the Meisels' next-door neighbour. Local volunteers also signed up for service. The best-known former resident to enlist was Robert von Schultz, the village's now dispossessed landlord.

Most of those too young, too old, or physically unable to fight remained in the village, working in the fields and the woods as they had always done. Some of these villagers were employed at the Gatow airfield, where a noticeable increase in activity could be discerned. Given that the runway was orientated so that the aircraft flew directly over their houses, the villagers couldn't help but notice that more planes were taking off and landing at the airfield.

To prepare for the war, an air-raid siren was installed at the Drei Linden. It was considered central to the village and therefore in earshot of most people. The villagers dug trenches, built bunkers and practised air-raid drills in readiness for possible aerial attacks. Although there would be no enemy raids until August 1940, the Luftwaffe put a number of anti-aircraft guns to the north and west of the village, positioning them so that they could shoot down any planes hoping to bomb the airfield. Teenage boys were trained to be *Flakhelfer*, or gun assistants. Hearing the siren sound, they would run to their posts, help operate the gun, and seek potential targets flying across the night sky.

Other than this, the start of the war had little impact on village life. School classes continued unchecked, shop shelves were adequately stocked and church services were well attended. The outbreak of war didn't seem to affect the Berlin settlers either. Even while the nation readied for war, lawyers, artists and film stars continued to arrive in their chauffeured cars to spend the weekend at their cottages. That is, until the weather became too cold, and their houses were closed up for the winter.

On 18 January 1940, Eliza gave birth to a son, whom they called Thomas. Now that they had two children, the Meisels felt an urgent need to resolve their interest in the lake house. They were accustomed to owning things – houses, music rights, businesses – and the fact that they were tenants made them feel uncomfortable. The house didn't feel like it was theirs; if they owned the property, they could decorate it the way they liked, and throw away any furniture they found ugly or unnecessary. Either they would find a way to purchase the property, they decided, or they should look for somewhere else.

On 17 February, four weeks after the birth of his son, Will travelled to the tax office at 33–34 Luisenstrasse in the Berlin suburb of Moabit. There he met a bureaucrat recorded only as 'J.A.', who confirmed that the state had seized the Glienicke property from the 'Jew Alfred John Alexander' and that, under the terms of the Law for the Revocation of Citizenship, it was now owned by the Third Reich. If Will was interested, they would indeed be willing to sell him the lake house.

'J.A.' then suggested a price of 3,030 reichsmarks – less than 25 per cent of its true worth – a sum which included the buildings, the leasehold arrangement with Schultz, along with the furnishings and furniture that the Alexanders had left behind. A week later, Will and Eliza Meisel wrote to the tax official agreeing to this proposal. Beneath their signatures they added the words *Heil Hitler*.

Though the land beneath continued to be owned by the Third Reich, the lake house itself was now owned by Will and Eliza Meisel.

11

MEISEL

1942

Early in the morning of 20 January 1942, a line of black saloon cars pulled up at a white-stoned building located on the edge of Wannsee Lake, just three kilometres south of the lake house in Groß Glienicke.

Out from the vehicles stepped some of the highest ranked members of the Nazi Party, the SS and the civil service. Among them were RSHA chief Reinhard Heydrich (one of Heinrich Himmler's deputies), Adolf Eichmann (head of evacuation and Jewish affairs for the RSHA) and Heinrich Müller (the head of the Gestapo).

The purpose of the meeting in Wannsee was to inform and co-ordinate the various government ministries regarding the so-called Final Solution to the Jewish Question. Over the course of the day, matters of racial purity were debated, along with methods of selection and transportation. The size of each country's Jewish population was circulated, and long discussions were held about who would be considered Jewish, such as the children of mixed marriages, converts and their descendants. With the selection policy established, the remaining question was one of logistics: how to transport the Jews to the camps and which Jews should be sent. Although some 250,000 Jews had already fled Germany during the previous decade, a little over 200,000 remained – along with the millions of Jews who lived in the countries that had been recently occupied, such as Poland, Holland, France and Denmark, as well as those who lived in nations that might be invaded soon, such as England, Ireland and Spain.

It was at this meeting, and shrouded in the highest secrecy, that a blueprint was agreed for the extermination of European Jewry. The decisions made at the Wannsee Conference were soon put into action, and could be seen not only in the streets of Berlin, Frankfurt and Hamburg, but also in those of Amsterdam, Paris and Budapest. Across Europe, Jews were seized from their houses and places of work, and then transported on mysterious trains to the 'East'.

In Groß Glienicke, word filtered through that former Jewish residents had been deported to Theresienstadt, including Alfred Wolff-Eisner and Anna Abraham. Similarly, Will Meisel discovered that two of his former composers – Willy Rosen and Harry Waldau – had been picked up at their Berlin homes and hadn't been seen since. Since the early 1930s, despite the worsening persecution of the German Jewish population, a very small number of non-Jewish music publishers and composers – fearful for their own lives or those of their loved ones – had left the country. The vast majority, including Will Meisel, chose to stay.

Will's company, Edition Meisel, had changed considerably over the previous few years. The majority of his staff had either been conscripted into the army or been let go, because the company could no longer afford their services. From the high point in the 1930s, when they had employed twelve people, they were now down to just three: the manager Paul Fago, the creative director Hanns Hartmann and Will himself.

Despite the loss in personnel, they were still able to sell the company's back catalogue of music. At this time, the radio broadcasters had an appetite for *Schlager Musik*, or popular music, which had blossomed in the 1930s and was something Edition Meisel excelled at. Light in tone and typically upbeat, the music reminded listeners of life's sentimental moments. Occasionally, Will agreed to compose a military march, with such titles as 'Wir sind Kameraden', but mostly he stuck to publishing non-political songs. Driving the company's success was Hanns Hartmann, who travelled the country, promoting the music to radio stations, music halls and bandleaders.

Like most of their friends, Will and Eliza Meisel read the Berlin newspapers to follow the war's progress. Yet, fully aware that such news was severely restricted by the Ministry of Propaganda and its leader Joseph Goebbels, they also listened to the BBC. For while the government had announced that it was illegal to listen to enemy radio stations – and that such a crime could be punishable by death – it was fairly simple to avoid being caught. Safest of all was to listen at the lake house, where they were spending an increasing amount of time, away from Berlin and prying eyes.

From the BBC they learned that the scale of the hostilities had widened and that the momentum had shifted. In June 1941, reneging on the pre-war pact, Hitler's forces had invaded Russia. A few months later, in December, the USA had entered the war, following the Japanese attack on Pearl Harbor. Then, in a series of long-range sorties, RAF planes dropped bombs on German cities at an increasing distance from Britain. Though the first British air attack on Berlin had taken place on 25 August 1940, a large-scale assault was only launched on 7 November 1941, when Bomber Command sent more than 160 bombers to drop ordnance on the German capital. Since the raid was at the very limits of these planes' range, the assault was ineffective, with most of the bombs missing their targets and more than twenty planes being shot down.

These aerial assaults, and the explosions that followed them, were visible to the villagers, given that Groß Glienicke was only twenty-five kilometres from Berlin's city centre. Even more apparent were the activities taking place at the Luftwaffe flight school. By early 1942, tens of thousands of technicians and pilots had been trained at the airfield, the numbers becoming so large that the instructors complained that the quality of tuition was deteriorating. Then, as a reminder of the conflict's proximity, the Groß Glienicke windmill was set on fire, preventing it from becoming an identifiable landmark for the Allies.

One night, a Bristol Blenheim bomber was picked up on the radar, as it flew in from the west on its way towards Berlin. The air-raid siren at the Drei Linden pierced the air and those who were on their way to the bunkers could see bright searchlights crossing the night sky, searching for the bomber. Suddenly, the plane was illuminated, paving the way for one of the anti-aircraft guns stationed in Groß Glienicke to track its target. The bomber was hit and the villagers heard the fierce screeching as it fell to the ground, ending with a loud boom and a ball of flame.

The next day, a policeman appeared at the village school, collected the older boys, and organised them into a search party. Walking in a long line, they made their way around the lake's northern tip. A short time later, the bodies of two soldiers were found close to the schloss, still attached to their parachutes. They both wore the uniforms of the Royal Canadian Air Force. Another parachute was found, but there was no trace of the third man. The deaths had a profound impact on the villagers. The war was not as far away as they had thought.

Seeking respite from their hectic lives in Berlin, the Meisels went out to Groß Glienicke most weekends. Thomas learned to walk in the gardens at the house. Peter mastered the front crawl in the lake.

They continued to hold lavish birthday parties at the house for their city friends. Movie and business acquaintances eagerly drove from Berlin, staying for dinner and a swim in the lake. Indeed, Will was so taken with the house that he wrote a song with a couple of the village's other musical residents, Hermann Krome and Hans Pflanzer: 'Groß Glienicke du Meine alte Liebe'.

Will was popular with the locals. He was an approachable man, happy to stop for a few minutes and chat about the latest news, the weather or whatever interested the villagers. Eliza Meisel was less liked, for she preferred to stay at the lake house and rarely ventured beyond the Potsdamer Tor.

Will could also sometimes be found in the Badewiese, the pub which was located next to the public beach. This is where Will preferred to socialise, for the Drei Linden was a little rough for his sensibilities. Built by the Niemann family in 1937, the Badewiese included a restaurant and a hall with a dance floor and four three-metre-high arched windows that overlooked the lake. Will liked to sit at the grand piano, performing songs requested by his friends. Sometimes these would be his own compositions, or those then popular on the radio. A favourite was 'Groß Glienicke du Meine alte Liebe'.

> You so close, so far from world affairs
> So pretty in summer and in snow
> The waves are playing
> And the willow trees are swishing
> One can hear the heartbeat of nature
>
> Groß Glienicke you are my old love
> You are my home by the quiet lake

The Meisels' commitment to the house motivated them, in 1942, to protect their asset by transferring ownership to Edition Meisel.

They had spent no significant sums improving the property, yet the official transfer price was now listed as 21,000 reichsmarks, only two years after they had purchased the 'seized' property from the Gestapo for 3,030 reichsmarks. When asked by neighbours, Will Meisel said that he had bought the house from the Alexanders back in the 1930s.

Meanwhile, as the war progressed, Will continued to improve his ties to the Nazi Party, in particular the Ministry of Propaganda. On 13 May 1942, he wrote to Dr Goebbels, hoping to gain the minister's support for his latest operetta, *Mein Herz für Sylvia*. 'I allow myself, with much respect, the request that you, the Much Honoured Reichsminister, would possibly allow me a little bit of your precious time for a short meeting so that I can ask something.' He ended the letter: 'I greet you with much submission, from the bottom of my heart.'

A few months later, Will issued another letter to the propaganda minister. Upon receipt, a functionary stamped the top right-hand corner of the document, confirming that the letter had been read by the minister. At the bottom of the page was a handwritten note from Goebbels himself, '*Schlösser Empfang!*', an instruction that Will would be met by Dr Rainer Schlösser, a senior official at the ministry. There is no record of what took place in this meeting, but after Will sent another letter the following year, this time requesting that Goebbels again sponsor *Mein Herz für Sylvia*, support was forthcoming and the operetta was produced in Berlin to great acclaim.

In late spring 1943, Will Meisel invited two colleagues, Ernst Nebhut and Just Scheu, to spend a few weeks at the lake house. In recent weeks, Berlin had seen a marked increase in the number of air-raids, making it hard for the publisher to focus on his creative work. Not only would there be fewer disruptions in the countryside, but he believed the lake's fresh air and cool waters might prove helpful for their productivity.

Ernst Nebhut was a lyricist with whom Will had worked before, and Just Scheu was a famous actor and a Goebbels favourite. The plan was that they would stay at the house while they wrote a new operetta, *Königin einer Nacht*, Queen for a Night. The story involved a duke who, wishing to avoid an arranged marriage, pretends to be a boxer, runs away to a hotel and, through a series of comedic events, ends up marrying his intended at the play's end. The music would be light and uplifting.

Working long hours, and often into the night, the three men sat around the piano in the Blue Room, developing new melodies and testing out the accompanying words. Sometimes, Will was dragged away to discuss a pressing business matter with Hanns Hartmann. At other times, they interrupted their labour to go for a swim or to eat one of Eliza's home-cooked meals, enjoyed al fresco on the veranda at the back of the house.

But the war was moving closer. There was no respite, even in Groß Glienicke. While working on the score, Will received a letter telling him to report for duty. Unwilling to serve, Will now marshalled his friends to write letters of protest. On 15 May 1943, the National Theatre Department wrote to the Military Personnel Department regarding the case of Will Meisel, arguing that it is 'of great importance that the above-mentioned be deferred from military service'. They added that Meisel must remain in Berlin in order to make changes to his latest operetta, which had been recently accepted by the Metropol Theater for the coming season. A few days later, Will heard that his service had been deferred. Reinvigorated, he and his colleagues refocused their energies. Finally, the operetta was complete, and they sent the finished work to the ministry for approval.

By this time, the Allies had proved that they had the capacity to send bombers as far as the German capital. Such raids had been restricted to a few minor sorties so far though, and, devastating as they were to the targeted building and its occupants, the vast majority of the city's residents remained unaffected. Now, over the course of the summer, the newspapers were full of stories of a full-scale aerial attack on Berlin. The anxiety grew to such a state that, on 6 August 1943, it was announced on the radio that Goebbels had ordered the evacuation of Berlin's non-essential population. The decision was covered by newspapers around the world, including the *Chicago Tribune*, who ran a headline 'NAZIS ADMIT EVACUATION OF BERLIN: FEAR OF BIG RAIDS TOLD BY GOEBBELS'.

Hearing of the evacuation order, the Meisels decided to stay at the lake house. In a letter to the village mayor, written on 6 August, Will announced that his family had now permanently relocated to Groß Glienicke. As part of the move, and given the shrinkage in the company's staff, the house would also serve as the official headquarters for Edition Meisel. The company's letterhead, brochures and catalogues were reprinted with the new address: Am Park 2, Groß Glienicke. Hanns Hartmann, the creative director, was still mostly on the road, selling the company's music. Paul Fago, the manager, could work from home in Berlin. When they needed to work together, they could do so at the lake house.

As ever, the Meisels quickly adapted to their new circumstances. Eliza pottered around the house, cooking meals, tending her vegetables and garden, and taking care of her younger son, Thomas. Will spent most of his time in the Blue Room, writing songs and fulfilling the few catalogue orders that were still arriving. Peter, meanwhile, who was now eight years old, attended the local school.

Located on the Dorfstraße, opposite the church, the elementary school was the village's only educational institution, known to many as the 'Bach School', after a well-liked former teacher. Classes started at eight in the morning and ran until three in the afternoon. The younger students, such as Peter, who were learning to read and write, worked with small blackboards and chalk, the older students wrote in ink. Sometimes on his way home, Peter came across his father wandering down the street, pencil and notebook in hand, jotting down a melody for his latest song. Father and son would then walk happily home together.

Peter was a good enough footballer to be picked to play against neighbouring schools. Yet his afternoons were filled not only with football. Once a week he participated in Hitler Youth activities with the other boys, at the sports field on the edge of the village. Dressed in uniform – brown shirt, dark trousers, with a leather strap stretched diagonally from waist to shoulder – Peter sang nationalist songs, marched and, when the weather was good, camped next to the lake. When the older boys took part in rifle practice using airguns at the Drei Linden, Peter played football outside with the younger conscripts.

Now that his family was living full-time in the village, Peter made friends with the local kids. In particular, he spent much of his time with the three brothers who lived in a two-storey stucco house behind the lake house: the Radtke boys, Gerhard, Erich and Burkhard. Their father, who had owned an independent gardening business, was now away, fighting in Norway for the German Army. Their mother, Gerda, was a young pretty blonde woman. Their uncle leased the caretaker's cottage from the Meisels.

The Radtke boys liked to play at the lake house, with its tennis court, climbing frame, and large wooden duck that was set in the ground and could be ridden like a rocking horse. Best of all, the Meisels had direct access to the lake. They could jump straight into the water, their knees tucked up, trying to make as large a splash as possible. Leaving the youngest, Burkhard, in the garden to play with Thomas, the two eldest Radtke boys and Peter would swim out to one of the two islands, where they played on a rope swing attached to a branch overhanging the water or paddled out in the Meisels' long red canoe. When it came to mealtimes, however, Gerda Radtke ordered her sons home. It would not be correct for them to eat at the Meisels' table, she said. If her sons had eaten with the Meisels, Frau Radtke felt that she would have had to reciprocate. Even though her own home was more substantial than her neighbours', she thought she might be embarrassed by their more humble furnishings.

At times when playing on the beach, the boys saw Eliza Meisel standing on the terrace singing songs from the films in which she had starred. The children found her shrill soprano hilarious, full of romantic yearning and urban intensity, so out of place in Groß Glienicke. Eliza never took kindly to their laughter, and would force the children to listen to the entire song – which, being well-behaved children, they did.

At other times, the children ran to the now abandoned schloss, which stood three hundred metres east of the lake house. Climbing over a low stone wall, they stole apples from the orchard or played on the swing at the rear of the estate. One day, venturing further, they discovered a tall barbed-wire enclosure that had been set up next to the schloss. Inside stood around twenty men who spoke a foreign language. Guarding them were a few German soldiers. The boys had heard rumours in the village that these men were French prisoners of war. Not wanting to linger, the boys ran off, with the sound of soldiers shouting behind them.

On 3 November 1943, the opening night of *Königin einer Nacht* was held at Berlin's Metropol Theater. Located at the heart of the city on the busy Behrenstrasse in the Mitte district, the theatre was a short walk from the main government offices and popular with workers at the SS/Gestapo headquarters, the Aviation Ministry as well as the Ministry of Propaganda.

As they entered the theatre, the guests walked past giant posters on either side of the main entrance announcing the show's stars: Friedel Schuster and Erich Arnold, along with the up-and-coming Maria Belling and the army's choir. Those on the VIP list – which included Hermann Göring, Joseph Goebbels, Heinrich Himmler and Hans Hinkel, the head of the Reich Chamber of Culture – were ushered towards the private boxes. As a gala event, the house was full, with an audience of over a thousand people. In the orchestra pit, the musicians awaited nervously for the conductor, Horst Schuppien, all wearing black evening tailcoats and trousers. Above the balcony, a chain of nymphs and cherubs held up a gilded ceiling, while heavy red velvet curtains protected the stage.

Also present, of course, and anxiously hoping that all would go well, were Will Meisel and his wife Eliza, along with the show's other creators. Will needn't have worried: *Königin einer Nacht* was a hit. The next day the reviews were unanimously positive, with one theatre critic writing a particularly ebullient notice under the headline: 'WILL MEISEL'S NEW OPERETTA GREAT SUCCESS AT METROPOL THEATER'.

Eight days later, on 23 November 1943, a bomb dropped by an Allied plane struck the Edition Meisel storage facilities at Passauer Straße in Berlin. In the ensuing conflagration, the company's entire back catalogue was destroyed. The only sheet music and recordings saved were those that had been temporarily stored at the lake house. For Will and his colleagues, it was hard to imagine how Edition Meisel could continue operating.

Early in the morning of 19 November 1943, the Groß Glienicke villagers were woken by the deafening rumble of over four hundred Avro Lancasters flying in from the west. They could not see the planes because the sky was thick with clouds, but with the roar of

1,600 engines ringing in their ears, they tracked the planes as they flew across the lake towards Berlin. A few minutes later, when the Lancasters dropped their loads, the sky to the east turned orange, purple and red with the colours of destruction. This was a significant escalation in the shape and scope of the aerial bombardments and marked the start of a sustained aerial campaign against Berlin.

Over the next few days and weeks, the air raids continued, and the devastation wrought by exploding ordnance was amplified by the persistent dry weather, resulting in rampant fires spreading across Berlin. By 17 December, a quarter of the capital's housing had been rendered uninhabitable.

Although the Allied bombardment was unrelenting, wreaking ever-worsening havoc on Berlin into the next year, *Königin einer Nacht* continued to be performed at the Metropol. Until one night, in the summer of 1944, after 155 performances, the theatre took a direct hit. The damage was so extensive that it was impossible for the playhouse to reopen. The operetta was closed indefinitely and the cast dismissed.

Shortly afterwards, on 1 September 1944, Propaganda Minister Goebbels declared that, given the need for every available man to fight in the war, all theatres would be closed. A few weeks later, on 18 October, the government announced the formation of the Volkssturm, calling up all able-bodied men, including those who had been previously excused like Will Meisel, in order to defend the fatherland. Realising that the ministry would still need a few artists to help him pursue his war aims, Goebbels compiled a thirty-six-page list of 1,041 men and women who were exempted. This 'God-gifted list' included Just Scheu, who had helped to write *Königin einer Nacht*. Conspicuously absent from the list, however, was the name of Will Meisel.

Facing the reality that he would be soon conscripted, Eliza and Will Meisel discussed leaving the country. There was nothing keeping them in Berlin. Most of his talent had been driven out of the country, his sheet-music catalogue had been destroyed and the theatres were now closed. They could no longer run the business. Even the lake house didn't feel safe. It didn't take long to decide. The only question was where to go. It was impossible to travel to one of the countries fighting Germany – the Meisels would be seen as the enemy. Meanwhile, the neutral countries – Turkey, Spain and Switzerland – were not providing entry visas. Will had heard of a colony of refugee artists that had been established in Bad Gastein, a spa town located in the Austrian Alps. Since its annexation in 1938, Austria was a part of Germany, so they would not need papers to travel there. Even better, they could speak the language.

Before leaving, Will spoke to Hanns Hartmann. Explaining that his family would soon be relocating to Austria, he invited Hanns to live at the lake house. Hanns was grateful for the opportunity. He and his wife, Ottilie Schwartzkopf, had spent the war ducking the attentions of the Gestapo, given her Jewish heritage and his run-ins with the party. While Hanns had criss-crossed Germany promoting Edition Meisel's back catalogue, Ottilie had remained alone in their Berlin apartment, unable to work and afraid to go outside. Hanns hoped that by staying out of Berlin they might avoid both the aerial bombs and the authorities. After discussing it with his wife, Hanns told his boss that he would be happy to take care of the lake house. Handing over the keys, Will reassured his colleague that they would be back as soon as it was safe.

12

HARTMANN
1944

Hanns Hartmann

Hanns Hartmann had first met Ottilie Schwartzkopf in 1922. At the time, he was twenty-one years old and she was thirty-seven. They had bumped into each other at the opera house of Essen, a city in western Germany, when Hanns was training to be an actor and she was performing under the name 'Ottilie Schott'. Born into a Jewish family in Prague, Ottilie had moved to Germany years before, hoping to build her career. Within a short time, Hanns and Ottilie were going out, unworried about people's mutterings about the age difference.

It wasn't long before Hanns decided he was more interested in management than acting and, in 1925, he secured a job running a theatre in Hagen, a city located fifty kilometres to the east of Essen. He was, at that time, the youngest theatre director in Germany. His next break came when he was appointed theatrical director for Chemnitz, a city in the far east of the country. He was now responsible for three venues including a theatre with 500 seats, an operetta hall with 800 seats and an opera house with 1,250 seats. With overall artistic and financial control, he oversaw hundreds of singers, actors, conductors, musicians, choreographers and set builders. He became known as a man who made fast decisions and was capable of both artistic originality and financial prudence. Meanwhile, Ottilie's career as an opera singer continued to flourish, and she appeared in performances across the country. In 1927, after five years of courtship, she and Hanns were married.

Then, in late February 1933, just a few weeks after the appointment of Adolf Hitler to the chancellorship, Hanns was told that he must choose between his wife and his job. Unable to imagine a life without Ottilie, Hanns made his decision and, on 9 March, was suspended. Then, on 7 April, following the enactment of the Law for the Restoration of the Professional Civil Service, and because of her Jewish heritage, Ottilie was banned from any public performances. Finally, on 30 June, still refusing to leave his wife, Hanns was permanently dismissed from his job.

Realising that he needed to find employment quickly, Hanns successfully applied for a position as director of another theatre company. He soon lost this job as well when the local Nazi Party banned him from the entering the building. Now desperate, Hanns worked as a secretary for a wealthy Czech businessman. A year later, he began approaching music publishers and composers, hoping to secure a job in the arts, one that he could perform under the authorities' radar. This was when he met with Will Meisel, and, in 1936, was taken on as the creative director.

Hanns flourished at Edition Meisel, quickly developing a reputation as a man who knew his own mind. He did not like to be dependent on anyone and could work the system. He was not prone to illogical thinking and was quick to dismiss a foolish idea – even if it came from Will Meisel. Often seen with a cigar in hand, he walked around the office, keeping an eye on even the smallest detail, taking down notes and calculations on a pad he kept in his pocket. Before long, and despite the difficult political situation, the business was benefiting from his savvy financial management.

Then, on 1 January 1937, Hanns Hartmann was excluded from the Reich Chamber of Culture, whose membership was a prerequisite for working in the professional arts. This was the last straw. A few days later, Hanns and Ottilie agreed it was time to leave the country. Contacting the Czech businessman, with whom he had previously worked, he negotiated a contract to manage one of his businesses in Switzerland. He would be paid 4,000 marks each month and gain Swiss citizenship. Two weeks before their departure the Czech businessman died from a sudden embolism. The deal was off. The Hartmanns would have to remain in Berlin.

Since the introduction of the Nuremberg Laws in 1935, Jews had been banned from marrying non-Jews. Yet an exception had been made for the approximately 20,000 couples – such as the Hartmanns – who had wed before the law's enactment. Regarding this group, the Nazis announced a series of increasingly complicated rules, depending on ancestry, gender and religious practice. As far as the Hartmanns were concerned, because Hanns was deemed an Aryan and head of the household, and because the couple did not attend synagogue, even though Ottilie was Jewish, they were considered 'privileged'. By contrast, those belonging to non-privileged mixed marriages were forced out of their homes and into cramped Jewish-only buildings, and had to wear a yellow star or J on their clothes.

In practice, such rules were interpreted differently depending on the local authority and the connections at the disposal of the couple. Nazi bureaucrats frequently punished even those declared 'privileged', dismissing them from employment or banning them from public organisations. Other tactics included harassment and being pulled in for questioning by the police or, worse, by the Gestapo.

Stuck in Berlin and faced with the rapidly escalating anti-Semitism gripping the capital, Hanns asked his boss for help. Through his lawyer, Reinhold Walch, Will Meisel then contacted Hans Hinkel, the head of the Reich Chamber of Culture. A short while later, Will Meisel told Hanns Hartmann that he had obtained a 'special permit', permitting the Hartmanns to remain in Berlin without harassment or fear of deportation.

Hanns had spent the start of the war assisting Will in the running of his publishing company. Much of his time was spent travelling around Germany by train, promoting the company's music to radio stations and theatre directors. When the business was moved to Groß Glienicke, Hanns drove back and forth from his apartment in western Berlin to the lake house. In 1943, Hanns was called to active duty, only to be let go seventeen days later, once his superiors discovered that his wife was Jewish. It was after this and other 'increasing difficulties', as he later noted in a four-page handwritten memoir – presumably alluding to both the increased Allied aerial bombardment and the dangers that his Jewish wife faced from the Gestapo – that he and Ottilie moved to Gloß Glienicke in the autumn of 1944, seeking calm and sanctuary.

The Hartmanns were not the only family who saw the village as a place of safety. According to local rumours, the director of one of Germany's largest record companies had moved into a house further down the shore. Apparently, having divorced his Jewish wife, he had remarried and relocated, hoping that his sons' Jewish parentage would not be discovered. The villagers chose not to denounce these runaways; perhaps they liked the idea that Groß Glienicke had become a safe haven. Or perhaps they thought it was none of their business.

There were others too, mostly professional families from Berlin with weekend houses near the lake, who now chose to live full-time in Groß Glienicke, hoping to avoid the worst of the aerial bombardments. Among this number was Hildegard Munk, the wife of Fritz Munk, whose weekend home stood next to the lake house. While her husband remained in the city, tending to the growing number of civilian casualties that were brought to his hospital, Hildegard stayed in the country, praying that her two soldier sons were safe, and that the war would soon end.

But if any of these refugees thought they could completely avoid the threat from the skies, they were wrong. It was around this time that a bomb fell on the farm owned by Wilhelm Bartel, located directly opposite the village church. Targeting the Gatow airfield, the bomb had dropped short, entirely destroying the stone and mortar farmhouse that had stood for hundreds of years. The air-raid siren had given the family good warning, yet there was one death, a Polish forced labourer. He had been unable to hide with the others because the Nazis had prohibited Poles and other Eastern European workers from entering air-raid shelters.

There were other bombs that came close to the village over the next months, falling either in the lake or outside the village. The residents were thankful that the most important buildings had so far survived the war, particularly their beloved church, the Potsdamer Tor and the schloss. The escalating aerial campaign did, however, cause disruptions to the electricity and water supplies. There were long periods when running water was no longer available and, despite knowing that this was where many of the local houses dumped their sewage, many settlers, the Hartmanns included, were forced to take their drinking water from the lake.

In the first few months at the house, the Hartmanns were able to purchase goods from the village shops – Frau Mond's grocery opposite the Drei Linden, Herr Reinmann's butcher's round the corner and Dettmer's bakery on Sacrower Allee. For a while, luxury items were available, such as coffee, meat, fruit and butter. These they purchased using money Hartmann had saved while working for Will Meisel. Aware that supplies might run out, the Hartmanns had stocked up, storing the items in the lake house cellar. When funds ran out, they bartered items of value left at the house, a few old pots, a coffee-maker, the bread machine.

On one occasion, Gerda Radtke sent six-year-old Burkhard to warn the Hartmanns that they should quickly find shelter. She knew that sometimes, depending on the wind direction, her neighbours failed to hear the air-raid siren that sounded at the Drei Linden. Burkhard later recalled running to the lake house and knocking on the front door with the diamond-shaped window. When nobody came, he knocked again, louder this time. Eventually the door opened a few inches and he saw the face of Frau Hartmann. She looked undernourished, pale and scared. Having relayed the news about the air-raid warning, Burkhard ran back to the safety of his own house. A few seconds later, the Hartmanns hurried outside to hide in the concrete pump house at the bottom of the garden. When Burkhard asked his mother why the Hartmanns could not join them in their wine cellar, which was dug deep into the ground, his mother explained: 'Because they are Jewish.'

The winter of 1944 descended on Groß Glienicke with the aerial assault on Berlin intensifying each day and the Soviet forces moving through Poland, advancing ever closer. It was a particularly cold November and December, the temperature remaining well below freezing. The house was not designed to be inhabited during such severe weather. Bundled up in multiple layers of clothing and blankets, the Hartmanns sat in front of the living-room fire, grateful for the wood they had gathered during the autumn. But feeding themselves was becoming increasingly difficult. While others in the village had animals on which they could survive – chickens, pigs, goats, cattle – the Hartmanns had no such supplies. Similarly, the vegetable garden that had been so well tended by Alfred Alexander, and which could have provided much needed provisions, had been neglected, and lay overgrown with weeds.

Around this time, Hanns contracted shigellosis, a severe form of dysentery caused by drinking polluted water, and suffered from chronic diarrhoea, stomach cramps and fever. With only his wife to care for him – there were no doctors then working in the village or nearby – Hanns lay in bed hoping that his symptoms would soon improve.

Their predicament worsened in January 1945, when the new year ushered in a massive storm. Thick white flakes fell for days, blanketing the garden with snow two metres high. It was exhausting to trek into the village. Even then, the cupboards of the few shops that were still open were nearly bare, following five years of war. With their supply of food almost depleted, Hanns and Ottilie stayed inside, listening to the radio, praying that the fighting would soon be over.

13

HARTMANN

1945

At the beginning of April 1945, over two million Soviet soldiers converged on Berlin from the east, bringing with them 6,000 tanks and 40,000 pieces of artillery. Their plan was to encircle the city, sending part of the Red Army to the north, and part to the south, with the forces converging to the west of the capital near Potsdam. For Hitler, holed up in his bunker in the city centre, it soon became apparent that fighting on would be in vain. With each passing day, the war was reaching a bloody crescendo.

Yet even at this late stage of the war, the villagers of Groß Glienicke were able to place telephone calls to friends and family in Berlin. In these conversations, as much as on the street or in the air-raid bunker, rumours were swapped, discussed and embellished. Those with radios could pick up BBC Radio transmissions from which they learned that American and British forces were fast approaching Berlin from the west through the cities of Cologne, Frankfurt and Düsseldorf. In Groß Glienicke, there grew a sense of ensnarement.

In previous weeks, the Hartmanns had witnessed wave upon wave of planes flying in from the west, over the village, across the lake and on towards Berlin. There were times in which the entire sky seemed to be filled with aircraft. The rumble of thousands of tons of explosives pummelling the city could be clearly heard, and for days and nights the firmament flared bright, as the capital's buildings burned on an industrial scale.

With the sirens at the Drei Linden going off every few minutes and the sound of artillery close by, the Hartmanns found it hard to sleep. At first, on hearing the approaching planes, they would duck instinctively. Before long, they became used to the noise: the scream of the engines, the barking of the guns, the booming of the explosions. If the windowpanes rattled and curtains and pictures fell down, that meant a bomb had fallen nearby. Sometimes the shells exploded so loudly they thought they had been hit.

Then, on Sunday 22 April, the sirens suddenly fell silent. Rumours circulated around the village that a ceasefire had been agreed. Others said that the Allies had stopped their overhead bombing to allow American tanks to approach Berlin. The next day Soviet fighter jets buzzed the village. This was the first time that the Hartmanns had seen low-flying planes. They did not strafe the village, instead focusing their firepower on the German troops who had gathered at the airfield. During the day there were more attacks, one after the other, on the Gatow airfield and the roads around.

With the prospect of a ground assault fast approaching, Hanns and Ottilie decided to hide in the pump house: a concrete bunker measuring four metres square buried into the slope running down to the lake. For the next few days they hid in the bunker, with only one water bottle and little food. It was cramped, dark and terribly cold, but they felt more protected than if they had stayed at the house, which was more likely to be attacked come the invasion.

They were not the only people to seek shelter away from their homes. With her husband still in Berlin working at his hospital, Hildegard Munk had also abandoned her house and moved into her neighbour's pump house. Joining her were five others: her neighbour, Ewald Kunow – the pharmacist – along with three girls from the village, one of whom had a baby. Like the Hartmanns, their thinking was that if the Soviets did come, they would probably want to requisition the houses; plus that concrete offered more protection than the wooden walls of the summer houses.

On 26 April, the sun rose over the lake, casting a red glow across its calm waters. For a while, shooting could only be heard in the distance, but then grew closer, louder and more frequent. Judging by the sounds, the most dramatic fighting was taking place just outside the village. The Soviets were attempting to take the Gatow airfield to the east of the village and the 67th Tank Regiment's base to the north. As one of only three airfields in the Berlin vicinity, Gatow had been operational until just days before, with thousands of German troops flying in, on their way to defend the capital. Now, the only planes flying were Soviet. The tank base, in contrast, was deserted, all of its vehicles, troops and supplies having been relocated to the east in an effort to halt the Soviet advance. By lunchtime the gunfire had stopped. It seemed that the Soviet troops had captured both of their targets.

It was now that three fleeing German soldiers knocked on the door of Gerda Radtke, the mother of the three boys who had befriended the Meisel sons and who lived just behind the lake house. Realising that the Soviets were close, and with her husband still away on service with the German Army, she suggested that the soldiers escape across the lake. Together, they dragged the Meisels' old red canoe out of the garage, and Gerda pointed them across the waters to the far shore, from where they might flee to Berlin.

A few hours later, the first Soviet troops arrived in Groß Glienicke. By now, there were only a handful of German soldiers left to defend the village. Two had carried a machine gun up the tight, winding stairs of the church steeple, in order to mount a defence from a high position. From their pump house, the Hartmanns could hear the rat-tat-tat as the Germans tried to hold off the Soviets. Brave as the attempt may have been, the result proved disastrous for both men and tower, as they were promptly blown up by the Soviet troops.

The fighting continued in the streets. At around four in the afternoon, three Soviet soldiers broke through the fence between the Munk and Kunow properties. Spotting a few German soldiers in the lake house garden, they started shooting. Some of the ammunition struck the Munks' house, leaving holes in the wall of one of the children's rooms. When one German soldier was shot, the others fled. Seeing the Soviets, Hanns Hartmann jumped out of the pump house, put his hands in the air and yelled, *'Ich Bolshevik! Ich Bolshevik!'* – 'I am a Bolshevik'.

Uninterested in Hanns, or his claims of solidarity, the soldiers pushed on up the shore. With the Soviets now gone, Hildegard stepped out of the Kunow pump house and covered the dead German soldier with branches and leaves.

Now that the German resistance was quashed, the Soviets arrived en masse. To the villagers' surprise, they drove neither tanks nor trucks, but instead straggled in as a ragged column of men on foot. Exhausted and malnourished, they seemed desperate for an end to the war. Their only vehicles were *Panjewagen*, four-wheeled carts pulled by horses, now loaded with items looted over the previous days.

That night, the Soviets returned to the lake house and the other homes along the shore. There they dug holes in the sandy gardens, covering themselves in blankets and quilts stolen from the houses. The following day, worn out by the fighting, the Soviets slept late. When they awoke, they began exploring the village. Hildegard hoped they would be safe in the concrete pump house. 'We were at their mercy,' she later recalled.

Her fears were realised when they heard the sound of a rifle butt thudding against their door. 'Send the women out!' a voice commanded. Frau Munk was terrified, as were the three young women. Herr Kunow came out, telling the soldiers that Frau Munk was an elderly woman, what could they want with her? The five Soviet soldiers took one look at her, agreed, but then grabbed the younger women, whom they wrestled, kicking and screaming, outside and into the houses nearby – the Kunow, Munk and Meisel homes. There, they were raped.

A hundred metres away, Gerda Radtke was hiding in her wine cellar, with her three sons and a few neighbours. They too heard a sharp rap on the door, and the same demand: send out the women. Gerda stepped forward and, reassuring her children, said she would deal with the problem. Outside there were six or seven Soviet soldiers, who seized Gerda, and her three sons, who were holding on to her. The soldiers bustled them up the stairs to the kitchen, where they raped Gerda, one soldier after another, in front of her sons. When Burkhard, by then seven years old, tried to stop them, the soldiers just batted him away. His mother tried not to scream, aware that her sons were watching, not wanting to scare them further.

After the attack, the soldiers returned to the cellar where they found the neighbours on their knees, begging to be spared. The soldiers allowed the villagers back to their homes, but informed Gerda Radtke that they were requisitioning hers. She would be allowed to live upstairs, while they would occupy the ground floor.

Over the next few days, word of the Soviet advances in Berlin filtered back to Groß Glienicke. Leaflets were dropped from the air into the village by passing planes, declaring that Hitler had been found dead in his bunker, having apparently committed suicide.

Finally, on 2 May 1945, Helmuth Weidling, the German commander of the Berlin Defence Area, unconditionally surrendered the city to

General Vasily Chuikov of the Soviet Army. The hammer and sickle now flew over the Reichstag.

Six days after the surrender of Berlin, the senior generals and admirals of the German army, navy and air force were flown to the capital and driven to the newly established Soviet military headquarters. There they signed the act of unconditional surrender in front of representatives from the British, American, French and Soviet governments. Following the German submission, the Soviet soldiers held one celebration after another at the barracks on Döberitzer Heath – in the old Olympic Village where Jesse Owens had practised his long jump nine years earlier. Each time there was a party, the Soviet soldiers would come to the Radtke house and take Gerda away. Often, she was gone for more than twenty-four hours. Once she escaped, but the soldiers found her and brought her back to their barracks. When they were finished with her, she would return deeply traumatised.

Gerda's house had also now been transformed into the local Soviet headquarters. But it was not only the ground floor that had been taken by the occupying forces. The small barn, which was located twenty metres from Gerda's house and eighty metres from the lake house, had also been requisitioned, and turned into a brothel where local women volunteered their bodies in return for food and protection.

The women of the village were not the only ones to suffer. As soon as they arrived, the Soviets began hunting down anyone they suspected of war crimes. One of the first to be seized was Wilhelm Bartel, the farmer whose building had been bombed during the war. Pointing at the Poles still working on the farm, and learning of the worker who had died in the bombing, they accused him of overseeing slave labour. He was loaded onto a truck and driven to Ketschendorf, a Soviet camp ninety kilometres east of Groß Glienicke. At least ten young men were also taken, including two sixteen-year-olds, who were accused of being part of the Werwolf resistance movement. Neither Wilhelm Bartel nor the youngsters were seen again.

14

HARTMANN
1945

At 7.15 a.m. on 30 June 1945, seven weeks after the war's end, a convoy of British trucks and jeeps – known as Staging Post 19 – set off from Hamburg in western Germany towards Groß Glienicke in the north-east. The mobilisation was part of a wider effort by Britain, France and America to match the Soviet forces in Berlin.

As the convoy trundled eastwards, the only other vehicles they passed were American and British jeeps travelling at speed, or trucks carrying troops. The carcasses of destroyed tanks and personnel carriers littered both sides of the road. The towns and villages they passed through were deserted. Nobody was walking on the streets; the only sign of human activity were the white flags hanging from people's windows and balconies. After a journey of 280 kilometres, they arrived in Groß Glienicke, and heeded for the Gatow airfield.

Since its capture at the end of April, the airfield had been under Soviet control. Now, following an agreement between the occupying powers, it was to be temporarily handed over to the RAF's Staging Post 19, and would be available for use by American, French, Soviet and British planes. According to the airfield's logbook – filled in each day by the British commanding officer – 'The aerodrome had been previously occupied by the Russians who, before departure, had taken nearly all the easily removable equipment etc. and left litter and confusion behind them.' In order to clean up the facility, the British 'hired local civilians to clear the airfield and secured permission from Russians to do this'.

Two weeks later, on 15 July, a group of dignitaries flew into Gatow. Their arrival was again recorded in the logbook. 'The great day began very quietly. At 9 o'clock when the security troops had taken up position it was already very hot. The tarmac now filled with distinguished personages. Russians being most colourful, including Deputy Commissar for Foreign Affairs, Andrey Yanu-arevich Vyshinsky, wearing a single large Marshal of the USSR star, plus a dozen Russian officers.' Next to arrive was an American plane, carrying President Harry S. Truman along with Generals Dwight D. Eisenhower and Henry Arnold, and Secretary of State James Byrnes. 'At 16:00 came the great moment for which the spectators had most eagerly awaited,' the logbook continued. 'The PRIME MINISTER'S SKYMASTER drew up on the tarmac, and excitement ran high when the steps, specially made for the occasion, were set in position and the familiar figure of the PM, with cigar, appeared. He was greeted by Field Marshal Montgomery and Air Marshal Sir Sholto Douglas and host of high ranking American and Russian officers.'

Churchill and Truman had intended to go straight to Potsdam, where they were scheduled to meet Joseph Stalin to discuss Europe's post-war future, but the Soviet leader was delayed for a couple of days due to a minor heart attack, so instead they were driven into Berlin for a tour of the damaged city.

Berlin was a wasteland. Many of the city's most significant struc-tures were in ruins, including the Reichstag, the Reich Chancellery, the People's Court and the Gestapo headquarters. The Berliner

Stadtschloss, the massive royal palace on the banks of the River Spree, was roofless and burned out. The city centre's main streets – the Kurfürstendamm, Unter den Linden and Friedrichstrasse – were a sea of stone and rubble.

An estimated 100,000 civilians had been killed during the Battle of Berlin. Over 300,000 Soviet soldiers died during the campaign. If one added in the hundreds of thousands who were captured and later died in the Soviet camps, German deaths in the Battle of Berlin exceeded one million.

Of the 4.3 million people who had lived in Berlin before the war, only 2.8 million remained. And this diminished populace now faced ruin. The Berlin air was so thick with smoke from the persistent fires that it was hard to navigate the streets. The city had no functioning water supplies or sewer system. Its transportation was non-existent. There was no heating fuel, no electricity and food was scarce. The telephone and postal networks had collapsed, as had most of the city's bridges and train tunnels. Over a million Berliners were home-less. As he was driven around the streets of the German capital, Churchill was shocked by the devastation.

On 17 July, the three victorious leaders met at the Cecilienhof in Potsdam, the same building where Adolf Hitler had met the Kaiser's son during the Day of Potsdam in 1933. This 176-room former royal palace was built on the shores of the Jungfernsee, some ten kilometres south of Groß Glienicke, and was now the venue for the so-called Potsdam Conference.

At first, the talks proceeded in a celebratory atmosphere. During the daytime, sitting in large armchairs at a round table in a wood-panelled room, conversations proved relaxed and positive. In the evenings, the leaders hosted lavish dinners and entertainments. Then, a week into the conference, on 24 July 1945, Truman casually mentioned to Stalin that the USA now had a 'new weapon of unusual destructive force'. The Russian premier replied that he was glad to hear it and hoped the Americans would make 'good use of it against the Japanese', but showed no special interest.

In the second week, tempers deteriorated as negotiations focused on the key outstanding issues of reparations, political control and territory. At the end of the third week, now exhausted, the Allied leaders announced the end of their deliberations: they would establish a process for the prosecution of Nazi war criminals with a trial slated to take place later that year in Nuremberg; there would be new external borders for Germany, Austria and Poland; and Germany would have to pay the Soviet Union reparations in compensation for the losses endured during the war, including 10 per cent of its industrial capacity. In contrast, the US and UK delegations did not insist on reparations, wary of provoking a backlash from the German people similar to that seen in the years after the First World War.

Also announced was the Allies' plan for the post-war administration of Germany. The country would be split into four zones, respectively controlled by the Americans, French, British and Soviets. In addition, the city of Berlin, located within the Soviet zone, to the east of the other three, would likewise be split into four sectors. It had always been Stalin's intention to control Berlin after the war's end, so it was with great reluctance that he agreed to this redrawing of Germany's internal borders. In effect, the western neighbourhoods of Berlin – including Wilmersdorf, Charlottenburg and Spandau – would now form a capitalist island within a sea of communist control.

On 6 August, four days after the conclusion to the Potsdam Conference, the Americans dropped a nuclear bomb on the Japanese city of Hiroshima, instantly killing 80,000 people and destroying 70 per cent of the city's buildings. On 9 August, a second bomb was launched on Nagasaki killing 40,000 people. Three weeks later, on 2 September 1945, Japan signed its unconditional surrender, during a ceremony held aboard the USS *Missouri* docked in Tokyo Bay.

The Second World War had finally come to an end.

The first map that came out of the Potsdam Conference placed the entire village of Groß Glienicke, including both sides of the lake, within the Soviet zone. But the British wanted their own airport. So, on 30 August 1945, they asked the Soviets for permanent control of the old Luftwaffe airport at Gatow, whose runway terminated a few hundred metres from the lake's eastern shore. The Soviets consented, and in return received land in Staaken, a few kilometres to the north. The result was that Groß Glienicke was separated from Gatow, with the boundary between West Berlin and East Germany now running down the centre of the lake.

The houses on the west of the lake – where the Meisel, Munk and Radtke homes stood – would continue to be located within Groß Glienicke and controlled by the Soviets. Meanwhile, the houses on the eastern shore were administratively folded into the village of Kladow and, from now on, would become part of the British sector of West Berlin.

At first, the agreements made at Potsdam had little impact on the village. The Soviets set up a border control at the Potsdamer Tor, while the British established their own control point at the Spandau Tor, a similar stone arch on the Berlin side of the old Groß Glienicke Estate. Villagers were able to cross between the zones without restriction, unimpeded if they wanted to travel for work, shopping, or to visit family members.

Then in September 1945, the Soviet Military Administration in Germany announced a series of land reform measures. Private properties would now be limited to one hundred hectares, equivalent to one square kilometre. Farms were seized, split into smaller units and redistributed to the landless. Forty-five per cent of East German land was affected with over seven thousand farms expropriated. Landowners, often accused of 'Nazi activities' and 'war crimes', were forced to find alternative employment. Many were also sent to labour camps that were located within East Germany, some of which had been established within former Nazi concentration camps.

However, the Soviet Military Administration had failed to prepare for the massive changes resulting from their reforms. For a start, many of the *Neubauer*, as the newly installed farmers were known, lacked sufficient machines to plough the fields or to collect the harvest, and most of those who had been tasked with running the farms lacked the knowledge or skills to achieve their government-directed goals. The results were immediate: food production collapsed, malnutrition rose, and with mansions and farm buildings now demolished, in ruin or in disrepair, the already limited housing stock was reduced yet further.

Groß Glienicke was spared none of this. The first consequence of the land reform was that the former workers of the estate were dispossessed of their houses, including families such as the Radtkes – even if they owned the properties outright. Next, twenty-nine current tenants were given the opportunity to buy the land they occupied. This included the Meisels who were now offered the chance to purchase the land underneath the lake house, even though they owned a residence in West Berlin. But as the Meisels were still in Austria, they were unable to take advantage of this opportunity. The final repercussion related to the schloss itself. As soon as they had taken over the village the Soviets had occupied the schloss – by now there was barely any furniture left since the Schultzes had removed anything of value back in the 1930s. The schloss represented everything that the Soviets disliked: an extravagant building, an unused resource, a symbol of feudal power and injustice. During the early days of their occupation, a group of Soviet soldiers even chiselled off the Wollank family crest from the top of the Potsdamer Tor.

Then, sometime during the extremely cold winter of 1945, a fire erupted in the schloss's upstairs sewing room. It was never determined if this was an accident or an act of arson. Within minutes, the alarm sounded at the fire station. Jumping into their truck, the volunteer firemen raced under the Potsdamer Tor, passing the gate to the lake house, down the dirt track, before arriving a minute later outside the schloss. They were met by a line of Russian soldiers who barred their way. Soon after, the British arrived, also carrying fire equipment, but they too were prevented from taking action by the Russians.

Since the schloss stood within the Soviet zone, the fire was clearly their responsibility. Yet the Soviets made no effort to put it out. Instead, they focused on removing the few items left inside the building. The blaze quickly grew out of control and the roof collapsed. The beautiful frescos in the hallway were destroyed, as were the sweeping staircase and the ballroom. By now, almost the entire village had gathered to witness the schloss's end; it was as if their old way of life was burning to the ground before them. This fire marked the climax to the terrors experienced by the villagers since Soviet troops had taken control.

For Burkhard Radtke, life in Groß Glienicke had been paradise for most of the war years. After 1945, he later recalled, it felt 'like falling into hell'.

Shortly after the Soviets arrived in Groß Glienicke, Hanns and Ottilie left the lake house. Hearing what had happened to their neighbours, they decided it would be safer to be in the capital than in the village.

Having closed the shutters, covered the furniture with sheets and locked the front door, they set off with their few belongings for

Berlin. There was no public transport at the time, and as Soviet drivers were unlikely to help a couple of struggling civilians, Hanns and Ottilie had to walk. It was a little over thirteen kilometres to their apartment in the capital's western suburbs, and the journey took them most of the morning. As they arrived in the Berlin district of Spandau, they found that the Freybrücke, the old iron bridge spanning the River Havel, had been blown up, forcing them to follow the other pedestrians and use a series of jerry-rigged structures to cross the river. Eventually, they reached their apartment at Giesebrechtstraße 9 in Charlottenburg. Here they waited, shocked by the devastation around them, but glad to be out of Groß Glienicke, and safe in the city.

Once again, the lake house stood empty. For the second time in its history, its shuttered windows endured a long summer, autumn and winter unopened and unwarmed by human company and the heat from a fire. Inside, the air grew stale and cold, while outside, a strange normality returned to the village.

In January 1946, an unexpected visitor arrived in Groß Glienicke. Hanns Alexander had spent the war in the British Army, rising to the rank of captain. Now he was back in Berlin working as part of a British war crimes investigation team.

Finding nobody at the lake house, Hanns walked over to the house next door, looking for Fritz Munk. It had been Professor Munk who had urged the Alexanders to flee Germany for their lives back in the 1930s. The two men greeted each other warmly. The Munks had survived; although the sons, Klaus and Peter, had taken part in campaigns in northern Italy and Russia, thankfully neither had been injured. Fritz did not mention what his wife had witnessed during the Soviet occupation.

Hanns's news was that almost all of the Alexanders had made it to England. He and Paul had served in the British Army from 1940. His parents were doing well, although he worried about his father's health. At the end of the war, Bella had lost her husband, when the car he was driving in south-west England had been hit by a plane just as it was landing.

His sister Elsie and her husband Erich had had a second son in 1942, Michael, and then — eager to assimilate, and worried about sounding too German — they had changed their name from Hirschowitz to Harding. Elsie, however, had found it harder to adapt than her parents or siblings. She missed Germany. Most of all, she missed the house in Glienicke.

In a letter home to his parents, penned in English, Hanns wrote:

I passed Glienicke. House OK. Garden very *verwildert* [wild], and looks tiny, as the trees etc are so big, that it looks much more closed in and smaller. Meisel is still living in it. Windows now painted red instead of blue-and-white. Munks are still alive and neighbours.

It would be decades before another member of the Alexander family would see the lake house.

15

MEISEL
1946

With Will Meisel and his family remaining in Austria, Hanns Hartmann was in charge of Edition Meisel. This was the first time that the creative director was able to run the business as he saw fit, without interference from his boss. Having re-established contact with his deputy, Paul Fago, who had remained in Berlin during the last months of the war, Hanns set about rebuilding the company.

First, he had to deal with the new Allied bureaucracy. Much like their Soviet counterparts, the British authorities had no sooner arrived in Berlin than they began assessing and then licensing the businesses operating within their sector. Licences could be granted, however, only if a business owner could be shown to have no connection to the Nazi Party.

On 7 June 1945, the West Berlin council sent a letter, typed on thin pink paper, to Hanns Hartmann.

Dear Mr Creative Director,
   Hereby I allow you to reopen the Edition Meisel in Wittelsbacher-strasse 18 under your personal management, as well as the Monopol and Echo Editions. Clearly the former owners cannot be in any way

directly or indirectly involved in the company or have any kind of influence on the artistic decisions.

With the company now officially permitted to do business, Hanns Hartmann and Paul Fago rebooted the operation. They contacted Berliner Rundfunk, the radio station which was broadcasting from the British sector, suggesting that they play the company's back catalogue. Then, taking advantage of the relationships developed before the war, they reached out to the music halls and other venues that had begun to emerge. Within a few weeks, with a trickle of orders coming in, it felt as if they were back in business.

As he made his way around Berlin, reconnecting with old friends and colleagues, Hanns Hartmann came to the attention of the Soviet authorities. Now in charge of the city's eastern sector, and believing that the arts were important to both building morale and political education, the Soviets asked Hanns to rebuild the Metropol Theater which had been bombed in 1944. While the theatre was being restored, he was told, the company could rehearse at the Colosseum which had served as a hospital during the war and was also in the Soviet sector. In return for helping out with the Metropol Theater, the Hartmanns were provided with new accommodation in East Berlin.

A few weeks later, impressed by his efforts, as well as his unimpeachable record, the Soviets asked Hanns to head the German Audit Committee, which would assist the occupying powers in their denazification of the arts.

The term 'denazification' was first devised in 1943 by the US military as part of their post-war planning to reform the German judiciary. Over the next few years it evolved into a more general programme of removing the Nazi Party's influence from the German population. At the war's end, over 8.5 million Germans, more than 10 per cent of the population, were members of, or affiliated to, the Nazi Party. As well as pursuing and prosecuting the Nazi high command, and those deemed to have committed war crimes or profited from slave labour, the Allies sought to purge Germany of National Socialist ideology, and rid the country of all remnants of Nazi rule – statues, symbols, street names and any organisation that had been connected with the party.

Following the occupation of Berlin, the implementation of denazification varied considerably between the four occupying powers. The Soviets chose to promote their own communist ideology rather than educate the population about their responsibility for war crimes. The Americans, by contrast, initially vowed to vigorously investigate every potential supporter of the party. It quickly became clear that the American approach would be impossible; the number of potential suspects was simply overwhelming.

In the end, the Americans chose to follow the British and French who were embracing a more pragmatic approach, zeroing in on the most egregious personalities along with those who wished to retain positions of responsibility. A hierarchy of guilt was established: Exonerated, Followers, Lesser Offenders, Offenders and Major Offenders. The Major Offenders – men such as aviation minister Hermann Göring, or Josef Kramer, the concentration camp commandant – would be dealt with at the war crimes trials that year in Belsen and Nuremberg. The exonerated were released. Those in the intermediate categories would be investigated and, if found guilty, punished using a variety of methods, ranging from imprisonment to being banned from holding public office or being forced to carry out manual labour.

As part of the denazification process, millions of Germans were asked to fill out a *Fragebogen*, or questionnaire. This six-page document – which was soon hated by the Germans – was then reviewed by a panel of inspectors, and if warranted, the subject of inquiry would be called in for questioning.

Early in August 1945, Hanns received a *Fragebogen*, which he completed on behalf of Edition Meisel. The company had been founded in 1926, he wrote, and it was owned one hundred per cent by Will Meisel. Yes, he conceded, Will Meisel had been a member of the Nazi Party, but none of the company's works had been used by the government, and nor was their content 'fascistic'. He said that the company could resume normal business as soon as the city's printing presses were operating again, and provided a copy of Edition Meisel's catalogue including a list of their well-known composers.

As to the future, he said, 'together with famous new authors, our plan is to set up programmes for German theatres and to write new plays. In addition we hope to sell and play foreign pieces.' There was no mention of the Jewish composers who had been attached to the company before the war. Of the eleven questions to which Hanns Hartmann had to respond, his only ambivalent answer was to number 9. Asked 'Which of the works cannot be played because of fascist or militaristic or racial tendencies?', he replied, 'None of these have tendencies, but some have to be checked and until then they will not be used.' On 29 August 1945, Hanns submitted the completed questionnaire and then, hearing nothing back from the British authorities, assumed that his answers had been satisfactory and returned his attention to the day-to-day issues facing business.

Over the next twelve months, Hanns endeavoured to balance his work for Will Meisel with his responsibilities to the Soviets. This proved difficult, however. While working to rebuild the Metropol, he experienced intolerable interference from the Soviets. With the memories of a dictatorship meddling in his artistic life still fresh in his mind, Hanns discussed the matter with his wife. All he says of this matter in his private memoirs is that he decided to 'leave Berlin for political reasons'.

The problem was that Hanns was now well known to the Soviet authorities. If the Hartmanns left for the British, American or French sectors, the Soviets might track them down and arrest them. In the previous months, there had been cases where the Soviet security police had crossed into western Berlin, snatched a suspect and dragged them back into the eastern sector. Already, a number of Berliners had been detained by the Soviet authorities and accused of espionage and, worse, connections with the Nazi Party. Those found guilty had been sent to the camps and had not been heard of since. Hanns wrestled with how best to escape the city.

In early autumn of 1946, having determined that it was safe to return, Will and Eliza Meisel left their 'Austrian holiday home' with their two sons, arriving back in Berlin on 15 September. With their office building destroyed and their apartment still in ruins, they moved into the house in Groß Glienicke, located as it now was in Soviet-controlled eastern Germany.

Soon after his return to Berlin, Will Meisel met Hanns Hartmann. Explaining his predicament with the Soviets, Hanns said that he and his wife would shortly be leaving. As such, he could no longer continue managing the company. While Will remained banned from ownership, pending his denazification process, Paul Fago would take over the helm. The two men said their goodbyes and promised to stay in touch.

A few days later, on 1 October 1946, Hanns and Ottilie Hartmann lined up at the border crossing in the Soviet sector carrying only a few belongings. Through his contacts, Hanns had secured false papers in the name of 'Mansfeld'. When it was their turn, they handed their travel documents to the guard and, after a cursory inspection, they were waved through. Relieved, the Hartmanns crossed into western Berlin and headed directly for the station. There they purchased a ticket to Hamburg, which lay deep in the British zone in north-western Germany, and boarded a train. From Hamburg they travelled to Cologne, where soon after the British appointed Hanns as director of North-West German Radio.

Now that the Meisels were living once again at the lake house, Will wrote to the Groß Glienicke *Gemeinde*, or parish council, asking if he could purchase the land underneath the house. The *Gemeinde* administration had been established soon after the Soviets had taken over the village and was made up of individuals who had no previous affiliation with the Nazi Party or the landlords, the Schultzes. Since the *Gemeinde* was in charge of local affairs, it was also responsible for the village's land reform programme. As tenants, Will and Eliza Meisel were still deemed eligible and, in return for a small fee, the transaction was complete. Finally, the Meisels owned both the land and the buildings of the lake house.

With Hanns Hartmann having fled Berlin, Will Meisel set about retaking control of his business. First, he decided, they must repair the building at Wittelsbacherstrasse 18 in Wilmersdorf, intending to use the location as both an office and a home. Next, he wrote to the British authorities asking that he be allowed to manage Edition Meisel. The response was clear and firm. In a letter from the Berlin council to the Information Control Unit (Theatre and Music Section), dated 21 November 1946, it was written that the company should continue to be run by Herr Fago, 'until the successful denazification of Mr Meisel'.

Frustrated by the intransigence of the British, Will informed Paul that he would be officially running the company. In the meantime, Will would continue his efforts to clear his name.

By the summer of 1947, the repairs were complete and the Meisels moved back into their home at Wittelsbacherstrasse 18. They were now too busy rebuilding their shattered lives to spend time in the countryside. Once or twice they drove out to Groß Glienicke to check on their property, but the village was difficult to reach, given the terrible roads and the Soviet and British checkpoints along the way. The post-war shortages had also made petrol prohibitively expensive.

By October 1947, two years after the war's end, the British denazification efforts had been proven only a partial success. More than 2.1 million cases had been examined by the British, resulting in 347,000 people being dismissed from their jobs and 2,320 people being prosecuted for providing false answers on their *Fragebogen*. Per capita, these figures were far lower than in the American zone. In response, the British authorities passed Ordinance 110, transferring the responsibility for the denazification process from the British to the German authorities. As a fail-safe, ultimate control remained with British commissioners, who could intervene in cases when they felt it necessary.

With millions still awaiting denazification, it was clear that the system could never catch up. By now, more concentrated on the emerging Soviet threat than worried about former Nazis, the British, French and American occupying powers agreed to rush the outstanding cases through the courts. These remaining cases were to be tried through summary proceedings, leaving insufficient time to investigate the accused. As a result, many of the judgements of this period had questionable judicial value. It was also decided that no new denazification cases were to be initiated from January 1948 onwards. Only ongoing cases would proceed to trial.

★

On the morning of 25 June 1948, Will Meisel entered Schlüterstraße 45, off the Kurfürstendamm in West Berlin, the same building that had previously housed the Reich Chamber of Culture, and where its commissioner, Hans Hinkel, had held his offices. Now it was occupied by the Intelligence Section of British Information Services Control. They had two main tasks: handing out licences to artists, actors and musicians, and overseeing denazification *Spruchkammer*, or tribunals. Will was here for the latter.

The *Spruchkammer* were run by twenty-two German staff and their remit had been defined in a four-power directive: 'Concerning the Removal from Office and Positions of Responsibility of Nazis and Persons Hostile to Allied Purposes.' The *Spruchkammer*'s decisions were subject to Allied ratification, but in practice were seldom overturned.

The lift had not worked since the days of Hans Hinkel, so Will walked up three flights of stairs before entering an elegant, wood-panelled room filled with rows of chairs facing a large table. The chamber was almost empty – there had been so many of these de-nazification hearings that they hardly awakened interest anymore. Eighteen months earlier, in December 1946, this same room had seen Wilhelm Furtwängler, one of Germany's most famous conductors, undergo his own denazification trial. Despite his close association with the Nazi Party, Furtwängler had been exonerated and allowed to return to work. Will Meisel hoped he would achieve the same outcome. To do this, he would have to demonstrate that he had been a *Mitläufer,* a nominal 'paper' member of the party, and had never supported its beliefs. It is worth noting that during his trial in the 1930s, Robert von Schultz had to prove the opposite: that not only was he a member of the party, but he also adhered to its ideology.

Furtwängler's tribunal had been overseen by the Americans, with the assistance of two Germans, from the German Audit Committee, including its chairman, a certain Hanns Hartmann. Will Meisel knew, however, that his former creative director was no longer in Berlin and, distressingly, would not be appearing as a witness in his trial.

On the stroke of ten, the six commissioners walked into the room, including the forty-year-old chairman and former communist, Alex Vogel. Also present were six witnesses, including Paul Fago. The chairman opened the proceedings by explaining that Will Meisel had been a member of the Nazi Party, had therefore been banned from running the company, and had now applied for reinstatement. He then invited the publisher to present his case.

Will Meisel started by providing a summary of his career, establishing his company in 1926, building up the music catalogue and then working on various films. The Nazi rise to power on 30 January 1933 had been a total 'surprise', he said, and that, three days later, Edition Meisel had been blocked from the radio because 80 per cent of his catalogue was made up of Jewish composers. He was known in the Ministry of Propaganda as a '*Judenknecht*', he reported, a slave to the Jews, and he had 'suffered a lot' for that.

He described his Nazi Party membership as an 'unfortunate step,' adding that he had joined the party to 'protect my business and the rights of the Jewish authors'. At this point Vogel interceded and said, 'In terms of business it was a fortunate move.'

Will was quick to counter that 'with hindsight, it was not the right thing to do', adding that after losing his Jewish financial director in 1935 he had hired Paul Fago, who was a Freemason, a proscribed organisation at that time. Later that year he had taken on Hanns Hartmann, whose wife was Jewish. Will said that he tried to help Frau Hartmann emigrate to England, and when they failed at this, he 'made good weather' with the Ministry of Propaganda, allowing Hartmann to retain his position, despite having a Jewish wife. He went on to say that when things became politically turbulent in Berlin, during the 'times of Jewish discrimination, the Hartmann couple had often slept in my private flat or in the company house in

Groß Glienicke. In short, until the end of the war I did everything to save the Hartmanns.'

Vogel pushed him on this point. 'Have Herr Fago and Herr Hartmann given statements on this?' Will replied, 'No, not in this manner.' The court was clearly puzzled by these omissions. Why, if he had been so helped by Will Meisel, had Hartmann failed to give a positive testimony? This was particularly odd, since Hartmann was a highly credible witness.

Worried that he was losing the panel, Will described how he had helped other Jews, first mentioning the estate agent who had found the lake house for his family back in 1937. 'I knew the property manager Herbert Würzburg,' he said, 'who was of Jewish descent, and I supported him until 1943 with money and food coupons. I also supported the Jewish composer Harry Waldau, commissioning him to produce work until 1943.' No one mentioned that in 1943 the sixty-seven-year-old Harry Waldau and the forty-four-year-old Herbert Würzburg had been rounded up in Berlin, and transported to the gas chambers of Auschwitz.

In order to prove that he was not directly connected with the Nazi regime, Will now called on former colleagues to testify. While it was common at such tribunals to call character witnesses, their testimonies were commonly known as *Persilschein*, or whitewash certificates, and were often discounted as unreliable by the judges. The first to take the stand was the music publisher's former lawyer, Reinhold Walch. Holding up the 1938 letter that Will had written to the head of the Reich Music Chamber, Hans Hinkel, Vogel asked the lawyer if he was involved with his client's attempt to purchase aryanised businesses. It was he who had pushed Meisel, Walch responded, as he had 'thought it was a good idea to buy those businesses'. Pointing out that this attempt to purchase Jewish properties had taken place only a few days after Kristallnacht which had terrorised Germany's Jewish population, Vogel then asked the lawyer if he thought he had 'given a good tip'. Walch replied, 'Yes.'

As part of the trial record, Will Meisel had been asked to submit an up-to-date copy of his *Fragebogen*, copies of which were included in the court papers. In question 121, Will had been asked, 'Have you or any immediate member of family ever acquired property which has been seized from others for political, religious, or racial reasons?' Will had said 'No'. To question 123 – 'Do you administrate Jewish properties which have been aryanised?' – he had again said 'No'. Finally, when asked to list the properties that he owned, Will had written that, in addition to his properties in Berlin, he 'owned a wooden house in Groß Glienicke which he had purchased from Dr Alexander in 1936'. Of course, Vogel and his fellow commissioners didn't know that the lake house had been aryanised in 1940, since those records were buried in the Gestapo archives, to which they had no access at the time.

In an effort to distract the commissioners, Will then interrupted the proceedings – this was not a usual criminal court in which only the prosecutor and defence put the questions – and asked his former lawyer about the efforts that he, Will, had made to protect Hartmann and his wife.

> Walch: I can only say that Herr Meisel didn't have a very good reputation [with the Nazis] because of the Hartmann issue. Hartmann was Meisel's manager, which was not allowed because he was not a member of the Reich Chamber of Culture. This led to certain problems. It was necessary to get him a work permit and to get special liberties for Frau Hartmann.

When Walch was asked who had suggested that he obtain a special permit for Frau Hartmann, he replied that it was Will Meisel and Hanns Hartmann, adding that he was not paid for these efforts.

Walch sat down and was followed by Wilhelm Lachner, who said that he worked in the music business and had known Will for twenty years. He told the court that he was 'often in Groß Glienicke, where he met the creative director Hartmann'. He added that there they listened to foreign radio together. He said that as well as Frau Hartmann, Will Meisel had helped other people who were 'impacted by the Nuremberg Laws', including the composer Willy Rosen. When Vogel asked whether he had seen one of Will Meisel's employees load the company car with Nazi propaganda and drive it to marches and parades, he said that he didn't know.

Finally came Paul Fago. He said that he had known Will for twenty-five years and had worked at his company since the mid 1930s. He said that 90 per cent of authors published by Will were Jewish, and after Jewish music was banned from the radio, the company fell into debt. 'I think he joined the party to save his company,' he said, adding that Will was 'neither a Nazi nor a militarist', and that even in March 1945 he had skilfully avoided serving in the Volkssturm, the people's militia. Contradicting Will's earlier testimony, however, Fago said that Edition Meisel had in fact published at least three militaristic songs.

The chairman of the proceedings then returned to the issue of Will purchasing Jewish properties. Herr Meisel had 'resisted' buying Jewish properties, Fago said, and was an 'opponent' of such deals. The only exception, he added, was Meisel's attempt in 1938 to purchase the Austrian publisher, Universal Edition.

It was at this point that Will jumped in again, asking Fago about the office tuning in to BBC Radio. Fago then confirmed that 'Meisel was brave enough to listen with staff to foreign programmes'. He had never seen Will with any Nazi Party sign inside the office, he added, nor did the staff greet each other with *Heil Hitlers*, nor were Nazi Party meetings held at the company offices. Will was constantly visited by famous writers and composers, he said, and had 'very dangerous conversations during these times for which we could have lost our heads'. When Vogel asked if this was an anti-fascist group, Fago said that it was, and that Will was part of it.

Vogel then said that the last document he wished to read out was written by Hanns Hartmann, and had been sent to him from Cologne, dated 31 May 1948. In his statement, Hartmann said that it had been his idea to purchase Universal Edition, to safeguard the interests of the Jewish owner while he was unable to own it himself. He said that he didn't remember Will trying to purchase other Jewish properties.

Critically, despite Will Meisel's repeated claims that he had protected the Hartmanns from the Nazis, Hanns did not mention his former boss's help. Nor did he say that Will Meisel had assisted other Jewish composers, or indeed that the Hartmanns had been allowed to seek refuge for more than a year at the lake house.

There are several interpretations for Hanns's lack of attendance, as well as his silence on his former employer's alleged support. Certainly, Hanns was himself busy with running the broadcasting organisation in Cologne, not to mention the fact that he wished to avoid contact with the Soviet security police who patrolled Berlin's streets. According to a statement given by Paul Fago to one of the denazification investigators prior to the trial, there existed a degree of 'hatred' between the two men, though 'most of the fights were about views on artistry'. In addition, Will likely exaggerated his role as saviour. Like other Jews who were married to Aryans, Ottilie would most likely have been protected from the worst excesses of the Nazi regime without the interference of the music publisher. In other words, Hanns felt no obligation to express his gratitude.

Following a final statement from Will Meisel, the commissioners retired to deliberate. It took only a few minutes for them to reach their conclusion that the publisher was indeed no more than a nominal member of the Nazi Party and that the evidence showed he was not a believer in their ideology. Furthermore, despite the publisher having tried to purchase Jewish companies in 1938, the commission took the view that he did not do so for personal gain or anti-Semitic reasons. As a result, the commissioners announced that they believed Will should be able to work again, a decision which would be forwarded to the British Military Government, where it would almost certainly be rubber-stamped.

Will rejoiced, realising how close he had come to disaster. It seemed that he had been cleared of any wrongdoing and would not receive any punishment.

Yet as Vogel and his staff delivered their verdict, a larger political story was gripping the city. For, the day before the trial, 24 June 1948, the Soviet authorities had announced that with immediate effect they would erect a blockade against the population of West Berlin. The effect was that the two and a half million inhabitants who lived in the Allied-occupied sectors were cut off from the rest of the world.

Berlin was under siege.

16

MEISEL
1948

Early in the morning of 26 June 1948, the plates and cups in the kitchen cupboard of the now vacant lake house rattled, as a Dakota C47 roared overhead, barely fifty metres above its rooftop. It was the first British plane to arrive at Gatow. The Allied-sponsored rescue mission for the people of Berlin, or what would become known as the Berlin Airlift, was underway.

Wanting to control all of Berlin, the Soviets had made a decision to force the issue by sealing the road, train and water routes into West Berlin. The only remaining access to West Berlin had been the three air corridors that cut through Soviet airspace. Calculating that their aircraft would not be shot down – based on the assumption that the Soviets would not wish to dramatically escalate the situation – the Americans, British and French had acted quickly. Within a few hours they had organised round-the-clock flights to support West Berlin's citizens. Located close to the city, and as one of only three airports available to the Allies, Gatow was an obvious staging post for the airlift.

The greatest need was coal, which was transported in large hessian

Gatow airfield, with the northern tip of Groß Glienicke Lake visible (top left)

sacks and made up the bulk of deliveries. Flour, rice, fish and potatoes were also flown in to Gatow, as were light bulbs, milk and mail. Before long, more than five thousand people were supporting the airlift operation at the British airfield. Once the planes had pulled up to enormous hangars, teams worked round the clock to unload the precious cargo. While the coal was transferred to boats waiting nearby on the River Havel, to be delivered on to West Berlin's power station, other goods were trucked into the city. At peak efficiency, a plane could be unloaded and ready for take-off within fifteen minutes. As the air traffic increased, planes were coming and going from the airfield every few minutes. At first there was only one runway at Gatow. Realising the enormous volumes that would be required to feed and heat the city, the British set about building a second.

At weekends, the village children would gather by the Potsdamer

Tor, jumping up and down with excitement as they waited for the next plane to arrive. If they were lucky, as they followed the plane's last few hundred metres to Gatow, parcels would rain down, each slowed by a tiny parachute. The children would scramble to grasp them, for they were gifts from the British, containing biscuits and chocolate.

One of the children chasing the planes was Lothar Fuhrmann. Then ten years old, he had moved with his family just a few months earlier into the Munks' property next to the lake house. The Munks were leasing their weekend house having chosen, at least for now, to focus their energies in Berlin.

Lother's father, Erich, had served in the army during the war, and at its end he had been held for a short period, accused of war crimes. The charges were dropped and he had been released. Before arriving in Groß Glienicke the Fuhrmanns had lived in northern Germany near the Baltic Sea. They had found the house through Lothar's uncle, who worked as Professor Munk's gardener.

Lothar Fuhrmann was fascinated by the airlift. Whenever he could, he raced over to the airfield along the old sandy path and past the ruins of the schloss. There, joining the other boys and girls, Lothar stood by the wire fence watching the planes as they prepared to land, their wheels almost scraping the village roofs and, with a roar and screech of engines, touching down just feet from where they were standing.

Some of the children had notebooks in which they scribbled the number and types of planes as they came and went. There were aircrafts of all shapes and sizes. The silver Dakota C47, for instance, a stumpy workhorse of a plane, and Gatow's most frequent visitor; or the Tudor 688, with a long thin body and an awkward wheel beneath the tail; or the enormous Handley Page Hastings, the largest transport plane the children would see, with four wing-mounted Bristol Hercules engines and a retractable undercarriage; the box-like, evergreen-coloured Lancaster, with its gun turret jutting out in front; or the Short Sunderland 10s, with their heron-like snouts and wing stabilisers, a seaplane that landed directly onto the River Havel. These last were used for transporting salt as they were designed to be impervious to corrosion.

As the months progressed, the activity at Gatow grew even more intense. On 10 October 1948, for example, there were over 442 landings at the small airfield, and the same number of take-offs. On 16 April 1949, there were 944 landings and take-offs, many of them during the night, resulting in a plane arriving or leaving Gatow every ninety seconds.

The American, French and British planes and their air crews were not the only ones responsible for the airlift's success. The West Berliners themselves displayed enormous stoicism, withstanding great physical and mental hardship so that their city was not taken by the Soviets. Berliners helped the crews unload the planes and transported the goods around the city; they distributed food and water to the elderly and sick; and they generally boosted morale. They also developed ingenious ways of getting around the blockade.

Late in the autumn of 1948, Will Meisel ventured out of West Berlin into the Brandenburg countryside. Though he was crossing from the city's British sector into Soviet-occupied Germany, such border crossings were allowed, and he was waved through by the guard. First, Will drove out to the lake house to make sure everything was in order. He hadn't visited for a while, and was glad to find it securely locked and undamaged. Then he approached some of the local farmers, hoping to trade pieces of his wife's jewellery for eggs, meat and fresh fruit, all of which had become scarce in West Berlin. Such journeys, or 'hamster trips' as they were known, were common at the time, but forbidden by the Soviet authorities. While crossing back into the city, Will had to hide his newly acquired goods – they would have been confiscated, had he been caught.

A few weeks later, Will Meisel contacted Bruno Balz, a composer known for his rousing lyrics with whom he had worked during the war, and suggested they produce a song celebrating the city's resistance and solidarity. In a short space of time, they wrote, 'Berlin bleibt doch Berlin'. Almost immediately the song became West Berlin's anthem, and was widely sung and hummed in the streets of the city. This catchy tune was Will's biggest hit since 'Ilona' in the 1920s.

> Berlin is still Berlin
> Nothing can change it!
> For us, it will remain Berlin
> The best city in the world.

Despite his pride in the city and its citizens, Will's professional life continued to frustrate him. After his success in front of the denazification panel, the German-staffed West Berlin council had written to the British Military Government's Theatre and Music Section on 14 September 1948, requesting that approval be given for Will to work once again. They concluded with the words: 'There should be no concerns to give Will Meisel a permit to operate his company.'

This request was first passed to the director of the British Cultural Relations Branch (Book Section) in Berlin, and then on to their head office in Hamburg. Attached was Will Meisel's 1938 letter to Hans Hinkel asking if he could purchase Jewish businesses, along with a letter in which George Clare, head of the British Licensing Control Section in Berlin, had written that 'this section would strongly object' if either Will or Eliza Meisel was allowed to 'hoodwink' the British Military Government, and that he 'strongly recommended' that Will not be given a licence to work in the music industry. In a reference to Will's creative director, Clare noted that 'Hartmann was the only person in the whole outfit who was ok'. Further down the letter, Clare summed up his opinion: 'Herr Will Meisel is as black a character as can be. He was also a party member since 1933 and has to await his denazification. This has, however, not prevented him from living very, very well since the end of the war.'

On 11 July 1949, more than a year after Will's denazification trial, the director of the Hamburg office wrote a brief memo to the Information Services Division: 'The following application has been rejected, and the file is returned for your retention.' To be prevented from working this long from the war's end was highly unusual. For this to happen to a composer and publisher of music, rather than a member of the SS or Gestapo, was even more noteworthy.

Why was Will Meisel still barred from work, given that the vast majority of former Nazi Party members had not only been exonerated but were busily rebuilding their businesses? The answer is that in these other cases, the British, American and French authorities had been unable to prove their suspect's guilt. Indeed, most of the British investigators were infuriated that so few Nazi Party members had faced justice. Their problem was that the necessary evidence had been destroyed during the war. This was why Will Meisel's letter to Hans Hinkel was so extraordinary, and damning. It was one of the rare examples where complicity in what had been a widespread crime to purchase Jewish properties could be proven.

For now, at least, Will would have to rely on others to run his business.

17

MEISEL
1949

By the spring of 1949, almost a year after the Soviets had cut off supplies to Berlin, it became clear that the Allies were winning the blockade. Making use of the British airport in Gatow as well as the French airport at Tegel and the American airport at Tempelhof, the Allies had run over 275,000 flights, providing more than 2.3 million tons of food, coal and medical supplies to the population of West Berlin. Having survived the brutal winter months of 1948, in which visibility was at times less than fifty metres, temperatures twenty below zero and snowstorms a regular occurrence, the crews were boasting that they could maintain the airlift for an indefinite time.

The realisation that their siege had failed was a bitter pill for Stalin and his supporters, for they would have to continue to live with American, French and British troops stationed in the heart of Eastern Europe. So, on 12 May 1949, the Soviets reluctantly lifted their blockade. This climbdown was in the face of increasing tensions between the Soviet Union and the West.

Eleven days after the blockade's end, on 23 May, the Allies merged their three zones of occupation into one new country: the

Bundesrepublik Deutschland (BRD), or the Federal Republic of Germany (also known as 'West Germany'). A West German constitution, the Basic Law, was also ratified. While inspired by the Weimar Republic, this new constitution differed in key respects to that of its predecessor. Perhaps most importantly, it enshrined the rights of the individual and declared that the government could never seize emergency powers. As a symbol of its independence, West Germany also adopted a new national flag, based on the black, red and gold tricolour of the democratic revolutions of 1848/9, and a new currency, the deutschmark. This independent West German state was a direct and inflammatory challenge to the Soviets, who had long fostered hopes that they would control the whole of Germany. Yet to many in Europe and around the world, the partition of Germany was the correct choice. As *The Times* declared, Britain, the USA and France must remain 'steadfast and resolute', now that the Germans had 'shown that they would prefer to have half Germany free than all Germany under threat from a communist dictatorship'.

The animosity between the world powers took a turn for the worse four months later, on 23 September 1949, when the leaders of the USA, Britain and Canada jointly announced that they had discovered 'evidence that within recent weeks an atomic explosion has occurred in the Soviet Union'. The world's newspapers reacted with shock. A *New York Times* column warned that the Soviet Union might soon have a stockpile of bombs sufficient 'to destroy fifty of our cities with 40,000,000 of our population', while the *Sydney Morning Herald* spoke of 'Alarm in Berlin'.

Two days later, the Soviets' official response was that they had been in possession of an atomic bomb since 1947, but that there 'was not the slightest grounds for concern'. That same day, an article in the *Tägliche Rundschau*, a Soviet-controlled newspaper published in East Berlin, hailed the announcement as 'good news for Germany' since the Americans no longer had a monopoly on the atomic bomb, and any government that used the bomb could 'expect an answer in kind'.

Twelve days later, on 7 October 1949, the Soviet occupation forces handed control of the eastern part of Germany to a new council of ministers, headed by the leader of the Socialist Unity Party (SED), Otto Grotewohl, and his deputy, Walter Ulbricht. Together they declared the establishment of a new country: the Deutsche Demokratische Republik (DDR), or the German Democratic Republic (also known as 'East Germany'). Germany had now formally split into East and West.

It was against the backdrop of these remarkable events that the Meisels read disturbing newspaper stories about Groß Glienicke.

One report concerned Gerda Radtke who, on the evening of 20 September 1949, had been tidying up after her three sons had gone to bed. The family now lived in Bullenwinkel, a hamlet located one kilometre west of Groß Glienicke, having been forced out of their house by the Soviets.

Around 10 p.m., Gerda looked out of her window and saw a Soviet soldier talking to the Tauffenbachs, an elderly couple who owned an orchard next door. It appeared that the soldier was offering an exchange to Herr Tauffenbach: an item of jewellery for some fruit. Thinking nothing of it, Gerda returned to her household duties. An hour or so later, she heard a scream from Frau Meier who lived on the other side of the Tauffenbachs: 'Frau Radtke, Frau Radtke, there's a fire at the Tauffenbach house!'

Rushing outside, Gerda saw flames leaping out of her neighbours' windows. Then she saw the body of Carl Tauffenbach lying across the doorstep, his head split open, his face and hands slashed, his wedding ring missing. As she stared on in shock, Herr Meier leapt on his bicycle and rode into Groß Glienicke to alert the fire brigade. When Gerda moved to enter the house, Frau Meier held her back, telling her she must not enter for fear of being trapped by the flames.

A few minutes later, the fire brigade arrived. Inside the living room they found the half-burned corpse of Carl's wife Valerie Tauffenbach, naked and with both of her arms cut off. Close to her body they discovered an empty gas can which had been used to start the fire. Walking further into the house and down into the cellar, they found a third body, Martha Greiner – a thirty-six-year-old fruit picker who worked for the Tauffenbachs – her legs broken, her breasts cut off and her stomach sliced open. Next to the body stood an ironing board and an iron, still warm.

It wasn't long before the NKVD, the Soviet security police, and the German Volkspolizei arrived. The Soviets ordered the firemen out of the house and prevented the German police from documenting the scene of the crime. The house was allowed to burn. That night, Gerda was visited by the NKVD, who asked her for a statement. She had seen the Russian soldier at the Tauffenbachs' front door, she told them, and would be able to identify him. After she had signed her name she was told that she must not tell anybody about what had taken place. Whilst it was still dark, the victims' bodies were loaded onto a military vehicle and taken to the small red-brick building beside the church in Groß Glienicke, which served as a morgue. Soon after, they were transported to Potsdam, where the remains were cremated. Despite repeated requests, Martha Greiner's ashes were never released to her devastated husband.

Two weeks after the Tauffenbach murders, another crime shattered the fragile peace. Two woodsmen were driving through the Glienicke Heath when their truck stalled. Leaving his companion to mind the vehicle, one of the men walked into Groß Glienicke to ask for help. When he returned he found his colleague lying terribly injured next to the truck, barely alive and with his skull caved in by a blunt object. The dying man's last words were that the criminals had been two men in Russian uniforms.

That same day, two dismembered and mutilated bodies were fished out of the sewage plant near the Soviet military base at Krampnitz, four kilometres west of Groß Glienicke. Then, on 5 October, the bodies of a married couple were found, again on the village outskirts, with their eyes cut out. Another body, the ninth, was discovered in the forest. The following day, the mutilated body of a cyclist was found six kilometres west of Groß Glienicke, towards the village of Fahrland. A few days after that, a mushroom hunter came across the bodies of two women in the woods just a few hundred metres north of the lake house. The women had been raped and their faces were so mutilated that they could not be identified.

West Berlin newspapers – indeed West Germany as a whole – became fixated on this story, running articles under headlines such as the *Tagespiegel*'s 'MURDERERS IN RUSSIAN UNIFORM – NEW VICTIMS IN GROSS GLIENICKE' and the *Rhein Echo*'s 'SOVIET MILITARY ADMINISTRATION COVERS UP GLIENICKE MURDERS'. Unsurprisingly, the DDR newspapers took a very different view of the story, epitomised by the *Berliner Zeitung*, whose headline read 'MULTIPLE MASS MURDER MADE UP', and who went on to say: 'The West German newspapers wrote articles about this event with the goal of defaming the Volkspolizei and the Soviets.'

One intrepid West Berlin reporter decided to investigate in person. Under the byline HH for the *Social Democrat* newspaper, the article opened:

> It could have been a magical hike around the Groß Glienicke Lake on this mild autumn day but the magic doesn't surface even though the sun is warm on the pale blue sky and the red, yellow and brown of the trees and bushes is very vibrant. All

this beauty is not felt strongly because on the other side of Groß
Glienicke there have been twelve murders in the past four weeks.

Crossing from the British sector into the Soviet zone, HH then
walked to the northern edge of the lake which 'used to be a summer
home for prominent actors, artists and businessmen', and spoke to a
few of the locals. One woman recalled that a 'friend told me that I
should stay away from this area as there is a lot going on in Groß
Glienicke', before adding that 'we all know, even the Volkspolizei, who
the murderers are, but it is better to keep your mouth shut'. Someone
else told him, 'If you are stopped by a Russian soldier or Volkspolizei
then you are in trouble.' As the journalist pointed out, despite the
beauty of their surroundings, the locals were in a 'fearful panic'.

The residents' theory was that the killers were encamped in the
barracks established at the old Olympic Village. There were more
soldiers than usual living at the Soviet base at this time, since hundreds
were taking part as extras in *The Fall of Berlin*, a high-budget production commissioned by Joseph Stalin that was then being shot on the
heath north of Groß Glienicke. People living in the village were now
too scared to leave their homes, especially at night, and when they
did go out, they went in groups. 'But', HH concluded, 'the people
only talk about this at home, with their families behind closed doors.
Their fear has taught them silence.'

Initially, the Soviet-controlled Ministry of Interior for Brandenburg
told the journalists that they hadn't heard of the murders. Only when
pushed did they acknowledge that the Tauffenbachs had been killed,
but not the others. On the other side of the border, the *Berliner Abend*,
a West Berlin evening newspaper, claimed that Soviet security officers
had forbidden the Volkspolizei from investigating the murders. More
specifically, the NKVD threatened to arrest both the mayor of Groß
Glienicke and the head of the Potsdam Criminal Police if they failed
to ensure the silence of every eyewitness. The only measure that was

put in place was that the Soviet soldiers barracked near Groß Glienicke were more restricted when it came to leaving the camp. No arrests were made in relation to the murders. This was in spite of reports that Gerda Radtke had seen the murderer clearly enough to identify him from a photograph.

Finally, on 19 October 1949, the chief of the Brandenburg Criminal Police, Herr Hoppe, took the unusual step of allowing a question-and-answer session with a journalist from *Neues Deutschland*, the official organ of the Socialist Unity Party (SED) and largest-selling paper in the DDR. Responding to stories about the other murders, Hoppe said that they were only investigating the Tauffenbach crime, and that no other corpses had been discovered. When asked about the articles in the Western press, he said, 'These have been written solely for the purpose of defaming the Soviet Union and the Volkspolizei. They do this to divert attention from the growing unemployment in West Berlin.'

The East German policy was to bury the story.

While the murders were occupying the front pages of newspapers across Berlin, these were not the only terrors troubling the residents of Groß Glienicke. On 23 August 1950, ten months after the police chief had spoken of 'defaming the Soviet Union', armed troops burst through the door of a house located on the southern tip of the Groß Glienicke Lake, and arrested its occupant: the Jewish politician Leopold Bauer.

Bauer was a well-known character locally and internationally. In the early 1930s, he had been active in the Communist Party, before fleeing to Paris with the rise to power of the Nazis. Imprisoned in France following the German occupation, he had then escaped in 1940, before being imprisoned again as a communist agitator in Switzerland.

After the war's end, Bauer had returned to Germany as a hero. Quickly promoted, he became chairman of the Communist Party for the Hesse region and then, in the summer of 1949, was appointed as head of the national radio station, Deutschlandsender. This was when he had moved to Groß Glienicke, since it was close to Berlin and offered him the peace and quiet he was looking for.

In early 1950, given the growing tensions between America and the Soviet Union following Germany's partition, Joseph Stalin had ordered a crackdown on anybody suspected of working for the West. It was now, a year after arriving in the village, that the thirty-seven-year-old Bauer was arrested. Accused of helping American spies, Bauer was charged with treason, and incarcerated in Potsdam prison. There 'Inmate Number 6' – as he was called – was brutally interrogated and ordered to confess. In a seven-page handwritten note, he stated: 'This is the last chance to tell my side of the story, to prove I am not an enemy, otherwise there is no reason to prolong my useless life.' After providing his biography he added, 'How should I prove that I am not an enemy if I am not an enemy? I have always fought for the working class and the party. I may have made mistakes but I am not an enemy of the people. I always had to work, sometimes I was not aware who I was working for.'

Two years later, in the spring of 1952, and as part of a series of 'show trials', Bauer was convicted in a Berlin court. Initially sentenced to death, he was then given twenty-five years' hard labour in a Siberian prison camp.

Whenever a resident of Groß Glienicke walked past Leopold Bauer's house, which stood empty having been confiscated by the government, they were reminded of his fate. It was another reason to be fearful. With the prospect of further, seemingly arbitrary, government oppression, such as that experienced by Bauer, and the knowledge that the authorities were unlikely to investigate the murders, let alone catch the criminals, the villagers of Groß Glienicke hunkered down. The most common strategy was to avoid all contact with the Soviet soldiers, or their counterparts in the East German security apparatus. The village had become a site of terror, not tranquillity.

Meanwhile, though the Soviet blockade was now over, the people of West Berlin felt more under siege than ever. They were surrounded by East Germany, whose politics and economics were looking increasingly different from their own, and threatened by the Soviets, who were building military bases closer and closer to the capital city. Unable to return to Groß Glienicke, Will Meisel focused on growing his business. In 1951, he had received his business licence, the authorities having finally relented. In celebration, Will framed the poster-sized licence and hung it on his office wall.

Four years after the war's end, mass migration became a problem for the newly established country of East Germany. Traumatised by the violence of the Soviet occupiers, and fearful for their economic and political future, hundreds of thousands of people were fleeing from East Germany to the West. The easiest route was through Berlin, for the border controls between East and West Berlin were more lax than between East and West Germany. People living in the Soviet-controlled parts of Germany made their way into East Berlin, crossed the still permeable border into West Berlin, and then applied for West German citizenship. In 1949, almost 130,000 people emigrated to the west. That number climbed to almost 200,000 the following year.

To counter this exodus, the DDR government imposed a series of ever tightening rules aimed at restricting border crossings. From this point forward, border guards were ordered to check people's papers more carefully. Anyone who was caught smuggling – food, luxury items, money – was immediately arrested and put in prison.

The DDR newspapers ran stories lambasting the inequality plaguing West Germany, and denounced its government, which they claimed was run by former Nazi Party members.

Nevertheless, the mass migration continued. In 1951, more than 160,000 made their way from East Germany to West Berlin and – via train, bus and plane – on into the Federal Republic of Germany. Meanwhile, scores of Groß Glienicke residents continued to commute from the village into West Berlin, where the salaries were higher, and paid in the more valuable western currency. At the same time, many of the West Berliners who owned weekend houses in Groß Glienicke sporadically visited the village, though scared of the violence and intimidated by having to cross into the Eastern bloc, if only to check on their properties.

The situation dramatically changed on 26 May 1952. While reading the morning newspapers, Will Meisel discovered that the DDR was closing the border between West Berlin and East Germany, with immediate effect. Even more significantly, the government had announced that if anyone wished to own property in the DDR they would have to live there permanently.

Given the impossibility of visiting the lake house, Will Meisel now contacted Ella Fuhrmann, Lother's mother, who was still living at Professor Munk's house. Will and Ella had met a few times, often exchanging pleasantries and catching up on the village gossip across the garden fence. During one such conversation, Will had gathered that Frau Fuhrmann was looking for new accommodation. She had been informed by the local council that her family must leave the Munks' house to make way for a teacher, a Herr Wißgott. Will wrote to ask if she might be interested in moving next door, at least until things became politically clearer. By return of post, Ella agreed.

Will Meisel was pleased. In Berlin he could attempt to recover his business sure in the knowledge that, for now at least, someone would be taking care of the lake house.

PART III

HOME

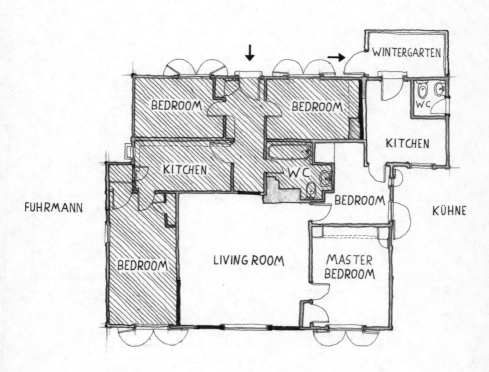

FUHRMANN

KÜHNE

WINTERGARTEN

WC

BEDROOM

BEDROOM

KITCHEN

KITCHEN

WC

BEDROOM

BEDROOM

LIVING ROOM

MASTER BEDROOM

December 2013

I have returned to Berlin, hoping to find one of Will Meisel's family members. After a few days I locate Sven Meisel, Will's grandson, who now runs the Edition Meisel music publishing company in Berlin.

Sven and I meet on the steps of a white-stone building on Köthener Straße in the city centre. At the end of the street, where a tall office building now stands, once ran the graffiti-splattered Berlin Wall, blocking access to the eastern part of the capital. Two blocks away lies the Potsdamer Platz, one of Berlin's main squares. After exchanging greetings, Sven gives me a tour of his music studios.

'This is where David Bowie recorded his Berlin Trilogy in the 1970s,' he tells me in perfect English as we walk through the Meistersaal, a wood-panelled hall with a small stage and a high ceiling. I follow Sven to the room next door where he points at a window. 'And that's where Bowie saw his producer kissing one of the backing singers,' he says. 'Do you know the song "Heroes"?' I nod. 'The line about kissing next to the wall, hearing guns overhead, thinking that nothing would fall? That all happened here.'

Back in his office, having explained more about who I am, and why I had sought him out, I ask Sven about the lake house. He suddenly becomes circumspect. 'What is your intention here?' he asks me. 'Are you trying to get the house back?'

I tell him that my objective is to gather information about the house so that I can save it from demolition. The question over who owns the house has already been settled, I add, it is the city of Potsdam.

More comfortable with my motives, Sven picks up the phone and asks for the file on the house to be brought up from his company archive, along with any relevant materials. A few minutes later we are looking at pictures from the war years, newspaper articles, court documents and old letters.

One of the photographs is of his grandfather, wearing white shirt and black trousers as he leans against a doorway. The doorway has a diamond-shaped window in it. It is the lake house. The man looks relaxed, happy, at home. The image shocks me. This is the first time I have seen evidence of other people living at the house, of others including it in their family histories. I find the picture disconcerting, as if it somehow undermines my own family's story.

Sven tells me that he never knew his grandfather, who died before he was born. I ask whether his grandfather was connected to the Nazis, and I am surprised by Sven's honesty. It is possible, he tells me, that his grandfather may have taken advantage of the situation. 'He was a complex character,' he says.

A few days after my return to England, I receive an email from my father. He asks how my research is going in Berlin and says that he has been doing a bit of digging himself. He has found documents relating to a second claim, he says, made four decades after that of Henny Alexander.

I double-click on the attachment and find a number files relating to a claim made by the Jewish Claims Conference on 11 November 1992. According to the documents, this claim was submitted on behalf of the Alexanders, but without the family's knowledge. This was not uncommon. The JCC made thousands of claims in the years after Germany's reunification in the early 1990s, their worry being that Jewish families might otherwise incorrectly submit a claim.

According to the files, it took almost two decades for the JCC's claim to process. Finally, in 2010, a federal department acknowledged that the Alexanders had indeed been 'persecuted by the Nazi government' and that their buildings in Groß Glienicke had been 'illegally seized'. In compensation, the family was awarded a little over 30,000 euros.

Leafing through the documents, I see that not only was this offer accepted but that my father and every single member of his generation – his brother, his sister and his cousins – had signed an individual waiver, nullifying any right to future claims. Looking to the top of the page I notice that the date the money was released was September 2012, just months before my first return to the house.

I send an email to various family members asking if they might be interested in helping me find out more about the house in Groß Glienicke; in digging out old photos and letters, in trying to piece together our family's story. To my surprise I receive several hostile responses.

One cousin says that he wants nothing to do with the house. After all, he says, we were persecuted by the Germans in the 1930s, and then disappointed ever since by a succession of German governments and lawyers.

One of the strongest reactions comes from my father. He asks, quietly, 'Are you really expecting us to dip our hands in our pockets . . .' In my head, I finish his sentence: 'when the house was stolen from us in the first place?'

18

FUHRMANN
1952

In the autumn of 1952, Ella Fuhrmann and her two children, Lothar and Heideraud, packed up their belongings at the Munk house and moved to the lake house.

For Ella Fuhrmann, it was only another trial to endure. Her forty-six-year-old husband, Erich, had died of stomach cancer the year before, and she was still grieving. She had liked living at the Munk house, but had known their stay there would only ever be temporary. A tall, thin, outgoing and energetic woman, Ella wasn't worried about taking care of the Meisel property, or the large vegetable plot, which should, she hoped, provide more than enough for her family.

In her conversation with Herr Meisel, it had been made clear that the Fuhrmanns would be caretakers, not tenants. This was still the publisher's house. As such, he didn't want anyone sleeping in the master bedroom and preferred that the living room not be used, and any belongings which he had left in the Blue Room – his piano, stool, posters and music – should remain untouched. Lothar, therefore, took the maid's bedroom next to the kitchen, while his eighteen-year-old sister slept with his mother in the spare room by the front door.

Despite the Meisels' minor adjustments and improvements, the house's interior looked as it had when the Alexanders had first moved in. The same high-backed wooden chairs standing to attention in the living room, the large red table and built-in benches, the wicker chairs on the veranda to the rear of the property and the cheerily painted walls. Some of the windowpanes had cracked and would have to be replaced, and with the house so long empty it took a couple of days to warm it up. Soon enough, though, it felt like home.

Outside, similarly, almost everything appeared to be as it had been. The caretaker's cottage – where Gerda Radtke's brother still lived – the greenhouse and the pump house were all still standing, though they needed some attention. The tennis court, however, was barely recognisable, with the white lines marking the edges of the playing area only just visible through the long grass. The veranda, to the rear of the house, with its porch roof and beaded columns, along with the orange-painted wooden shutters had all survived the tumult of the preceding years. Though older, taller and more dominant, the willow and pine trees continued to tower over the land, casting a wide swathe of shade over the steps that descended gracefully to the shore.

The other major changes were only evident at the foot of the garden. There was now a fence running along the lake's edge, demarcating the border between East Germany and West Berlin. This fence was made of thin wooden posts and limp chicken wire. Also, the long white jetty that had jutted into the lake, and which had launched a generation of children into the water, had been removed.

The border fence was so rickety that many of the posts had fallen over so it was easy for Lothar to clamber over and go for a swim in the lake. If spotted by one of the occasional border patrol boats, he might be shouted at, but this was a small price to pay for the enjoyment of a refreshing dip.

Since his father's death, Lothar had assumed additional responsibilities. At the new house, the worst involved emptying the septic tank. Each evening, he removed a metal sheet covering a large black hole in the ground, and then lowered a hose into the putrid-smelling liquid below. Walking down to the bottom of the garden, he would then check to make sure that the liquid was soon running out into the sandy ground next to the shore.

While the Fuhrmanns enjoyed their first summer at the house – eating outside, swimming in the lake, building wigwams in the woods – Lothar was looking forward to the winter. Once the lake froze over, he could walk on the ice, exploring the hidden coves and woods of the lakefront. The border patrol guards, such as there were, didn't seem to mind that he was on the wrong side of the flimsy chicken-wire fence – after all he was only a child. Indeed, they seemed to enjoy interacting with the local kids, given that fraternising with the adults was strictly forbidden. Nor was Lothar alone on the frozen lake that winter. Others from Groß Glienicke were there too, skating on the ice or sliding around in their boots like Lothar. There were also plenty of people close to the other, West Berlin, shore. The two groups didn't mingle, seemingly separated by an invisible line that ran down the centre of the lake.

Best of all were the winter storms which covered the steep slope between the house and the lake with snow. Lothar and his friends spent hours building ramps and jumps, and then, speeding down the hill towards the lake astride a solid wooden sledge. When they had grown tired of their races, they built giant ice caves, imagining themselves in some northern wilderness, or frozen forts, from which they threw snowballs, until, exhausted and chilled, they said goodbye and retired, each to their own coal-warmed house.

Cold was the Fuhrmanns' biggest problem. The house had been constructed as a summer residence and there was no insulation in the walls, cellar or attic. During that brutal winter, which sometimes fell to fifteen degrees Centigrade below freezing, Ella Fuhrmann covered the windows with blankets and the walls with newspaper. The living room had a chimney but Will Meisel had forbidden them from using this space. The fireplace in the cellar channelled hot air up to the master bedroom and the Blue Room, where Will Meisel had his music studio, but these rooms had also been decreed off-limits. The only heated room was the 2 x 3 metre-wide kitchen, which became the centre of their lives. All meals were taken here, with Ella cooking on the coal-fired stove in the corner which had two heating plates on which a large kettle constantly simmered. There the family huddled around the pull-down table, holding mugs of steaming tea in their hands, talking about their days, playing games or listening to the radio.

One Sunday in early 1953, Lothar walked towards the Potsdamer Tor with his sister and mother. Dressed in his suit, he was on his way to the village church to be confirmed. This confirmation cere-mony was a rite of passage in which he would seal his commitment to Christianity and his community.

Lothar had turned fourteen the previous October, and conse-quently was one of the oldest children arriving at the church that morning. Inside, he was greeted by Wilhelm Stintzing, the congrega-tion's tall, wiry, thirty-nine-year-old pastor. Over the previous year the village's confirmands had studied Protestant rites and customs, and the catechism. Now, however, there were no more discussions of ethics or morality. Instead, a few Bible verses were read, a handful of hymns were sung, and then the pastor blessed the young boys and girls in front of him. With the service complete, Lothar would be treated as an adult member of the congregation. From this point on, when adults addressed him, they would use the more respectful word *Sie*, rather than the informal *du*.

Lothar's was one of the last big groups to be confirmed in the village, for it was around this time that the politburo in Moscow passed the 'Measures for the Recovery of the Political Situation in the DDR', including a provision for a socialist alternative to the Christian confirmation ceremony known as the *Jugendweihe*. During this new ceremony the children would be asked to pledge themselves to the 'great and noble cause of socialism'. Afterwards, they would receive flowers and a book, *Weltall, Erde, Mensch (Universe, Earth and Man)*, which was stridently anti-religious. The first such *Jugendweihe* ceremony took place in East Berlin, and with political favour, its popularity grew exponentially. As a result, from a high point of more than thirty children per year in the early 1950s, the number of confirmations in Groß Glienicke fell by the end of the 1960s to less than three.

Other traditions soon began to disappear: on Christmas Eve, for example, it was customary for the village to gather together to sing carols. Yet with the border now dividing Groß Glienicke in two, half the congregation were now unable to attend the service. While Pastor Stintzing had built a new church in Kladow – partly constructed of stones salvaged from the ruins of the schloss – for the villagers who now lived on the lake's geographic eastern side (the political West), the community had been fragmented. As an expression of their faith, or perhaps as a protest, the parishioners who had been cut off from Groß Glienicke walked along the lakefront, candles in hand, singing carols. When their voices could be heard across the water in Groß Glienicke, a few of the villagers lit their own candles in solidarity.

Late in the evening of 5 March 1953, the Fuhrmanns heard an announcement on the radio: Joseph Vissarionovich Stalin, Secretary of the Central Committee of the Communist Party and Chairman of the Council of Ministers, had died. He had suffered a stroke resulting from high blood pressure and hypertension.

In the Soviet Union, Stalin's death sent shock waves through the political establishment and triggered a power struggle within the country's ruling elite. For much of the DDR population, the news sparked hope. Only the year before, the ruling Socialist Unity Party had announced an intensification of Sovietisation within the DDR. As part of this policy shift, the government would impose a series of punitive new measures upon its citizens: taxes and work quotas were to be increased, and the price of food supplies and heating oil was to rise. Worse still, the political oppression had been ramped up, with Protestant youth groups now banned and 'capitalist' dissidents pulled off the streets and jailed.

Three months later, on the morning of 17 June 1953, protests erupted across the DDR. The largest demonstrations were in East Berlin where over 100,000 people took to the streets. Marching along the main thoroughfare of Under den Linden, they sang the West German national anthem, demanding unity, law and freedom. One group of young men even climbed the Brandenburg Gate and tore down the Soviet flag flying there. Work stoppages and strikes were also declared in over 250 of the country's towns and cities, with some estimating that as many as half a million people participated. In Potsdam, for instance, citizens occupied the district offices of the court, party and police. Unrest also broke out in various towns to the north of Groß Glienicke, including Kyritz, Wittstock, Neuruppin and Pritzwalk.

Panicked by the uprising, the DDR government called on the Soviet military for support. Before long, Soviet tanks were rumbling through the Berlin streets, while the Volkspolizei shot at protesters near the Brandenburg Gate and the Potsdamer Platz. The protesters threw bricks and bottles at the police, and rolled cars over in an attempt to halt the tanks. By the end of the day, fifty people had been killed, over a thousand injured, and thousands more arrested and jailed. Trials were held over the next few days, resulting in the execution of more than two hundred people.

The Berlin unrest did not, however, spread to the streets of Groß Glienicke. The few who were inspired to demonstrate had travelled to East Berlin and Potsdam, while the others, more cautious or more afraid, remained in the village. The following day they learned the official explanation for the unrest. According to the *Neues Deutschland*, the protests had been deliberately provoked by Western agencies with the aim of disrupting the progressive policies of the DDR. Such stories provoked a series of comments from the party's senior leadership, who argued that the younger generation was being corrupted by Western culture, particularly through films and music that celebrated rebellion. These youngsters, they said, were becoming *Halbstarke*, or half-strengths. They would have to learn to support the socialist revolution and to embrace the opportunities offered by the East.

Such statements were being made as the partition between East and West was becoming increasingly delineated. Berlin's division, for instance, impacted on the services that had previously supplied the entire metropolis. Electricity and telephone systems were now separated, with each sector now managing its own network. Meanwhile, East and West Berlin's water supplies were controlled independently, with the exception of the suburbs in the far west of West Berlin, whose supply was provided by a DDR water plant located in Groß Glienicke. The sewage system, however, which ran underneath the city irrespective of political boundaries was jointly managed; it would simply have been too expensive to create different tunnels and pipes.

While buses and trams were operated separately, the trains were more complicated as many of the lines ran across the city. Most trains which had formerly traversed the capital now stopped and turned back at the border. Those few Western trains that continued to run through East Berlin did not stop. Later, the highly guarded empty terminals through which they whistled became known as *Geisterbahnhöfe*, or ghost stations.

Throughout the division of Berlin, the city's overground train system, known as the S-Bahn, was managed and maintained by the East Berlin authorities. Many of the workers who maintained the S-Bahn in West Berlin lived in East Germany, including Groß Glienicke. Each day, on his way to school, Lothar would see villagers cycle past, as they made their way to the border crossing at Staaken, ten kilometres to the north. There they had their identity documents inspected, before crossing into Spandau in West Berlin, and then taking an S-Bahn to whichever station or depot they worked at.

In the summer of 1957, the lake house turned thirty. On the surface, the structure seemed to have weathered the years with grace. The wood siding was flawless and well varnished, the roof was smooth and unblemished, and the veranda to the rear of the property was level and free of moss. On closer inspection, however, there were signs that the house required attention. The windows needed a new coat of paint, the top bricks in the chimneys could do with a repointing, and with a family now living at the house year-round, the meagre kitchen was proving inadequate. And the deterioration was likely to continue, given that the Fuhrmanns were 'caretaker' residents only, and had neither the money nor the skills to renovate themselves.

Ever since they had moved into the property, the Fuhrmanns had taken Will Meisel's instructions seriously, occupying only one half of the house and avoiding the forbidden rooms. The publisher's furniture remained covered with sheets. The cupboards, bulging with his film-star wife's clothes, smelled of mothballs and stale air. The

Edition Meisel sheet music that lay on the piano had curled at the corners, after long exposure to the sun pouring in through the large windows.

The sense of abandonment and emptiness that filled the home became more palpable when Lothar's sister left to live with her aunt in Potsdam. It is no surprise then, given the shortage of housing stock that had persisted since the massive property destruction in the Second World War, that the *Gemeinde* decided to find another tenant to share the house.

19

FUHRMANN AND KÜHNE
1958

On 16 September 1958, a van drew up to the lake house. In it were Wolfgang and Irene Kühne, their two children, and all of the family's possessions.

Irene was enchanted. Green and red apples hung ripe on the trees in the orchard at the top of the property. The garden was lush and the view across the lake was beautiful. As they approached the front door she saw a woman through an open-shuttered window. 'Who's she?' She asked her husband. This was Frau Ella Fuhrmann, he explained, the woman with whom they would be sharing the house.

Earlier that summer, Irene Kühne had had enough. For more than two years she had lived in a dark, damp basement apartment in Potsdam. The basement was bad for the health of her children, three-year-old Hartmut and one-year-old Rosita. Yet despite repeated promises, Wolfgang had failed to find them anywhere better.

Even worse, her husband's father and stepmother, who lived

next door in a larger, cleaner and brighter apartment, were getting out of control. Every day, it seemed, they treated her more cruelly. It was easy to predict when they would erupt. As soon as they started drinking, typically around lunchtime, they became aggressive and combative, and would then begin to shout and criticise her. To make matters grimmer, Irene's sister, Ursula, had recently left for a holiday in Dortmund in West Germany with her husband and children. A few days later, she had sent Irene a letter telling her that they would not be coming back, that they wanted to build a new life in the West. Irene felt depressed, unloved and trapped.

It hadn't always been like this. She had liked Wolfgang when they'd first met. She had also felt sorry for him. His own mother had died when he was a child and his stepmother would beat him for the slightest transgression. Then, during the war, though still only a young boy, Wolfgang had spent long, noisy, cramped hours, as an anti-aircraft auxiliary. The couple had met eight years after the war's end at a dance in Potsdam. She was small, pretty, and training to become a nurse. He was a tall and angular young man, with a square chin and an infectious smile. As a builder, he had ample work, given Potsdam's extensive bomb damage. In 1955, after dating for two years, they married. They were both twenty-one years old.

In the last year or so, Wolfgang's work had tapered off and he had spent more time at home, drinking with his father and stepmother. His temper had soured, and he didn't help with the children. Money was hard to come by. After a particularly boisterous drinking session one evening, Irene had snapped, and told Wolfgang that she was at the end of her tether and that he needed to find a job. Realising that his wife was serious, Wolfgang promised to do better. Over the next few days he went looking for employment in Potsdam, visiting construction sites and asking if they needed help.

It was then that Wolfgang heard that the border patrol regiment in Groß Glienicke was recruiting and dropped off an application. To his delight, he was told that he could start at once. His new job would involve driving a truck for the regiment. His military rank would be lance corporal, and his contract would run for three years. But with his new position, they said, came additional responsibilities. Before he could start work he must report for a meeting with the Ministry for State Security (MfS), more commonly known as the Stasi.

Wolfgang Kühne

The Stasi had been created in February 1950, five months after the foundation of the DDR. Its official motto was 'Shield and Sword for the Party', a clear indication of its political imperative. Established under the guidance of the Soviet secret police – and formed from the K5 department which had been tasked with investigating political crimes within occupied Germany – the Stasi was answerable directly to the SED leadership.

Following the 1953 uprisings, the Stasi's functions included recon-
naissance and counter-espionage work in West Germany and West
Berlin, uncovering and eliminating 'anti-democratic' organisations
and activities within the DDR, border police work, and providing
protection for political functionaries. By 1958, the Stasi employed
over 17,000 people, and oversaw a network of between 20,000 and
30,000 unofficial informants, equivalent to approximately one in
every 450 adults in the DDR. Their role was to spy on the domestic
population. While some were little more than occasional sources of
information, others held more formal roles, requiring them to sign
a formal contract. At this time they were known as *Geheimer Informator*
(GI), or secret informants.

Wolfgang arrived on time for his recruitment meeting on 13 August
1958. The interview took place in the office of a Stasi operative,
Helmut Zschirp, based at the Groß Glienicke border patrol barracks.
On the desk in front of him lay Wolfgang's file and application.
Wolfgang, Zschirp had read, could speak no foreign language, nor
did he have any relatives outside of the DDR – he had conveniently
forgotten to mention his sister-in-law in Dortmund – and had no
relatives who had worked for the Nazis. He was therefore politically
clean. The file also included a physical description of the candidate:
thin, with blond hair, an oval face and having a slight stutter.

One thing troubling the recruitment officer was a sentence that
had been underlined in red: 'Kühne has participated in political education. However, he focuses on negative discussions, revealing that he
has little trust in the politics of the DDR. In this matter lots of
questions remain over him.' On a more positive note, 'Kühne accom-
plishes simple tasks satisfactorily.'

Attached to the file was a handwritten note from Zschirp's superior,
First Lieutenant Hermann, which recommended that Wolfgang be
recruited despite 'several weaknesses which point towards ideological
confusion . . . Kühne has enough intellect to work as a secret

informant.' The operational objective for recruiting Wolfgang, it was written, should be 'to bolster the number of informants working in the truck drivers department as they only have one now and that does not meet security standards'.

Zschirp started by asking the 'candidate' about the current political situation. Wolfgang said that he feared the 'enemy gathered in Berlin threatened to take over our troops and communities', and that he didn't want his family to 'experience enemy forces penetrating our land and starting an atomic war'. Zschirp then explained that he wanted Kühne to work as a secret informant. He would be expected to collect information on his family and co-workers, preparing written and oral reports and meeting at times and places designated by his handler. Most importantly, Wolfgang must never disclose his work to anyone, not even to his wife. In return he would benefit from the state's patronage – a better quality of life, and a better home.

After consenting to these terms, Wolfgang wrote his 'commitment letter', the content of which was dictated to him. Compared with the neat handwriting on his truck driver's application, this note was uneven, the blue ink seemingly applied with varying pressure, as if he wavered during the writing.

Commitment

Because of the current political crisis in the world and the continuing threat of the atomic arms military build-up in West Germany, I have understood that it is necessary to protect our borders and to hinder such threats or acts that try to disrupt our peaceful development. On this understanding, I agree to inform the Stasi in writing on anything that will hinder the development of our peaceful workers' and farmers' state. I will provide my written reports openly and honestly. My working for the Stasi will be an unofficial relationship and I will always come to the meetings with the Stasi punctually. I will keep this to myself and not disclose to my wife and family or colleagues. I will sign the reports I hand in with the code name:

Ignition Key

If for some reason I cannot attend meetings with the MfS I will let my superiors know in advance. If the connection is lost I will try and re-establish it.

It was signed 'Lance Corporal Wolfgang Kühne'. The recruitment now complete, Wolfgang was told that his first task was to provide a 'detailed description of his family and their political views', as well as any 'deficiencies in the vehicle department'. They agreed to meet two weeks later.

Later, the file would be reviewed by Zschirp's superior, a certain Operation Group Leader Beick. At the bottom of the report, Beick added a handwritten note: 'In future, please persuade other candidates not to come up with such senseless code names.'

Once home, Wolfgang told Irene the good news. He said that he had a new job driving trucks for the border patrol regiment in Groß Glienicke. Even better, he had found them somewhere to live, beside a gorgeous lake. What he didn't say was that they would be sharing the house with another family nor how he had secured their new home.

This was how Irene Kühne came to be standing outside the lake house with her children as Wolfgang greeted Frau Fuhrmann. Irene assessed the situation. It would be a tight squeeze perhaps, but anything would be better than living next to her in-laws in Potsdam. Frau Fuhrmann came over to say hello. She seemed pleasant, friendly, although perhaps a little too chatty. She offered to show them round.

Ella Fuhrmann explained that the house was owned by Will Meisel, a famous music composer who lived in West Berlin. At first, she had been taking care of the property until the tensions improved between East and West. But, given that it had been six years since they had last been seen, she assumed that the Meisels were not coming back.

The Fuhrmanns would live in the right-hand side of the house. They would have the two bedrooms by the front door, the main corridor, the kitchen and bathroom, as well as the room with the piano and the blue ceiling. The Kühnes would live in the left-hand side. They would have the small room containing a wooden bunk bed, the living room and what had been the master bedroom. They would also have use of the room where the chauffeur had once lived and the cupboard-sized toilet, which could only be accessed from the outside. They would therefore have no inside toilet, nor a bath or hot water. From now on, the Kühnes would have to wash outside, rain, snow or shine. But it would have to do. Many people didn't have indoor plumbing, and the children would love growing up by the lake. They would have to make some alterations, but fortunately her husband was a builder.

It didn't take Wolfgang long. First, he built a brick chimney in the chauffeur's annexe, stretching from the floor, through the attic and then the roof. He installed a cupboard with a work surface on which to prepare food, a small table and four chairs, and a two-ring electric stove. This would be their kitchen. With winter coming, and having heard from the Fuhrmanns how cold it could get in the house, Wolfgang removed the draughty French windows that led from the living room onto the veranda overlooking the lake and, in their place, built an insulated wall into which he inserted two large windows. To decorate, he pasted flower-patterned paper onto the wood panelling. Next he sealed up the fireplace and, in a final effort to reduce even the smallest draught, he covered the brick chimney with brick-patterned wallpaper, concealing the thirty blue-and-white Delft tiles. Then he installed a coal-burning stove in front of the fireplace, connecting it to the chimney with metal pipes and fabric tape.

After that, he set about clearing the master bedroom, removing and storing the oversized oak bed and its heavy wool-stuffed mattress in the garage by the main gate. When he went to move the large gold-edged mirror that hung on the wall to the left of the bed, he was startled when a cluster of small photographs of scantily clad women fluttered to the floor. Irene assumed they had been left by Will Meisel.

Finally, he built a small extension onto the front of their section of the house. The sides were formed of cheap plywood, within which Wolfgang inserted windows, and on the floor he laid narrow pine planks. The purpose of this two-metre by three-metre *Wintergarten*, or conservatory, was to keep the cold away from the kitchen. What had once been a simple, symmetrical wooden cottage, memorable for its straight lines and pretty exterior, had become a botched product of East German utilitarianism.

The Groß Glienicke community council provided all the materials Wolfgang needed. In return, the Kühnes were told that they had to pay a nominal rent each month at the post office into an account marked 'Meisel' – money that would be handed back by the state to pay for maintenance and upkeep. The Meisels never received a penny.

To wash, the Kühne family filled a large metal tub outside and then heated it with an immersion coil. This process could take over an hour and was both uncomfortable and laborious, especially in the winter. It wasn't quite clear why they couldn't share a bathroom with the Fuhrmanns, who after all had inside running hot water, but it had never been explained to Irene and she decided not to ask.

Whatever the problems, their new life was infinitely better than before. They were now living in a charming little house next to a lake. Her children had plenty of space to play in and, while they had to share the house, doing so was much better than being abused by her in-laws. To cap it all, her husband even had a new job.

20

FUHRMANN AND KÜHNE
1959

Ignition Key appeared on time for the first meeting with his Stasi handler.

Unsure what to expect, he felt anxious and insecure. He attempted to evade the handler's probing as best he could, saying that he hadn't had time to complete his tasks, and didn't see the purpose in gathering information on his family as 'he didn't have any relatives in West Germany'.

Then Ignition Key was asked about his colleagues. Had he noticed if they had committed any 'political misdeeds'? Ignition Key responded that while it 'was possible that a few of the truck drivers used the petrol vouchers for their own usage', he could not name anyone specifically. Trying to keep his handlers happy, and gaining a little confidence, he promised that he would pay more attention in the future. He did have one piece of information though: while drinking at the Drei Linden he had heard someone complaining about the state of the country. Delighted that Ignition Key was at last sharing a real titbit of information, the handlers asked for the man's name. Apologising, Ignition Key said that the drunkard was unfamiliar to him.

On 9 February 1959, Ignition Key met his handlers once again. This time he said that he would like to pass along a report on Herr Gerdner, who also lived in the village and was his manager at the truck department. Ignition Key said that when he was returning an airgun he had borrowed, he had noticed that Gerdner's television was tuned to a Western station. Having been thanked for this report, Ignition Key was told they would meet again on 19 February 1959 at 12.30. The rendezvous would be held at a place code-named 'The Barn'.

Shortly afterwards, the Kühnes took possession of a large television set, becoming one of the few families in the village to have such a luxury.

Lake house, 1960s

Though they lived side by side, the two families did not spend much time together. Wolfgang kept busy with home improvements: building a new garage next to the house, in which he kept his tools, with room to spare for the car he hoped one day to own, along with a number of sheds for his chickens, geese, and pigs. Before long, Wolfgang was known in the village as '*Schwein Kühne*', piggy Kühne.

Irene was happily occupied with her two children and housework. Then, in the spring of 1959, she realised she would have even less time on her hands, for she was once again pregnant.

Ella Fuhrmann meanwhile occupied herself in the garden, tending to her fruit trees and vegetables, and tidying up after her son. Now twenty years old Lothar was busy working, having secured a job installing milk machines for the state-owned company KLF. He was not only proud of his salary, but also of his company van. It was a matt-grey B1000 Wartburg and, while not in great condition, he loved to drive it fast along the narrow country lanes to his customers' farms. Officially Lothar only worked from 7 a.m. to 4 p.m., but most weeks he was obliged to clock in an additional five to ten hours. The van also gave him the mobility to travel to Potsdam, where he and his friends visited the bars, hoping to meet girls.

On most days, the Fuhrmanns and Kühnes had no contact. If they saw each other in the garden, or at the shops, they might greet each other, but no more than that. Twice the Fuhrmanns looked after the Kühne children, but for some reason this never became a habit. They never shared meals or invited one another to birthday parties. Although they held the keys for each other's houses, the two families were not friends.

While the house was just about able to absorb its additional residents, the lake was having a harder time. When the little weekend houses had first been built in the late 1920s, the planning department had assumed that they would be used infrequently. In consequence, the authorities had allowed these first homeowners to build gravity-based septic systems next to the lake. But now, with all the cottages filled with full-time residents, the sheer quantity of black water over-whelmed the rudimentary systems. To make matters worse, the sewage from the National People's Army (NVA) barracks on the edge of the village also flowed directly into the water.

Green algae began spreading across its surface, at first in small spots, then joining up to form a massive blanket which blocked the sun from the water, further depriving its deeper levels of oxygen. The consequences were dire: the water turned acidic and soon the plant and fish life died off. Meanwhile the shoreline's greenery – ground elder, iris, mountain ash – began to vanish, swamped by touch-me-nots, an aggressive weed whose pink and yellow berries can leap more than five metres when its seed pods open.

Yet Groß Glienicke was still considered an attractive place to visit by the West Berlin media. In 1959, the *Berliner Morgenpost* wrote:

Whoever travels to Berlin these days should also take a look at Groß Glienicke. Not only because the fauna and flora is so relaxing and interesting but mainly because of its political statement. In only a few other places does the division of our city becomes so vivid and clear . . . If you reach this region, turn down your music and leave the football in the car! Something like that should be written in a travel guide, for Groß Glienicke is one of the prettiest suburbs of our city, a small settlement between water and forest, under windy trees and a wide-open sky.

On 5 December 1959, a little boy was born. Irene and Wolfgang named him Bernd. Yet another person to squeeze into the lake house. He was a good infant, sleeping through the night and eating well. Yet even the most angelic baby cries from time to time, and his little yells of hunger, or longing, pierced through to the Fuhrmanns' side. The house was feeling more crowded by the day.

★

On 21 October 1960, Ignition Key received a message from Stasi Operative Schneider: appear at 5.30 p.m. at a secret location code-named 'Garage 21'. Given that he hadn't written any memos, and still had nothing to report, Ignition Key decided to go for a drink at the Drei Linden instead.

Thirty minutes later, Schneider tracked him down. Clearly disappointed, the operative attempted to engage Ignition Key in a more general conversation about the DDR's political situation. He was distressed, however, by the informant's lack of interest, noting that he repeatedly glanced at the clock on the wall. At the end of the conversation, Schneider asked Ignition Key to investigate a certain Herr L, who lived in the village and also worked as a truck driver. In addition, he was told to confirm if Herr L or Frau L were stealing food from the regiment's kitchen. Ignition Key agreed to look into this and to report back next time.

Ignition Key failed to turn up not only for the next meeting, on 19 December at the 'Clubhouse', but also for the backup meeting set four days later at the 'Hall Rental'. On 3 January 1961, Schneider finally located Ignition Key and asked him what he had discovered about the L family. Trying to put his handler off, Ignition Key once again said that he hadn't been able to gather any information. When pressed, he confessed that even though he was constantly in contact with the L family he did not want to inform on them since they were friends. To do so, he said, 'would be to his friends' disadvantage.'

Ignition Key's career as an informant was in peril. In a final report, written on 22 February 1961, Schneider concluded that Ignition Key 'was not honest and did not report well on shortcomings and failures'. For him to be of '*Nutzeffekt*', or 'use-effect', would require 'further education'. Worse, Schneider had heard from another informant that Ignition Key was stealing groceries, coal and potatoes from his food truck and using the truck for private purposes.

In conclusion, Schneider wrote, Ignition Key 'is dishonest and closed towards our Organ'. The one saving grace, he noted, was that the informant had never revealed his secret work to others. A few days later, Wolfgang's Stasi contract was terminated.

At the end of March 1961, a late-winter storm rolled into the village. For more than a week, snow fell on the lake house. With school cancelled, the Kühne children dressed warmly and, using whatever they could find – tin trays, plastic bags, rubbish-bin lids – like Lothar before them, they slid down the snowy slope below the terrace, stopping well before the flimsy wire fence that ran along the shoreline.

After months of sub-freezing weather, the lake was still frozen and Wolfgang helped the children onto its slippery expanse. It wasn't too hard to scramble over the fence, and there really wasn't any risk from the border guards who paid the children no attention. There they joined the villagers, some of whom skated as others sailed by on home-made ice boats, most simply walked, enjoying the monochrome tranquillity.

It had been a good three years for the Kühnes. They had a third child, and a happy if crowded life at the house. Wolfgang was working for the military and had managed to get safely in and then out of the Stasi. And while the three-year contract for his truck-driving job would soon come to an end, he could easily find another job, if not in the village, then in Potsdam.

21

FUHRMANN AND KÜHNE
1961

On Sunday 13 August 1961, Wolfgang Kühne was woken by the noise of construction. Oddly, the racket seemed to be coming from the lakefront.

From his bedroom Wolfgang could hear the whine and thud of heavy machinery, along with a chorus of pickaxes chipping away against rock and sand, and every so often the house shook.

Wolfgang rose, opened the front door, walked round to the back of the house and was amazed by what he saw: between the house and the edge of the lake, less than forty metres from where he stood, scores of soldiers were milling about. By the shore, bulldozers were pushing the flimsy fence into the water. Nearer the house, holes were being dug and filled with concrete; spools of barbed wire were unwound. More soldiers were working to the left and to the right, all the way up and down the shoreline. He was stunned. With no notice of these works, Wolfgang couldn't make sense of what he was seeing.

Back inside, Wolfgang turned on the television to find out what was going on. For the protection of the DDR citizens, the announcer explained, the authorities had decided to build a barrier between East

Berlin border fence, Groß Glienicke Lake, 1961

and West. It was now illegal to cross this boundary. The border patrol guards had been given permission to shoot anyone who tried. The next day the DDR newspapers lauded the decision to erect the barrier, with a commentator from the *Neues Deutschland* writing: 'Children are now protected from child-stealers; families are protected from the blackmailing snoopers of the human trafficking headquarters; businesses are protected from the head-hunters; people are protected from the monsters.' Under the headline 'DEFIANCE OF THE SABRE-RATTLERS', the *Tribüne* wrote: 'Deep satisfaction fills us trade unionists of the DDR at the decision of our government to stop up the West Berlin rat hole.'

Since the start of that year, Walter Ulbricht, the DDR leader, had been pushing Nikita Khrushchev, the Soviet premier, for a solution to his country's mass emigration crisis. Despite the closing of the external border between East and West Germany, over three and a half million East Germans had emigrated to West Germany between

1949 and 1961, mostly through East Berlin where the border had remained relatively open. This exodus comprised almost 20 per cent of the entire DDR population. Not only did this outflow concern Ulbricht from an ideological standpoint, undermining the people's pride in the socialist mission, he also knew that the country would not survive if it continued to haemorrhage people to the West. It was simply too easy to cross from East to West Berlin. So on 1 August, after deciding that the British and Americans would not oppose the building of a barrier, the two leaders agreed to a plan. They would build a permanent barrier between West Berlin and East Germany, making it as close to impossible to cross.

The barrier would have a profound impact on Groß Glienicke. While the border in the village had been closed for some time, it had still been possible – with a short bus ride to Staaken and then an S-Bahn train – to visit West Berlin. Families would now be unable to see each other, and those with jobs in West Berlin would lose them.

Though no member of the Communist Party, Wolfgang *did* believe in socialism and thought that the East German experiment, with its promise of greater distribution of wealth, had more to offer him than the capitalism of West Germany. After all, didn't the Kühnes have this wonderful house beside the lake? Never a Nazi Party member and always a stern critic of all they had done, especially to the Jews, Wolfgang had been disturbed to read in the press how many former Nazis were employed by the West German government. Despite the inconvenience of the barrier and the added security hassles, Wolfgang believed that 'the government's politics were good'. If the border was there to protect them, then so be it.

Irene Kühne was less accepting, disagreeing with the border fence in principle. Why should the government stop her travelling to West Berlin or indeed West Germany? While she was grateful for all that the DDR had done for them, Irene had family in Dortmund whom she would now not be able to visit.

Little Bernd Kühne didn't really understand the fuss. It was a hot day and, ignoring the building work and the guards, he crawled under the fence and made his way to the shore and then into the lake. To her horror, Irene spotted him struggling in the water, but was unable to reach him because of the fence. In the end, a guard helped the small boy out. As he handed Bernd back across the barrier, he urged Irene to keep better control of her children.

In the early weeks and months of the Anti-Fascist Protection Barrier, as it was known in the East, or the Berlin Wall, as it was called in the West, it was still possible for enterprising East Berliners to cross the border zone and make it to West Berlin. They brought ladders, jumped out of windows from buildings next to the Wall and hid in the boots of cars. As the DDR government spent increasing funds to seal the crossing, these attempts became more difficult.

From their back door, the Kühne family watched as the Wall was gradually fortified. Additional space was cleared between the new border fence at the lake's edge and the house. Everything was then removed: the few remaining willows and black alders on the shore, the apple and cherry trees on the terraces, the terraces themselves, the fences that Dr Alexander had built down the edge of the property to the lake, the pump house, the steps down to the shore, even the tennis court.

Next, a second barbed-wire fence was added, topped with razor wire thirty metres from the lake's edge, and only ten metres from the back of the house. Between the two barriers developed a no-man's-land that would become known as the 'death strip' or the 'killing zone'. In the middle of the death strip, a three-metre-wide concrete path was built. This the border patrol police patrolled every hour, in a green cabriolet.

Over the next few years, the Wall was enhanced still further. Trigger wires were laid to alert the patrol guards whenever someone tried to escape. Fifteen-metre-high concrete towers were erected at intervals along the Wall, giving the guards a view up and down the border as well as across the lake towards West Berlin. Every few hundred metres, a tall post was erected from which hung giant *Krieg* lights that shone all day and all night. Mines and large metal spikes littered the lake shore. Next, the barbed-wire fence by the lake was replaced by an outer wall, which was made up of precast three-metre-high concrete sections, on top of which was laid a long metal concrete tube. Then the wire fence near the house was replaced by a concrete inner wall which was 2.5 metres high. It was now impossible to see the lake from the garden.

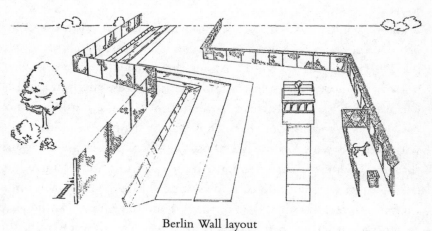

Berlin Wall layout

Finally, a metal wire was strung along the inside of the inner wall, to which German shepherds were tethered by a lead that enabled them to run up and down the death strip, searching for possible escapees. Early each morning the Kühnes and the Fuhrmanns heard the rumble of a truck as it drove up the border patrol path, stopped in front of each kennel, and ladled out food for the hungry animals.

As with many of their neighbours, they grew fond of these dogs, throwing them scraps from dinners and summer barbecues. Yet, wise to the possible canine corruption, the border patrol guards rotated the dogs' sentry posts to ensure that they did not become too familiar with the nearby inhabitants.

With the Wall now in place, the villagers were not only cut off from West Berlin, they also had to live with the physical presence of a giant concrete structure just a few metres from their homes. Another immediate consequence was the creation of the *Grenzgebiet*, the border security zone. This ran parallel to the Wall at distances varying from less than fifty to one hundred metres. Only those with permission were allowed to enter the zone, and access to non-residents was limited to special circumstances. Applications to enter could take many weeks to be processed.

In Groß Glienicke, this border security zone started in the north of the village, running along the Potsdamer Chaussee, and then down the Dorfstraße to the south. Along these roads metal signs were posted at hundred-metre intervals on which were written in English, German, French and Russian: 'Attention here is the border, do not pass without permission.' Each sign was held up by a pole striped with red and white paint, like those of old barbershops, to ensure that nobody missed the warning. All the lakefront homes, including the Meisels', were considered to be within this zone. From this point forward, to return home, the Fuhrmanns and the Kühnes would have to show their passes to the soldiers who were standing guard at the Potsdamer Tor.

Two things now became clear. First, and this was good news as far as the two families were concerned, the Meisels would never be coming back. They were now official tenants, rather than caretakers. As a result, the remnants of Will and Eliza's life were removed: the piano was hauled to the garage, the sheet music was thrown away, and any clothes left in the cupboards were divided up between the families, the rest handed to the community council.

The second was sadder, at least as far as the Kühne and Fuhrmann children were concerned. For although they lived in the lake house, it was now impossible to swim in the lake.

22

FUHRMANN AND KÜHNE
1962

Sitting alone at the table, twenty-four-year old Lothar Fuhrmann worried that he was going to spend the night alone. His friends were all out on the dance floor, each with a partner, and each apparently having more fun than him.

The social evening was held at the Nedlitz fire station, a twenty-minute bus ride from Groß Glienicke. Lothar was tall and well built, and he'd made an effort to look presentable, with his dark pleated trousers, a white shirt unbuttoned at the collar, and his hair slicked back. He looked good, he thought, which made his lack of dance partner all the more galling.

It was then that a young woman walked over to him. Dressed in a knee-length skirt and blouse and carrying two beers in her hand, she handed over a bottle and asked if he wanted to dance. Taking a quick swig, Lothar said yes, stood up and followed her onto the floor. Her name was Sieglinde Bartel.

Over the next few weeks they went out several times. One of their favourite spots was the village's Badewiese bar and dance hall where Will Meisel had played his music back in the 1940s. Now the property was state-owned and the four arched windows overlooking the lake had been blocked up in an effort to prevent people from climbing through and attempting an escape. Lining up with the others when the doors opened at six, Lothar and Sieglinde paid their ten marks before entering the building. Inside, the heating was turned up, and while Western music was prohibited, the small band – a guitarist, an accordionist and a saxophonist – stood on a raised stage to the rear of the hall and played with enough rhythm and energy for the youngsters to have a good time.

As one of the few dance halls in the area, the Badewiese attracted locals as well as soldiers from the NVA barracks to the north of the village and Soviet troops. This sometimes caused problems, for there were often more single men than single women, and when fights broke out, it was not uncommon for a Soviet military policeman to brandish his weapon. When that happened, the Badewiese would empty, then, after a brief pause shivering outside in the cold, the youngsters would return to the dance floor.

A few months after they started dating, Lothar and Sieglinde decided to marry. Despite their engagement, Sieglinde lacked a pass to enter the border security zone that ran along the Wall, and was forbidden from spending nights at her fiancé's house. Breaking such rules risked arrest and even jail. Nevertheless, on 2 April 1963, Lothar and Sieglinde invited all their friends for a wedding-eve party at the lake house. That evening, over twenty people managed to evade the border patrol officers standing guard at the Potsdamer Tor.

Some brought cake and wine, others cold meats and cheese. Everyone brought an old china plate, for this was a traditional *Polterabend* party, which takes place the night before a wedding. To avoid being heard by the patrol guards, who every hour walked along the border patrol path less than thirty metres from the back door, the revellers held the party inside. They squeezed into the Blue Room – which appeared more spacious without the piano and piano stool – and, sitting cross-legged on the floor, on the couch, or on one of the chairs brought in from the kitchen, toasted the young happy couple.

Late into the evening, and now merry from all the schnapps and beer, Lothar and Sieglinde led the group outside. There, in a moment of frivolity and carelessness, and with a cry of '*viel Glück!*', or good luck, they threw their chinaware to the ground, the shards scattering noisily on the grey flagstones by the front door. The crash of the plates resounded in the silent night air and, realising that someone was sure to investigate — nobody wanted to be found without the correct paperwork — the friends quickly said their goodbyes, and hurried off into the night.

The next day the bride woke early and set about clearing up the mess. Around noon, they dressed. Sieglinde wore a lilac-coloured skirt and matching jacket, streaked with silver beading. Her hair was plaited and tied up in a crown decorated with small wild flowers. Lothar wore a formal dark suit, with a white shirt and black shoes.

They had ordered a taxi to take them to the village community hall on Seepromenade, but by 1 p.m., the allotted time for the service to begin, the taxi had not turned up. With Sieglinde increasingly anxious, Lothar asked Wolfgang Kühne for a lift. A few minutes later the couple were on their way in their neighbour's ancient DKW F7, spluttering and backfiring so loudly that Sieglinde commented there was no need for any tin cans to trail behind.

Finally arriving at the community hall they found the main doors locked. Being careful not to trip in her high heels, the bride opened the cellar door and the pair snuck in through the back entrance. An hour later, now officially married in front of a civil magistrate, the newly-weds were on their way — the taxi having turned up by now — to Sieglinde's parents' house for a reception.

A few days later, Sieglinde informed the *Gemeinde*, the local parish council, that she had moved into the lake house at Am Park 2. Shortly afterwards, she revealed to a shocked Lothar, and then to his mother, that she was pregnant. It soon transpired that she was not the only one.

On 29 August, Irene Kühne gave birth to a baby girl she named

Marita. Two months later, Sieglinde and Lothar Fuhrmann's son Dietmar was born. A year later, Sieglinde became pregnant again, and when a daughter named Sabine was born, on 26 January 1965, everyone realised that it was time for the Fuhrmanns to find a new place to live. There were simply too many people crammed into a small space.

In February 1965, with the help of the *Gemeinde*, Ella Fuhrmann and her family moved to Rehsprung 23 in Groß Glienicke, on the south side of the village, some four blocks from the lake. Lothar was sorry to leave his childhood home, yet he was relieved to have more space, away from the prying eyes of the neighbours, away from the *Krieg* lights that shone all night, and away from the scary-looking border guards.

The house had given the Fuhrmanns many happy years. Now it was time to move on.

If the Fuhrmanns were pleased with their new accommodation, the Kühne family members were happier still. For now they had the house all to themselves. Irene quickly set about commandeering the rest of it. Each child was allotted their own room, with Bernd given the Blue Room on the south-west corner of the house.

Irene claimed the Fuhrmanns' kitchen for her own, and asked Wolfgang to tear down the wall that separated it from the maid's bedroom where Lothar had slept. With a long pine table and six chairs, the family could now sit comfortably during mealtimes. Irene could also use the cellar, which was accessed through a trapdoor next to the kitchen pantry, and there, on metal shelves arranged in neat rows, she stored potatoes in brown paper bags, as well as jars of pickled cucumbers and onions, and compotes that she made from the garden's copious cherry and pear harvest.

Best of all, the family now had a bathroom, with running hot water. It had been seven years since they had moved into the house, and at last they had an indoor toilet. Wolfgang added a chimney to the Blue Room to make it more comfortable in the winter, and extended the bathroom. Finally, since they no longer needed them, he removed the small kitchen and toilet in what had been the chauffeur's annexe, and knocked a door into Ella's old bedroom. Bernd, now six years old, began running circuits around the house's interior: from the bed in his Blue Room to the kitchen to the spare bedroom, where his sister slept, to the chauffeur's annexe, where his brother now slept, on to the living room and into the master bedroom, back to the living room and then returning to his bedroom. When the clamour of banging doors and footsteps drove his mother mad, she would shout for him to play outdoors.

With the Fuhrmanns gone, and two of the rooms enlarged, the lake house appeared very spacious. At last, it felt fully theirs. So much so, in fact, that Wolfgang began laughingly to call it their *Kleine Villa*, and *Villa Wolfgang*.

View of Berlin Wall from Groß Glienicke Lake

PART IV
VILLA WOLFGANG

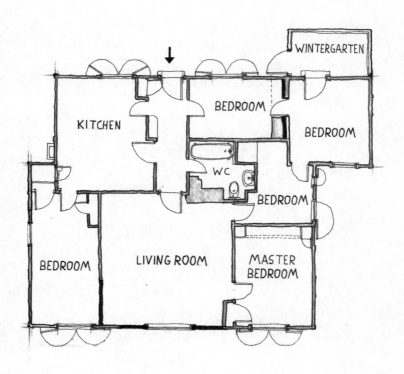

January 2014

I am sitting in a small Groß Glienicke cafe with Bernd Kühne, Wolfgang's son. He wears work clothes: paint-spattered blue trousers, an old pair of running shoes and a navy-blue parka. He is eager to talk, but tired. Now fifty-four years old, he tells me he has problems with his kidneys, and that he has just come from the hospital where he has undergone dialysis, a treatment he has to endure three times a week.

We speak about his life, about his parents and how he remembers the house. He answers each query calmly, candidly, never seeming to tire or take offence at my intrusion. During our conversation many customers come over to say hello to Bernd. He is a man well liked in the village.

At one point Bernd tells me that, during the DDR era, his was one of the few families to have a telephone in the village. I ask if this is significant. He pauses, and says that it might be evidence that someone in the house worked as an informant. 'Your father?' I ask. 'Not my father,' he says, 'but perhaps my stepmother, his second wife.'

Hoping that I am not crossing too many boundaries, I ask Bernd if he's ever wanted to see his father's Stasi file, his stepmother's, possibly even his own? I tell him that it can take up to three years to see a file once an application has been submitted. He pauses again. I imagine him weighing the risks: might he find out something he could later regret — a girlfriend who spied on him, a work colleague who reported on him, perhaps even a family member who exchanged information for profit? Yes, Bernd says, he would very much like to see what they have, if I can find it.

As we're picking up our coats, Bernd talks about his childhood at the house, about the other family who had lived there before them: the Fuhrmanns. They knew the Meisels, he thinks — a widow and her son. The son might still live in the village.

I thank him, and rush back to our hotel to telephone my researcher. There has always been a gap in our knowledge of the house – a missing inhabitant or inhabitants between the Kühnes and the Meisels. The researcher calls back, excitedly – she's found him. He's suggested that we meet.

A few days later I am walking to the lake house with Lothar Fuhrmann and his wife Sieglinde. Now in their seventies, they are both dressed in large sweaters, loose trousers and tired-looking boots. It is their first return in almost fifty years, despite living less than two hundred metres away.

As we pass through the overgrown meadow above the house, they see the building for the first time. 'Nay, nay, nay,' moans Sieglinde. She appears shocked at the house's dilapidated state. Tears slide down her cheeks, 'This is so terrible,' she says. Her husband is equally taken aback. 'It was so beautiful when we used to live here,' says Lothar. 'Not any more.'

At first Lothar and Sieglinde speak freely as they walk around the property. They talk about their romance, their time living at the house and the changes that have swept the village. For them, it was 'normal' to grow up next to the Wall, and they 'became used to it'. They also say that life was better before the Wall came down. At least then, they say, childcare and housing were free, food was cheap and jobs were plentiful. Travel restrictions and government surveillance were a small price to pay for such benefits, they tell me.

Despite the years that have passed, they are still able to describe the house as it was in extraordinary detail. From what they say, it appears that the house changed very little from the days of my grandmother's childhood.

Their excitement is infectious, and I begin asking more questions. I have read a lot about the Wall, its politics and construction, and I want to understand just what it was like to live within its shadow. 'What did you and your friends do for fun?' I ask. 'What was your daily routine?' and 'How could you have a relationship while living in the border zone?'

But as I press, the Fuhrmanns grow quieter. 'It is personal,' they say as we walk back. 'And besides, why would anyone care about our story?'

On my return to England, despite their earlier lukewarm response, I am eager to share my research with my family — the secrets I've unearthed about the house.

A few weeks later, we gather at my aunt and uncle's flat in central London. In front of me sit twenty family members: my parents, uncles, aunts and cousins. I am anxious. This feels like pitching an idea at a business meeting. Telling myself to relax, I start to talk.

I show them pictures from the 1930s along with those from the 1940s, 1960s and 1990s, explaining how the house has changed over the years. I recall my meetings with people who remember the house and the stories that they shared. Finally, I tell them about the city of Potsdam's intention to demolish the house.

I had expected interest, possibly even thanks. Instead, I hear anger and resentment. One cousin tells me that I am being sentimental, that the family had never spent much time at the house. When I mention the film shot by Dr Alexander from the 1930s — the wide-grinned kids playing football on the lawn, Elsie and Bella splashing around in the lake — he shuts me down. Another relative raises practical concerns, suggesting that it will be impossible to organise such a project from England. I hear myself saying that what is required is a 'leap of faith', and realise that even I find these words unconvincing.

I am not totally surprised by the resistance. After all, we have painful history here. Their anger and fear echo the emotions that I had myself felt before spending time at the lake, before I had met the people who lived there. Yet I am disappointed. While I had never thought that they would forgive what had happened in the past, I had hoped that my family would be open to something new, that they might be interested in a exploring a different future.

Realising that the meeting is a disaster, I try to wind it down. 'OK then,' I say. 'Thank you all for coming . . .'

Then, one of my younger cousins speaks up. She says that she is excited. She is ready, whenever, to fly out to Berlin, to meet the locals, to roll up her sleeves, and begin clearing up the house. Another says that it could be an opportunity to heal, a chance to start afresh. And a third adds that if we are honouring all of the families who lived in the house, then there is 'real power to this idea'.

After two hours of honest and sometimes bruising communication, the meeting comes to a close. There appears to be some support for the project, but there is also an equal amount of resistance. I wonder how I am going to move this forward if I can't even persuade my own family.

23

KÜHNE
1965

On 27 May 1965, many in Groß Glienicke were surprised to learn that they would soon experience a royal fly-by.

Those villagers secretly watching West German television saw the live broadcast pictures of a plane approaching RAF-Gatow. Inside, the broadcaster announced, was Queen Elizabeth II and her husband, the Duke of Edinburgh, arriving as part of the first visit by the British head of state to West Berlin. Those who were quick enough ran outside and were just in time to see a red, white and blue plane roar overhead, readying for landing at the nearby airfield.

The Queen's trip followed on from President John F. Kennedy's visit two years earlier, which had attracted massive international media attention, especially his declaration of '*Ich bin ein Berliner*'. Since that time, it appeared that the West had decided not to force the issue of the separation of Berlin into two cities. While they considered the Wall an affront to democracy and all that the West held dear, they feared what would happen if they attempted to break through the barrier. Similarly, the Soviet Union, though outwardly outraged by the build-up of American and British forces in Berlin, and still desperate to gain control of the entire city, was thankful that the mass exodus from the DDR had dramatically fallen since the construction of the Wall, averting a collapse in the country's economy. The situation was far from ideal for either side, but tensions seemed to have lessened in the years since the Wall had been built.

According to *The Times* two soldiers rolled out a red carpet to the side of the plane as soon as the royal aircraft had slowed to a stop. In a pale yellow coat and matching yellow hat, white handbag, white gloves and white heels, the Queen walked down the plane's steps, at the bottom of which she was met by the West German Chancellor Ludwig Erhard and the Berlin mayor, Willy Brandt – who handed her a bunch of red flowers.

After inspecting the British troops at the airfield, the royal party drove in an open-topped black Mercedes through the streets of West Berlin, which were, as reported by *The Times*, 'deep with happy crowds'. As the vehicles slowed, the Queen and her husband stood up, smiling and waving at the masses who, in return, cheered and fluttered palm-size Union Jacks. Some reports estimated that over one million people, almost half of West Berlin, had turned out to see the Queen.

At the Brandenburg Gate, the cars paused, while the mayor pointed at the Wall and explained its history and fortifications. Seeing two DDR sentries standing at the Wall, the Duke of Edinburgh waved, without eliciting a response. On the far side of the barrier, some eighty metres down Unter den Linden, a crowd of five hundred East Berlin citizens had gathered – but, according to *The Times* journalist, over one hundred policemen blocked their view.

Leaving the Brandenburg Gate, the Queen was driven along the Berlin Wall to the Potsdamer Platz, and then on to West Berlin's town hall in Schöneberg, for an afternoon rally, attended by over 100,000 people. As she sat on a dais above the steps of the sandstone town hall the crowd chanted 'E-li-za-beth, E-li-za-beth'.

Speaking first, Willy Brandt thanked the Queen and her country for their years of support, and his words were met with cheers and clapping from the crowd. He continued: 'Today we have been able to show ourselves as we would like to be, relaxed and friendly. In this we have been helped by Your Majesty's dignity, but also, if I may speak frankly, Your Majesty's charm.'

When the Queen stood, the crowd immediately hushed. She spoke of her admiration for the people of Germany. 'Nowhere is the tragedy of a divided world made more evident than in this city. While other cities have enjoyed twenty years of peaceful redevelopment and progress, Berlin has never ceased to struggle for her existence.'

The final speaker was the chancellor who, having said that Germany's desire for reunification would not be stalled by the 'wall of tyranny', ended by shouting out, 'Long live the Queen.' His chant was echoed by the crowd.

Much of the royal visit was covered by Radio in the American Sector (RIAS), which was hungrily devoured by the villagers of Groß Glienicke, Wolfgang and Irene among them. The visit was, however, not reported by the East German media. To Bernd's family, this was yet more evidence that the press could not be trusted.

By now, it was apparent that the villagers could be separated into three new categories. The first were the believers. These included the party apparatchiks and the ardent communists, who, despite all evidence to the contrary, continued to cling to their revolutionary precepts. Then there were those who didn't believe all they heard, who could see through the lies of the party bosses, and who sang the obligatory songs and abided by the laws they knew to be inane or, worse, unjust and dangerous and yet kept silent. Members of this group might confess their doubts in private, but never in public. The final group were the dissenters, those who bravely rejected the status quo and called for its replacement. This was the smallest of the three groups, and many of its members were harassed by the Stasi, held without trial and tortured. The Kühne and Fuhrmann families belonged to the second group.

That September, Bernd Kühne attended his first day at 'School Number 2', one of three in the vicinity.

As his family lived within the border security zone, Bernd had first to walk through the checkpoint at the Potsdamer Tor. The passes of any adult were carefully checked and only when approved was a button pressed, the light changed from red to green, and the person was waved along. As a child, and a familiar face, Bernd was swiftly nodded through.

Turning left on the Potsdamer Chaussee, Bernd passed the Drei Linden, and then took another left onto Dorfstraße, past the church and into the school. As the school building was also located within the *Grenzgebiet*, and as the vast majority of the schoolchildren's parents lacked permission to enter the border security zone, most had to drop their children fifty metres from the school's front door.

Inside, Bernd was ushered to his classroom and introduced to his fellow students. Later, before lunch, the children were walked up to the Drei Linden, which was now state-owned and had been converted into a school canteen. Back in class that afternoon, Bernd asked his teacher, 'Why can't we drive to the West?' His classmates sniggered at the question, making Bernd feel self-conscious and stupid. He decided he didn't like the building, the students or the teachers. He much preferred the familiarity of his own home, his garden and the animals in the sheds. After the class had quietened down, the teacher looked at Bernd and said kindly, 'We cannot drive to the West because we cannot afford roads.' Not knowing any better, Bernd believed this statement, though he was left with a nagging doubt. At the end of the day he walked home in tears. It was only after considerable encouragement from his mother that he returned to school the following morning.

Bernd's core subjects were German, Mathematics, History and Russian. He, along with his classmates, was expected to join the Thälmann Pioneers, a national youth organisation named after Ernst Thälmann, the former head of the German Communist Party. Each week Bernd attended 'lectures' at which he and his classmates had to repeat lines such as: 'We Thälmann Pioneers are friends of the Soviet Union, and protect peace while hating the warmongers.'

During the spring they took part in outdoor activities, much like the scouts, learning survival skills and basic orienteering. Bernd and his fellow Pioneers wore blue scarves, a symbol, according to the organisation's manual, 'of our devotion to the cause of the working class and its party, the Socialist Unity Party of Germany'. They were told that it was their mission to love nature and all its beauty. A highlight of each meeting was the raising of the national flag, during which a leader would call out, 'We want to prepare for peace and socialism,' before the children shouted back, 'Always ready!'

On 13 August 1966, dressed in their Thälmann Pioneers uniforms, seventy boys and girls walked out of School Number 2 for a field trip. Carrying flowers and gifts which they had made with paper and glue, and accompanied by their teachers, they made their way along the Dorfstraße towards the barracks which housed the border patrol guards of Groß Glienicke Regiment 34.

Thälmann Pioneers meet soldiers, Groß Glienicke

As they approached, an armed guard lifted the barrier, and the children were ushered inside towards the parade ground. There they were met by a long line of neatly dressed border patrol guards. Together, soldiers and children would celebrate the fifth anniversary of the building of the Anti-Fascist Protection Barrier.

Having handed their gifts to the soldiers, a few of the children were invited to hold one of the guards' rifles. After photographs were taken for the local newspaper, the children went for a swim in the regiment's swimming pool. Afterwards, they were shown a film which explained the work of the border patrol soldiers and how they protected the republic.

According to the editor of the *Chronik*, the state-controlled village chronicle, the event was a 'great success'. Once the children had thanked the soldiers for protecting the border, as a result of which 'they could study in peace and quiet', they returned to the school to resume their classes.

★

As he grew older, one of Bernd's favourite school pastimes was to gather small sticks with his friends during morning break and then throw them over the border fence, which ran along the back of the school playground, trying to set off the trigger wires. Most times they missed, but if they were lucky, and the stick was heavy enough, they struck the first wire, which let out a green flare. If a teacher saw them, he would yell, 'Don't throw sticks at our Anti-Fascist Protection Device!'

On a few occasions, they were able to hit the second wire, sending a red flare into the sky. Within minutes three or more trucks would arrive, and troops would pile out, looking for the suspected escapee. When none could be found, the troops would confer, glare at the schoolkids, and then reset the trigger wires. As soon as the troops left, one of Bernd's friends would shout, 'Let's go and see the fireworks!' and he and his classmates would try to hit the trigger wires again.

Though no great lover of team sports, Bernd enjoyed running. He showed ability as a sprinter, but was truly impressive over longer distances. Before long, his teachers noticed his talent and Bernd was selected for races against other schools. He developed a reputation among his peers and began to take pride in his skill as an athlete.

While Bernd made friends at school, he wasn't able to invite them home, unless they too had passes permitting them to enter the border security zone. This was one of the most annoying aspects of living at the lake house. Birthdays were a particular challenge. It was sometimes possible to sneak some friends past the guards, but next to impossible to get everyone through. Indeed, even if they had been able to, many of the parents would have forbidden their children, given the risks.

★

Despite the frustrations of living so close to the Wall, the Kühnes soon settled into a routine. In the evenings, after supper, they often watched television in the living room. There were two domestic channels available, DDR1 and DDR2, and the family gathered each evening to watch the news and the variety show *Ein Kessel Buntes*. Of more interest were the shows broadcast by the West German channels – ARD and ZDF – which they could pick up from the antenna tower positioned five kilometres south-east of the village. Their favourite shows were *Am Laufenden Band*, similar to *The Generation Game* in the UK, and *Einer wird gewinnen*, a quiz show with contestants from around Europe. They also watched a lot of sport, particularly football and Formula One. Whenever the West German shows had finished the family made sure to switch the TV back to a DDR channel in the unlikely event that someone stopped by.

By the late 1960s, many more people had television sets in the village. Teachers at Bernd's school would often quiz the children on their family's viewing habits. One trick was to ask the children which clock was showing on the TV news. If they replied with 'rectangle', then the teacher knew that their parents were watching *Aktuelle Kamera* on DDR at 7.30 p.m. But if they said the news had a circular clock, then the teacher would know that *Tagesschau* was being watched, an 8 p.m. news programme carried by the Western channel ARD, and the child's family would be reported to the authorities.

And then there was the radio. Like most of Berlin's population, Bernd's favourite station was RIAS, which since 1946 had been broadcasting American culture into West Berlin and beyond. He liked to listen to the weekly chart show, singing along to the popular British and American songs then unavailable on East German radio.

*

On 13 June 1967, when Bernd was seven years old, he and his family attended Groß Glienicke's seven hundredth anniversary celebrations. The local party bosses had decided to use the event, held over three days, as an opportunity to highlight the benefits of socialism. The programme ran to six pages and was printed on glossy white paper. At the village sports hall there were games for children and, for the adults, an exhibition entitled 'From feudalistic village to a socialist community at the border to West Berlin'. Down the road at the Drei Linden, they were holding 'a forum for intelligence'. At the beach bar, party officials gave awards to 'outstanding citizens'. Later, there was dancing, accompanied by a Soviet music ensemble. There was also a forum where women were educated about 'socialist health policies and the healthy development of our children'.

At the Drei Linden event, Johannes Sieben, one of Bernd's teachers and the editor of the *Chronik*, captured the mood of the day. At the end of a long speech about the village's history, he said, 'The leading men of the capitalist industry have been chased away, so that they cannot stretch out their hands for profit any more, and we now have this barrier to West Berlin to stop future capitalists.' As people clapped, Sieben concluded, 'We have been good citizens, we have done it right because we the people of Groß Glienicke are very happy with getting along with the border patrol guards, and support their work protecting our borders.'

In the years since the Wall was constructed, the number of people who crossed the border from East Berlin to the West had fallen from over 200,000 in the first seven months of 1961 to a few hundred per year. By 1965, seventy-seven people had died attempting to cross the Wall, ranging in age from eighteen to eighty. Most had been shot by DDR border guards as they attempted to escape. Typically, the government-controlled DDR media did not cover the story of those who died while trying to escape across the Wall. The exception was if a border guard died while on duty, they were then lionised for their patriotic service. When the government was unable to conceal civilian deaths, they were justified by the DDR media as a legitimate defence of national borders. On the other hand, the Western media widely covered these deaths, prompting protests and condemnations, which in turn damaged the DDR's reputation and fuelled anger towards its leaders.

By now, the Wall had become the most prominent symbol of the ongoing Cold War, a physical reminder of the conflict between the two global powers. To the East German government and the Soviet Union, it represented an assertion of their independence from the West, as well as a practical barrier against emigration. To the USA and its allies, it embodied the servitude suffered by the people of Eastern Europe, an affront to Western ideals of democracy and freedom.

The drama, complexity and fraught negotiations of the Cold War were played out on a small scale at the so-called 'Bridge of Spies', where captured Soviet, American and British intelligence agents were swapped. Spanning the River Havel, the bridge formed a border crossing between West Berlin and Potsdam in East Germany, and lay only three kilometres south of Groß Glienicke. The first exchange took place on 10 February 1962, six months after the Berlin Wall was erected. From one end of the bridge, the USA released Colonel Vilyam Genrikhovich Fisher, who five years earlier had been found guilty of running a spy ring in New York. From the other side, the Soviets sent over Francis Gary Powers, an American pilot who had been captured two years earlier when the Soviets shot down his U2 spy plane as it flew over its airspace. A second exchange took place in 1964, when Konon Molody, a Soviet agent who had acquired British military intelligence, was swapped for Greville Wynne, a British intelligence officer captured in Budapest. While celebrated in the West, such exchanges were not covered by the DDR media. Officially, the only news items available to Bernd Kühne and his family were the one-sided stories circulated by the East German newspapers and radio: accounts of how Fisher had thwarted the US government and was being feted as a hero in Moscow; and of how Gary Powers had been shot down as the result of a Soviet pilot's superior skills; how Greville Wynne had confessed at his trial in Moscow and had been sentenced to death.

Yet the escapes from East Germany and the spy swaps were not the only border crossings taking place at this time. For some, life in the DDR appeared more attractive than that in West Germany.

Surprisingly, perhaps, this was true of a few British soldiers working at Gatow. By the early 1960s, a section of Britain's Gatow military base had been transformed into Britain's most important intelligence gathering operation in central Europe. Officially known as Royal Signals Detachment RAF Gatow, this unit monitored communications traffic between East Berlin and Moscow. To handle the sheer volume of data that needed to be translated and analysed, the British recruited hundreds of young linguists through their Russian Intelligence Corps, most of whom had little or no military training. One such example was the writer Alan Bennett; another was future TV producer Leslie Woodhead. During long shifts, the teams listened to the airwaves, seated in rows of desks situated in a secret bunker towards the back of the base. Another of these young recruits was a certain Brian Patchett, a scruffy-looking, long-haired, twenty-five-year-old who had grown up in Coventry.

It was on 9 July 1963 that Brian Patchett's name first appeared in the British newspapers. Under the headline 'BRITISH CORPORAL DEFECTS TO THE EAST', *The Times* reported that Patchett had requested asylum, giving the reason that he was 'no longer prepared to work for the revanchists who are preparing for war'. The soldier had been missing since 2 July, the paper said, adding that an army spokesman confirmed that he had not taken any secret documents with him. An investigation by the British Army was quickly launched and it was soon discovered that Patchett had fallen in love with a twenty-one-year-old German girl, Rosemarie Zeiss. Zeiss had grown up in East Berlin but, hoping to study law, she had crossed into West Berlin a few months before the Wall was built. Her parents still lived in the DDR, where they ran a state-controlled restaurant. Patchett had met Zeiss at Gatow, where she had worked for a short time at one of the base's shops and had been devastated when Zeiss had ended their relationship because it 'was becoming too serious'. In a letter to Zeiss dated 21 June 1963, Patchett had confessed that he didn't like working at Gatow and was frustrated that his requests to be relocated to another base had not been accepted: 'the army refuses to move me out', he wrote. Anxious lest he be trapped on the base, he concluded: 'I've only got one way to run.'

In a confidential memo to the British Cabinet, the War Office concluded that Patchett was a 'lone wolf with no particular friends in the unit', and that 'there is no evidence that the defection was a steered operation'. In a final report, the director of Military Intelligence, Marshall St John Oswald, wrote that the cause of the defection was a combination of an unstable psychiatric history, a poor home background, unhappiness about his posting as well as his girlfriend breaking up with him. On 7 November 1963, following a series of inquiries from a Member of Parliament who had been pressing the government to return Patchett's belongings to his family, Oswald wrote that 'it is obviously desirable from the army point of view to let the Patchett case die a natural death if possible'. The items would be returned to the family 'and held on Patchett's behalf'.

Brian Patchett was one of only twenty-three members of the British Army based at Gatow who defected to the East, at a time when tens of thousands of young people in East Germany were considering fleeing in the opposite direction.

24

KÜHNE
1970

Berlin Wall with view of Groß Glienicke Lake and islands

Despite living in the shadow of the Wall, with all its extraordinary features, the local residents tried to establish a normal life. By the start of 1970, the Kühne family had developed a firm daily routine.

The first task of a winter morning was to light the oven in the kitchen. This was Bernd's job. At 6 a.m., the ten-year-old would be woken by his alarm. Climbing out of bed and wrapping himself in a warm jacket, he would venture outside to grab an armful of wood from the stack by the chicken shed. Back indoors, he fanned the embers in the grate before carefully adding the logs. Once the fire was roaring, he added a few lumps of coal from the metal scuttle standing next to the stove. It was dark outside and the windows in the kitchen were covered with ice; he could not see through them.

When the stove was warm, Irene would begin breakfast, typically toast and scrambled eggs. The smell of the food would wake the others and before long the family was sitting around the kitchen table. Everyone drank tea poured from a large yellow urn. If there was enough time, Irene would tell her four children, often still in their pyjamas, that they could go back to bed for a few minutes if they wanted.

On their way to school, the kids had to pass through the barrier at the Potsdamer Tor. Bernd, his brother and sister Marita would not stop, but his sister Rosita would normally slow down enough to say good morning to the soldiers. Since they learned Russian at school, rather than English or French, it was an opportunity to practise. Sometimes she brought the guards a slice of cake, a boiled egg, or a piece of bread with honey that she had been given by her mother – she felt sorry for these young men so far from home, and was always rewarded with a nod and a smile. Once she was even given an old Red Army medal.

With the kids at school, Irene went about her chores. She cleaned the kitchen – the breakfast plates, the pots and pans. She washed clothes in a tub in the bathroom, hanging the wet items on a rack in front of the fire. Then she would sit in the living room and knit. Each year she made a fresh set of jumpers, hats, gloves and scarves for her children, from the same dark red wool, all that was available at the village shop. While Bernd and Hartmut gladly wore their home-made woollens, their sisters refused. They didn't want people to think that they were wearing their brothers' clothes.

Irene spent the afternoon shopping. There were two main stores in the village. Konsum Shop Number 422 was part of a national grocery cooperative and was located on Wilhelm-Pieck-Allee, the road which ran behind the church and was renamed after the DDR's first president. It was here that Irene could buy soap and powder, vegetables and pasta, margarine and beer. This shop was run by Ingeborg Tauschke, a tall, friendly woman and an active member of the Socialist Unity Party. Despite the puff pieces in the newspaper – in which locals declared that Frau Tauschke 'has good opening hours and you are served very well', and 'the shelves are clean and always full', and 'there is as much choice as in Potsdam' – the truth was that Irene and the rest of the villagers knew that you could buy the same goods in Konsum 422 as you could in any other shop. After all there was only one brand of washing powder and, one brand of toilet paper, one brand of sausage, one brand of cigarettes.

The village's other big store was known as 'HO' for Handelsorganisation, a state-run general store located next to the Drei Linden on the Potsdamer Chaussee. Here Irene could buy nails and glue, hooks and planks of wood, insect spray and bleach. There was a butcher in the southern part of the village, which Irene rarely needed to visit, thanks to the chickens and pigs they kept at home. As with most shops in the DDR, the trick was knowing when to turn up. The best time seemed to be just after the deliveries were made, at three o'clock in the afternoon or so, but even this was no guarantee that the shelves would be stocked.

When Frau Tauschke renovated her shop, the local newspaper ran a full-page story; a sign, perhaps, of how significant the shop was in village life, and how little else was going on – at least that the authorities would allow to be published. As part of the celebrations, the local schoolchildren were asked to write a poem about the improvements, the best of which was published in the paper.

Most happy are the saleswomen
They have less stress now
Because they don't have to serve any more
They have time to smoke a cigarette.

The family's evenings were filled with cooking dinner, more cleaning up, watching television and bathing. As darkness fell early for most of the winter, the children were typically in bed by eight, allowing Wolfgang and Irene some time to themselves.

Often, Wolfgang would go out for a beer at the village pub with friends, or even with one of the border patrol guards. On one occasion, he spent an evening with a colleague who also lived in the security zone next to the Wall. They met at the Drei Linden and after a few beers they had become fairly drunk. On the way home, they passed through the barrier at the Potsdamer Tor and chatted good-naturedly with the guards. At one point, filled with alcoholic exuberance, Wolfgang's friend grabbed one of the soldier's Kalashnikov and started messing around, pointing it at the sky, pretending to shoot.

Within seconds the situation grew tense. The soldier snatched the weapon back, while his comrade roughly grabbed Wolfgang's friend. The drunken pair were arrested and taken to Potsdam police station where they were separately interrogated. Only when it became clear that Wolfgang had played no part in the inebriated antics was he allowed home. His friend was locked up and, upon release, he and his family were ejected from their comfortable house close to the Wall and relocated to a town far from the border, his friends and his job.

In the summer months, the children played outside while Irene and Wolfgang worked in the garden, growing and harvesting large quantities of beans, strawberries, potatoes, asparagus, cucumbers, lettuce and tomatoes. The chickens did not need much attention and it was the children's task to collect the eggs and feed them. They also cultivated honeybees, who swarmed around a cluster of hives near the apple orchard. The honey and eggs were so plentiful, and so good, that Irene sold what they did not need to the local shop.

The family was not wealthy, by any stretch, but rarely wanted for anything. Wolfgang found steady work transporting groceries to the soldiers at the NVA barracks, and although it did not pay well, it won him the respect of the border guards – a relationship that was vital if he and his family were to remain in the house by the Wall.

Late at night on 19 March 1970, Bernd Kühne was awoken by shouts from next door. Slipping on a pair of shoes and a coat, he ran to the fence and saw, to his horror, that the Munks' old weekend house was on fire. The Wißgotts, the tenants who had been living there since the 1950s, were standing near the Wall, pleading with the border patrol guards for assistance.

Wolfgang soon joined his son outside, and seeing that the guards were refusing to help, instructed him to run to the fire station that stood on the other side of the Potsdamer Tor. While Bernd was gone, Wolfgang grabbed a hose and drowned his roof with water to protect it from the sparks now cascading from the neighbours' property and blowing in the night breeze across towards his 'villa'.

At the fire station, Bernd pressed the alarm button. A few moments later, a fireman came outside and told him that the fire engine was unable to come because it was experiencing technical problems. Instead, they sent word to the Potsdam fire station who took another forty minutes to arrive. By then it was too late. The Munk house had burned to the ground.

Wolfgang and Irene invited their now homeless neighbours to stay the night. Over restorative glasses of schnapps they were told that the fire had started in the chimney, which had not been cleaned for years. Glad that he had improved the ventilation of his own chimneys, Wolfgang vowed to clean them out regularly.

The next day, the *Gemeinde* found a new place in the village for the Wißgotts to live. Once the ruins had cooled, Wolfgang dug up the old bricks that had formed the walls of the Munks' kitchen, cleaned them of soot and mortar, and used them to build a small wash-house next to the lake house. With the Munks unseen for twenty years, and with no prospect of their imminent return, why let such good materials go to waste?

At the age of fourteen, Bernd graduated from the Thälmann Pioneers, and was inducted into the party's senior youth movement, the Freie Deutsche Jugend (FDJ), to which 75 per cent of the East German youth belonged. The majority of those who did not participate chose not to for religious reasons. His new uniform consisted of grey trousers and a blue shirt with a bright yellow rising sun emblem embossed on one sleeve, and a red handkerchief around his neck. In the FDJ, Bernd continued to attend weekly lectures on the virtues of socialism, chanting: 'FDJ members – Friendship!', and was taught new songs to sing. 'Forward, Free German Youth!' was a typical example.

> Forward, Free German Youth!
> Have faith in the party
> Be prepared and determined to fight
> If hazards befall us!
> Our time needs happiness and peace
> Friendship with the Soviet Union!

The FDJ had a distinctly military cast. Learning marksmanship was compulsory, and the children had to take part in outdoor activities, such as clearing up a local park. Bernd hated the special FDJ blue shirt and frequently chose not to wear it. His teachers disapproved of his rebelliousness, but they didn't punish him.

Some afternoons, Bernd's parents took him and his siblings to Potsdam. While Irene and Wolfgang shopped or drank at a bar, Bernd wandered the streets with his brother and sisters, or with a friend. His favourite activity was collecting stickers found on West German cars parked in-between the more ubiquitous DDR Trabbis. Making sure that nobody was looking, Bernd would peel off the sticker − advertising Esso, or Dunlop, or Beck's − and hide it in his pocket. Later he would add them to his collection on his bedroom wall. Bernd loved West Germany and dreamed of moving there. He was caught only once, arrested by the police and taken in for questioning. When his parents heard what had happened they said, 'Never do it again.' Their scolding scared him much less than the police had.

In order to purchase better quality, less readily available items − jeans, the latest chart hits − Bernd would often stand in line for over an hour to purchase whatever was available. If he didn't like it, he could always swap it later with a friend.

When Bernd asked his parents, as he frequently did, why they hadn't fled to the West when they'd had the opportunity, before the Wall was built − after all, they could have simply walked across the frozen lake − his mother would say, 'We didn't think the Wall would last so long', and his father would snap. 'Life isn't so bad in Groß Glienicke,' he'd say, urging Bernd to 'make the best of things'.

Since the creation of West Germany in 1949, its leaders had consistently asserted that they did not recognise the country to their east. Instead, their constitution was based on the premise that the East would one day rejoin the rest of Germany. Consequently the DDR was not recognised as a country by the USA, UK, France and other Western powers either. It also meant that neither Germany was a member of the United Nations.

This impasse began to change in 1969 when Willy Brandt, the former mayor of West Berlin, was elected chancellor of West Germany. Calling for a *Neue Ostpolitik* he argued that a 'normalisation' between the two halves of Germany would benefit those wishing to see their families, it would help trade, and it would reduce international tensions.

On 12 August 1970, Brandt flew to Russia and signed the Treaty of Moscow, acknowledging the borders between East and West Germany and renouncing the use of force. A few months later, on 7 December, he signed another treaty, this time in Warsaw, finally recognising the borders between Germany and Poland that had been settled at the Potsdam Conference. These two agreements were ratified by the West German parliament on 17 May 1972. Five months later, on 16 October, the East German government announced that anyone who had fled the DDR before 1 January 1972 would no longer face prosecution and, most importantly, would be allowed to visit the DDR without risking arrest.

Then, on 21 December 1972, Brandt signed the 'Treaty concerning the basis of relations between West Germany and the DDR', in which official relations were opened between the two countries, despite stiff opposition from conservative politicians. As a result, both nations now acknowledged each other's diplomatic representatives and, on 18 September 1973, they were both accepted as members of the United Nations. With these improving relations, it became possible for West German citizens who had left the DDR to see their families in the East.

That autumn, Irene Kühne was shocked and delighted to receive a letter from her sister, Ursula. They hadn't seen each other for more

than fourteen years, ever since Ursula had failed to return from her
'holiday' in Dortmund. She and her husband had well-paying jobs,
a nice house with the latest appliances, a modern car, and they could
travel to France, the Netherlands and England whenever they liked.
Ursula had benefited from the economic boom that had blossomed
in West Germany in the 1950s and 1960s. In her letter, Ursula said
that she would take advantage of the recently relaxed travel restrictions, and visit Irene in Groß Glienicke.

A few weeks later, Bernd and Wolfgang were on their way to the
village shops when they saw Ursula, her husband and children waiting
anxiously in their expensive-looking black Mercedes near the
Potsdamer Tor. They had managed to get as far as the border security zone, but no further. Having warmly embraced his in-laws and
their children, Wolfgang suggested that they keep going. Ursula said
that she had never seen her sister's house and was willing to risk it,
but her husband was nervous of the soldiers guarding the border
area.

Wolfgang instructed Bernd to stay behind with his uncle and
cousins and jumped into the Mercedes with his sister-in-law. Taking
the wheel, Wolfgang crept up to the guards manning the barrier. As
he passed by several times a day, they waved him through. They
didn't notice Ursula who was lying on the back seat covered with a
blanket. A few minutes later, they arrived at the house, and the sisters
were reunited.

Despite presenting a united front to Ursula, and proudly showing
their guest around the lake house and its garden, Irene and Wolfgang's
relationship was beginning to fray.

Not long after the Fuhrmanns left, Wolfgang began drinking
heavily again, often by himself. His liquor of choice was Apfelkorn,

a drink made from 100 per cent wheat spirit blended with apple juice which he would sip throughout the day, sitting in his rocking chair in front of the fire.

Concerned by her husband's descent into alcoholism, Irene began hiding his booze – a futile exercise, as Wolfgang found increasingly remote places to store it: the canoe in the garage, behind the fireplace in the cellar, under the beehives.

His moods became dark and bitter, Irene later remembered. At first he berated her, complaining that she wasn't doing enough around the house, wasn't taking proper care of the children, didn't pay him enough attention. Gradually he turned violent. He hit her, threw bottles at her, shoved her to the ground. It became so bad that Irene made sure that she was not in the house when he was drinking or, if she realised too late, would hide in the garage.

Seeing Irene with a bruised face and discoloured arms, her friends urged her to leave Wolfgang. She was tempted, she told them, but what about the kids? She would leave him, she said, once they had grown up.

The Kühnes' situation was becoming desperate. Wolfgang was caught drinking at his new job, driving a truck for the city of Potsdam refuse department, was banned from driving, and dismissed. Now unemployed, he spent almost all his time at the house, which gave him additional opportunities to drink, and to abuse Irene.

Realising that staying at home was not a viable option, and that the family needed another source of income, Irene made enquiries about employment. Soon she found work at the village post office, which was situated on Dorfstraße, in a building that had once housed horses and cows. There were three rooms in all, separated by thick stone walls. In the first was a high table where customers stood to seal their post and stick on stamps. On the walls were notes explaining to the public how they could send mail to the West. Irene worked at a desk in the second room, to the left of the entrance, selling stamps, and lottery tickets – which were popular among young people – and receiving cheques. In the third room, workers sorted the mail.

Irene was also given the responsibility of receiving and transmitting telegrams. This meant she was given a telephone at home. To call out, she first had to dial 81 to reach the Potsdam operator who would then connect her. The network was very slow and there were frequent misconnections. The Kühnes were now one of only two families in the entire village with a telephone. The other family allegedly worked for the Stasi.

When the telegrams arrived at home, Irene wrote them down and handed them to Bernd, who ran them over to the recipient, sometimes getting a tip. Initially, the white plastic telephone sat in the living room next to the television; later it stood on a stool in the corridor. The children were ordered never to touch it. Although Irene could have called her sister in Dortmund at any time, doing so would have been dangerous as she knew all calls were monitored by the Stasi. At best Irene would have lost her job, and her family would have been moved out of the border zone; at worst she would have ended in prison.

Eventually, Wolfgang used his 'good connections' to redeem his driving licence. Once back at his old job, he instructed his wife not to work any more, but despite her husband's order, Irene continued her shifts at the post office. A détente of sorts was established at the house, with Wolfgang and Irene retreating into his or her corner. While the political situation was steadily improving, a different kind of cold war had spread to the lake house.

25

KÜHNE
1975

Bernd had now become a serious runner. He was not only faster than all the other lanky teenagers at his Potsdam school, he was faster than anyone his age in Brandenburg. By the age of sixteen he was racking up times that were consistently in the top five for the entire country. He might even be good enough to make the Olympics.

To be the very best, he was told, he would have to continue training, build up his strength and win competitions. If he managed all that then, at the age of eighteen, he would attend the Berlin Children and Young People's Sports Academy. This would be a major coup for Bernd and his family. Students who attended the Sports Academy received benefits that others could never hope for. They were paid in foreign currency and were allowed to purchase goods at the Intershops, which sold luxury items from the West – coffee, electronics, jeans – unavailable at the typical Konsum and HO shops. As a successful athlete, he would be taken care of for the rest of his adult life. He would be given a top-of-the-range car and a lavish house. Best of all, as far as Bernd was concerned, he would be allowed to travel to the West.

Bernd's preferred distance was the 1,500 metres, but he was also quick at the 800 metres and 3,000 metres. He trained every day, lifting weights at the gym, doing press-ups, and running endlessly. Most days he ran a ten-kilometre loop, from his house, under the Potsdamer Tor, through the Glienicke woods and along the road to the village of Seeburg, and then back.

Bernd slowly progressed to become one of the DDR's elite young athletes. Each year after Christmas, he attended a two-week sports camp in Tanna, a small town close to the Czechoslovakian border. Here he was instructed on nutrition and health management, hygiene and weight training, and watched films of world-class runners in action.

Every morning Bernd took a little brown pill, the size of an M&M. He had been taking these pills since he was eleven years old. His coach told him that it was a vitamin supplement. Wolfgang and Irene not only knew about these 'supplements' but reminded him to take them every day, believing that they would improve his performance and his chance of success. Before competitions, Bernd drank a special vegetable soup that had been carefully prepared by his coaches. The soup would help him run faster, he was told. He was also instructed not to swim before a big race, or to stay out in the sunshine.

Bernd's dream of Olympic glory was part of a wider obsession sweeping the country at this time. Despite having a population of only sixteen million people, East Germany consistently excelled in international sporting competitions and athletics had become a national pastime. From 1976 to 1988, the DDR gained the second highest number of medals in all three summer Olympics it took part in, well ahead of West Germany. This was improved upon at five winter games, with four second-place rankings and a first at the 1984 Winter Olympics. Their success was achieved through a combination of methodical selection of children at a young age, a training programme that was both scientific and rigorous, and the widespread use of doping.

Motivated by material success, not to mention athletic fame, Bernd continued with his schedule.

One spring evening in 1977, Bernd noticed several abandoned sacks of wheat lying in a field behind the village church. Feeling bored, and fancying a ride, he decided to tell his father about his discovery. After all, the bags would be easy to steal, and the family's chickens would be grateful for the additional food.

Having mounted his black two-stroke Simson moped – which his parents had purchased to make his journey to school easier – Bernd set off in the direction of Potsdam where his father was working. It was dark, and cold, and with the wind blowing fiercely as he increased his speed, he was glad to be wearing his jacket.

Arriving in Potsdam, he turned left onto Berliner Straße, the main road heading west through the city, and continued past the Bergmann Hospital, towards his father's workplace. Suddenly, he was thrown into the air. He had ridden into a large hole where workmen had been repairing tramlines. There had been no signs or flashing lights to warn him.

When he regained consciousness the first thing that he saw was his mother standing next to his bed. She was crying. He had been in a coma for three weeks, she told him. He had been thrown, head first, into a stack of iron bars, suffering multiple fractures. Doctors had rushed him into surgery, and removed his left kidney. They had saved his life.

Bernd was stunned. He couldn't remember the accident, and was confused by what his mother was telling him. The last thing he recalled was being on the bike on the way to see his father. For the next few weeks he remained in hospital, unable to walk and groggy from all the pain medication.

As soon as his mind cleared he realised the consequences of the accident: he would never be able to compete again. Devastated, Bernd asked the doctors if there was anything they could do. They said that he had been fortunate, lucky to have survived. If the accident hadn't been outside the hospital he wouldn't have made it.

A year later, after graduating from school, Bernd found a job driving trucks for a state-owned company based in Potsdam. He was soon transporting car parts manufactured at the Groß Glienicke Max Reimann factory as far away as Prague.

Though employed full-time, Bernd continued to live at home with his parents. For entertainment, he and his friends drove over to Potsdam, which boasted a better range of bars and restaurants than Groß Glienicke. One day he travelled with a friend to the Pressefest, the annual party thrown by Potsdam's newspaper in the Pfingstberg park. There, walking across the lawns beneath the old royal palace, Bernd spotted a beer stall. As the queue was over fifteen metres long, he wandered to the front and spotted a pretty girl with blonde hair and blue eyes. 'Hey, doll,' he called out, 'can you grab me a couple of beers?' To his surprise, she replied, 'OK.' A few minutes later they were sitting under a tree drinking together.

They talked for hours, late into the evening. Her name was Gabriella, or Gaby, as she said everyone called her. She was seventeen-years-old, friendly, energetic and fashionably dressed in tight-fitting Levi's and a T-shirt covered by a Wrangler jean jacket. She told him that she worked at a petrol station, and sometimes received tips in Western currency, which she spent on luxury items at the Intershop.

They started dating. Since she didn't have a permit to enter the border security zone, they mostly met at her parents' house in Potsdam, or at one of the city's many pubs. Sometimes they went to the Saturday-evening disco at the Badewiese in Groß Glienicke, which was still the village's most popular gathering place for young people. From the dance floor, they called out for their favourites,

Intershop, East Berlin, 1979

songs by Western groups such as AC/DC, the Beatles, Queen and Abba, as well as DDR bands, such as City and Puhdys. Always aware that there were likely to be Stasi informers in the room, the DJ made sure that there was a balance between the Western and Eastern songs.

As they became more serious, Bernd told Gaby that he wanted to take her to his home, but was worried about the risks. After much discussion, and not a little alcohol consumption, they decided to try. Having grown up in the border security zone, Bernd knew the patterns of the guards who stood by the barricade at the Potsdamer Tor, especially when they were likely to be most vigilant. Taking Gaby by the hand, Bernd guided his girlfriend along the Potsdamer Chaussee, past the entrance to his house, past the Munk property, and then into the Kunows' garden. This way they could avoid having her papers checked. Careful not to attract attention, they snuck along the edge of the property towards the Wall, and then turned left, clambering over the Munks' fence, across their garden, and then across the fence to his own house.

Once inside, and by now laughing with excitement and relief, Bernd showed Gaby around the house and introduced her to his family. Wolfgang and Irene were not too pleased. They told Bernd that if he was caught, it wouldn't be just him who would pay the consequences – arrest, interrogation, losing the house, or worse – it would be them as well. Despite their admonishment, Gaby spent the night at the lake house in the Blue Room with Bernd.

The next morning at breakfast Wolfgang was friendly, asking what Gaby did and about her family, but Bernd's mother and sisters were cooler. In front of Gaby, Irene told Bernd not to bring her back to the house. Bernd replied that he would do what he liked, and told his mother to mind her own business.

Over the next few months, Gaby often stayed at the house, always sneaking through the Kunow property, and always careful not to be caught. Relations with Bernd's mother did not improve though. She would tease Gaby about her appearance or manners. For instance, when Gaby placed her shoes in the wrong place, she asked why the girl didn't know how to behave properly. Bernd defended his girlfriend, but Irene's comments were unrelenting. After a few of these family rows, Wolfgang took his son aside and reassured him that things would get better.

Finally, Bernd had had enough. On the morning of 2 July 1980, he told his parents that 'As Gaby is not wanted here, I will go with her'. He packed a bag, and the two of them left the house. At the *Gemeinde* office, Bernd said that he was now over eighteen and needed a place for him and his girlfriend. The person in charge of allocating housing said that they were in luck. A few hours later, the young couple moved into an apartment on the second floor of the Drei Linden, at a rent of six marks per month.

On 14 August 1981, Bernd and Gaby were married at a civil ceremony in Potsdam. Afterwards, they threw a party in the garden of the Drei Linden which over fifty people attended. To the guests' delight, Bernd played a compilation tape he had recorded from RIAS. It was an eclectic mix, including Queen's 'We Are the Champions' and City's more plaintive 'By the Window'.

Four months later, Gaby gave birth to a daughter whom they named Michelle. The village offered the couple a ruin of a house on Seepromenade, a kilometre south of where his parents lived. It too was a lakefront house, and its access to the shore was similarly blocked by the Wall. As such, it was located within the *Grenzgebiet* and so, even though he had lived within the border security zone for most of his life, Bernd and Gaby had to obtain permission from the Stasi to live at their new home.

It took five months, but on 30 April 1982, their application was accepted, and Bernd promised his bride that he would transform their new house into a 'jewel'. Five days later, before he was able to start work on the house, he was called away to commence his mandatory military service.

In the 1980s all East German men between the ages of eighteen and twenty-six had to spend eighteen months in the National People's Army (NVA). Established in 1956, seven years after Germany's partition, the NVA was the main armed force of the DDR.

Initially, the NVA had been a voluntary organisation since the government worried that mandatory service might encourage young men to flee to the West. Conscription had been introduced in 1962 after the Wall was built and the borders made secure. By 1982, when Bernd joined, the NVA had grown to almost 200,000 men. Uniquely, for the East European countries under the control of the Soviet Union, it was possible to refuse to participate for ideological reasons, though such conscientious objectors would often later experience discrimination.

As a key arm of the government's security apparatus, the NVA was kept under close political control. By the 1980s, over 95 per cent of the office corps were members of the Socialist Unity Party, and all of its officers were vetted by the Stasi. Such political control was considered imperative, given that one of the NVA's key tasks was to prepare for the possible invasion and capture of West Berlin. As part of this plan, which had been developed by the NVA's high command in conjunction with its Soviet counterparts, the main incursion would focus on the fence that bordered the British Gatow airfield base near Groß Glienicke. Indeed, rather than the typical concrete barrier, this section of the Berlin Wall was made of easily penetrable metal mesh. What the NVA didn't know was that the British airbase commander was ordered to offer no resistance in the event of an attack, and to flee the base as soon as possible.

When he arrived at the NVA training camp, Bernd was given the basic uniform, a dark green camouflage jacket and trousers, a green cap and black boots. Having grown up next to the NVA base just north of the village, Bernd was familiar with its culture of elevated security and highly strung soldiers. As part of his training, he was not only taught how to operate and clean a gun, but he also had to participate in political education classes, to memorise yet more slogans, such as 'For the Protection of the Workers' and Farmers' Power'. Most of his time in the army was filled preparing for rapid deployment in the event of a NATO attack; endless drills in which Bernd had to dress quickly, run to a parade ground, and present himself to a supervising officer. As a result, the conscripts were usually on high alert.

Throughout the next eighteen months of his service, Bernd kept his head down, doing what he was told. Consequently, he was considered both militarily competent and politically reliable. On his last day in the army, on 28 October 1983, Bernd was invited in for an interview. As soon as the man entered the room, wearing a long brown leather jacket and a confident, intimidating look, Bernd knew that he was from the Stasi.

Stasi officers were often recruited from conscripts. Such candidates were considered particularly suitable if they or their family members had been party members, or had acted as informers during their military service. That Bernd's father had been a Stasi informer – a fact of which Bernd was unaware – would have helped his standing.

Potential recruits had to be recommended by their military unit's political officer, along with the local Volkspolizei and the chief of the local Stasi. Once approved, candidates had to pass a series of exams, which tested their intelligence as well as their political reliability. If successful, they would then complete a rigorous two-year training programme at the Stasi college in Potsdam.

Mentioning passport control, the stranger asked Bernd, 'Do you want to work for us?' There was no discussion, simply the request for a 'yes' or 'no'. Bernd knew that if he said 'yes', he would be given a nice car and maybe some extra money. What he didn't want, however, was to become one of those people who everyone knew worked at the Ministry for State Security, who everyone feared. People in the village could tell who was in the Stasi. It was how they talked, how they acted. One giveaway was the car they drove, particularly a certain kind of Lada.

Indeed, by the early 1980s, the Stasi had a large presence in Groß Glienicke. Liking the proximity to Berlin and the surrounding countryside, many senior Stasi officers had dachas in Groß Glienicke. In addition, the Ministry for State Security's legal section owned a large retreat on the shores of Sacrower See, the lake located one hundred metres to the south of Groß Glienicke Lake. Here, its officers could spend a relaxing weekend. The Stasi's military section also operated a group of wooden cottages on Bayerstraße in the village, where its members could spend the weekend, albeit in less style than their legal comrades. Unsurprisingly, Bernd was more than familiar with the customs and benefits of working for the Stasi.

With the Stasi officer still sitting in front of him, Bernd made up his mind. He was not the right person for the job, he told him. He didn't want to work for the State Security organisation. A few days later, Bernd returned home to his wife and child in Groß Glienicke.

26

KÜHNE
1986

After his military service, Bernd resumed his job as a truck driver for the company in Potsdam and, during the evenings and weekends, set about repairing the dilapidated house on Seepromenade.

He and Gaby liked to socialise. Whenever they could find a babysitter, they went out for drinks at the Drei Linden or the Badewiese (although it had been officially renamed Hechtsprung, or Fish Jumping, in an effort to distract the citizens from the fact that it no longer had beach access, everyone still called it Badewiese). They also co-founded the Groß Glienicke Carnival Club, a local committee aiming to arrange more events for the village's young people. As its first creative director, Bernd organised a Mardi Gras, a three-day celebration involving dancing and extravagant costumes.

Bernd also took Gaby and Michelle to visit his parents at the lake house. Although Irene and Wolfgang were welcoming, it became clear to him that life at home had grown steadily worse. His parents often argued, or sat silently in separate rooms. Irene later recalled how Wolfgang's excessive drinking, and the violence that usually followed, finally forced her to move out. Bernd's parents were officially divorced in early 1986. With his wife now gone, and his children having moved out, Wolfgang found himself alone at the lake house.

As he was once again living in the border security zone, Bernd came into frequent contact with the authorities. At one point, for instance, he was visited by the Volkspolizei who wanted to know why he had assorted building materials in his backyard. To a suspicious eye, they said, it was possible that he could use the wooden planks and iron bars to climb over the Wall. Once he had explained that he was merely building a shed, the police left him in peace. Bernd suspected that someone had informed on him.

Shortly afterwards, a neighbour who was leaving the area asked if Bernd would like to take on a little job that he would no longer be able to perform. When Bernd asked him what this was, the man said that he was helping the Stasi by 'keeping an eye out for people who tried to escape across the border'. Thanking him, Bernd demurred, and wished his neighbour good luck with his move.

But this was not the end of Bernd's contact with the Stasi. By now, the security organisation had become even more powerful. With a staff of over 90,000 people, and another 180,000 people working as informers – equivalent to one informant in every seventy citizens in the DDR – the Stasi was intent on keeping a close watch on its population. Perhaps because of his refusal to work for the organisation, the Stasi had kept a file on Bernd. In one note dated 24 February 1986, the Central Filing Department reported that Bernd Kühne, or 'K', 'works well and is reliable. He has a positive attitude and takes part in social activities.' They added that he 'is not associated with negative people. K lives within the border security zone. There are no negative comments.' Not content with reporting on just Bernd, the Stasi file provided an additional commentary on his family.

The Ks live in Groß Glienicke. The marriage and family life seems harmonious and orderly. He had a good relationship with his father, who is divorced and lives in Groß Glienicke. His mother has moved away. His family seems to be normal and they are living according to their income without anything noteworthy. There are no reports about his in-laws.

While Bernd was unaware of such reports, he knew that both he and his family – like most of the East Germany's population – were probably subjects of Stasi surveillance. To deal with such intrusion, he kept to himself any criticism that he might feel towards the state, to be shared only with the limited few that he trusted.

In 1987, aged fifty-three Wolfgang Kühne married again. He did not like living by himself, and was eager for company, someone to take care of him. His bride's name was Ingeborg Rachuy, or Inge as everyone called her. She was Wolfgang's boss at the city of Potsdam cleaning department.

Inge was four years his senior and had six children of her own. Shortly after moving in with Wolfgang, Inge's seven-year-old grandson, Roland, arrived at the house. Roland had lived in a children's home in Potsdam since he was five, having been removed from his mother, a substance abuser who had spent time in prison. Roland was allowed to select his bedroom, and with all of Wolfgang's children now gone, he had three to choose from. He picked the spare room, the first room to the left on entering the house. Having spent so much time in institutional housing, Roland made no effort to decorate or to make the room his own. And, with his mother in prison, his father absent, and his grandmother and step-grandfather increasingly incapacitated by drink, Roland was often left to his own devices.

A tall, thin, athletic-looking boy with short dark hair and sad eyes, Roland loved nothing more than playing with a football on the front lawn: shooting at an unmanned goal, honing his dribbling skills, bouncing a ball on the tip of his foot, knee, chest and head, and then back onto his foot. He was often joined by Rex, Wolfgang's brown-and-white mongrel, who eagerly chased after the ball. Even at such a young age Roland's talent was noticeable and it wasn't long before a coach spotted him, and he was invited to play for the village team, the Rot-Weiß.

Over the next few years, Wolfgang and Inge spent most of their time inebriated, becoming almost entirely withdrawn from the world. As his drinking escalated, so Wolfgang's efforts to maintain his villa slowed. Now well into its fifties, the lake house was looking its age. Its exterior needed a coat of paint, as did the windows and the shutters. The garage roof had caved in. The walls of the animal sheds were cracked, the vegetable garden had become overgrown with weeds, and the beehives stood empty.

According to Bernd, there was one exception to this inactivity. One evening, after a day of heavy drinking in which he had stared long and hard at the living-room fireplace, Wolfgang had an idea. Taking a sharp knife to the fake brick wallpaper that still covered the chimney, he carefully removed a square of wallpaper one metre high and half a metre wide. There they were. The blue-and-white Delft tiles, in five rows of six: the child on a rocking horse, the man watering his plants, the windmill on a hill overlooking a lake, the carpenter making a casket, the woman in a large hat walking in her garden. The tiles reminded Wolfgang how much he loved the house; he felt proud of his efforts all these years to care for the property.

Delft tiles in lake house living room

Bernd visited less and less, the gradual deterioration of his childhood home depressing him. His father and stepmother appeared to be always drinking or drunk, and paid little attention to Roland, a fact he reminded them of whenever he visited. Bernd focused instead on his family – Gaby gave birth to a boy, Christian, in 1987 – working hard at his job, and building a new life for himself.

Like many of his friends, Bernd was desperate to leave the village. Ever since he was a boy he had wanted to live in the West. From the programmes he watched on Western television, he felt golden opportunities lay just on the other side of the Wall. He had spoken about his dreams of a better life with Gaby, but he was scared. He had heard of people trying to escape; a few had succeeded but most had failed. He knew that an escape was technically possible, but understood that there were real risks, both to him and his family.

The most famous local escape incident involved a twenty-four-year-old guard from Behrenshagen near the Baltic Sea named Ulrich Steinhauer. Steinhauer had been stationed with Border Regiment 34 at the barracks in Groß Glienicke. An unenthusiastic employee, he had been counting the days until his release.

Scene of Ulrich Steinhauer murder, with Steinhauer's body visible, far left

On 4 November 1980, Steinhauer was assigned as the guard leader at the Staaken–Schönwalde border section, some six kilometres north of the village. There he was joined by a soldier named Egon Bunge, a recent posting to Groß Glienicke. A little after 4 p.m., as they were walking along the barrier, Bunge flicked a switch to deactivate the border communication system and clicked off his gun's safety catch. Steinhauer was startled. 'Don't fool around,' he said, before removing the machine gun from his own shoulder. According to his later testimony, Bunge issued a warning, 'I'm taking off now, throw down your weapon!' and fired two shots over his colleague's head. When Steinhauer did not lower his weapon, Bunge fired five rounds at Steinhauer and then rode his bicycle to the Wall, climbed up and over, and turned himself over to the West Berlin police.

The Stasi's initial report stated that Steinhauer was found dead in front of the barrier with bullet holes in his back and side. 'They were standing in the area of the non-manned towers along the border patrol path. Steinhauer's weapon was not loaded. He did not shoot from it,' stated the report. 'The guilty party, Bunge, was without doubt aiming at him.'

Ulrich Steinhauer's death became a cause célèbre for the DDR authorities, who used it to build a narrative of the West's villainy, and the heroism of a young DDR soldier. The story sent the small village of Groß Glienicke into shock. Over the next few weeks and months, the town spoke of little else, bombarded by successive media reports. There was a ceremony in which Steinhauer was posthumously promoted to sergeant; another in which he was awarded a medal 'for service to the people and fatherland', by the East German defence minister, Heinz Hoffmann. A street in Groß Glienicke was even renamed Ulrich Steinhauer Strasse.

Yet it was another escape, which took place on 10 March 1988, that most impressed Bernd. That evening, some of Bernd's former colleagues were drinking in a local bar when the conversation turned to the West and a trip *dort drüben*, or 'over there'. One said that he knew of a truck loaded with propane gas canisters that they could drive through the checkpoint. The drunker the men got the better the idea sounded. A few hours later, the men climbed into the truck and, with the siren blaring and engine roaring, drove at full speed towards the barricade at the Glienicke Bridge border crossing in Potsdam.

As it happened, the barrier was not properly locked, and, travelling at over fifty kilometres per hour, the truck easily smashed through, narrowly avoiding the alarmed border guards. As they crossed the bridge, a few of the canisters bounced off the truck, crashing into the glass window of one of the guard huts.

This last attempt may have inspired Bernd Kühne, for in the spring of 1989, while having a few drinks at a party in Groß Glienicke, Bernd and one of his cousins decided to see West Berlin for themselves. Around seven that evening, they grabbed a ladder from the garden and carried it to the first inner wall. This they climbed before jumping down, laughing uproariously, on the other side. Tripping the first alarm wire as they crossed to the outer wall, they were seen and chased by a guard. But before the guard could act, Bernd and his cousin were quickly over the second wall. Next came the lake, which at that stage in spring was very cold, and in the water was yet more fencing and possibly mines that they would have to make their way around. Fuelled by alcohol and adrenalin, however, the two men swam across the lake to the West Berlin shore, a distance of around five hundred metres. There they scrambled out at Ludwig's Restaurant, where they were met by a barking dog and the puzzled owner.

As soon as they had explained their adventure, the restaurant owner silenced his dog and invited the pair in for beer and sausages. Hours later, at midnight, Bernd said it was time for them to go home. The restaurant owner was incredulous that his guests would want to return to East Germany. 'My wife will be furious if I don't go back,' said Bernd, nervous about having to swim across the freezing lake again. There was a better route, the restaurant owner told them, over the large metal gate through which the border patrol crossed from East to West. And so, after a few encounters with a series of holes large enough to trap a small bear, and still giggling from drink, they finally made it home, without meeting a single soldier or border patrol guard.

Bernd had now had his taste of the West. What would it be like to live there? he wondered.

27

KÜHNE
1989

On 7 October 1989, a large crowd gathered on the Potsdamer Chausee in Groß Glienicke. Everyone was there: the mayor, the editor of the *Chronik*, members of the FDJ and Thälmann Pioneers, residents, representatives from the border patrol regiment and local media. For today was the fortieth anniversary of the foundation of the DDR, and the mood was upbeat.

The anniversary march was part of a larger four-day 'Festival of Freedom' taking place in Groß Glienicke. According to the programme that had been circulated by the council, the village would also host a 'dance programme for the elderly' at the Badewiese, a mini-football tournament at the sports fields, a concert by the band Take It Easy, along with an 'information sharing' event at the community hall.

Such celebrations took place within a context of growing national dissatisfaction. Increasingly envious of the economic success enjoyed by their neighbours in West Germany, and inspired by the protest movements now gripping many East European countries – spearheaded by Poland's Solidarity trade union – many DDR citizens began to hope for political change. So, as they walked down the main street through the village of Groß Glienicke, behind banners proclaiming forty years of freedom and development, most took part only out of duty.

A few kilometres away, in East Berlin's city centre, the DDR leader Erich Honecker stood on a platform overlooking an enormous parade. As tens of thousands of soldiers, volunteers, tanks and missiles passed by, he waved and nodded. Next to him stood Mikhail Gorbachev, the general secretary of the Soviet Union, officially in Berlin to lend support to his East German counterpart. The tension between the two leaders was palpable. While Honecker believed he could simply outmuscle the country's growing dissent, Gorbachev was urging the socialist government to listen to their people. Warming to the Soviet leader, some in the crowd yelled 'Gorbi, Gorbi, Gorbi' and 'Gorbi, help us!'

For his speech, Honecker shouted into an array of microphones: 'Socialism is a young society, and yet it exerts a great influence on international developments. It has brought about social change and will continue to do so. Its existence gives hope, not only to our people, but to all of humankind.'

But few in the DDR still believed that socialism had brought *positive* social change to their country. Two days after the DDR's fortieth anniversary celebrations, over 70,000 protesters took to the streets of Leipzig, a city to the south of Berlin. This was the largest demonstration in East German history. Angry that they could not travel out of the country and worried for their economic future, the crowd called for political reform. People chanted '*Wir sind das Volk!*', or 'We are the people', a reminder that the DDR should be governed by its citizens, not by a few party bosses. Despite fears that the police would crack down on the protesters, an assault never materialised. The city authorities had been surprised by the demonstration's size, and without clear orders from Berlin, had pulled back their forces. A week later, on 16 October – in what would become a tradition of Monday protests – over 120,000 people took part in the next Leipzig demonstration. The following day, having lost the confidence of his colleagues, Honecker stepped down as head of the DDR politburo. He was replaced by the more moderate Egon Krenz, who now disclosed that the country was facing bankruptcy.

The people were fed up with their government, and protests spread to small towns and villages across the country. Meanwhile, thousands of people attempted to leave the DDR. Pretending to take holidays, they travelled to Czechoslovakia and Hungary, hoping that they might find passage to the West. In Prague, thousands of East Germans climbed over the fence of the West German embassy and requested permission to leave for West Germany. With each day, the pressure mounted on the DDR government to take radical action.

Sitting in comfy chairs in their living room, Wolfgang and Inge watched the events unfolding on the evening news with growing alarm. It was 9 November 1989, and the lead story was a government press conference that had taken place just minutes earlier.

During the press conference, Günter Schabowski, the sixty-year-old Berlin party boss and politburo spokesman, read from a statement and, to the disbelief of many, said that it would now be easier for East Germans to travel abroad. This policy had been approved only a few hours earlier and was meant to take effect the following afternoon, so as to allow time to inform the border guards. When one reporter asked when these regulations would come into effect, Schabowski paused for a few seconds, and then said, 'As far as I know, effective immediately, without delay.' His comments came as a surprise to his colleagues in the politburo and the security services.

Wolfgang and Inge sat glued to the news, watching with amazement, and some anxiety, as their world was turned on its head. At first, the live television feed showed hundreds and then thousands of East Berliners gathering at the city's border crossings. By 10 p.m. a seven-kilometre-long line of Trabbi cars had formed next to the crossing at Staaken, just north of Groß Glienicke. At the Brandenburg Gate in the middle of Berlin, a crowd of over ten thousand cried out 'Let us through' and 'Tear down the Wall'.

Meanwhile, Stefan Lorbeer, the kommandant of the Groß Glienicke Border Regiment 34, whose head office was based a few hundred metres from the lake house, was receiving increasingly frantic calls from his officers. What should they do? Should they let the people through? Should they push them back? Should they use force? Desperate for orders, the kommandant tried to call the central office in Berlin, but the lines were down. He tried the telex and the secure lines, but neither of these were working either.

A decision had to be made. At first, orders were relayed that the border guards should locate the 'more aggressive' people gathered at the gates, and then mark their passports with a special stamp, thus preventing their return to the DDR, revoking their citizenship in effect. It soon became clear that this policy would not work. Many thousands still wanted to be let through.

Calling the border guards in Staaken, Kommandant Lorbeer said that force should not be used, and that the people should be let through. At 10.45 p.m., the gates were opened, and a first wave of people were allowed into West Berlin. Lorbeer then ordered forty officers to hurry to the border crossings where they could lend their support.

At 00.30 a.m., Peter Kaminski, a major in the Groß Glienicke border patrol regiment, received a call at home telling him to come to the base 'right away'. Hanging up the phone, he realised that he hadn't been given any additional orders, nor had he been told the context, which surprised him. Feeling unsure and a little unsettled, he walked outside to his car and was further surprised to hear the loud rumblings of tanks from the nearby Soviet base in Krampnitz. Why were the Soviets on manoeuvres in the middle of the night? he wondered.

At his regiment's offices, he was informed about the evening's activities and told that they were now in a state of high emergency. His first task was to fill out the necessary paperwork associated with this increased threat level, and then return for a briefing. At 1.30 a.m., Kommandant Lorbeer met with seven of his most senior officers, including Kaminski, and told them that, 'From this moment on, every citizen can travel to West Berlin.' He then ordered them to lock away all their weapons, as he didn't want anyone to get shot.

Early on the morning of 10 November, and still watching television, Wolfgang and Inge followed the journey of a DDR journalist reporting live from West Berlin. As images of cheering crowds, modern shops and tall office buildings filled their screen, they couldn't believe their eyes. How had it all changed so quickly, and how would their lives be affected?

As soon as his step-grandson woke up, Wolfgang told him the news. Roland asked his *opa* if they could go and see the lake. Wolfgang said it was too dangerous, the political situation too uncertain. But, seeing the excitement in the ten-year-old's eyes, and after checking the news once again, Wolfgang relented.

Grabbing a sledgehammer from the shed, and with Roland jumping up and down next to him, Wolfgang walked round the house and up to the inner wall. He looked to see if he could see or hear any guards and then, when he thought it was safe, or at least safe enough, and after a brief pause to steady himself, he took a swing at the Berlin Wall.

The noise was frighteningly loud. Surely someone would come to see what was going on. But nobody came and, emboldened by the images he had seen on television, he took another swing, and then another. It was surprisingly easy, and within an hour, the hole was large enough for them to crawl through. Despite the racket he'd made, there was no jeep full of angry soldiers waiting for them, nor was there a snarling German Shepherd – apparently they had been relieved of their border patrol duties.

Now unworried about being caught, they walked across the thirty-metre-wide 'death strip', carelessly leaving their footprints in the sand, stepped over the border patrol asphalt path, and up to the second, taller, concrete wall. The pair were joined by Rex who had followed them through the gap in the first wall, and was wagging his tail excitedly. After a few blows with his sledgehammer, a crack appeared in the wall and before long, they were through.

And there it was, the lake, two steps from the Wall, less than fifty metres from his back door, grey, cold, its surface rippling in the chilling winter's breeze. First obstructed but still accessible in 1952, blocked off in 1961, and unreachable ever since. While Wolfgang stared across the water, still stunned by the tumultuous events of the preceding few hours, Roland picked up a stick and threw it in the water. Rex didn't have to be asked twice and jumped in, water splashing as he paddled towards the stick, clenched it in his jaws and returned to the shore, shaking the water off his coat and onto Roland, who shrieked with laughter.

Sensing it was time to leave, Wolfgang, Roland and dog went back through the hole. Now on the other side of the wall, there were guards waiting for them. The pair were escorted into a waiting vehicle with Rex barking furiously, and driven to the Groß Glienicke Border Regiment's quarters. There they were taken to a small windowless room and asked a series of questions. While it was true that the political situation was rapidly changing, they were told, this did not give citizens permission to damage state property.

Two hours later, and having been sternly warned not to repeat that day's actions, Wolfgang and Roland were released. Just a few days earlier, they would have suffered far more serious consequences. Realising how fortunate they had been, given their behaviour, the pair walked home, chastened but elated.

To reach West Berlin from Groß Glienicke, villagers had to drive to the border crossing at Staaken, ten kilometres to the north, and wait in a long line, which at times stretched for many kilometres. In the days following the first mass border crossing on 9 November, people began expressing their unhappiness that they couldn't have their own crossing in the village. After all, they had been able to walk from the Russian to the English checkpoint in the 1940s, and before that, there hadn't even been a border.

Hans Dieter Behrendt, the officer in charge of the Glienicke Bridge checkpoint, and Peter Kaminski, the major in the Border Regiment, were asked to establish a temporary crossing in the village. Together with the West Berlin police, they surveyed the land and decided that the most suitable spot would be three hundred metres north of the lake house, within walking distance of the entrance of the Gatow airfield.

A 100-metre-wide section of wall that had previously barred the villagers was torn down, and a new crossing was built, complete with sentry post and retractable metal gate. Well before daybreak on the morning of 24 December 1989, over two hundred people formed a calm line in front of the border crossing, chanting good-naturedly, 'Open up the Wall.' They were met by smiling border guards and tables decked with oranges and bananas.

Border crossing opens at Groß Glienicke

At 8 a.m. the barrier swung open and the Gross Glienicke villagers rushed forward, across a fifty-metre-wide wasteland – which until a few days ago had been the 'death strip' – to a large crowd of West Berliners, who greeted them with cheers, shouts and laughter. Television crews captured the scenes: reunited families hugged, strangers danced with each other, hundreds of men and women climbed on top of the Wall and symbolically chiselled at the concrete. Later such people would become known as *Mauerspechte*, or wall woodpeckers.

The mayors of Groß Glienicke and Kladow made speeches as brass bands played traditional songs and people danced in the street. A sense of amazement and excitement hung in the air. At six that night, the police declared that they would be closing the border again. The government had announced that the border would be permanently opened in the new year, but for now, they pleaded, please would everyone return home?

Much like his father, Bernd was unwilling to wait. With a sledge-hammer in his hands, Bernd Kühne walked to the bottom of his garden, and started pounding at his section of the Wall. After an hour or so, he broke through. This was an extraordinary feeling, for a man with no memory of life before the Wall – Bernd had been only two when the first border fence had been built.

Bernd Kühne's child on border path

It did not take long for Bernd to begin marking the territory as his own. His children carried their scooters to the bottom of the garden and rode them up and down the border patrol path. The family took photographs of each other posing in front of the Wall, and of a smiling Bernd leaning out of one of the control tower's windows. Then, using red, blue and yellow, they spray-painted across the inside of the concrete barricade – which only days before they had been forbidden to see – with slogans such as '9.11.1989', 'Viva', 'Peace' and '*Hier ist nicht*'.

For Wolfgang, Inge and many others of their generation, the dramatic changes were received with a mixture of shock and apprehension. What would this mean for their jobs, their houses, their pensions, their food? Everything they owned they owed to the DDR government, they felt. While at times they had criticised the state for its lack of efficiency and intrusiveness, at least they had never gone hungry. Now in his late fifties, and suffering from acute liver disease brought on by drink, Wolfgang was extremely worried.

His son, in contrast, was overjoyed. For Bernd and many of his friends, the Wall coming down meant opportunity, better pay, an improved standard of living and choice: over where to live, what to listen to, how to run your life. He was also thinking about the lake that had been tantalisingly out of reach for as long as he could remember. At last they could swim.

The following spring, Bernd built a little jetty from the shore at the bottom of his garden. The air was warm and the water tempting. Smiling, he watched as his son put on his swimming shorts, tore off his shirt and jumped with joy into the Groß Glienicke Lake.

Otto von Wollank and staff in front of Schloss
(*Groß Glienicke Chronik*)

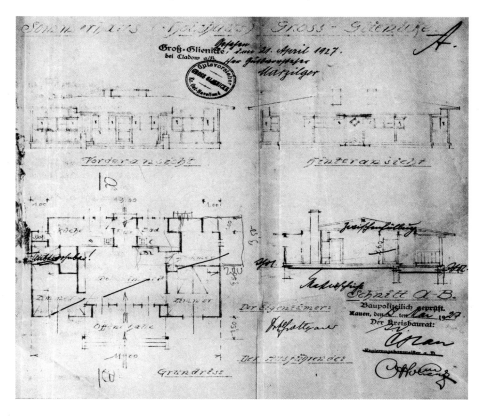

Lake house sketch and plans, 1927
(Alexander Family Archive)

Alexander family in Kaiserallee apartment (Back row: Ernest Picard, Bella, Alfred, Elsie. Middle row: Hanns, Elisabeth Picard, Lucien Picard, Amalie Picard, Henny. Front: Paul). (Alexander Family Archive)

Groß Glienicke living room by Lotte Jacobi, 1928
(Alexander Family Archive)

Lucien Picard at the lake house by Lotte Jacobi, 1928
(Alexander Family Archive)

Robert von Schultz during inspection of Stahlhelm troops, 1933
(Bundesarchiv Berlin)

Left: Meisel family at
lake house, 1940s
(Edition Meisel GmbH)

Bottom left: Gestapo letter seizing
property at Groß Glienicke, 1939
(Potsdam Landesarchiv)

Bottom right: Will Meisel's letter
to Hans Hinkel asking to purchase
Jewish properties, 1938
(Bundesarchiv Berlin)

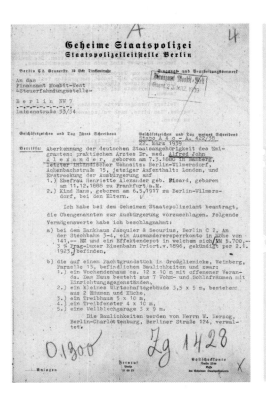

Sozialdemokrat

R. 244 • 4. JAHRG.　　　BERLIN • DIENSTAG, DEN 18. OKTOBER 1949　　　PREIS 15 PF. AUSW. 20 PF.

„Volks"polizisten Opfer der Glienicker Mörder

Von Sowjetsoldaten in der Nähe der Försterei Nedlitz bewußtlos geschlagen und ausgeplündert

Potsdam (Eigenbericht). Die schon zur Tagesordnung gehörenden Überfälle sowjetischer Soldaten auf die Bevölkerung im Gebiet von Groß Glienicke, die bereits zur bestialischen Ermordung von elf Deutschen geführt haben, forderten jetzt ihre ersten Opfer in den Reihen der „Volks"polizei. Eine aus zwei „Volks"polizisten bestehende Streife, die die deutsche Bevölkerung vom Betreten der in den sowjetischen Mordhuben unsicher gemachten Waldgebiete fernhalten sollte, wurde am Sonntag in der Nähe der Försterei Nedlitz von mehreren Sowjetsoldaten überfallen, bewußtlos geschlagen und restlos ausgeplündert. Einige Stunden später wurden die zwei Polizisten von einer anderen Streife gefunden. Sie wurden wegen ihrer schweren Verletzungen in das Städtische Krankenhaus Potsdam eingeliefert.

Da die Sowjetbehörden die Mordtaten der Besatzungstruppe totschweigen und die sowjetdeutschen Dienststellen angewiesen haben, jede Untersuchung zu unterlassen und alle Personen, die über die Verbrechen Aussagen machen, sofort festzunehmen, sind auch im Hinblick auf die neuen Opfer der sowjetischen Bestien Maßnahmen getroffen worden, um das Bekanntwerden dieser Bluttat unmöglich zu machen. Die neuen Opfer wurden sofort in die Polizeigefangenenabteilung des Krankenhauses isoliert, um keine Berichte in die Öffentlichkeit dringen zu lassen.

Westmächte müssen handeln!

Stalins Bündnisangebot an Deutschland erfordert Revision der Politik

...arts (dpa-Reuter). Die Ersetzung des Besatzungs... durch einen vorläufigen Friedensvertrag mit ...deutschland wird jetzt auch von der einfluß... ...hen Pariser Zeitung „Le Monde" gefordert. ...hen bereits in der vergangenen Woche der ...doner „Economist" dafür eingetreten war. Die ...onde" erklärt, Stalin habe in seinem Schreiben ... Pieck und Grotewohl ein deutsch-sowjetisches ...dnis angeboten. Selbst wenn die Zugeständ... ...e, die den Deutschen in der Sowjetzone gemacht ... häufig mehr Schein als Wirklichkeit seien, ...nötigten sie die Westmächte doch zu einer

gegenüber einer Einbeziehung Westberlins in die Bundesrepublik und das Fernhalten Westdeutschlands vom Europarat nicht mehr zu verantworten.

Wenig Einsicht in London

London (dpa-Reuter). Reuters diplomatischer Korrespondent erfährt aus berufener Londoner Quelle, daß die amtlichen Stellen Großbritanniens nicht für eine Revision der Grundlagen eintreten, auf denen der Status der Deutschen Bundesrepublik beruht. Nach Londoner Ansicht kann der Austausch diplomatischer Vertreter zwischen der UdSSR und ...

beeinflussen. Als einzige Änderung in Westdeutschland, die sich unmittelbar aus der Entwicklung in der Ostzone ergeben könnte, werde von britischen amtlichen Stellen ein neues Statut der Westberliner Sektoren bezeichnet.

Spezialist im Liquidieren

Berlin (dpa). Am Montag ist der frühere Sowjetbotschafter in Ungarn, Puschkin, zum Chef der Sowjetischen Diplomatischen Mission bei der „Deutschen Demokratischen Republik" ernannt worden. Auf Vorschlag von „Außenminister" Dertinger hat Wilhelm Pieck den stellvertretenden Leiter der Hauptabteilung Interzonen- und Außenhandel, den Kommunisten Appelt, zum Chef der Deutschen Diplomatischen Mission in Moskau ernannt.

Westalliierte Beamte in Berlin erklärten gestern zu der Ernennung Puschkins, dessen Hauptaufgabe werde in der Konsolidierung der Sowjetzonenregierung und den Regierungen der anderen Volksdemokratien bestehen. Britische Kreise wiesen auf die Rolle Puschkins in Ungarn hin und betonten, daß er aus seiner ungarischen Tätigkeit eine große Erfahrung auf dem Gebiete der Liquidierung von „Verrätern" mitbringe. Im Lager der sowjetzonalen Politiker werde sein Erscheinen ein nicht geringes Grauen hervorrufen. Eine Reihe dieser Politiker täte gut daran, sich vorsorglich zu überlegen, ob sie zu gegebener Zeit ihr „Geständnis" als Rechts- oder Linksabweicher ablegen wollen.

Aus unterrichteten SEP-Kreisen verlautete, daß der außerordentliche Sowjetbotschafter Semjonow noch in dieser Woche zum Chef der Sowjetischen Kontrollkommission für die Ostzone ernannt werden ...

Sie lesen heute:

S. 3: Das Terrorurteil gegen vier Berliner Falken

　　　Schwarzarbeit schädigt Stadtsäckel

S. 5: Der kolportierte Widerstand

Berlin-Hilfe im entscheidenden Stadium

Bonn (Eigenbericht). Während des ganzen Montag fanden in der Bundeskanzlei Beratungen über die Angliederung der Westberliner Wirtschaft an die Bundesgebietes statt. Die Bedeutung der Konferenz ergibt sich aus den Namen der Verhandlungspartner. Von der Bundesregierung nahmen außer dem Bundeskanzler Vizekanzler Blücher, Wirtschaftsminister Erhard und Bundesminister Kaiser teil. Als Vertreter Berlins waren der Berliner Oberbürgermeister Ernst Reuter, der stellvertretende Oberbürgermeister, Frau Louise Schroeder, der Berliner Stadtkämmerer Dr. Haas und der Präsident des Berliner Industrieausschusses West, Baurat Spennrath anwesend.

Die Berliner Vertreter hatten Gelegenheit, den Bedarf und die Hilfsansprüche Berlins konkret darzulegen. Wie unser Korrespondent erfuhr, forderte die Berliner Delegation u. a. Großaufträge für Berlin, die durch Regierungsgarantien zu sichern sind. Ferner wurden Steuererleichterungen als Anreiz für die Erteilung laufender Aufträge an Berliner Firmen und für die Verlegung von Zweigstellen

'Volkspolizei are victims of Glienicke murders', *Sozialdemokrat*, 18 October 1949
(Zeitungsabteilung der Staatsbibliothek)

View across Wall from northern tip of Groß Glienicke Lake
(Der Bundesbeauftragte für die Unterlag des Staatssicherheitsdienstes)

Left: Wolfgang Kühne commitment page in Stasi file, 1958
(Der Bundesbeauftragte für die Unterlag des Staatssicherheitsdienstes)

Right: Bernd Kühne
DDR passbook
(Bernd Kühne)

West Berliners at Groß Glienicke Lake with Wall in background
and lake house hidden by trees (Heinrich von der Becke)

Bernd Kühne's son jumps in lake, 1990
(Bernd Kühne)

Clean-up Day, 2014
(Sam Cackler Harding)

City of Potsdam handing over key to author, April 2015
(Friederike Gröning)

28

KÜHNE
1990

In the days following the the Wall's collapse, hundreds of thousands of East Germans crossed into West Berlin. Some stayed just for a day, marvelling at the luxurious shops and the bustling streets. Others arrived for good, hoping to make new and better lives for themselves in the West.

In the meantime, as soon as the Wall came down, West Berliners began arriving in Groß Glienicke. The locals had hardly enough time to digest the seismic political changes before they had to worry about whether the roofs over their heads would be snatched away.

Long-term Groß Glienicke residents now found strangers trampling through their vegetable gardens, declaring 'this land used to be mine' and 'we need to talk to the lawyers about getting it back'. Black Mercedes saloons cruised the village streets, slowly pulling up to houses as windows were wound down and photographs were taken. Such activities seemed predatory and destabilising. Some of the locals felt they were being taken advantage of by their cousins from the West.

★

The four decades since the war's end had been good for the Meisel family. Once he had finally been given a licence to work, six years after his initial application, Will Meisel had transformed his company into one of the strongest music publishing houses in Europe. His efforts were recognised in November 1962, when the German government awarded him the Federal Cross of Merit, and then again in September 1964, when he was presented with the Paul Lincke Ring. In an interview with the *Telegraf* at this time, when asked if he had any regrets, Will said: 'I am not someone who lives in the past. Yet, as with many others, we have lost so much.' He then paused, and added, 'We used to own a big property in Groß Glienicke on the water with a tennis court and a boat. Maybe my sons will get it back one day.'

Will Meisel never forgot the lake house. In May 1965 he had asked his lawyers to make a financial claim under a West German scheme established to compensate those who had suffered economic loss following the Soviet occupation of East Germany. The Meisels' argument was persuasive: they had purchased the house and its contents from the tax office in 1940; they had purchased the land from the state in 1946; then in 1952 they had been dispossessed by the DDR.

However, on 16 December 1968, a representative from the Düsseldorf-based department that handled such applications wrote back saying that the Meisel claim had been denied. Their investigation had found that the Third Reich had seized the property from the 'racially persecuted' medical doctor Alfred Alexander, and then sold it to the Meisels. 'As far as the files here are concerned,' the bureaucrat wrote, 'there is nothing relating to the plot of land in Groß Glienicke which Meisel is said to have acquired.'

Will Meisel never saw this reply, however; nor did he visit the lake house again. For in April 1967, he caught an infection while attending a spa at Badenweiler, near the French border. He was taken to Müllheim Hospital but died from a stroke on Saturday 29 April. He was sixty-nine years old.

The family was shocked by his death, for Will had appeared so healthy and had continued working until the very end. His wife and sons had been planning an extravagant seventieth birthday party for him that September.

The national newspapers carried effervescent obituaries that celebrated the great composer's life. They listed his most famous songs, many of whose melodies people could still hum, if not sing, by heart. Yet their father's death did not dampen his sons' drive. Over the next few years, they continued to publish Edition Meisel's still popular back catalogue from the 1930s, 40s and 50s. At the same time, they nurtured and promoted new artists through the recording side of the company. At the German Song Contest in 1968, Meisel's artists won each of the top six places. A year later, another of their artists, Giorgio Moroder, released 'Looky Looky', which went gold in France, Italy and Brazil. Soon they were attracting world-class acts, including Elton John, the Troggs, Boney M and Donna Summer. It wasn't long before the Meisel Group was representing songs as varied as 'Stand By Your Man', 'Sugar Sugar' and 'Rocky', distributing the Beatles' catalogue in Germany, and recording superstars such as David Bowie.

They had fulfilled their father's wishes, except for one thing, to get back the old lake house. This is how, a little over a year after the Wall came down, fifty-five-year-old Peter Meisel found himself knocking on the front door of the house in Groß Glienicke. Peter explained to a startled Wolfgang and Inge Kühne that he was the son of Will Meisel, the former owner of the house, and said that he had spent many happy weekends and summers here as a boy. Peter said that the property was his, and that he wanted to tear it down and build a larger house in its place. A country retreat, he said, just like it was for my father. Promising Wolfgang employment in the West, Peter Meisel repeated his claim: 'It all belongs to me.'

Leaving a card with the visibly shaken Kühnes, Peter Meisel walked down the road to the house of Burkhard Radtke, the boy he had played with at the lake all those years before. After a brief catch-up, Peter asked if Burkhard would be willing to sign an affidavit swearing that the Meisels had purchased the house and were the rightful owners. Baulking at the request, Burkhard said it was not how he remembered it. Hadn't the Alexanders built the house, only to have it stolen from them by the Nazis?

Disappointed that he wasn't walking away with a statement of support, Peter returned to West Berlin and, a short while later, instructed his lawyer to explore ways of repossessing the house. After all, his family's purchase of the property from the state, including the land, building and furniture, was well documented. Their property had been unjustly seized, without recompense, by the DDR. It was only fair that the property be returned or, at the very least, that they be compensated.

The Meisels, however, were not the only family to make a claim on the house following German reunification. In the early 1990s, a lawyer lodged a claim on behalf of the Wollank family, arguing that their estate had been illegally repossessed in 1939. Included in their claim was the land under the lake house.

After Otto and Dorothea von Wollank's tragic deaths and the estate's forfeiture to the authorities, the Wollanks were now much diminished. The few heirs who remained had moved away from the area to rebuild their fortunes. Their case was quickly dismissed, however: the courts ruling that they had lost their estate through mismanagement. This was no cause for a claim under German law.

The spring of 1991 also saw the arrival in Groß Glienicke of Cordula Munk, the granddaughter of Professor Fritz Munk, a teacher who had lived in West Berlin all her life.

Born in 1944, Cordula had only the faintest memories of her

family's weekend house. Her parents told her that she had learned to crawl in the Groß Glienicke front garden, but of this she had no recollection. Her father and uncle had advised against her visiting; the house for them was irredeemably coloured by its dark history.

Parking next to the Potsdamer Tor, Cordula pushed through a gate and walked along the top section of her family's lot. There she discovered four men living in little shacks, each no more than 4 x 4 metres wide. They were former border patrol guards, they told her, now jobless and otherwise homeless. Once she had explained her purpose, she walked towards the lake, eager to see the Munks' old family house.

All she found of the old wooden cottage were a few yellow ceramic tiles from the kitchen, scattered and half-buried in the ground. She and the rest of her family had known about the fire from a newspaper article they had been sent by friends in the village, but she was surprised at the extent of the damage. Nothing of the house remained. The old lime tree was still there, however, now grown so big that someone had built a rickety tree house in its branches. There was rubbish everywhere – old tyres, abandoned building materials, plastic bags – and the garden was wildly overgrown.

Seeing a stranger next door, Wolfgang Kühne walked over to Cordula. 'Hello,' he said. 'What are you doing here?' Cordula smiled and joked, 'It's OK, I know who owns this land!'

Having explained who she was, Cordula listened carefully as Wolfgang described the chimney-flue fire of 1970, about how slow the fire brigade had been to arrive, and how the Kühnes had watched distraught as the fire destroyed the Munks' house.

Cordula was conflicted, heartbroken that the old house had burned down but also relieved. With nobody living in the house, it would be far easier to regain control of the property.

Back in Berlin she made a decision: she would build a new cottage in Groß Glienicke. Nothing too fancy; perhaps a small wooden house,

like her grandfather's. As to the four ex-border guards, and their huts
at the front of the land, they could live there as long as they chose.
She wouldn't feel right throwing them off the land. The plot was
big enough to share, so long as they allowed her to live in peace and
quiet by the lake. They could be her tenants.

In the summer of 1991, almost two years after the first East Berliners
had broken through the Wall and thirty years since he had first been
woken by the sound of building work, Wolfgang once again heard
the heavy rumble of mechanised wheels from the lake's shore. Whilst
the Wall had been torn down in Berlin's city centre over a year before,
much remained standing in remote villages such as Groß Glienicke,
away from the lenses of the foreign media.

First the inner wall, nearest the house, was pulled down. The
concrete fragments, now shattered and in pieces, were loaded onto
dumper trucks and removed to Berlin, where they were heaped onto
a massive pile that had been formed from the remains of the former
Wall.

Next came the lamp posts, the watchtowers and the tripwires in
the death strip. Each was methodically demolished, taking care not
to harm any nearby building or injure any tree. The workmen then
addressed the most intimidating of all the security structures, the
high wall that ran along the lake's edge. Reaching three and a half
metres from the ground, the diggers pulled at the long horizontal
concrete tubes from the top of the barrier. Each section thudded
noisily to the mud below, forming a neat row of unconnected tubes,
as if a gas pipeline was about to be laid. Once the tubes had been
removed, the bulldozers set about dismantling the remaining wall.
Surprisingly little force was needed. With its jaw clamped tightly
onto the top of the wall, the machine hoisted the concrete panels

vertically from the ground in three-metre-long sections. Beyond the outer wall, the workmen found a line of sharp metal spikes, as well as bundles of barbed wire, long rusted in the lake's water, that had been pushed in after the first fence had been replaced in the 1960s.

Soon all that remained of the Berlin Wall was the narrow concrete border patrol path, which wound along the entire length of the Groß Glienicke Lake. Someone in authority had decided to leave it, perhaps as a reminder of the surveillance and security measures that had until recently dominated the village and the people who lived here.

All that remained of the lake house's garden – the elegant terraced embankment, the cascade of steps, the pump house, the tennis court, the ornamental pond and the jetty – was a roughly landscaped slope, overgrown with brambles and thorny shrubs, a thirty-metre-wide strip of barren, wheel-rutted and muddy land, a small cluster of thin-trunked birch trees that hugged the edge of the lake, and then the lake itself: unchanging, calm, full of potential.

View of the house from the lake shore, 1990s

In the weeks and months that followed the Wall's removal, the fog of euphoria gradually cleared. For many, the young mainly, the most immediate effect was that they could now travel to West Berlin, where they hoped to find new and better paid jobs, and diverse opportunities. For the rest, the older generations mostly, the impact was less dramatic.

Following the merger with West Germany, the DDR-era stores – Konsum and HO – that had served Groß Glienicke for more than three decades, closed down, unable to compete with the quality and range of items offered by those in West Berlin. In their place new shops appeared: a bakery selling French pastries and cappuccinos, a supermarket offering eight types of cereal as well as high-quality steak, two cafes, a Greek restaurant and a kebab shop. Equally significant, buses started to run again, taking villagers from the stop next to the Potsdamer Tor to Spandau, from where the passengers took an S-Bahn into the centre of Berlin.

Shortly after the Wall came down, the village experienced another loss when the Badewiese burned to the ground. It had been a cultural icon for over fifty years, providing a venue for many of the village's most memorable social events. The official cause of the fire was never determined, though many suspected the owners of arson in an attempt to claim the insurance money.

More pressing was the spike in unemployment. Once the DDR collapsed, hundreds of villagers discovered that they were without jobs. The Max Reimann car parts factory, the border patrol barracks and the Stasi conference centre were closed. The villagers who worked at the government-subsidised companies in Potsdam, East Berlin and surrounding towns and villages also lost their jobs. Those retaining their jobs discovered that their work lives were profoundly altered. Unions were frowned upon, longer working hours were expected, and retraining was often required, something that the young quickly embraced, but the more mature workers both struggled with and found demeaning.

Worse still, many of the benefits of living in the DDR suddenly disappeared. Where working parents had previously enjoyed free childcare, many now had to pay. Anyone deemed ineligible for social welfare was obliged to pay for health insurance. And now that it was no longer subsidised by the government, the cost of food increased, with dramatic hikes for even the simplest items, such as potatoes and rice.

With its beautiful surroundings, proximity to Berlin, and relatively cheap housing stock, Groß Glienicke soon became known as an attractive place to live. As a result, the population quickly rose. Before long, over three thousand people were living in the village. Most of the newcomers had been born in West Germany or West Berlin. These new residents either settled into houses that had been quickly erected following the fall of the Wall, or reclaimed homes lost when Germany had been partitioned.

As part of the reunification treaty, which came into effect on 3 October 1990, it was agreed that property that had been expropriated during the DDR period would undergo a process of *Rückübertragung*, or retransmission. Seized land would be either returned to its previous owners, or they would be offered compensation. In practice, there were many exceptions. If the property had been sold fairly, or if the seizure had been in the public interest, then the current property owner might avoid retransmission. Most significantly, assets that had been confiscated during the Soviet occupation – between 8 May 1945 and 6 October 1949 – would not be returned. In these post-war years 3.3 million hectares of land had been redistributed, amounting to almost a third of the entire country.

In Groß Glienicke, numerous families were forced to give up their homes, often to families far wealthier than themselves, who would use the houses as holiday retreats. Some were able to delay their departure, claiming tenants' rights, but even then DDR rents had typically been far lower than market rates in the West, and once landlords had increased the payments accordingly, most could not afford to stay. From the Westerners' perspective, the houses were theirs, and while the tenants had benefited from decades of subsidised rent, they believed that they had every right to reoccupy their own homes. Given the housing shortages, many DDR residents unable to remain in their homes moved out of the village.

Following reunification, the villagers also found themselves with an unexpected leader. The local Social Democratic Party (SPD), whom many had expected to be elected to office, became distracted by internecine battles. Into this vacuum stepped the party which for fifty years had governed the DDR, now renamed the Party of Democratic Socialism (PDS). Although it was able to muster less than 5 per cent in the polls nationally, in Groß Glienicke the PDS thrived. Supported by many of the troops who had previously worked on the border, they had put forward a young candidate who articulated the ill feeling held by many in the village, frustrated about the changes that had taken place since the Wall had come down. His election pledge was that he would 'shelter' the village from the West and all the unwanted changes. That was how in 1994, Peter Kaminski, the former border regiment major, became the mayor of Groß Glienicke.

One of Kaminski's first acts was to announce that the border patrol path that had previously run along the Wall would now be open to the public. Of course, the owners of the lakefront houses had hoped that, following reunification, their houses would be reunited with the land that ran down to the shore. Now they would have to contend with cyclists and walkers, instead of border guards and military vehicles. The Wall had gone but, in Groß Glienicke at least, divisions remained.

29

KÜHNE
1993

On a cold April morning in 1993, a commanding voice could be heard from the end of the lake house garden. Walking down the sandy lane, past abandoned washing machines, tyres and broken furniture, came Elsie Harding.

She was wearing a black mink coat, a black-and-white scarf, thick black trousers and black pumps. Her curly white hair was cropped short and her lips were painted a bright red. In one hand she held a lit cigarette and in the other a black leather handbag. She was accompanied by six of her grandchildren, all wearing long coats, woolly hats and scarves, one of whom was recording their arrival on a small video camera. As they approached the cottage, Wolfgang's dog, Rex, barked loudly. A few seconds later, Wolfgang appeared, wearing blue work overalls, a thick woollen sweater and a fluffy Russian hat.

'Good morning!' said Elsie, in perfect German. 'I have come to show my grandchildren where we once lived. We don't want the house back or anything'.

'This house is yours?' asked Wolfgang.

'Yes, this was our house . . .' replied Elsie.

'Are you one of the Alexanders?' interrupted Wolfgang, his voice rising with excitement.

'Yes, that's right,' said Elsie, handing him a large bottle of whisky.

'Come in, everyone, come in, please,' said Wolfgang, opening the gate and ushering Elsie and her family towards a front door with a diamond-shaped window.

It had been twenty years since Elsie's previous attempt to visit the house, an attempt thwarted by the Wall and its security restrictions. Her husband Erich had sadly died of a heart attack in 1981 but, indomitable as ever, she had soon returned to work, guiding German tourists around Britain's castles and cathedrals, chain-smoking, recounting the island's democratic and fair-minded values and, when she saw fit, letting her elderly clients off the bus for a toilet break. She had spent the following years by herself in a north London third-floor flat across the street from the house in which Sigmund Freud had lived, cultivating her terrace garden and her memories on her days off.

Then in January 1990, Elsie received a surprising letter in the post. Her childhood sweetheart, Rolf Gerber, had invited her to visit him in South Africa. Rolf's wife, Ruth, had died of lung cancer a few months earlier, and with his own health now failing, he was eager to see Elsie again. A few days after arriving, Elsie had moved into his house in Cape Town. After almost sixty years apart their relationship resumed from where it had left off in Berlin.

They now had time to catch up, quiet moments in which they talked about the old days, and shared their feelings for each other. He remembered the lovely times he'd had with the Alexanders in

Glienicke in the 1930s. She told him proudly about the accomplishments of her children and grandchildren. They took walks together, visited museums and restaurants, and when Rolf grew too ill to leave his bed, Elsie sat by his side, reading stories, talking about the news of the day. During this time, Elsie returned home, to see her family in London. But, before long, she was back in Cape Town.

Rolf's daughter Betty was glad that Elsie was there. 'She really cared about him,' she later recalled, 'and he was very fond of her.' Elsie kept him company, ensured he wore a jersey when he needed one, and that he had the food he liked to eat. 'Thank God for Elsie, that's all I can say,' said Betty. Finally, the doctors wanted to move him to the hospital but Betty wouldn't allow it. Elsie was in the house and supported Betty's decision. Still conscious, though now in considerable pain and waning fast, Rolf retained his sense of humour. 'I had a wonderful life,' he said. 'They put dogs down, why not me?'

Elsie was at his bedside when, on 17 January 1993, Rolf died. A few days later, her daughter, Vivien, flew out to South Africa to be with her mother. The memorial service was held at the Cape Town Reform synagogue. Elsie sat with Rolf's family.

While Elsie felt sad not to have spent more time with Rolf, she was grateful to have been with him for his final years. A few weeks later, after packing up Rolf's house, Elsie returned home to London, to live by herself once again.

Perhaps it was this remembering of past times in Berlin with Rolf that had prompted Elsie. Or maybe it was because she had just turned eighty years old herself. Either way, three months after Rolf died, Elsie decided to take her grandchildren to Groß Glienicke.

★

Inge Kühne, Elsie Harding and Wolfgang Kühne at the lake house

In the living room, Elsie and her grandchildren met Inge. Wearing a flowery housecoat, slippers and oversized round glasses, she greeted them in a friendly, if guarded way.

Inside the house it was dark and gloomy. Neither the standard lamp nor the light dangling from the ceiling was illuminated, while the pot plants and the net curtains hanging from the curtain rail blocked any natural light from entering the room. A threadbare blue carpet covered the living-room floor; the walls were covered with characterless pink paper, and the once-white square-patterned ceiling was yellowed by smoke. A line of knick-knacks and candles stood on the windowsill. Where there had once been a large red table and built-in benches, now stood a plump grey sofa and a similarly coloured love seat. Against the opposite wall stood a television, its screen flickering, the sound almost muted. Around the television stood a large wall cabinet, filled with yet more knick-knacks, ornamental plates and house plants.

Elsie turned to the fireplace and said, 'My father collected these tiles and brought them from Belgium.' Then, pulling out a sepia-colour photograph from her bag, she beckoned Wolfgang over, and told him to '*Pass auf!*', pay attention! As she passed the photograph of the Delft tiles to Wolfgang, she used the informal *du* – appropriate for family, friends and young children.

'How nice, thank you,' Wolfgang said, smiling as he took the photograph, apparently unperturbed by her bossy manner.

'That is where we sat,' Elsie continued, pointing to the sofa, 'and over there was a door to my bedroom,' she said, gesturing to the corner now covered with wallpaper, '. . . and there was my parents' bedroom . . . and there was my brothers' bedroom.' Then, facing the windows with the pot plants, she added, '. . . and here in front of us was a big veranda.'

'I built the wall later, this one with the windows,' explained Wolfgang, somewhat apologetically.

'Can you go to the lake?' asked Elsie.

'Now you can, but when the Wall was here you couldn't. It ran along there,' he said, sweeping his finger from left to right between the house and the lake.

Walking back towards the front door, Wolfgang said, 'This is where Frau Fuhrmann used to live. Do you know her?'

'No,' said Elsie, following close behind.

'Frau Fuhrmann lived here with her son. After they left we took down the wall because the kitchen was too small.'

'How clever!' said Elsie, and then, pointing at the small room by the front door, added, 'This used to be my grandfather's room.'

'This is where Roland now lives,' said Wolfgang, opening the door.

'Ah, hello, Roland!' called Elsie.

Wolfgang closed the bedroom door, not wanting to disturb his thirteen-year-old step-grandson, who neither said hello nor ventured out of his room to greet the former inhabitant.

Back in the kitchen, Wolfgang gestured to a small electric stove in the corner: 'We're renovating at the moment – this is where a simple brick oven used to stand.' He then led the group down to the lake, pointing out and remembering the many changes to the cottage, the pump house and the garden.

Finally, it was time to say goodbye. Wolfgang invited them to come back in the summer, 'when it's nicer'. Shaking hands, they all smiled and said their thanks. Wolfgang and Elsie swapped telephone numbers and then gave each other a warm hug. As they walked back to the van Elsie lamented that where there had once been raspberry bushes and cherry trees, there was now a wasteland of dead grass and rubbish, and then added that her brother, Hanns, would have found the visit very interesting, though he would not have wanted to reclaim the house.

'They have always been thinking', Elsie said sadly of the Kühnes, 'should we renovate, or will those people want it back?'

At the house, Wolfgang and Inge felt relief. They had been surprised by Elsie's visit, but glad that, unlike the Meisels, she had no intention of throwing them out. For now, at least, it seemed as if the house was theirs.

Although there looked to be no major changes at the lake house for the time being, the village was undergoing its own dramatic changes. In early 1994, given that the Soviet forces were now withdrawing from Berlin, and the British no longer wished to incur the financial burden of running Gatow, the new German federal government announced that they would be regaining control of the airfield.

For almost fifty years the airfield had been occupied by Soviet and then British forces. During that time, Gatow had been visited by prime ministers, politicians, and even Princess Diana. The end to the British rule at Gatow was marked on 27 May 1994, with a final royal visit by Prince Charles. The day was commemorated by a series of carefully orchestrated ceremonies and speeches, culminating with a 'Farewell Britain' parade to the beat of a big bass drum. According to *The Times*, the event marked 'the beginning of a long farewell to the city . . . part of the grand retreat of Western and Russian armies from united Germany.' Three weeks later, on 18 June, the handover formalities were complete, and Gatow was officially ceded back to German control. For a short while, the airfield remained open to air traffic, but without the need for another regional airfield, it was closed. Over the next few years, the NVA barracks adjacent to Gatow were knocked down – including the old *Panzerhalle*, which had been a squat for an art collective since the fall of the Wall – and the area was redeveloped as a housing estate.

The villagers welcomed the airfield's closure, and with it the noise and flashing lights of night-time flights. But it soon became apparent that the redevelopment would not benefit them. The new houses were priced out of their reach, and too few in number to accommodate the growing number of locals who had been displaced in any case.

Many of the Easterners felt they had become victims of history. After the collapse of the DDR, they had been expected to adapt to the culture and economic realities of the West. Almost none of what they had been familiar with had survived into the 1990s. There was no more party or Stasi, no more processions or Pioneers, no more guaranteed state employment or housing. Very few visible aspects of Eastern culture remained: the traffic lights' green arrow, prompting vehicles to turn right; the *Sandmännchen*, a character from a DDR children's television programme; and the *Ampelmännchen*, the cutely hatted man that flashed green on pedestrian crossings, who survived only after Berlin-wide protests.

This cultural war expressed itself in Groß Glienicke as a debate over street names. Many of the newcomers wanted to change Kurt-Fischer-Straße – named after the head of the Volkspolizei – and

Wilhelm-Pieck-Allee, named after the DDR's first president. The newcomers, with the support of some of the 'old' Groß Glienicke residents, won this battle, with the streets renamed as Am Gutstor and Sacrower Allee respectively.

A battle was also waged over the monument to Ernst Thälmann, the leader of the Communist Party during the Weimar Republic. Many argued that this too should be removed, but others, led by the radio journalist Winfried Sträter, said that it should be preserved as a reminder of the village's history. In the end, Sträter's proposal won. The tension between those in the village who had been born in the East and those born in the West remained.

30

KÜHNE
1999

Lake house, 1990s

By 1999, having lived at the lake house for forty years — by far the longest of any inhabitant — Wolfgang had left his mark upon the property.

It was not just his clothes in the cupboard, his shoes by the front door, or his empty bottles in the cellar. From the walled-in French windows to the wallpapered kitchen, from the chimneys teetering above the roofline to the lopsided *Wintergarten* that still guarded the front facade, from the half-collapsed chicken shed to the overgrown vegetable patch, evidence of his work could be seen everywhere.

Early on the morning of 25 March 1999, Wolfgang told Inge that he was going to collect some eggs. From the kitchen window, Inge watched as he walked across the yard to the chicken enclosure. Closing the metal gate behind him, she saw him stoop and then collapse. Rushing out, she found her husband short of breath and unable to speak. She half-dragged, half-carried him back inside, and called the doctor. For some reason she did not call the emergency services. More than six hours later the doctor arrived to examine Wolfgang, who was still unable to speak, and said that he might have suffered a stroke, but they would not know until they conducted tests. Shortly afterwards, Wolfgang was transported to the Bergmann Hospital in Potsdam, the same building in which Bernd had awoken from his coma.

Inge phoned the family. 'Your father isn't well,' she told Bernd. 'He was picked up by the ambulance. They're not sure about the diagnosis.' Bernd drove over to see his father. Wolfgang was now conscious, and could smile, but still could not speak. The doctors confirmed that he had indeed suffered a stroke. A week later, on 2 April, Bernd returned to the hospital to be told by a nurse that his father had died. Wolfgang was sixty-five years old.

Six days later, on a mild and drizzly Thursday morning, Wolfgang was buried in the small cemetery next to the Groß Glienicke church. It was a secular service, attended by Inge, Wolfgang's four children and a handful of friends from the village. In all, fewer than twenty people were present. The coffin was lowered slowly into the ground, and then, starting with Inge, each mourner took a small shovel and dropped earth onto the coffin.

Soon afterwards, Inge Kühne decided to move out: she would be unable to look after the lake house by herself. The house was still without central heating and it was unlikely that she would be able to fire up all the stoves needed to keep the place warm. The exterior siding needed a coat of varnish, some of the tiles were missing from the roof, the trees – now growing dangerously close the house – needed to be pruned. So in May 1999, Inge told Roland she would soon be moving into an old people's home in Potsdam.

A few weeks later, Inge set about emptying the house of most of its contents. She sold the beehives and the garden equipment. She took with her the bed from the master bedroom, the grey love seat from the living room, as well as a few personal belongings, and squeezed them into her new accommodation. With the exception of the kitchen furniture, the rest was either sold or given away.

Shortly after his father's funeral, Bernd himself was rushed to hospital. His one remaining kidney had collapsed. When he asked his doctor what might have caused the problem, he was told it was probably the 'vitamin pills' he had taken as a boy. Since the Wall had come down, there had been numerous documentaries on television investigating the doping of young athletes in the DDR, and he concluded that the pills had been steroids or worse.

A month later, when Bernd finally returned to the village, he discovered that the house was almost empty. He was furious. His father had promised to pass substantial savings on to his children; his stepmother had offered him the pick of his father's best suits. It was the last time he visited the house in which he had grown up. He never spoke to his stepmother again.

Bernd contacted his lawyer to find out if he could lodge a claim on the lake house. After all, his family had lived at the property since 1958, far longer than any other occupant. There had been no news from the Meisels since Peter's visit in 1991. It would be a shame to see the house go to ruin.

It didn't take long for the lawyer to respond: since they had only ever been tenants, the Kühnes would be unable to establish an ownership interest. As to who actually owned the property, the lawyer had no idea. Presumably, the local government would resolve the matter soon.

As Inge was leaving the lake house for the last time, she handed the front-door keys to her grandson. 'It's yours to enjoy,' she told him.

Roland – known as Sammy in the village – was by now nineteen and working as an apprentice carpenter in Potsdam. When he realised that the house was his, he invited a friend, Marcel Adam, to join him. Two years younger than Roland and a foot shorter, Marcel was also an apprentice carpenter, albeit at a different firm. They had known each other for over a decade, having both attended the village school.

With his grandmother now gone, Roland and his friend organised their new pad. Roland dragged his mattress into his grandparents' room, along with an old television set and a wooden chair. Meanwhile, Marcel had use of a suite of three rooms: the spare bedroom which had been Roland's, the chauffeur's annexe that had once served as the Kühnes' kitchen, and the small bedroom next to it. Lugging a bed from his parents' apartment, along with some personal belongings, Marcel made the space his own. The kitchen remained as it was, including the table, chairs, washing machine and cooker. The Blue Room where Bernd had slept was left empty.

Having transformed the living room into a games room, with two monitors set up back to back, two consoles and two chairs, the boys spent hours immersed in games such as *Command and Conquer*. The built-in bookshelves installed by Wolfgang in the 1970s remained in place, but Inge's knick-knacks and house plants were replaced by unwashed plates, empty beer bottles and magazines.

Rarely cooking for themselves, the boys ate *döner*, wrapped in folded paper plates, purchased at the kebab shop that had opened in a corner of the old Drei Linden building. They had grand ambitions for the house. While they played video games, they discussed the improvements they would make: painting the bedrooms and patching up the crumbling chimneys, hanging new lights and bringing in some modern furniture, filling in the holes in the bathroom floor — at one point a rat stole the pants Marcel had left lying by the bathtub. They also planned the parties they would host and debated which music they would play. Most of all, they discussed girls. Who in the village they fancied. What it would take to get girls to move in with them.

Marcel, Matthias and Roland

Before long, their fantasies came true. The house played host to huge parties every weekend. Each of the boys had a girl staying with them, they were drinking vast quantities of alcohol, and smoking weed. The only thing that did not happen were the home improvements, although they did organise for a repairman from the local government to fix the chimneys.

When summer came, Roland and Marcel and ten friends constructed a permanent camp at the water's edge, erecting an array of tents of various shapes and colours. During the day they headed out into the lake in two pedalos and two rowing boats, taking food and a large box of beer, slowly making their way to the islands at the centre of the lake, or joining up with friends further down the shore. When not on the water, they took turns riding bicycles down the steep slope from the back of the house, along the makeshift jetty and into the water, or competed as to who could perform the most somersaults off the rope swing that had been tied to one of the lakefront's willows. Towards the evening they would congregate on the roof of the house, smoking, drinking and telling stories.

At night, the campers were often joined by thirty or forty friends and acquaintances. Sitting around a fire, they sang along as a ghetto blaster blared the latest chart music from Berlin's new radio stations, Fritz and Energy. Sometimes, Roland and Marcel called in requests on the mobile phone they shared. One favourite was 'Dark Place' by Böhse Onkelz, a punk anthem lamenting the mistreatment of young people, with lyrics such as 'We wait for death wasting our time doing what you expect of us'. Not all their requests were as morbid. 'Waiting for Tonight' by Jennifer Lopez was frequently asked for by Roland's friend Matthias, and whenever the radio station obliged, the group would cheer and, at the appropriate moments, sing out 'Waiting for Matthias'.

Around the village the property became known as the *Strand*, with people agreeing to see each other 'later at the *Strand*'.

Occasionally the boys organised a bigger event – over two hundred people crammed onto the property for a birthday party held for Marcel's girlfriend for example – but usually their gatherings were informal, and everyone was welcome, providing guests brought their own alcohol and drugs.

The neighbours mostly tolerated the parties taking place at the *Strand*. When the noise became unbearable, Cordula Munk called the police, who would then visit, ask the boys to 'turn things down a bit', and move on. It became violent only once, when an elderly neighbour threatened to hit Marcel, only to be promptly punched by one of Marcel's friends.

Throughout this period, the boys continued to care for the house in their own way. Marcel was particularly eager to maintain a tidy living space. The front lawn was occasionally trimmed with an old mower Marcel had borrowed from his parents. The small pond Wolfgang had dug in front of the house was replenished with fifty goldfish given to Marcel by his father. Roland took on the responsibility of keeping the pond clean and the goldfish fed, often sitting next to it on a plastic chair like his step-grandfather, watching the fish swim round and round.

People who visited the house at this time commented that, while it was untidy and unkempt, it was not a wreck. The walls were intact, the electricity remained on, the stoves were well cared for, the windows weren't cracked and the plumbing worked. Inevitably, however, given their hard living, the boys' jobs suffered. Persuading a friendly doctor to write a note saying they had some illness, they frequently missed days at work. When they did show up, they were often hung-over and unable to perform their duties. Sometime towards the end of the summer of 2000, Marcel's employer threatened to throw him off his apprenticeship if he did not radically improve his behaviour. Hearing that their son's career was now in jeopardy, Marcel's parents told him that if he didn't move back home, they would cut him off.

Realising that it was time to become a little more serious, Marcel moved back home. After living at the house for a little over a year, the party, at least for Marcel, was over. Not long after Marcel left, Roland was dismissed from his apprenticeship. Without a regular source of income the house quickly, deteriorated.

The stoves fell into disrepair. There was so much rubbish piled up on the floor that it was hard to walk around the house. Roland spent most of his time holed up in his bedroom under the covers. Yet when Marcel visited, often bringing two servings of *döner* from the kebab shop, he noted that the house was still structurally in good repair. It just needed a good clean-up.

In early 2003, Roland was visited by representatives of the city of Potsdam's property department. As the city had officially absorbed the village of Groß Glienicke earlier that year, the house was now their responsibility, they told him. The city planned to redevelop the site, they added. Roland could leave the property voluntarily, or he would be forcibly evicted.

Roland realised that he had no choice. The house had been fun, but it was time to go. With the help of Marcel and some friends, he bagged all the rubbish in the house and arranged for the local council to pick it up. He sold what furniture he could, packed his belongings, and closed the windows and shutters. Unsure what to do with the front-door keys, he put them on the kitchen shelf, and walked out, leaving the front door unlocked behind him.

PART V

PARCEL NUMBER 101/7 AND 101/8

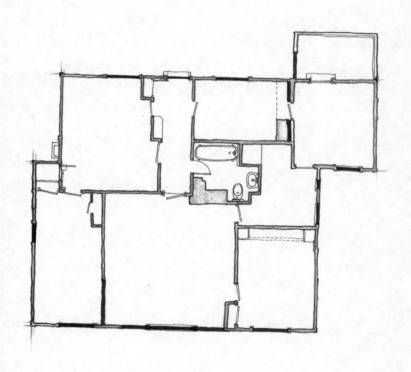

February 2014

Once again, I am back in the village. It is a freezing cold midwinter night. My researcher and I are sitting in my rental car next to a floodlit pitch a few hundred metres from the entrance to the Gatow airfield. From the driver's seat, I can see a group of men chasing a white football across the green artificial turf. We are waiting for the game to finish and, hopefully, if he is willing, for one of the players to talk to us.

I have known for a while that Roland was the last person to live at the house. But all efforts to locate him have failed. He has refused to respond to my messages on Facebook. A note left at his home address in Groß Glienicke goes unanswered.

A contact in the village has agreed to speak to Roland on my behalf. I just want to talk, I say. I give the contact my mobile number, and a few days later, I receive a response. Roland is willing to meet. I am given the address of a Greek restaurant and a time. After four hours of waiting I realise he's not going to show up. His elusiveness makes me wonder if it was Roland who was responsible for the house's dilapidated condition.

Now in the car by the football pitch I coach my researcher. 'When it's time, just try and get him to talk for two or three minutes,' I suggest. Still smarting from being kept waiting at the restaurant, my researcher is wary. 'At the very least we have to establish the basic facts,' I continue.

A little while later, the game finishes, and my researcher heads into the cold. From my rear-view mirror I follow her progress. At the mesh fence that encloses the field I see her stop in front of a tall thin man with dark short-cropped hair, wearing a red hoodie, black shorts and boots. I wait anxiously. Will he agree to talk?

Then they walk together, slowly up the concrete path towards the car park, before stopping underneath a street light. I watch the clock: one minute passes, two minutes, then another. Soon they are beyond five minutes. At ten minutes, Roland's friends, who have been patiently waiting in a nearby car, honk their horn. The conversation wraps up. It has been eleven minutes in all. Way beyond my expectations.

My researcher returns to the car, closes the door and blows into her hands. 'It's freezing out there,' she says with a smile. 'And?' I ask impatiently. 'What happened?' She tells me that Roland was eager to share stories from his time at the house. It is clear, she says, that he loved the place. His years there were the best of his life, he told her.

At the end of the conversation, she reports, Roland apologised for not replying to our requests. 'I just never got round to it,' he told her. He even rejected her offer of fifty euros for his time.

It has been a year since my first research trip to the family's house. A year since the civil servants at the city of Potsdam informed me that the house was set to be demolished to make way for new homes.

Since that time I have become friendly with many of the villagers, recording their testimonies, gathering their memories. I have visited numerous archives in both Potsdam and Berlin. Now, with the help of local historians, I submit an application asking that the state of Brandenburg register the house as a 'Denkmal', or protected monument. In my application, I share what I have learned: how the house was first built, the story of those who lived there, the history it has seen.

A few weeks later I hear word. The specialist from the state of Brandenburg has visited the house but was unimpressed by its construction. Overgrown by trees and bushes, and filled with rubbish as it was, he didn't enter the property to survey the interior (other members of his team looked inside, he says). In a letter, he explains that there is not enough of the original structure left to warrant preservation and that the house itself is of insufficient interest. Apologising for being the bearer of bad news, he informs us that our application to register the house as a historic monument is rejected.

Bitterly disappointed, I turn to my friends in the village, asking for their advice. They suggest that I meet with the Groß Glienicker Kreis, the group dedicated to preserving the village's cultural and natural heritage. Made up of historians, botanists and artists, both professional and amateur, the Kreis had already shown considerable interest in the history of the house (three years earlier, it turns out, they had published a booklet about the history of the Jews in the village).

A few days later, I am sitting at the dining-room table of the Kreis's president, Dieter Dargies, along with several of its members. Having explained my efforts, I ask for their support. I am surprised by their response. Not only do they believe the house to be of critical historic significance, but they are willing to work hard to ensure its survival.

Over coffee and cake we discuss various options. They tell me that it will be hard to overturn the official's report. To do so, we will have to demonstrate not only that the house has unique value, but the effort to save it has overwhelming community support. It will have to be something persuasive, something extraordinary, something that touches people's hearts. They suggest we organise a day in which members of my family join with residents of the village to clean up the house and garden. They call this a 'Clean-up Day'.

31

CITY OF POTSDAM
2003

Before the convulsions of 1989, the local council would have completed some basic renovations in the now vacant house and then offered it to a new tenant. Perhaps it would have gone to a young family like the Kühnes or the Fuhrmanns, or a professional couple like the Meisels or the Alexanders. But this was 2003, and the federal government was too busy restructuring the economy to worry about local housing needs.

Complicating matters further, the lake house had been built by a Jewish family and seized by the Nazis. Such properties were considered toxic. Intractable problems that were best avoided. For now, nobody took responsibility for the house, known only to the local authority as parcel number 101/7 and 101/8.

With the property abandoned, it became vulnerable to squatters. Sometime during the winter of 2003, a collection of Russians, or possibly Serbs, moved into the house. Nobody is clear where these people came from, or how they even found the house, considering it was located two hundred metres from the main road and invisible from any public spot.

When Cordula Munk first spotted the house's new inhabitants, she contacted the city of Potsdam. It took two or three calls, but eventually the city kicked the squatters out. Inevitably they returned. The winters were cold and the empty house had become an easy place to shelter.

The squatters, however, had no interest in improving their living conditions. They smashed the bathroom sink, upended the bathtub, ripped the boiler off the wall and plugged up the toilet with paper and dried excrement. As a result, the bathroom became totally unusable. Even worse, they broke the glass in the ceiling window, allowing rain to pour into the bathroom. A ghostly trail of black mould started to spread underneath the room's peeling wallpaper.

Boys' Room

They also destroyed the kitchen. Inge's washing machine now stood on its side with its door torn off. Dirty crockery was piled in one corner, an orange plastic shopping basket filled with old lamp fixtures in another. The pantry – its shelves lined with yellowed plastic paper dotted with blue and grey seashells – was left bare, save for a couple of pot lids and a flowery teapot.

The squatters adorned the living-room walls with red and blue graffiti: 'Fuck you man' read one; 'Seku is a wild boar' declared another. Someone drew a hammer and sickle and the letters YPA, standing for the Yugoslav People's Army, onto a piece of drywall and discarded it on the rubbish-strewn floor. The small room next to the fireplace was completely filled with bottles, cans and other detritus.

Next door, in what had been the spare room, they smashed the window; broken glass now littered the ground, along with various pieces of broken furniture. In a parody of the two-adult, two-children ideal, someone had drawn a sketch showing two stick figures, above which was written '*Kinder T und K*' – standing next to a house with smoke curling out of its chimney, a little tree and a Trabbi car.

They transformed the master bedroom into a drug den. Flimsy mattresses, piled high with unzipped sleeping bags, pillows, sofa cushions and clothes, all stained with beer, cheap wine, blood, ash and urine – now lay on the floor. Under the window, a small table stood caked in red, blue, yellow and white melted wax, a clay jar containing cigarette butts and a metal spoon stained by heroin's oily residue.

At the back of the cupboard by the front door, three ageing rock stars gazed out from curling posters that had been stuck, probably by Bernd, to the wood panelling. In front of them lay a sea of unpaired shoes, the top half of a plastic Christmas tree, more plastic bottles and scraps of wallpaper.

In the spring of 2004, following further calls from the neighbours, the city of Potsdam finally took action, nailing rough-cut rectangles of plywood over the windows and doors. They also drained the plumbing and turned off the water supply, winter-proofing the property and preventing the pipes from exploding. Finally, they erected a fence around the property, and installed a wide metal gate marked with a large white 'Private' sign.

32

CITY OF POTSDAM
2004

The pulsating electronic music and the drunken shouting of lyrics made it impossible to sleep. It sounded like the ruckus was emanating from the lake shore.

Susanne Grunert, who lived in one of the modern brick homes that had been built next to the lake house, groaned and climbed out of bed. Telling her husband, Volker, that she would find out what was going on, she slipped on some shoes and headed out of the door. The beach parties had almost stopped since Roland had left the previous year, and she had hoped they weren't going to start up again. She didn't have a problem with young people enjoying themselves, but she had a meeting early the next morning, and she really needed some sleep.

Opening the gate that separated her garden from the lake house, she walked down the bank towards the noise, her way illuminated by the light cast by the shoreside fire. Closer now, the lyrics were more distinct, and she was able to catch a few of the words. She heard 'Germany', 'fighting' and 'Hitler'. Six bald men, all dressed alike in shiny black leather boots, green army trousers and leather jackets were standing round the fire.

Seeing her approach, they quickly quietened. She asked them to 'please keep the noise down'. They grunted their assent and she walked back up the slope to her house. A few minutes later the noise started up, louder than before. Sleep was impossible.

Now furious, she rose from bed again, determined to put a stop to it. This time she brought her fierce-looking German Shepherd. As she approached from the trees, one of the men called out, 'Oh, it's Snow White!' 'Yes,' she replied, 'and her wolf!' Seeing the snarling dog, the skinheads packed up their few belongings and staggered south down the shore.

The next day when Susanne took her dog for a walk along the lakefront, she found white swastikas sprayed along the former border patrol path.

The Grunerts had first visited Groß Glienicke in April 1999. At the time they were living in Mannheim, in the far west of the country near the French border. Volker had been offered a good job in a Berlin bank – Susanne could run her insurance business from anywhere – and they were looking for a place to live, ideally somewhere with plenty of space for their then one-year-old son and three-year-old daughter. Seeing an advert in the newspaper, they had driven out to the village and were shown the plot next to the lake house. 'I felt it was a good place to live,' Susanne later recalled. Working with a Berlin architect, they had built their house quickly, and by the summer of 2000 had moved in. It was close to Berlin and a great place for the family to hike, cycle and run.

They had been relatively untroubled by Roland and Marcel's parties, tolerating the noise and the mess of the garden. But they were less happy with the squatters who had moved in after Roland had left. One man in particular scared Susanne. He was tall, emaciated and painfully thin, with a dark brown beard and a tatty plastic bag clasped in his hand. He snuck in late at night, just before dark, and left very early in the morning.

Like Cordula Munk, who lived on the other side of the abandoned property, the Grunerts had made numerous phone calls to the city. When the squatters had eventually been evicted, they were thankful. Since that time, Volker had observed the neighbour's increasingly wild yard, which lay on the other side of his fence and only ten metres from their back door. It might benefit from a little attention, he had thought to himself, and, given that the place was abandoned, nobody would complain if his family made use of it.

Shortly after Susanne's encounter with the neo-Nazis, Volker took it upon himself to mow the lake house's lawn. Soon, the family was taking picnics in its garden, letting their dog roam freely through the overgrown vegetable patch, walking down to the shore for dips in the lake.

When he was four years old, the Grunerts' son, Chris, was given a mini-motorbike – a Yamaha PV50. All he needed now was a circuit. Before long, Volker was clearing the steep bank between the lake house and the shore. Once the ground was free of bushes, trees and other obstacles, he watched as Chris learned to drive up and down the steep, muddy circuit. When he had mastered the loop, Chris and Volker added ramps, jumps and other obstacles. The slope between the shuttered little wooden house and the lake was perfect for their off-road tricks. Over time, the tall metal gate between the two properties, made as it was from fencing reused from the Berlin Wall, was left permanently open. The garden next door had, in effect, become the Grunerts' playground.

On at least one occasion, Cordula Munk looked over her fence and saw the Grunerts' son practising. 'Stop this,' she shouted. 'This isn't your property, it's the Alexanders'.' When Chris ran to his mother and said that Cordula had yelled at him, the two neighbours held an impromptu meeting in the no-man's-land of parcel number 101/7 and 101/8. Susanne said that Cordula shouldn't yell at her kids. Cordula said that she was being antisocial and that her kids shouldn't be playing on land that wasn't theirs.

From that day forward the two avoided each other. Thinking that his family could benefit from the additional space, and that it might be a sensible long-term investment, Volker approached the city of Potsdam to ask if he could buy the land. He was told that it would be impossible, given that the owner of the property was unknown. Despite the city's rejection, and the argument with the neighbour, he continued to mow the grass and to use the property for his garden furniture.

The house itself remained untouched. It was around this time that a new tenant moved onto the plot: a red fox who had found a way into the brick cellar through a crack in the foundation. There she gave birth to a litter of seven, emerging at night to scavenge, eager to feed her cubs, seemingly happy to have found a hideaway away from humans and their disturbances.

Nature now took over the abandoned house.

The vixen and her family continued to live in the cellar. A pair of raccoons moved into Wolfgang's decrepit garage. From time to time, an owl perched on a high leafless branch of the dead silver birch, which threatened to fall onto the house.

The flat ground between the house and the Potsdamer Tor became a meadow, filled with tall wild flowers and grasses. Ash-leaved maples and black locust trees spread across the slope beneath the house, reclaiming the thirty-metre-wide swathe that the border patrol guards had cut down forty years earlier. Their long branches now blocked off the view of the lake, their roots criss-crossing the stairs that had once so neatly led down to the shore. The brickwork to the rear of the house buckled with tree roots. Ivy snaked its way up the corners and into the gutters.

The lake house began to fall apart. The shutters' rich orange paint was pale and stained, its surface cracked and flaking. The diamond patterns were now so faded that they were visible only from a certain angle. The paint on the soffit, which ran under the narrow eaves, bubbled up and peeled off, exposing the soft raw wood underneath.

Tree growing through bricks next to the lake house

341

The pointing in the three chimneys installed by Wolfgang in the 1960s began to crumble. The roof, untended for more than a decade, cracked and was vulnerable to the winter storms. When it rained, a torrent of water funnelled from the rusted gutters into the foundations, and during cold periods formed an upside-down mountain range of jagged icicles.

One year, worried that the foxes still living in the cellar might be carrying rabies, Volker Grunert called a local hunter to take care of the 'problem'. The hunter was unsuccessful: the foxes fled and the hunter was himself arrested after a neighbour called the police saying that they had heard an illegal firearm being used in the village.

Later that night, the foxes returned to their den in the cellar. For the time being they would continue as the custodians of the lake house.

As the house fell into dereliction, the village around it grew prettier by the day. Inspired by the rise of the Green movement, the governments of Berlin and Potsdam now agreed to clean up the lake with federal support. Starting in 1994, local volunteers and government workers began clearing the lake of refuse – oil drums, asbestos tiles, lead piping, barbed wire – which the DDR authorities had dumped into the water. The West German Army deployed frogmen who defused and removed the mines that still littered the shallow lake bed. Next, the Spandau district of Berlin – whose boundary stretched to the eastern side of the lake – paid millions of euros to remove thousands of tons of algae from the lake's surface, before pumping oxygen into the waters through long plastic pipes. Soon after that native fish species were reintroduced, carp and pike among them, establishing a healthy population within a couple of years. The results were miraculous, with the Groß Glienicke Lake eventually declared one of the cleanest lakes in Europe.

This environmental push was mirrored in other local projects. The massive military training grounds at Döberitzer Heath, some 3,400 hectares of marsh, shrubland and forest, which had housed the Olympic Village in the 1930s and later the Soviet Army, was purchased by an environmental documentary-maker, cleared of ordnance, and converted into a park. In 2008, European bison were released, the first to roam the woods around Groß Glienicke for over a hundred years, as were a herd of Przewalski's horses, which in 1969 had been declared extinct in the wild.

To many, it appeared as if balance was returning to the area.

By 2012, the village population had grown to more than four thousand people, with over half of that number hailing from the former West Germany.

At the start of the twentieth century, Groß Glienicke was largely split into two distinct groups: the independent farmers and those who lived and worked on the estate. Then, in the 1920s, a third group was added: the affluent weekenders from Berlin. By the 1960s, the villagers could be divided according to their political affiliations. Half-a-century later, the groups were harder to discern. East Germans mixed with West Berliners, a new generation emerged unaware of their country's complex history.

Much like its residents, the village's housing stock had also diversified. Many of the modest wooden homes and stone buildings from the 1930s were still standing, often next to ugly concrete tower blocks built during the DDR period. And now alongside these, were giant architectural marvels made of steel and glass, rising up along the lake's edge.

Groß Glienicke had become an attractive destination once again. Thousands of day-trippers travelled down from Berlin, eager to get away from the city and to have access to the cleaned-up lake. The lakeside trail created from the former border patrol path became heavily used, often congested by dog walkers, cyclists, runners and families pushing buggies during the summer months.

It was around this time that a few of the original lakeside homeowners became agitated. They pointed out that when their families had purchased the properties, in the 1920s and 1930s, their land had run all the way down to the lake shore. Some had their homes seized by the Nazis. Others had lost property when the DDR government had built the Wall through their gardens. For many, seeing the public walk across land they considered their own was yet another dispossession.

Some landowners erected 'Private' and 'No Trespassing' signs where the trail cut through their gardens. These were largely ignored by walkers and cyclists, who wandered off the path to picnic, some even borrowing homeowners' boats for afternoon paddles on the lake. In response, several disgruntled residents took to building fences along their property's edge, effectively splitting their land in two: the land above the old border patrol path, and the land below between the path and the lake's edge. A few took more aggressive action, digging up the border path and building barricades made out of chunks of asphalt, dirt and fencing sections from the old Wall. One such barrier was constructed by the lake house. So when bikers and hikers approached this part of the trail, they were forced down to the lake's sandy shore, before rejoining the path on the other side.

In 2012, after years of filing paperwork and dreaming of building a large home on the site of their childhood *Weekend-Haus*, the Meisels finally received the verdict of their claim: they would receive neither possession, nor a single euro in compensation. The state would not compensate anyone who had acquired land during the 1945–49 Soviet land reform, nor would they reward anyone who had purchased property that had been aryanised.

Later that year, the city of Potsdam planning department met to discuss development proposals for the village of Groß Glienicke. Of the many ideas circulated only one gained traction: the *Bebauungsplan* (Pre-Plan) Number 22. The proposal was simple: to knock down the lake house and develop the 200 x 30 metre plot on which it stood for the construction of affordable homes for low-income residents. With little discussion, the *Bebauungsplan* was approved. It was only a matter of time before the house by the lake would be knocked down.

In the summer of 2012, a group of developers walked onto the property. Trees to be felled were striped with paint. The parcel's dimensions were measured and noted on clipboards. The number of houses that might fit on the lot was calculated. And then the developers left, closing the metal gate behind them.

The foxes would have to find a new home.

33

CITY OF POTSDAM

2014

On 5 April 2014, fourteen members of my family travelled from London to Groß Glienicke.

At ten o'clock in the morning, we set to work. Removing the plywood that covered the windows, running power from the Munks' house to illuminate the interior, and loading hastily constructed tables with light refreshments. Before long the locals arrived. Carrying forks and rakes, shovels and gloves, loppers and shears, and pushing wheelbarrows and bicycles, they joined in. Soon there were over sixty of us helping to clear the house and its garden. Villagers and historians, politicians and lawyers, accountants and journalists, all eager to conserve the property's precious history.

This then was the idea, to demonstrate the property's value through action, rather than word. If it was important enough for all of us to turn up, from both sides of the North Sea and a multitude of backgrounds and interests, overcoming searing memories and bitter heartache, then surely the house had worth?

A giant twenty-metre-long skip had been deposited in the garden and soon it was filling up with refuse. Without orchestration, people laboured together. My uncle and cousin wrestled an old washing machine out from the kitchen. A neighbour dragged out old carpets, ably assisted by my cousin's eight-year-old daughter. My father and the village mayor lifted a wheelbarrow filled with bottles and old clothes up and into the container. Kneeling on the ground, with an apron wrapped around her waist, my aunt cleaned a pile of old flower-patterned crockery with the assistance of one of the villagers. As people walked by, they stopped to admire the kitchenware. The designs were DDR classics, they said, and should not be thrown away.

Meanwhile, another team quietly sawed, hacked and cut away at the overgrown garden, whose branches and leaves had grown so close to the lake house's exterior walls. As these amateur archaeologists proceeded, they unearthed treasures: the metal gate next to which Wolfgang had greeted Elsie back in 1993; the flagstones at the front of the house, where Lothar and Sieglinde had broken their wedding plates in 1963; the patio of white stones to the rear of the house, where Elsie's grandfather, Lucien Picard, had taken his afternoon naps in the 1930s. Discoveries were also made inside: in a hole in the living-room floor I found a photograph of Roland, Marcel and their friend Matthias, all wearing what looked like paper Burger King crowns. Others uncovered a newspaper from 1927 stuffed behind a wall in the small bedroom, and then the living-room door boarded up by Wolfgang Kühne, through which Will Meisel had once walked to play the piano in the Blue Room.

By lunchtime, all the rubbish had been removed from the house, its floors swept clean and its windows prised open. For the first time since 2000, it was possible to stand in the living room unencumbered by the fumes of old clothes or dust from decaying furniture.

Now empty the house was suddenly full of potential. A bed could go here, a chest of drawers there. In the corner of the living room, perhaps, a sofa and some shelves, in front of which might stand a coffee table and a television. Maybe a small fridge in the kitchen, along with an electric stove and a washing machine. The walls could be painted this colour or maybe stripped and varnished, as they had been back in the 1920s.

Only now was it possible to generate a feel for the place, its dimensions, its layout; the way that the various rooms worked together. The home seemed much larger on the inside than appeared to be the case from the outside. More than this, jolted into life by the collective effort, and belief, of more than sixty people, the house suddenly felt alive again.

After the locals had left, my father and I took a walk along the lakefront. The border patrol path was busy with cyclists, runners and dog walkers. I asked my father what he thought about the morning's activities. 'As you know, I had my doubts,' he said. 'I came here to support you. But I have to tell you I think it's extraordinary. The people I've met. Their excitement about saving the house.' He stopped, I turned round to look at him, and then he added, 'You can count me in.'

Clean-up Day, April 2014

That evening, over a hundred people gathered in the large room that served as Groß Glienicke's community centre. This building had once been the elementary school, where Bernd and his friends had thrown sticks over the Wall hoping to trigger the alarm wires. There were a number of villagers present, along with members of my family and a handful of local politicians. I had been invited to talk about the house and what we were attempting. I felt nervous, unsure of the response, eager to strike the right tone.

Beside me stood Winfried Sträter, the village's deputy mayor, who was giving a presentation on the fate of the Jews in the village. From the loudspeakers we heard the voice of Adolf Hitler and then that of Heinrich Himmler, both declaring that the Jews must be exterminated for the greater good of Germany.

Once the recordings ended, the deputy mayor explained that these facts would have been suppressed in Groß Glienicke during the DDR years. The authorities maintained that West Germany alone was responsible for the horrors of the Third Reich. After all, how could the DDR, built on a staunch anti-fascist foundation, be home to Nazis? I was impressed that he should play these audio files to this gathering, made up as it was of former DDR citizens and Jewish refugees. I was also shocked that, seventy years after the war's end, I considered such a move to be bold.

Then it was my turn. As my words were translated by one of my village friends, I ran through a slide show: pictures of my family's time during the 1930s, sketches of the house and floor plans. At one point, when a photograph appeared of a young lady dressed in white – white trousers, a white blouse and white shoes – someone from the crowd called out, 'Who's that?' Before I had a chance to answer, my father stood up.

'That's my mother, Elsie,' he said in German.

Nobody spoke for a moment, and then somebody asked, 'You speak German?'

'Of course,' said my father, then adding, demurely, 'though not very well.' Various people called out that he spoke beautifully. They encouraged him to continue.

And I realised that something had changed, something real. A warmth had crept into the crowd, a togetherness. There was no longer a sense of us and them: of villagers and city folk, of Germans and English, of persecutors and victims. For the first time, the people in the room seemed to recognise that we were all families of Germany.

In the days following the Clean-up Day, numerous articles appeared not only in the Potsdam and Berlin newspapers, but also in national papers, such as the *Frankfurter Allgemeine Zeitung*. Through emails and telephone calls, the locals told me that the politicians had been overwhelmed by the Clean-up Day, the fact that so many family members had flown in from England, and that such a large number of the villagers had taken part. More than this, they were taken by the story of the house itself, seeing it as a rare opportunity for commemoration, as well as reconciliation.

On 7 May 2014, the city of Potsdam legislature met to discuss what they were now calling the 'Alexander Haus'. After a positive discussion they voted unanimously to support the following resolution:

7.23 Alexander Haus

The city assembly of the State Capital Potsdam recognises the efforts to preserve the Alexander Haus on Groß Glienicke Lake and to revive it as a place of commemoration of the German-Jewish history, the reconciliation and meetings. The State Capital Potsdam will support the aim to make the Alexander Haus open to the public as a place of commemoration on the shores of Groß Glienicke Lake.

Realising that someone would have to assume responsibility for the property, if and when it was saved, a group formed of members of my family and representatives from the village set up a charity, registered in Germany for just such a purpose, called 'Alexander Haus'. Shortly afterwards we received a warm letter from the mayor of Potsdam, in which he added his support to the project.

Yet we still lacked the *Denkmal*, or monument status, for the house. Without that, it would be impossible to guarantee the protection of the house in the long term and next to impossible to raise the funds necessary to restore it.

Nevertheless, we hired an architect who produced a thorough report detailing the architectural history and context of the house, and listing its original features, as well as those that had either been altered or required replacement. To his surprise, he wrote, the house was in better structural condition than anticipated. Together with this report, we included newspaper articles that described the overwhelming community and family support as demonstrated by the Clean-up Day, along with letters of endorsement from the city of Potsdam, and submitted the package to the State of Brandenburg authorities.

And then we waited.

EPILOGUE

A few months later, on 27 August 2014, I returned to Berlin once more, and to the house. Dressed in a navy-blue suit and white shirt, I stood on the newly revealed front patio, anxiously waiting for the event to begin.

Gathered around me were local residents, politicians and representatives of the Groß Glienicker Kreis. We were joined by members of the Potsdam and Berlin media. Today was officially a press conference, but to me it meant something far more. After introductions had been made, I walked over to the front door, carrying a hammer and two nails. Next to me was the representative from Potsdam's historic preservation department. With our bald heads, stubbled chins, dark suits and stocky bodies, we looked absurdly similar, brothers even.

As the preservationist held a thin white metal tile against the wooden siding, I hammered in the nails. On the tile was a blue shield and the word '*Denkmal*', the official sign that the state of Brandenburg had entered the house onto its list of protected buildings. The house had been saved.

Denkmal ceremony, August 2014

I had, by this point, spent months in the village, interviewing scores of people and reading the testimonies of many more. I had studied old architectural drawings and planning files. I had broken into the house and investigated its darkest corners, searching for clues to its past. And with village residents and members of my family, I had helped clean the house from years of neglect and decay. I knew these walls so well now – but perhaps not well enough.

Soon after the house received monument status, I was speaking to a neighbour and confessed that I had not yet been out on the water. He was shocked – surprised. Laughing, he offered me the use of his boat – 'You'll have to row,' he said, 'but it's worth the effort.'

The next morning, my wife and I stood on the shore. It was a sunny, calm and beautiful day. Large puffy white clouds floated across the wide-open sky, casting perfect reflections on the lake below. Untying the rope that had been wrapped around a tree, we launched the boat. As we pulled out I could see the lake house – dark, decrepit, overshadowed by trees. Tidier perhaps, but still a ruin.

It was, however, becoming easier to imagine what it had once been. The white wooden jetty jutting into the lake. The sandy beach. The children playing in the water. Growing in the shallows was a small forest of reeds, just as there would have been in my grandmother's day. A white-beaked mother duck shepherded her three baby ducklings away from us as we headed into deeper waters. There were no motorboats on the lake, no sailing boats, or jet skis. The water was crystal-clear. A pair of young boys were paddling their dinghy towards one of the small islands at the lake's centre. A family stood on the public beach preparing for a swim. Two scuba divers dolphined under our boat, propelling giant air bubbles towards the water's surface.

After a twenty-minute paddle, my wife and I pulled up at a lakeside restaurant, the very same place that Bernd had 'escaped' to more than twenty-five years earlier. There I drank a beer, my wife sipped a coffee, and we shared a plate of cold meats and pickles.

I thought again about the first trip I had made to the house, in 1993. On the aeroplane, my grandmother had given me the black J woven onto a yellow silk background. At the time, I thought she was imparting an important message: *This is my history, and this is your history. Do not forget.* But as I had pieced together the story of the house, I'd discovered that Elsie had left Germany before Jews were forced to wear such yellow badges – that she had never worn this piece of cloth. My first reaction was shock that she had lied to me. Then came laughter at her brazen attempt to manipulate me. Now, finally, I understood that there was a difference between truth, and what is true. My grandmother may not have worn the piece of cloth, but she had been persecuted. Her family had been uprooted, nearly destroyed. Her husband's family had lost so many. My grandparents had been forced to start again, to build new lives for themselves – in England. And yet Elsie still felt a connection to Germany. The house was important to her, she was saying, and it was important to us – as much a part of our history as it was hers.

As I looked out over the lake that day I finally understood why the house's inhabitants had all been so fond of it. Despite life's difficulties, despite all the upheavals, it was, indeed, a soul place.

Groß Glienicke Lake

POSTSCRIPT

In April 2015, we reached an agreement with the local authorities: in return for the city of Potsdam handing over the management of the property to our Alexander Haus charity, we would take responsibility for renovating the house and making it available to the public.

We can now set about repairs – fixing the roof and the gutters, mending the floors and the walls, repainting the diamonds onto the shutters – restoring the home to its former glory.

A hundred years after Otto von Wollank's estate had run into economic trouble after the First World War; after the collapse of Imperial Germany, the Weimar Republic, the Third Reich, communism and reunification; after five families had fallen in love with the land, only to be dispossessed; after twelve years of being abandoned, the house at last has a brighter future.

Whatever the outcome, *The House by the Lake* is a story of hope. It demonstrates that while we humans can experience terrible suffering, in time we are indeed able to exercise our capacity for healing. And if we manage that, a century of pain, joy and dramatic change will have had a positive outcome. One thing is clear: a new chapter in the story has just begun. It will be fascinating to see what the next hundred years will bring.

While it is true that the house has now been officially protected, and cannot be demolished or redeveloped, much still needs to be done. Money must be raised to restore and maintain the house, to transform it into an education centre and exhibition space to remember and celebrate the families who lived there: a place of remembrance, reconciliation, relaxation and joy. To do this we will need help.

For more information on the house by the lake, please visit

www.AlexanderHaus.org

NOTES

Prologue

1 'the village of Groß Glienicke . . .' The name of the village has been
  spelled various ways over the centuries. It can be found as Groß or Gross,
  Glienicke as well as Glienicker. According to a note written in 1961 in
  the *Chronik*, the village chronicle, 'Groß Glienicke' was actually adopted
  'because it sounded more official'.

Chapter 1

13 'it was known as the "Ribbeck Estate" . . .' Indeed, only the year before
  Otto's horseback tour of the estate, one of Germany's most renowned
  writers, Theodor Fontane, had written a poem about Ribbeck, who
  lived in a nearby estate, and the pear tree that grew in his garden. This
  poem, which celebrates the charm and generosity of the landed gentry
  quickly became popular in Germany, and later, required learning by
  every German schoolchild. In the poem, once the landlord dies, he asks
  that a pear seed be buried on his grave, and 'From the silent dwelling,
  after three years / The tip of a pear tree seedling appears / And year

after year, the seasons go round / Long since a pear tree is shading the mound.'

14 'three hundred or so villagers . . .' From his travels through the Brandenburg Mark, or region, Fontane describes visiting Groß Glienicke. He mentions the population of the town as well as his visit to the village church.

15 'Nineteen years earlier . . .' Prussian troops were supported by other north German states. The German siege of Paris ended on 28 January 1871 and the Franco-Prussian War finally concluded in May of that year.

16 'Its Friedrich Wilhelm University boasted an impressive list . . .' Later the university would be known as Humboldt University. Since 1901, over twenty-nine academics associated with the university have won Nobel Prizes, including Max Born, Hermann Emil Fischer, James Franck, Robert Koch, Max Planck, Erwin Schrödinger and Albert Einstein.

18 'On 18 February 1890 . . .' The details of the purchase are contained in the files at the Brandenburg land registry, Potsdam. According to the purchase contract, Otto Wollank was living at Yorkstrasse 5 in Berlin at the time, and the money was received by the court on 19 February.

19 'gütig und mitfühlend . . .' This characterisation comes from an unpublished manuscript, *Chronik der Berliner Wollanks*, written in 1978 by Dr Waldemar Wollank.

Chapter 2

23 'Three days later, on 19 April, Kaiser Wilhelm instructed . . .' Kaiser Wilhelm II had taken a particular interest in the modernisation of agriculture. Only the year before Otto's ennoblement, he had ordered that all farms pasteurise their milk in an attempt to curtail an outbreak of foot-and-mouth disease. The information on the ennoblement of Otto von Wollank can be found at the Geheimes Staatsarchiv Preußischer Kulturbesitz [I. HA, Rep. 176 Heroldsamt, Nr. 10775]. According to Harald von Kalm, in his book *Das preußische Heroldsamt*, most ennobled persons in Prussia were military officers, followed by estate owners and civil servants/judges.

29 The *Kaiser Reich*, which had . . .' The official name of the empire both in the constitution of 1871 and in the constitution of 1919 was simply Deutsches Reich.' More commonly, the periods are known as 'Second Reich' (1871–1918), 'Weimar Republic' (1918–33) and 'Third Reich' (1933–45).

30 'More than twenty men had died in the conflict . . .' The War Memorial in Groß Glienicke on Dorfstraße lists the names of twenty native-born soldiers who died in the First World War. This list, however, is not complete, nor does it include those injured. The pre-war population of the village was a little under four hundred adults, approximately 120 were men and 280 women.

31 'Born in 1897 . . .' According to his marriage certificate found at the Potsdam City Archive, Robert von Schultz's full name was Carl Robert Christoph von Schultz von Vaschvitz, and his parents were Christoph Theodor Albert von Schultz (from Rügen) and Anna-Sofie von Schultz von Essen (from Berlin). The marriage certificate also said that Schultz was born on Sponholzstrasse 1 in Schöneberg, Berlin.

Chapter 3

38 'After his mother's death . . .' At this time, it would have been extremely rare for a German or any other doctor to hasten the death of a terminally ill patient. Two months earlier the first ever bill attempting to legalise euthanasia had been introduced into the Oregon legislature, which had caused a storm of protest around the world. The *New York Times* carried editorials condemning the bill and the *British Medical Journal* asserted that 'America is a land of hysterical legislation'. The discussion of medical euthanasia, let alone the *practice* of medical euthanasia, became widespread in Germany only after the 1920 publication of Karl Binding's and Alfred Hocke's book, *Permitting the Destruction of Life not Worthy of Life*. Therefore, Dr Alexander's decision in 1906 to end his mother's life not only ran contrary to the prevailing norms, but

could have resulted in him receiving harsh punishments, from both his medical board and the country's justice system.

39 'Acknowledging his efforts during . . .' Over 100,000 German Jews, out of a population of 550,000, served during the First World War. In 1916, following anti-Semitic accusations that Jewish soldiers avoided battle, the German Army conducted a *Judenzählung*, or Jewish census, that found that almost 78 per cent of Jewish soldiers saw front-line duty. In all, 12,000 Jewish soldiers died during the war and over 30,000 were decorated for their service.

43 'the day-to-day construction would be overseen by the master carpenter . . .' As part of their training, carpenters would have completed a mandatory *Walz*, a year of travelling during which the apprentice learns his trade. These 'journeymen' continued their practice from medieval times through to the 1930s when they were stopped by the rise of the Nazis, who felt that the trade guilds posed a threat.

45 'Following Otto Lenz's design . . .' According to Jörg Limberg, a wooden-house specialist from the City of Potsdam's Monument Preservation Department, the *Wochenende* exhibition did not include designs by Paul Baumgarten, but he speculates that perhaps Alexander and Munk were 'inspired by the exhibition's houses and their special details and gave the order to Baumgarten to design these houses'. It is worth noting that, according to Bettina Munk, her family's house (and therefore the Alexanders') was designed by Baumgarten. It is also worth noting that in an interview, Alfred Alexander's daughter Bella remembers that the architect who designed her father's clinic on Achenbachstrasse 15 was employed to design the weekend house in Groß Glienicke.

Chapter 4

57 'Some, like Einstein . . .' In 1929, Alfred's patient Albert Einstein built a wooden cottage in Caputh, a village four kilometres to the south of

Potsdam. Though they might not have acknowledged it, these professionals belonged to the *Wandervogel*, the so-called wandering bird movement: romantic city dwellers, harking back to a pre-industrial period when life was slower and less stressful.

57 'One visitor was the photographer Lotte Jacobi . . .' Born in West Prussia, Lotte Jacobi lived for many years in Berlin, but fled to New York in 1933, eventually settling in New Hampshire. Lotte Jacobi was arguably one of the most renowned female photographers of the twentieth century. Of the many photographs that she took of the house and family only eight remain. On each she signed her name 'Jacobi'. Alfred made postcards using two of the images and handed these out to his friends. On the back of the postcard was printed 'Haus Dr Alexander'.

Chapter 5

61 'Somehow both drivers . . .' By coincidence, the wife of the driver for Otto von Wollank was the Munks' family cook in Groß Glienicke.

61 'The *Vossische Zeitung* . . .' The *Berliner Lokalanzeiger* also covered the crash, though it revealed slightly different details.

62 'On 1 October . . .' The source for the meeting at Koch's office comes from Landesarchiv Berlin (File: A rep 349/1214/a).

63 'the three children appeared satisfied . . .' This would not be true of Horst von Wollank's heirs. Following his death in 1932, his wife, and later his children, would challenge the will all the way to the highest German court, eventually losing in the 1950s. Horst's cause of death was registered as influenza by the Wollank family historian. A slightly different story comes from his son, Helmut von Wollank. According to Helmut, Horst died because he refused to go to hospital when he suffered an inflammation of his diaphragm. Helmut also confirmed that his father never served in the First World War, despite being of eligible age. Though there are no records to confirm this, it is logical, given his early death, to deduce that he was excused service because of ill health.

65 'An article published in the *Der Stahlhelm* newsletter . . .' A little later, this same newsletter published a cartoon about Ullstein, the company that published Berlin's main newspapers and which was owned by a Jewish family, mocking it for cowardice during the First World War.

65 'we tell our aims with an honest . . .' Quoted from *Anti-Semitism in the German Military Community and the Jewish Response, 1914–1938*, by Brian E. Crim, taken from *Der Stahlhelm* issue 23 May 1926. Later, the Stahlhelm would be criticised by the Nazi Party for not being sufficiently anti-Semitic, even allowing some Jews to be members of this veterans' organisation, despite the fact that their constitution explicitly forbade Jewish membership.

66 'Labourers who lived close to the estate . . .' This description comes from Erich Kurz in a statement submitted on 1 July 1967 to the village *Chronik*. It was later denied by Robert von Schultz's daughter, Katharina von Kitzing, in a statement made on 25 September 1990 (also to the *Chronik*), in which she wrote: 'According to the previous statement there were "*Prunkgelage*" at the schloss, these I would have noticed as I was a daughter in the house. Of course there were feasts but they were family affairs mostly . . . In conclusion it was not the parties that caused the mismanagement of the estate it was the poor profit from agriculture from 1934. Also the German Wehrmacht took away some of the land for the training company for troops in Dallgow-Döberitz. In the end they had to sell it to the tax department, apart from the little lake and the park where my grandfather and grandmother are buried.'

Chapter 6

71 'Many of the country's leading newspapers . . .' In Elsie's home town, the *B.Z. am Mittag* and *Vossische Zeitung* were both published by the Jewish-owned Ullstein company, the latter being edited by Hans Zehrer who was married to a Jew. Meanwhile, the *Berliner Abendpost* was edited by Manfred George and the *Berliner Tageblatt* was edited by Theodor

Wolff, both of whom were Jewish. Many of those writing for magazines and anti-Nazi publications such as *Die Weltbühne* were also Jewish.
76 'Finally, in a carefully choreographed moment . . .' In an interview with
Hildegard Munk, recorded by her son, Klaus, and her grandson, Matthias,
on 3 August 1984, she remembered that a few days after the Enabling
Act was passed a party was held at the Leopold Palace to celebrate the
inauguration of Franz von Papen as vice chancellor. Attending this lavish
gala were the Alexanders' neighbours from Glienicke, Professor Fritz
Munk and his wife Hildegard, who had been invited by Papen. Seeing
a slight man standing alone on the other side of the large hall, the professor
approached: it was Adolf Hitler. According to the story told by Hildegard,
ten years earlier, in 1922, as Fritz was on his way to Brazil for a conference, someone in the military had asked him to carry a stack of pamphlets
to Rio. These flyers described how 'in Munich there is a young labour
leader who wants to combine socialist and patriotic ideals.' Now, a decade
later, the topic of Brazil came up in conversation and Fritz reminded the
chancellor about the pamphlets. Laughing, Hitler said, 'I realised later
that 60 million Germans were more important than 60,000 German
Brazilians.' Hildegard also recalled that it was after the Papen gala that,
like many others, they learned about the killings and the persecution and
that, in 1934, she and Fritz realised their interest in Hitler had been
mistaken: 'we suddenly saw Hitler for who he was, and we were afraid,'
she said. Later, Fritz Munk was told by a party member 'be careful, you
are on the black list'.
81 'A few weeks later, on 4 June 1933, the family gathered . . .' Indeed,
according to their son Peter Sussmann, Bella and Harold has been so
anxious that Bella receive a British passport as soon as possible that they
participated in a civil ceremony at Hampstead Town Hall in London a
few weeks before the formal wedding service in Berlin.
84 'on the history of the village, the Wollanks' lawyer . . .' Erwin Koch
wrote a history of the village in October 1935. His lengthy report was
included in the Groß Glienicke *Chronik*. In this he wrote: 'Compared

with 1838 there is 75% less land in the village being used for farming. The land lost was used either by settlers or for training camps for military. They mostly gave the unproductive land away.' Later he wrote, that the 'settlers had a strong impact on the village'. One result was that the 'village has more income and a bigger budget, but having sold land the farmers' income is less.'

85 'After swapping pleasantries, Professor Munk spoke frankly . . .' This memory comes from Fritz Munk's son, Peter, who I interviewed in July 2014 sitting in the garden of the Munk weekend house in Groß Glienicke. Peter qualified this as follows: 'I don't know anything else about the rest of the conversation; however, I know, from later conversations, that this was an important situation for both men. But as I said, I was twelve years old at the time.'

Chapter 7

89 'finally stood trial at the end of August . . .' The file on Robert von Schultz's time in the SA and his subsequent trial can be found in the Bundesarchiv Berlin (File: VBS/4001006331).

90 'On 2 November 1935, Adolf Hitler attended . . .' The Luftwaffe Museum that is now located at the Gatow airfield contains a useful permanent exhibition about the airfield's history from the 1930s to the present day.

Chapter 8

92 'To memorialise the day in crisp 16mm . . .' In 2013, I was listening to an interview with Bella conducted by her nephew John Alexander, and came upon a passage in which she referred to film that her father had taken in Berlin. After sending an email to my family members asking if they knew anything about this, I received an email from Bella's son Peter Sussmann, letting me know that 'there might be some old canisters in the attic'. A few weeks later the canisters' contents were transferred

from 16mm to digital format. The results were extraordinary: three separate films shot in the early 1930s of the family's time at Groß Glienicke, the quality near perfect, showing the Alexanders enjoying life before the terror of the Third Reich.

95 'In the afternoons, she kept an eye on her grandfather . . .' Lucien's obituary was published in the *Berliner Börsenberichte* newspaper: 'Lucien Picard, 80, well-loved banker and Swiss Counsal to Frankfurt, died, Basel, Switzerland, 22 December, 1935. Born, 25 October, 1855, in Hegenheim, in the Alsace, to Sophia Dreyfus, the daughter of the founder of the Swiss Dreyfus Bank. By the time he retired in 1922, as the managing director of Commerz & Diskont Bank, Berlin, and partner in Lazard Speyer-Ellisen, Frankfurt, he was the "Doyen of German banking".'

97 'In due course, Elsie invited Erich . . .' As it happened, Erich's father was a freemason in the same lodge as Adolf Abraham, a Jewish dentist who, with his wife Anna, purchased a plot in Groß Glienicke at Seepromenade 41, about a kilometre south of the Alexanders' house. Intending to live in it full-time when they retired, the house the Abrahams built was more substantial than that of the Alexanders'. Stunning in design, its garden landscaped by famous landscape architects Karl Foerster and Hermann Mattern, it was featured in architectural magazines. With the rise of the Nazi Party, pressure increased on the Abrahams. In 1936, their only son Hans fled to England with his family. On 3 March 1939, Adolf Abraham died of a heart condition, and in September 1940, after she had been forced to dispose of her Berlin properties under the Nazi regime, Anna sold the house in Groß Glienicke to Friedrich Wintermantel, a family contact. On 4 March 1943, Anna was picked up from her apartment at Georg-Wilhelm-Straße 12 in Berlin and deported, first to Theresienstadt, and then, on 18 May 1944, to Auschwitz, where she was murdered. Hans Abraham died in 1950 and his widow moved to New York where she died in 2004. After the war, the house was first occupied by locals and Soviet officers and then used as a doctor's surgery. Later, the writer Helga Schütz lived at the house with the film director Egon Günther. In the

1990s, Hans Abraham's widow made a restitution claim, but finally agreed with the heirs of Fritz Wintermantel that they should retain the house. The house and its garden are again lived in by descendants of Fritz Wintermantel, have been beautifully restored, and have been listed as a *Denkmal*, or a historic monument. In April 2015, a '*Stolperstein*', or memorial plate, was laid at Georg-Wilhelm-Straße 12, Berlin, in memory of Anna Abraham.

97 'Hearing the news, Rolf now wrote . . .' According to Vivien Lewis, Elsie's daughter, Rolf visited London before the war. He took Elsie to the Café Royal on Regent Street, and asked her to leave Erich. 'I have decided that I love you,' he said. 'Come and live with me in South Africa.' Elsie declined.

98 'The next day, driving a black Austin 7 . . .' In an interview given at her home in London in 1993, Elsie told me that this was their first car, that it had been given as a wedding present, and that they called it 'Charlie'. Later they transported the car to London, but when the war started, because they were enemy aliens, they were forced to sell it. 'We made four pounds sterling,' she said, 'and then we had a very good dinner on it.'

101 'before Henny could leave Germany she would have to pay the *Reichsfluchsteuer* . . .' The Reich flight tax was introduced during the Great Depression in 1931, before the Nazis seized power, to prevent capital flight. However, the Nazi government used the flight tax to force all emigrating Jews to part with the bulk of their wealth. The Nazis put in place a further hefty fee for transferring assets abroad (the *Dego-Abgabe* levy), which increased over time. The Reich flight tax, the *Dego-Abgabe* and other measures by the Nazis meant that emigrating Jews often lost more than 90 or even 95 per cent of their savings in the late 1930s.

102 'in the old Prussian military grounds on Döberitzer Heath . . .' The Olympic Village is still preserved, including the room in which Jesse Owens slept, the enormous swimming pool, the running track and the food hall, and can be visited.

103 'She carried her black Erika typewriter . . .' This typewriter is now in the possession of Elsie's grandson, James Harding, the head of BBC News.

104 'But his wife had made the decision . . .' Later, Elsie would say that if she hadn't made the unilateral decision to leave Germany, her husband would have died in Auschwitz.

104 'They were now refugees . . .' Now in London, the family attempted to assimilate to the new culture. Despite his international renown, Alfred had to retake his medical exams, forcing him to temporarily relocate to Edinburgh, where he took up studies. With her husband away, Henny attempted to rebuild a social life within the immigrant community, and Hanns and Paul started apprenticeships in London. Meanwhile, Bella, who had left Berlin four years earlier than the other family members, happily busied herself as an English housewife. Of all the children, Elsie found it hardest to adapt to the new country. Living in a small, frigid flat in central London, she missed the efficient heating system of their apartment in Berlin. Here, every few minutes the gas fire stopped and would not restart until she had fed the meter with coins. She found the English to be cold and lacking passion. To make matters worse, she could not acclimatise to the damp and dreary weather, and thought the food unappetising. Harder still, despite her efforts to speak the language, she retained a thick Berlin accent and was consequently shunned by the local population who distrusted foreigners, particularly Germans. Her longing for home, especially for the peace and quiet of Groß Glienicke, was only tempered by her former country's increasing belligerence. Elsie worried that her adopted country and that of birth might soon be at war. On 20 September 1937, Elsie gave birth to Frank Alexander Hirschowitz, my father. Later, his last name was changed to Harding. Then, on 19 July 1940, Erich was arrested and interned under Prime Minister Winston Churchill's policy of rounding up all potential 'enemy aliens'. Convinced that the safest solution was to send Frank overseas with his nanny, Elsie wrote to Erich suggesting that she purchase boat tickets for the USA. At

first Erich resisted, but in the end bowed to his wife. In a letter of 26 July 1940 he wrote, 'Give endless kisses to Frank, let's pray he gets to the USA all right and let's hope with God's help we will see him again in our home.' A week later, on 4 August, Elsie replied, updating him on the travel arrangements: 'I do hope we have done the right thing. It breaks my heart, but I still think it is for the best.' Torn between protecting her son and keeping him close, Elsie did not know what to do. Her son's reluctance did not help. When she started packing, Frank told her, 'I don't want to go on the boat, Mami.' It was 'heartbreaking', she wrote to Erich. Then the boat was delayed, and finally, after 'spending the day crying', she returned the tickets to Cunard and was refunded her money, having told them that she 'could not go through with it'. Once it had been agreed that Frank would not be sent to the USA, Elsie wanted to take him to Erich, so that he could see that his son had remained. It was difficult to gain a permit to visit the internment camps, so Elsie asked her doctor to teach her how to faint convincingly. Once she felt she had mastered the technique, she visited the Home Office and, having demonstrated her frail state, secured the necessary paperwork to visit her husband. After a long train journey, a bus ride and an arduous walk, she and Frank found themselves outside the camp in Prees Heath near Crewe. Soon after, Erich appeared, and through tears and uttering thanks, he was able to touch his son's little fingers through the barbed wire.

Chapter 9

112 'Five foot eight and of medium build . . .' Details about Will Meisel are included in the *Fragebogen* he filled out in 1945, and are available at the Landesarchiv Berlin.

112 'The sub-lease was for three years . . .' A copy of this lease along with the inventory and other legal documents related to Alfred Alexander and the house are available at the Landesarchiv in Potsdam (Files: Rep 36A/G52, Rep 36A/nr 430, and 2aIII/F18613).

113 'August Wilhelm Meisel was born . . .' A number of files on Will and Eliza Meisel exist at the Bundesarchiv Berlin (Files: R55/20207, R/9361/V Signature 81419, R/9361/V Signature 147724, R/9361/V Signature 110383, R/9361/V Signature 128869).

114 'Shortly afterwards, one of Will's composer friends . . .' This conversation was retold in the Edition Meisel publication *100 Years of Will Meisel*.

117 'Several were huge hits . . . Otto Wallburg . . .' Otto Wallburg (also known as Otto Wasserzug) was one of the most famous actors in Germany's silent and early sound film era. In 1933, he fled Germany for Austria. According to the Yad Vashem Victim Database, in 1940 he was picked up in the Netherlands, deported to Westerbork transit camp and later deported to Theresienstadt on 31 July 1944, and then on to Auschwitz on 29 October 1944, where he was murdered at the age of fifty-five.

117 'given that over 80 per cent of his composers were Jewish . . .' What happened to Meisel's Jewish musicians? Willy Rosen escaped to Netherlands, was then deported and murdered in Auschwitz on 29 September 1944. Kurt Schwabach fled to Palestine. Jean Aberbach emigrated to the USA and started his own publishing company, Hill and Range, recording songs by artists including Elvis Presley. Harry Hilm fled to the Netherlands, hid during the war and continued writing after its conclusion. Later, Hilm sued Meisel for unpaid royalties. The files on this suit are at the Landesarchiv Berlin (File: C Rep 120/899). In a telephone interview, Charlie Hilm – Harry Hilm's son – told me that his father left Germany without help from anyone, 'everyone was on their own'. Friedrich Schwarz fled to France where he penned the song 'I Have No Homeland' with the subtitle 'Jewish tango'. Hans Lengsfelder moved to the USA in 1932, adopting the pseudonym Harry Lenk. Harry Waldau was deported on 2 March 1943 from Berlin on Transport 32 and murdered in Auschwitz later that month. Hans May fled his native Austria, ending up in England, composing over a hundred film scores. Robert Gilbert fled first to Austria, then France,

finally to the USA, returning to Germany after the war as a musical translator.

117 'Will later said of this loss of Jewish talent . . .' In an interview in the *Telegraf*, on 8 August 1965, with Rudolf Brendemühl, Will Meisel remembered the Jewish musicians who used to work for his company in the 1930s and said: 'My love still belongs to the stage and music, but we don't have any librettists any more, the cupboard is bare because of the fate of the Jews.' In his article on Will Meisel, the musicologist Raymond Wolff criticises the composer for the use of the word '*Schicksal*' – fate – as being too neutral, as if it were an accident.

118 'By the end of the day . . .' Other well-known people joined the party on 1 May 1933, including the philosophers Martin Heidegger, Arnold Gehlen and Erich Rothacker. According to Raymond Wolff – a musicologist who wrote a chapter called 'Will Meisel: Das Allroundtalent' in a book about musicians from Neukölln, Berlin – Meisel's joining the party in May 1933 was 'not atypical for a music composer, but he was not a political person, he never wrote a political song'. Will Meisel joined the party, Wolff added, because he 'felt insecure'.

118 'Within a few weeks . . .' At this time there was a general drop in the production of popular music. According to figures gathered by Sophie Fetthauer (and interpreted for me by music historian Michael Haas) from contemporary trade magazines, the following are the number of registered new releases for popular music, dance music, tango, jazz, etc: 1928 (1,503), 1929 (2,011), 1930 (1,563), 1931 (1,159), 1932 (1,023), 1933 (1,031), 1934 (888), 1935 (1,070) and 1936 (1,182). From this it appears that there was a drastic reduction following the takeover of the Nazis, followed by a recovery as new, presumably party-approved works were made available.

118 'There he saw a dark-haired young woman . . .' This comes from an untitled interview with Will and Eliza Meisel in 1965, held by the Deutsche Kinemathek – Museum für Film und Fernsehen in Berlin, which holds a thick file of articles on Will and Eliza Meisel. Later in this same article, Eliza said about this first meeting: 'We got lucky and then we got lucky.'

119 'On 3 July 1934, they bumped into . . .' It is possible to view at least two of the films of Eliza Illiard at the Deutsche Kinemathek, along with photographs of both Eliza and Will Meisel.

120 'a certain Herr Mertens . . .' Eliza Illiard was the stage name of Elisabeth Pieper. On 18 September 1934 the political leader of the Nazi Party's Theatre and Film Department wrote a letter to the president of the film guild to which Illiard belonged: 'I do not want to miss the opportunity to tell you that Miss Eliza Illiard Mertens is employed at the Metropol Theater. The premiere will be on 24 September 1934. Besides, Miss Illiard plays the leading role in the film *Lauf ins Glück* . . . Miss Illiard was born in Czechoslovakia and was married to the Jewish man Mertens which we informed you about on 30 January of this year. I thought you would like to know.' This letter can be found in the files at the Bundesarchiv Berlin (File: R/9361/V signature 110383). As a film and operetta star, Illiard was obliged to demonstrate the purity of her genes. A letter on 21 September 1934 from her film guild to the Nazi Party confirmed that she had done so since 'She brought her proof of Aryan ancestry. From her papers you can see that she was born Pieper from Cologne, her parents are both born German.'

120 'On 12 March 1935 . . .' According to the Landesarchiv Berlin index on registrations: 'Elisabeth Mertens was born 25.03.1906 in Cologne. She was married. She came to Berlin on 02.08.1934 from Dresden and lived in Emserstrasse 37/38. On 01.11.1934 she moved to Kastanienallee 21 in Charlottenburg.' The Landesarchiv Dresden could not find Elisabeth Pieper's marriage certificate to Herr Mertens, but they did find her name mentioned in a book that shows she lived in Zeschaustrasse 4 in Dresden in 1933. However, Herr Mertens was never registered to that address. Despite considerable effort, I was unable to find the first name or the fate of Herr Mertens.

120 'Even more memorable than his narrow moustache . . .' Much of the information for this section comes from the West German Broadcasting (WDR) archives. Hanns Hartmann's father, Joseph Hartmann, was a locksmith. His mother, Elisabeth Kohlen, was a homemaker.

Chapter 10

122 'the three-page typed inventory . . .' The items in each of the rooms were carefully registered; for example, in Elsie's bedroom were: 2 beds, 1 chair, 2 small pink tables, 1 folding table with an inkstand, 1 cushioned bench and 1 mirror. The inventory is held by the Landesarchiv Potsdam (File: 'Dr Alfred Alexander' – Rep 36A/nr 430).

126 'Believing that the Alexanders . . . half its actual worth . . .' Two years later, the Berlin tax office would value these same assets as worth 12,200 reichsmarks on the open market, according to a letter from the tax office in Wilmersdorf north, Berlin.

127 'Walking across the road . . . Wolff-Eisner . . .' Dr Alfred Wolff-Eisner was recognised internationally for his work on immunology, particularly the development of a diagnosis for tuberculosis, the Calmette Wolff-Eisner reaction. The research carried out on the Wolff-Eisner family was conducted by the Groß Glienicker *Kreis* as part of their survey of Jewish families who lived in the village before the war.

127 'The authorities and citizens of Groß Glienicke . . .' Günther Wittich, who was born in 1927 and grew up in a house opposite the schloss, remembered the Wolff-Eisner house on Seepromenade being burned down during the Kristallnacht pogrom. This was his first experience of anti-Semitism. He recalled that the SA were present in village, with many people wearing uniforms. He also remembers Robert von Schultz in the Stahlhelm, playing with the Schultz children, walking around the schloss, and going out on the lake. In a separate interview with another member of the village, I was told that the names of those involved with the Wolff-Eisner arson are known, though this person would not reveal the information to me and asked to remain anonymous.

129 'sent on 22 March to the Berlin tax office . . .' In a letter sent on 12 May 1939, from a Dr Lücker of the Wilmersdorf North tax office to the Moabit West tax office, it was written: 'Alfred Israel Alexander, born 7.3.1880 in Bamberg, and his wife Henny Sara née Picard, born 11.12.1888

in Frankfurt am Main, last resident at 15 Achenbachstrasse, W 15, emigrated to London on 25 March 1937 [*sic*]. On 1.1.1937 their total assets amounted to 145,000 reichsmarks. 36,250 reichsmarks was paid as Reich flight tax. The assessment of the assets is based on an estimate . . . Alexander also owns a wooden house in Groß Glienicke located on a plot of land which does not belong to him. Assessed value 12,200 reichsmarks (Nauen Aktenz. III / 26A).' The file is held by Landesarchiv Potsdam (File: Rep 36A/nr 430).

130 'Quietly, almost without notice, the Gestapo had taken ownership . . .' The Landesarchiv Potsdam has the Gestapo files for Dr Alfred John Alexander. In these files are a bundle of correspondence between the Gestapo and Dr Alexander's former patients written after the Alexanders had left the country. Not content with collecting mere physical assets, the Gestapo had written to the former patients to collect any outstanding debts. Though such bills were as little as three hundred reichsmarks, the authorities were determined to pursue even the smallest claim. It must have been quite a shock to receive such a collection letter, for the patients would have realised that the Gestapo now knew that they had been treated by a Jewish doctor. It is interesting to see how the various patients responded. One promises to immediately make good on his debt. Another sends pages of documents detailing the purity of her Aryan lineage. While a third argues that the debt is not valid as the Jewish doctor had failed to cure him.

133 'There he met a bureaucrat recorded only as "J.A." . . .' This meeting was documented in an internal memo: 'The cooperation of the landowner Wollank would be desirable, so that in the event that Mr Meisel were to fall behind with the rent in future, the Reich will not be deemed liable. Repeated letters to Wollank have, however, remained unanswered. Mr Meisel has now explained that Wollank has died. The estate is being managed by administrators. Moreover, the Groß Glienicke estate has been acquired by the Luftwaffe. As the lease agreement only runs until 31 March 1942, the risk for the Reich in selling is less than the sale

value. In addition there is very little risk pertaining to Meisel (well-known composer).'

133 'seized the Glienicke property from the "Jew Alfred John Alexander". . .' The J.A. memo went on to say that the Alexanders' property and rights seized by the Reich included, 'among other things, the rights from the lease agreement of 30/3/27 between Alexander and the landowner Wollank in Groß Glienicke regarding plot number 3 on the vineyard of the Groß Glienicke estate. The Reich also owns the rights to the ownership of the buildings erected on this plot (house, summer house, garage, glasshouse with 2 hotbeds) in addition to diverse items of furniture (bedroom furniture, dining table, garden set, a small portable cooking stove, hall furniture, 2 more bedsteads, some used and partly broken outdoor furniture and other household goods).'

Chapter 11

134 'Early in the morning of 20 January . . .' The discussions that took place that day are memorialised at the Wannsee Conference Museum, in south-west Berlin. In my opinion, this is the world's most informative Holocaust exhibition, providing a comprehensive and compelling overview of the background, administration, and execution of the so-called Final Solution.

135 'In Groß Glienicke, word filtered through . . .' Over the years there had been many notable Jewish residents living in the village. According to research carried out by the Groß Glienicker *Kreis*, some of the Jewish families who lived part- or full-time in the village included: Dr Adolf Abraham (dentist), Rudi Ball (ice-hockey star), Max and Wally Blaustein (perfume exporters), Dr Rudolf Leszynsky (scholar and insurer), Dr Richard Samson (physician), Josef Schmeidler (merchant and managing director), Robert Salomon Weitz (whose son was John Weitz, the novelist and fashion designer, and whose grandsons, Chris and Paul Weitz, produced the films *American Pie* and *About a Boy*, among others), Fritz Wertheim (businessman), and Alfred Wolff-Eisner (doctor and researcher).

135 'a very small number . . . left the country . . .' The Hungarian composer Béla Bartók, for example, professed strong anti-fascist views, and fled to the USA in 1940. Ralph Benatzky, Karl Rankl and Robert Stolz had Jewish wives, making their decision to leave German-occupied Austria more straightforward. Others, like Karl Amadeus Hartmann, lived in internal exile during the war, refusing to work with the Nazis or to have their work performed in Nazi-occupied Europe. Then there are the examples of those who joined the Nazi Party but later claimed not to hold Nazi sympathies. Some of these last cases were shunned in the post-war years, such as Max Butting and Eduard Erdmann, while others, such as Will Meisel, were not.

137 'The war was not as far away . . .' According to a handwritten note made on the side of his marriage certificate, and archived at the City of Potsdam archive, Robert von Schultz died on 13 September 1941 in Voranova (in what is today Belarus), while serving on the Eastern front. Underneath this note it was added that the death certificate 3/1942 had been 'sent to a mail address in Rügen on the Baltic Sea'. Yet despite his being the last landlord of the Groß Glienicke Estate, no service or memorial was held at the village church. Another death provoked more of a response. On 14 May 1943, Georg, the Crown Prince of Saxony, drowned while swimming in the Groß Glienicke Lake. The gossip in the Drei Linden was that, because of the prince's public statements against the Third Reich, the Gestapo was somehow involved in his death.

138 'Indeed, Will was so taken . . .' Though the song was registered in 1950 with GEMA, the German copyright music authority, it is probable that it was written much earlier. Meisel spent little time in the village after the war and, given the brutal Russian occupation, it is unlikely that he would have been motivated to write the song after 1945. Additionally, one of the co-writers of the song, Georg Wysocki, left the village in 1948, as reported by his daughter, Gisela Wysocki. According to Sven Meisel the song may well have been written in the 1930s.

140 'On 15 May 1943, the National Theatre Department . . .' To see the correspondence regarding Meisel's military service, see Bundesarchiv Berlin (File: R55/20207).

141 'Hearing of the evacuation order . . .' On 6 August, Will Meisel, wrote the following letter to Mayor Buge of Groß Glienicke: 'Dear Mayor. Because the Gauleiter Goebbels ordered everyone to leave Berlin my family (7 people) is staying during the winter in my house in Groß Glienicke, parcel 3, Weinberg. The house has 6 rooms and under-floor heating. I need 250 *Zentner* of coal and 100 *Zentner* of *Brikette* for the washing house, the bathtub and kitchen, as well as for the pre-heating 1 room-meter of wood. *Heil Hitler.*' This letter is held by the Landesarchiv Berlin (File: C rep 031-01-02 Number 1281/2).

141 'Peter, meanwhile, who was now eight years old, attended the local school . . .' In a letter to the editor of the village *Chronik*, Peter wrote that he spent two years in the village primary school of Groß Glienicke. There were forty-eight other students who were taught by one teacher. 'The education wasn't very well organised and structured,' he wrote, but he gained 'a broad general knowledge'.

142 'Once a week he participated . . .' Peter was younger than the typical entry age of ten. He was a member of the most junior Hitler Youth league, known as the *Pimpfe*, the name for a boy before his voice changes.

143 'On 3 November 1943, the opening night of *Königin einer Nacht* . . .' The Metropol Theater is now the location of the Komische Oper on Behrenstraße in Berlin.

144 'Those on the VIP list . . .' The invite list for the Metropol Theater is based on one from 23 August 1938, which was attached to a letter sent by the theatre's director, Heinz Hentschke, to the Ministry of Propaganda but the list is unlikely to be have been substantially different. The list can be found at the Bundesarchiv Berlin (File: R55/20.204, p. 338).

144 'the reviews were unanimously positive . . .' Another critic, Theo Fürstenau, said that the show included 'a little bit of sentimentality, a few jokes, pretty girls that cover only enough of their beauty to be in

good taste, and some ingratiating music, [*Königin einer Nacht*] is freshly polished to shine, and blinds the eyes of the audience'. He went on to say that 'Will Meisel gave the entire show a light mood with his easy-to-like melodies which . . . will stick in the mind'.

144 'Eight days later, on 11 November 1943 . . .' According to Hanns Hartmann's *Fragebogen*, written in August 1945, the Edition Meisel storage facility on Passauerstrasse, Berlin, burned down on 23 November 1943. The family's home at Wittelsbacherstraße 18 was bombed in February 1944, and it was only then that the Meisels moved permanently to Groß Glienicke. In truth, the family was already spending much of their time by the lake. Hartmann goes on to say that the business returned to Wittelsbacherstrasse 18, Berlin, on 7 June 1945, even though it was yet to be built.

146 'Since its annexation in 1938, Austria . . .' Austria was known by the Nazi Party as *Ostmark* until 1942. Thereafter it was known as *Donau und Alpen Reichsgaue*. On 10 May 1945, Bad Gastein was liberated by the Americans, a day one of the composers hiding out with the Meisels remembered as follows: 'War can be totally exaggerated; it is not bad if you stay away from it all in Gastein. Because here with a lot of talent you can lead a civilised and free life, and have a happy end. The bad times are over, never to return, we can breathe out, and we can speak English.'

Chapter 12

149 'Often seen with a cigar in hand, he walked around the office . . .' These details come from a biography of Hanns Hartmann published in *Fernsehen Information* on 1 November 1960 (nr 31/1960).

151 'a bomb fell on the farm . . .' This account comes from Hans Joachim Bartel who still lives on the family farm opposite the church in Groß Glienicke. He was five years old at the time of the explosion and hiding in the barn at the back of the farm with his siblings. His family had lived in the village since 1800, when his great-grandfather had moved

there. 'Everything was in flames,' he recalled, 'my parents' house was totally destroyed.' Another bomb had fallen in the lake before this; he remembered picking up the glass from his bed afterwards. Later, when the Russians came, he recalled being very scared. They knocked on the family's door with bayonets, and there were at least ten tanks in the village for two weeks or more. The family moved into the cellar and the Russians took over the main house. They made his mother taste the food to make sure it wasn't poisoned. 'This worked out well for us, as we had plenty of food,' he said.

152 'When Burkhard asked his mother . . .' This story was recalled by Burkhard Radtke in an interview with the author in August 2014.

Chapter 13

155 'With the sirens at the Drei Linden going off every few minutes and the sound of artillery . . .' Many of the details from this page and the next come from an anonymous diary that was written in April 1945, at the time of the Soviet troops' arrival in Groß Glienicke. I found a copy of the diary pasted into the village *Chronik*. Here is an excerpt: 'We have survived our first attack from low-flying planes. But they are not targeting Glienicke, they are targeting the troops that have gathered nearby. During the day there were more attacks, one after the other, apparently also attacking the airfield, and the roads around the airfield . . . There have just been several plane attacks one after the other. And you can hear them flying away in the distance. Now hardly any artillery, at the moment it is almost silent. You can hear the birds outside. What will the day and night bring?'

155 'Hildegard Munk had also abandoned her house . . .' Hildegard Munk's memories are recorded in an audio interview with her son Klaus and grandson Matthias.

156 'As one of only three airfields in the Berlin vicinity . . .' One of those to land at Berlin-Gatow just before the war's end was Albert Speer, architect and minister of armaments and war production. On 23 April, Speer flew into Gatow from Hamburg, and from there he drove in a

black BMW to Berlin, where he would be one of the last to speak to Adolf Hitler in his bunker.

156 'Realising that the Soviets were close . . .' The description of Gerda Radtke's time during the Soviet occupation was provided by her son, Burkhard, who still lives in Groß Glienicke. Of the Soviet occupation, Burkhard said, 'That's when the misery started. I thought it could not get worse . . . but it did.'

157 'Seeing the Soviets, Hanns Hartmann jumped out . . .' This story is told by Hildegard Munk. In her recollection, Hildegard suggests that Hartmann was hiding in a hole in the ground – it is likely that she was referring to the pump house that was built into the embankment between the house and the lake. In Hartmann's handwritten memoir, entitled 'My Life's Path' and dated 9 September 1950, a copy of which is held by the WDR archive, he confirmed that he was living at the house in Groß Glienicke when the Soviets arrived, writing: 'from 1944 (autumn) increasing difficulties until the marching in of the Russians on 26 April 1945 (Groß Glienicke)'.

159 'Six days after the surrender . . .' The exact time of the signing was shortly after midnight in Berlin on 8/9 May 1945. Negotiations on the text had delayed the signing. In the Western countries, 8 May became Victory in Europe Day. In the Soviet Union, Victory Day is celebrated on 9 May, because the surrender had been made at 00.43 hours Moscow time.

160 'Neither Wilhelm Bartel nor the youngsters were seen again . . .' Wilhelm Bartel, the thirty-six-year-old who owned the farm opposite the church, had been a member of the Nazi Party, and during the war he had been responsible for an agricultural commission. Upon their arrival in the village, the Russians accused him of organising slave labour from Poland and Ukraine. According to his son, his family was not told of his death until the early 1950s, and even then they were not sure where or how he had died. For the next few decades they desperately tried to find information. The NKVD suggested that he might have been taken to the Soviet camps at Buchenwald and Saschsenhausen, but

when they travelled to these sites the family found no new information. It was not until 1996, after the Wall came down, that his family learned through the Red Cross that Wilhelm Bartel had died of a lung infection at a camp near Ketschendorf and that he had been buried in a mass grave next to a wheel factory. In all, tens of thousands of German prisoners of war and civilians were deported to Ketschendorf, including 1,600 children between the ages of twelve and sixteen. Over 4,600 people died during the camp's existence between 1945 and 1947.

Chapter 14

162 'Two weeks later, on 15 July . . .' Harry Truman had replaced Roosevelt following his death on 12 April 1945, and a few days into the conference, Churchill was replaced by Clement Attlee, who took office on 26 July. For a description of the arrival of the dignitaries and the early days of RAF Gatow, see files at the National Archives in Kew (for instance, File: AIR 29/461).

163 'Churchill was shocked by the devastation . . .' Over a million Berliners were now homeless. Churchill was 'much moved' by the devastation, the people's haggard looks and threadbare clothes, as recalled by Martin Gilbert in *Churchill: A Life*.

164 'the Americans dropped a nuclear bomb . . .' The number of deaths that can be attributed to these bombs, resulting from long-term radiation effects, are often estimated as 135,000 for Hiroshima and 50,000 for Nagasaki. Some say the figures could be as high as 150,000 and 75,000.

165 'But the British wanted their own airport . . .' On 1 August there were five officers and sixty-one other ranks under the command of Captain Smeddle. By the end of that month RAF Gatow was manned by 2,479 personnel, including 697 civilians. At this time the airfield was used by British, French, American and Soviet planes, with around twenty take-offs and landings each day. In the first logbook it was noted that the army's laundry facility could not cope and that soldiers should make

'private arrangements' with the local women. In a meeting held on 22 August, it was agreed that the base would change its name from 'Staging Post 19' to 'RAF Gatow', and the air officer commanding stated: 'The AOC did not want any fracas with the Russians but was convinced that the way to prevent both looting and incidents was to show from the outset that we had force, were interested, and were always on the go, and then it would get about that this was a bad place to try any nonsense.' The food at the camp was not much loved, as evidenced by a poem published in *Airline*, the base's magazine, and entitled 'Airmen's Mess': 'Monday, Tuesday, Wednesday / Breakfast is always the same / Beans beans and more beans / They give us all a pain / Thursday, Friday, Saturday / Breakfast just the same / Yes! Quite right you guessed it / It's blasted beans again.' For more on the early days of the British forces in Gatow there are a large number of files at the National Archives in Kew (for instance, Files: AIR 28/296 and AIR 55/52).

165 'The Soviets set up a border control at the Potsdamer Tor . . .' The security was lax at these controls until the border was officially closed in 1952. In an interview, Pastor Stintzing recalled football matches being played between the Soviet and East German guards on one side, and British and West Germans on the other, in the woods near the derelict schloss in 1948/1949. There was also an unofficial kiosk at the border providing food and hot drinks to the guards. Whenever senior officers visited the border, the kiosk's owner would hide until they had gone. Later, this entrepreneur was imprisoned for continuing to run the kiosk.

167 'Then, sometime during the extremely cold winter . . .' As a child, Günther Wittich had played with Robert von Schultz's son Carl Christoph. When he heard the siren on the night of the schloss fire in 1945, he had run to the fire station and returned on the truck, as a member of the brigade. Arriving at the schloss he found a group of Russians blocking their way; they had no guns and did not speak German. He was shocked by their inaction and believes they started the fire on

purpose. 'The villagers gathered around watching the blaze,' he recalled. 'They were very sad thinking of old times.'

Chapter 15

173 'Hanns received a *Fragebogen*, which he completed . . .' This is available at the Landesarchiv Berlin (File: C Rep 120/ 899).

174 'In early autumn of 1946 . . .' According to Meisel family legend – as printed in the book *100 Years of Will Meisel* – September 1946 was the start of the 'next phase' of the publisher's rebirth, and the third time that Will Meisel would have to build the company from scratch: the first was in the 1920s when he was a young man starting out; the second time was in the 1930s, when the Nazis had forced him to let go of all his Jewish artists and the company had faced collapse; and now again, in the 1940s, following the war and the destruction of the family business by Allied bombs. In fact, Will Meisel did not regain control of his company until 1951.

175 'From Hamburg they travelled to Cologne . . .' Later Hartmann would become the first director of the national broadcaster, WDR.

176 'More than 2.1 million cases . . .' The slow-down in prosecutions can be seen by comparing the October 1947 figures to those of the following spring. By the end of April 1948, 2,326,257 people had been screened within the British zone (excluding Berlin), of which 358,466 had been removed from office, and 2,456 had been prosecuted for making false statements on their *Fragebogen*. By April 1948, there were 308 denazification review boards operating within the British zone. During that month, of the 37,797 appeals pending, only 2,428 had been reviewed, of which 2,209 were upheld. See National Archives in Kew (Files: FO1006/126, FO1056/268 and FO1032/1057).

176 'Per capita, these figures . . .' The Americans fared equally badly, despite their officious intentions. In March 1946, the Law for Liberation from National Socialism and Militarism came into effect, turning over

responsibility for denazification to the Germans. To implement this law, 545 civilian tribunals were established under German administration, with a staff of 22,000. Even this was far too small a number to handle the enormous volume of cases. By February 1947, only half of the submitted 11,674,152 *Fragebogen* in the American zone had been processed, fewer than 168,696 had faced trial, 339 had been classified as Major Offenders, 13,708 as Lesser Offenders, and of these, only 2,018 had custodial sentences.

176 'These remaining cases were to be tried through summary proceedings . . .' In 1951, the West German government granted amnesties to lesser offenders and ended the programme. The British denazification files can be found at the National Archives in Kew (Files: FO1012/750 and FO1056/268).

177 'Despite his close association with the Nazi Party, Furtwängler . . .' Furtwängler's tribunal in December 1946 was overseen by some of the same characters active in Meisel's case: Alex Vogel, Dr Loewe, Dr Flören, Wolfgang Schmidt, Mühlmann, Neumann, Müller-Ness and Rosen. For some reason his panel featured eight people and Meisel's only six. For a cinematic account of Wilhelm Furtwängler's denazification trial, see *Taking Sides*, with Harvey Keitel and Stellan Skarsgård.

178 'Hartmann . . . would not be appearing as a witness in his trial . . .' In an effort to better understand Hanns Hartmann, I spoke to Birgit Bernard, an archivist at WDR. Dr Bernard said that Hartmann was considered by his colleagues to be 'a very honest man' who was 'not interested in people's past'. Unlike many of his contemporaries, he hired a number of people for the broadcaster who had some previous links with the Nazis. In an email, Petra Witting-Nöthen, another archivist at WDR, wrote the following: 'The relationship between Hartmann and Meisel it is difficult to say. [Hartmann] knows the Meisel family. He sent Greeting to Will Meisel's parents. But the relationship was formal, they don't use the German *Du*. I think Will Meisel was his chief and the owner of the firm, Hartmann was only the financial director. The letters after the war show a reserved relationship between them.' It is

worth adding that, in his unpublished memoir, Hartmann did not mention the assistance that Meisel claimed to have provided to Hartmann's wife: helping her flee Germany and obtaining a work permit.

178 'On the stroke of ten, the six commissioners . . .' The trial record can be found at the Landesarchiv Berlin (File: C 031-01-02/1281/1-3).

178 'including the forty-year-old chairman and former communist, Alex Vogel . . .' Alex Vogel had been a communist since the age of eighteen. He had been arrested in the months after the Nazis seized power and then he fled Germany, but returned in 1935. During the war he served in the Wehrmacht and then in a penal battalion, until he deserted in 1944. There were rumours that Vogel worked for the Gestapo, spying on the Russian embassy.

179 'Vogel pushed him on this point. "Have Herr Fago and Herr Hartmann" . . .' Eighteen months prior to Meisel's tribunal one of the members of the denazification commission, Dr Flören, interviewed Paul Fago on 30 December 1946 about the relationship between Will Meisel and Hanns Hartmann. According to the file note written by Dr Flören: 'On the question of whether there has been a hatred between Hartmann and Meisel, Fago said yes and no. Meisel without doubt has been doing a lot for Hartmann simply through allowing him and his wife to stay in Glienicke during the worst times. On the other side Hartmann assisted Meisel on professional matters. The question is did Meisel help him only for these reasons? Meisel has always been the ideas man but needed help to put these into actions. He has Hartmann and Fago by his side supporting him. Most of the fights were about views on artistry because Hartmann wanted to reach a high level where Meisel wanted simple operettas. Mr Fago also had problems with Meisel but it was the way of Meisel that he never broke relations which he needed for his professional work.' This file is kept in the Landesarchiv Berlin (File: C 031-01-02/1281/1-3).

179 'In order to prove that . . .' Will Meisel had a history of being less than forthright in his questionnaires. For example, on his first Nazi Party questionnaire in 1941, he declared that his wife was a Protestant like

himself, and then on subsequent documents he said she was Catholic. He was not the only one to dissemble in official documents. On the CV attached to her British questionnaire, Eliza Meisel wrote on 9 October 1947 that her artistic career stopped in 1935. In fact she starred in a 1941 film titled *Ehe man Ehemann wird* (see Bundesarchiv Berlin File: R/9361/V, signature 128869).

180 'Of course, Vogel and his fellow commissioners didn't know . . .' The Gestapo and Berlin tax department files for Dr Alfred Alexander are held by the Potsdam Landesarchiv. Vogel did not have access to these during the trial as they did not form part of the records that were captured at the offices of the Reich Chamber of Culture.

181 'The chairman of the proceedings then returned . . .' Will Meisel gave a lengthy submission as part of the court proceedings, written on 13 February 1947. Along with a letter which asked for 'full denazification', he included a filled-out questionnaire, a book titled *Will Meisel: Life and Songs*, a photocopy of an article, along with sworn affidavits from friends and colleagues attesting to his good character. There was also a witness statement, written by Will himself, which ran for nine pages and included headings such as 'Why I Joined the Party' and 'Political History'. Will's statement concluded with the following passage: 'Despite the twelve-year reign of terror, I have remained true to my democratic sentiment and mode of operating – and, as this composition proves, I undertook, insofar as the modest powers of an artist would permit, to work against the party and the machinery of war. I need lower my eyes before no one. I was, am and will remain a democrat! A heedless and hasty signature in no way identifies me with Nazi terror practices . . . The past twelve years have been very difficult because of my "anti" attitude. In my position as publisher I had to represent the interests of my authors before the competent authorities. Fist in pocket, I had to present a mask to the outside world. Denouncers were to be found among my best friends. I could erect a monument to myself today – considering my lack of caution – for so skilfully having evaded the concentration camp.

I had not only to represent the interests of my author-clients but also my own interests as a composer. On top of that there was the finalising of performance commitments for my wife, the singer Eliza Illiard. After all, one had to make a living in this state. However, I believe that in the arts world there is none who could condemn me. The witnesses I have listed in the following will attest to my "anti" sentiment and the measures I took against the Nazi Party.' See Landesarchiv Berlin (File: C 031-01-02/1281/1-3).

182 'Vogel then said the last document . . . written by Hanns Hartmann . . . from Cologne . . .' On 1 September 1947, Hartmann became director of Radio in Cologne. On 25 May 1955, he was elected to the board of the newly formed WDR and became its first creative director, running the company until 1960. He received the Bundesverdienstkreuz, Federal Cross of Merit, in 1959. He died on 5 April 1972 in Mindelheim, Germany. His wife, Ottilie, died at the couple's apartment in Cologne on 26 July 1966.

182 'In his statement, Hartmann said that it had been his idea to purchase Universal Edition . . .' Universal Edition was founded in Vienna in 1901 and, until his death, was managed and owned by Emil Hertzka. The company published many of the world's greatest composers, including Strauss, Mahler and Bartók. After his death in 1932, the ownership of Universal Edition passed to Jella Hertzka, Emil's widow, who fled Austria after Germany's occupation in March 1938. The company was aryanised soon after. It returned to family ownership after the war. In 1800, Peters Edition was founded in Leipzig, and was built into one of Europe's premier publishing houses. Its catalogue featured Brahms, Bruch, Dvořák, Liszt and Wagner. Through the late 1930s it was owned and managed by Henri Hinrichsen, until the company was aryanised in 1939. In 1940, Hinrichsen fled to Belgium, until he was caught and deported to Auschwitz, where he was murdered on 17 September 1942. Following the reunification of Germany the company was returned to the family.

Chapter 16

184 'the Americans, British and French had acted quickly . . .' The Berlin
Airlift was primarily delivered by the USA and UK, as can be seen by
comparing the number of flights – Britain (85,870), USA (189,963) and
France (424) – as well as the Tons of Cargo transported – Britain
(541,940), USA (1,783,573) and France (896). While not delivering as
many tons as her two allies, France did allow its airport at Berlin Tegel
to be used as part of the airlift, and oversaw its reconstruction to allow
for greater air traffic. At the time, France was focused on the Indochina
War, which had started on 19 December 1946. Additional flights were
operated by other countries, including New Zealand, Canada and South
Africa. The British transported 23 per cent of the total 2,325,000 tons,
and manned 31 per cent of the 277,000 flights. The details can be found
in the F540 reports, at the National Archives, London (Files: Air 28/1034
and Air 28/1207).

188 'Attached was Will Meisel's 1938 letter . . .' Major Sely was in overall
charge of Will Meisel's case, a man known by the British as being
particularly determined. In a letter sent on 28 May 1948 from the British
headquarters in Hamburg to the Information Services in Berlin, Brigadier
Gibson wrote that he was tired of the 'witch-hunting by Sely' and he
wanted to stop him 'inventing the rules' when it came to denazification.
See National Archives, London (File: FO 1050/603).

189 'Herr Will Meisel is as black a character as can be . . .' This document
is filed at the Bundesarchiv Berlin (File: R/9361/V, signature 147724).

Chapter 17

192 'Around 10 p.m., Gerda looked out of her window . . .' This account
comes from Burkhard Radtke, who I interviewed in the summer of 2014.

195 'There were more soldiers than usual . . . extras in *The Fall of Berlin* . . .'
The film was a two-parter, commissioned by Joseph Stalin, directed by

Mikheil Chiaureli, and lasting 167 minutes. Over 10,000 extras were used in the production, much of which took place west of Berlin close to Groß Glienicke. The Soviet Army provided five divisions, including four tank battalions and almost two hundred aircraft. At one stage the military manoeuvres proved so realistic that they caused alarm at the nearby Gatow airfield, according to reports filed at the National Archives in Kew. Classified as a documentary, the film was released on 21 January 1950 and was watched by 38 million people in the Soviet Union. The film was also shown in the DDR with all members of the Volkspolizei required to watch it.

195–6 'The only measure that was put in place . . .' The murders continued through to the mid-1950s, though it is not clear if the culprits were connected beyond being linked to the Soviet Army. Hans Dieter Behrendt, who was later in charge of the border crossing at the Glienicke Bridge, and lived in Groß Glienicke from the 1970s, remembers the case of a couple who were murdered in 1955 by Soviet soldiers while making a black-market deal in Kemnitz, a few kilometres from the village. The Volkspolizei arrived to investigate, he said, bringing sniffer dogs with them. The crime scene was only 800 metres from the Soviet base. The dogs followed the trace to the base, right to the halls where hundreds of soldiers were sleeping. The kommandant of the base would not let the police onto the base, and shouted: '*Schluss! Hier nicht mehr*', or 'Stop! Do not enter.' The kommandant went into the hall and told his men that if the guilty did not step forward immediately then everyone would be punished. A few moments later, two suspects stepped forward. 'I am not sure what happened to them, maybe they were sent back to Russia,' said Behrendt. He added that he had heard from other officers that the DDR press office did not cover such stories, they were 'taboo', because the 'Russians wanted to keep up the positive image of the country, and socialism'. He thought that such cover-ups happened frequently. As the years progressed things 'got better and became more safe', he said. The Russians took measures to stop the abuse, preventing the soldiers from leaving the base. They investigated the crimes that they heard of and punished them more consistently. He recalled that the Russians came to his door in 1945 and 1946 frequently demanding jewellery, money and women. His family kept the door locked. 'The majority of people hated the Russians,' he added. In the days before they occupied his town, his family fled towards the oncoming American forces. 'Everyone was scared of the Russians,' he said. 'Nobody was scared of the Americans.'

196 'This was in spite of reports that Gerda Radtke had seen the murderer . . .' Burkhard Radtke told me that his mother had seen the murderer with burns on his arms walking through Groß Glienicke in the days after the event. As they passed, the Russian shook his head, implying that she must not reveal his identity to anyone. Despite this, Gerda reported him to the police. At first the police did not believe her, but eventually they arrested him. When the soldier saw Gerda at his trial he shouted out that his friends would hurt her and her children. Because of this threat, the family was allowed to move back into the village where they would be less isolated. In my interview with Burkhard, he reported that his mother was scathing of the West Berlin press coverage of the murders. He pointed out that though the victims were attacked with an axe, this was not the same as being mutilated.

197 'Two years later, in the spring of 1952 . . .' In 1955 Leo Bauer was released from Siberian prison camp and deported to West Germany. For a time he worked as a journalist, editing a number of publications, before becoming an adviser to Willy Brandt. He died in Bonn in 1972. His file can be found at the Stasi Archive [File: MfS HAIX 24458].

197 'With the prospect of further, seemingly arbitrary, government oppression . . .' Murders and home invasions were not the only crimes taking place in the village. On 8 October, the *Tagesspiegel* newspaper reported that on the previous Sunday at 8 p.m., people had been standing at the bus stop in Groß Glienicke when they heard cries for help and then saw people in Russian uniforms cycling away on bicycles. Two days earlier, the article continued, several people in Russian uniforms broke into an

apartment on Tristanstraße and stole jewellery and furniture to the value of several thousand deutschmarks. This was the twelfth break-in since the start of the month that had been reported in the village.

Interlude: December 2013

204 *'The JCC made thousands of claims . . .'* According to a list posted on the Jewish Claims Conference website in 2015, twenty-five Groß Glienicke properties that had been owned by Jewish families are still to be claimed.

Chapter 18

207 'In the autumn of 1952, Ella Fuhrmann . . .' Ella Fuhrmann arrived from Pomerania in 1947 with her two children. Two of her brothers were living in Groß Glienicke at the time, near to the lake house.

210 'Inside, he was greeted by Wilhelm Stintzing . . .' Pastor Stintzing became the village pastor in 1947, a position he retained until 1967. Once the village was split, following the Potsdam Conference, he continued to provide pastoral care on both sides of the border. Throughout his time in the village he was allowed to cross back and forth, which he did by bicycle. About the Wall, he told me that 'it was paralysing, it slowly rolled into us that we could not go to the other side', and then 'slowly people got used to it'. He told me that many of his congregants spoke to him about the Wall and about fleeing to the West, but always in private. In June 2014, Groß Glienicke church held a reception for Pastor Stintzing to celebrate his hundredth birthday.

Chapter 19

219 'By 1958, the Stasi . . . oversaw a network of between 20,000 and 30,000 unofficial informants . . .' This number would increase to 45,500 by 1971, and then, by 1989, to 91,015 full-time operatives. This final

number represents a ratio of 5.5 MfS personnel per thousand citizens, far higher than the ratio in the Soviet Union (1.8 per thousand) and Czechoslovakia (1.1 per thousand). By 1968, the number of Stasi informants reached 100,000, rising to approximately 180,000 by mid-1975, and peaking in 1989 at 189,000. Many informants had only a short relationship with the Stasi, with about 10 per cent starting or ending contact each year.

219 'At this time they were known as *Geheimer Informator* (GI) . . .' After 1968, Stasi informants were known as *Inoffizielle Mitarbeiter* (IM), or informal staff.

221 'Later, the file would be . . .' The Wolfgang Kühne file can be found at the Stasi Archive (Files: MfS AIM 1768/61 B and P and MfS AIM 1768/61 B and A). Stasi documents regarding the border regiment's activities in Groß Glienicke are kept in their Berlin archive (Files: MfS HA IX 1096, HA I 19543, and HA IX 5529).

Chapter 20

226 'Though they lived side by side . . .' The neighbours had differing recollections as to the closeness of their relationship. According to Lothar and Sieglinde, they did not spend social time together and, besides taking care of Irene Kühne's children once or twice, did not interact in any way. Irene remembers things differently. She recalled that 'we had birthday parties together, invited each other over to eat, and had cake and tea in each other's living rooms. We always had the Fuhrmanns over.' She also said that Ella Fuhrmann 'was very talkative, very calm and friendly and that she spoke about her husband a lot'. Irene added that Ella's husband died in the war, while Lothar said his father died of cancer in 1951.

229 'Ignition Key failed to turn up not only for the next meeting . . .' Around this time, a court case about the lake house was taking place in West Berlin. On 12 December 1960, the case of Alexander vs Deutsches

Reich was held in Court Room 149, on Am Karlsbad in West Berlin. Open to the public, the proceedings were presided over by a civil judge, a Dr Kiworr. Working with a Berlin lawyer, Henny Alexander was demanding that the German government pay out compensation for the assets that had been stolen from her family, including gold, silver and bank deposits, as well as the structures they had built in Groß Glienicke and the household goods contained within. Will Meisel appeared as a witness in the case and, reading from a prepared statement, he explained that he had rented the land from Dr Alexander before the war and then directly from the Wollanks. He had only a few documents to demonstrate those times, he said, as most went missing when his property was bombed during the war. Sometime after 1940, he said, he had paid 3,000 reichsmarks to the Alexanders via their lawyer, Dr Goldstrom, for the buildings and the inventory. Then, 'unable to pay the remaining amount to the Alexanders', as by that time Dr Goldstrom had 'also left the country', he had paid 3,000 RM to the Berlin tax office. He was not asked to provide proof of this purchase, nor was the Alexanders' representative offered an opportunity to refute that a deal had been made between the Meisels and the Alexanders. As to the items contained within the house, Meisel added that 'a large part of the furniture was built in so you could not move it. We left everything as it was, so it should still be there.' He concluded by saying that 'I also want to point out that we did not bring any of the inventory to West Berlin. We received notice that the land was managed by the Groß Glienicke community and, based on what I know, it is rented out now.' Next, Eliza Meisel took the stand. Having taken the oath, she stated her name, birth date and place of residence. She then confirmed that while her husband's statement 'should be true', she could not 'remember the details of the transactions'. A month later, on 3 January 1961, the court pronounced its verdict: The government was ordered to pay the Alexanders 90.34 deutschmarks (about £300 in today's money) in compensation for the building and the inventory. The Alexanders were not to be paid anything, however, for the furniture that had been left at the house, based on the Meisels' assertion that they had not removed any of the items to their home in West Berlin. This was the last time that the Meisels and Alexanders had any form of communication, until I met Sven Meisel in 2013.

Chapter 21

232 'Despite the closing of the external border between East and West Germany . . .' Until the permanent barricade was erected in August 1961, a significant number of East Berliners were able to travel to West Berlin. Many commuted for work, but others crossed the border for different reasons. Ursula Dargies, for instance, attended a boarding school in West Berlin since she was forbidden from attending an East German high school because her father was a priest. Every weekend she returned to East Berlin and was able to carry almost any item with her, with the exception of West German literature. In 1960, she moved with her parents to West Germany.

234 'Next, a second barbed-wire fence. . .' Part of the description of the Wall being built in Groß Glienicke over the course of the 1960s comes from Helga Schütz, who moved into a house two hundred metres down the shore from the lake house on Seepromenade. Describing the fortification of the Wall in the mid-1960s, when the fence was replaced by the concrete wall, Helga recalled, 'For one moment it looked like a beach, a flattened beach.' When asked how she felt about the Wall being built between her house and the lake, she said, 'The Wall was not the problem, the situation was the problem,' and then added, 'We didn't believe it was happening, it was one step and then the next.'

Chapter 22

238 'The social evening was held at the Nedlitz fire station . . .' The descriptions come from Lothar and Sieglinde Fuhrmann, who I met in 2014.

241 'In February 1965 . . .' The dates of residence for the house by the lake can be found, for the post-war years, at the city of Potsdam archive.

241 'If the Fuhrmanns were pleased with their new accommodation, the Kühne family members were happier still . . .' The description of the Kühnes' early days at the house come from Irene, who I interviewed at her apartment in Potsdam in the summer of 2014.

Chapter 23

250 'In a pale yellow coat and matching yellow hat . . .' The details of this visit were reported in *The Times*, 28 May 1965, under the headline BERLIN CROWDS CHEER THE QUEEN.

251 'By now, it was apparent that the villagers could be separated . . .' This analysis comes from Sylvia Fiedler, who was born in Groß Glienicke in 1963, lived there until 1982 and later was executive editor for a local newspaper. 'People adapted to the situation,' she said. 'Some people would say "don't tell me stuff as I will have to share it".'

253 'On 13 August 1966, dressed in their Thälmann Pioneers . . .' According to the *Chronik*, by 1966 the village was comprised of the following: 1,719 residents of whom 501 were male working-age adults and 628 were female working-age adults, with 215 pensioners, eighty-seven teenagers, and the rest children under fourteen years of age. Of these, 104 worked for the Volkspolizei, 282 worked in Potsdam, ten in Berlin, 110 worked at the Max Reimann factory, fifty-one were farmers, thirty-five in retail, and the rest were spread across various professions (such as taxi drivers, hairdressers and electricians).

254 'According to the editor of the *Chronik* . . .' The Groß Glienicke *Chronik* was started in 1956 by Johannes Sieben, one of Bernd and Lothar's schoolteachers. Halfway between a scrapbook and a local newspaper, the *Chronik* would become the official history of the village for the next forty years. As a party-sanctioned initiative, the *Chronik* came with its own yellow-covered instruction manual. Considered politically

reliable and well respected within the community, Sieben was hand-picked by the local party representatives to edit the *Chronik*. In one entry, Sieben explained his view of the *Chronik*: 'In these books you can see how the socialist development of the people's education is reflected.' Elsewhere, in an article for a local newspaper, the *Potsdamer Blick*, he clarified the purpose of the *Chronik*: to capture the 'historic epoch' in which they then lived, and 'In the future, knowledge-hungry youth will read this and add to it and learn about the origins of socialism and be thankful for this'. Whenever Sieben attended an event that he considered of historical importance – a speech by a local party chairman, the seven hundredth anniversary of the village, an anniversary of the *Chronik* itself – he wrote a short report and pasted it into the *Chronik*. To this he added stories published about the village in the Potsdam newspapers. For example, Sieben's view of the Wall was: 'our government took the necessary measures to protect our freedom and secure our borders against West Berlin. Of course these measures are painful to the citizens, to the inhabitants of this rural beautiful landscape. This border protects us from agents and saboteurs and allows us to build our peaceful republic.' After the fall of the Wall, the *Chronik* was edited in a more liberal fashion, residents were able to contribute stories, even adding material from before 1989. By 2015 there were forty-seven volumes of the *Chronik*.

255 'On a few occasions, they were able to hit . . .' Bernd was not alone in enjoying this game. The Groß Glienicke border patrol regiment major, Peter Kaminski, recalled that his children often played it. When the trigger was struck, a signal was sent to the nearest watchtower, causing a flashing red light to illuminate the part of the fence that was hit. Kaminski and the other guards called these 'disco lights'.

256 'In the evenings, after supper, they often watched television . . .' The Western television reception in Groß Glienicke was strong, as it was in large parts of the DDR. Those areas where it was weak were known as *Tal der Ahnungslosen*, or 'Valley of the Clueless'. The two main areas of

poor signal were in the far north-east next to the Baltic Sea and the far south-east, near Dresden.

258 'The first exchange took place . . .' There would be two other exchanges at Glienicke Bridge. In 1985, twenty-three American agents who had been held across Eastern Europe were exchanged for one Polish and three Soviet agents. Finally, in 1986, the dissident Anatoly Sharansky and three Western agents were swapped for the sleeper agent Karl Koecher and four other Eastern agents.

Chapter 24

264 'Irene spent the afternoon shopping . . .' The description of shops in the village comes from my talks with various residents, including Burkhard Radtke, Günther Wittich, Irene and Bernd Kühne, as well as articles archived in the *Chronik*.

264 'As part of the celebrations, the local schoolchildren . . .' This poem is featured in an article archived in Volume 3 of the *Chronik*, page 50.

267 'At the age of fourteen, Bernd . . . was inducted into the party's senior youth movement, the Freie Deutsche Jugend . . .' The FDJ was formed on 7 March 1946 as the party's youth league. By 1989, 2.3 million were members of the FDJ, close to 90 per cent of the DDR's fourteen-to-twenty-five-year-olds.

269 'These two agreements . . . on 17 May 1972 . . .' It was around this time that Elsie Harding took her daughter Vivien to see the lake house. It was then impossible, however, to visit, given its location within East Germany's border security zone, so they drove to the West Berlin side of the Groß Glienicke Lake to look at the house. Vivien later recalled that her mother held a pair of binoculars to her eyes and pointed to her old house just visible above the Berlin Wall on the other side of the lake. 'That is Glienicke, that is the house,' she said. 'You can see how close the house was to the lake, you can see how beautiful the surround-

ings are.' Frustrated by not being able to visit and inspired by her mother's stories, Vivien said that she felt a mixture of powerful emotions. Her mother, by contrast, appeared cool and businesslike. While she was willing to show the house – it was a physical object, a fact of history – she was not willing to express feelings.

270 'Not long after . . . Wolfgang began drinking heavily again . . .' These memories were shared by Irene Kühne when I met her with her son Bernd at her Potsdam apartment in the summer of 2014.

271 'His moods became dark and bitter . . .' The Fuhrmanns do not remember any abuse or violence taking place between the Kühnes while they were at the house between 1958 and 1965. 'It was a wooden house,' Lothar said, 'we would have heard such a thing.' If Irene's memories are correct, then Wolfgang's abuse likely started after the Fuhrmanns left in 1965.

272 'Eventually, Wolfgang used . . .' The word 'connections' was commonly used within the DDR as a euphemism for contact with powerful, secret or criminal individuals. Such individuals might work freelance on the black market or might be operating officially through the army, the Stasi or other government service.

Chapter 25

274 'Before competitions, Bernd drank a special vegetable soup that had been carefully prepared by his coaches . . .' Anabolic steroids were widely distributed to athletes in the DDR, including children. They were often taken orally, in the form of a pill, and the recipients were typically unaware of what they were taking. Though particularly prevalent in sports such as swimming, track and field athletes were also given such drugs. According to the Institute of Biochemistry, at the German Sport University in Cologne, the synthetic anabolic steroid has numerous side effects, including increased risk of a heart attack, liver damage, mascu-

linisation of women (deepening of voice, hair growth and infertility), and in men, erectile dysfunction and prostate disease. Some have estimated that as many as 10,000 DDR athletes were doped.

275 'One spring evening in 1977 . . .' Around this time, on 28 January 1977, a child who attended the Groß Glienicke school, located next to the Wall, was struck by a stray bullet. According to the Stasi report, the shot came from a nearby rifle range. The injured child was taken to hospital and later recovered. See Stasi Archive in Berlin (File: MfS ZAIG 23717).

275 'Having mounted his black two-stroke Simson . . .' Simson was a German company which produced popular guns, bicycles, motorcycles and cars. During the period of National Socialism, the company was seized from its Jewish owners, the Simsons. The Simson became one of the best-selling mopeds during the DDR period. The bikes were produced in Suhl until 2002.

278 'Finally, Bernd had had enough . . .' The date that the couple moved into the Drei Linden is noted in Bernd's Stasi file. According to the file, Gaby officially moved into the apartment on 27 May 1981, a few months before their marriage, but in practice, she lived with Bernd from the start.

279 'As such, it was located within the *Grenzgebiet* . . .' The request to move to the border security zone was noted in Bernd's Stasi file, stating that 'There are no restrictions for him to move to the border zone'. A note in Bernd's file on Gaby added that 'There are no contrary indications from her work history'.

280 'On his last day in the army, on 28 October 1983 . . .' Bernd's Stasi file records his army record as follows: 'Army – 2 STK – Soldier – 4.5.1982–28.10.1983'. See Stasi Archive, Berlin (File: MfS BV PDM, Abt XIX, ZMA 3218).

281 'particularly a certain kind of Lada . . .' The Lada car that Bernd was referring to was probably the Lada 2107, the luxury model that was frequently driven by members of the Stasi.

Chapter 26

283 'They also co-founded the Groß Glienicke Carnival Club . . .' According to the editor of the *Chronik*, the Carnival took place on 5 March 1987 and Bernd 'took it very seriously, and that is why the event was so successful'.

287 'He had heard of people trying to escape . . .' There were other escape attempts in the village, some of which were known to Bernd and some not. Detailed reports were compiled by the Stasi of each known attempt. Here are two examples. On 23 June 1971, an unnamed typesetter, who was married and had two children, drove towards the Wall in the forest just north of the village. Dropping his motorbike, he walked towards 'B Tower', reaching the Wall at 20.38. He was immediately shot at, with fifty-four rounds fired. He was not hurt. At 21.20 he was arrested and later imprisoned. According to the file, the attempt was prompted by 'his family breaking apart, and unhappiness at his workplace'. Another escape attempt took place on 3 August 1987, this time ten kilometres north of the village, at 02.15. Three people between twenty and twenty-four years old climbed over the Wall using a ladder. Seven shots were fired by border guards but nobody was injured. A letter was later found at one of the successful escapees' homes. It read: 'A bird in a cage cannot be happy.' These files can be found at the Stasi Archive in Berlin (Files: MfS HAII 4647 and MfS HAI 14441).

288 'The most famous local escape incident . . .' Details of this case can be found in the Stasi Archive in Berlin, including a trove of newspaper articles, as well as a copy of the Stasi preliminary report (Files: MfS HAIX 5529 and MfS ZKG 1477).

289 'The Stasi's initial report . . .' This report can be found at the Stasi Archive [Files: MfS HAIX 5529 and MfS ZKG 1477].

289 'Ulrich Steinhauer's death . . .' For years, the case wound its way through the West German court system, with Bunge's sentence, much to the dismay of East Germany, gradually reduced from murder to

manslaughter, as the courts tried to balance his right for freedom with Steinhauer's right to life. Complicating matters, Bunge's testimony was deemed questionable when a forensic team found that Steinhauer had been shot in the back. But there were also problems with the DDR evidence, given that the border patrol had removed the body soon after the shooting, only to return it later that day, to allow West German television cameras to film it. Moreover, the border patrol could not remember where they had first discovered the two guards' weapons.

289 'Yet it was another escape . . .' Details of this event come from Bernd Kühne, as well as General Hans Dieter Behrendt, who was in charge of the Glienicke Bridge at the time of escape, and who I interviewed in the summer of 2014.

Chapter 27

293 'With each day, the pressure mounted . . .' According to Hans Dieter Behrendt, 'The situation in DDR was shit! And we all knew it. We knew Honecker was weak, something had to happen, everyone knew that things could not continue as they were, all the institutions – Stasi, military, government, regiment, police – were all fighting each other.'

294 'the kommandant tried to call the central office . . .' Peter Kaminski suspects that this break in communication was caused by some senior members of the Stasi who wanted to stop the revolution from taking place. Hans Dieter Behrendt vehemently denies this, saying that the Stasi never stopped communications.

294 'Calling the border guards in Staaken . . .' According to Hans Dieter Behrendt, the kommandant of the border regiment in Groß Glienicke gave permission for pedestrians to cross the border but not cars. He disagrees with Major Kaminski on this. He says that in charge that day was a border guard called Horst Wieting, who called passport central control in Berlin for advice when the cars turned up, and said that he 'didn't know what to do'. Their response was simple: 'Open the border.'

297 'Hans Dieter Behrendt, the officer in charge of the Glienicke Bridge . . .'
In the days after the fall of the Wall, Behrendt visited a newly opened
border crossing and found East and West German guards sitting together
drinking coffee. When they saw a senior officer arrive, the guards jumped
up and apologised. 'We are so sorry,' they said. Behrendt told them to
relax. 'Don't worry, drink, eat.' Later he told his boss, who reprimanded
him about the lack of discipline, but Behrendt replied: 'You can't tell
me what to do any more.'

Chapter 28

301 'Long-term Groß Glienicke residents now found strangers . . .' The
West German press was bursting with articles proffering advice on how
to regain land in the East. One headline on 9 February 1990 read: TENS
OF THOUSANDS WHO HAVE LOST EVERYTHING IN DDR ASK THE QUES-
TION 'HOW CAN I GET MY CONFISCATED PROPERTY BACK?' Another
read: THE WEST REAL ESTATE AGENTS ARE ALREADY WAITING FOR
STARTING ORDERS! Another: HALF OF THE ALEX [ALEXANDERPLATZ]
WITH THE MAST BELONGS TO US! Such articles advised their readers
that 'West German companies can buy land in DDR' and 'West Germans
can inherit plots of land from children, parents, siblings'.

302 'His efforts were recognised in November 1962, when the German
government . . .' His former creative director, Hanns Hartmann, received
this same award on 30 January 1959.

302 'In an interview with the *Telegraf*. . .' In this same interview, in which
he was asked about his current efforts, Will Meisel said, 'I still have ideas
for musicals but nobody is interested any more.' Turning to Eliza, the
journalist asked about her career, pointing out that when she was a
young starlet she had appeared in the film *Paganini* and had received
more fan mail than the heart-throb Iván Petrovich, and in another film,
Petersburg Nights, a critic had described her as 'blindingly beautiful'. 'I
am here now fully for my husband,' said Eliza demurely. 'That is what

he likes because he always wants to be centre of the family.' Meisel added that he had given his wife a box set of her recorded songs for her birthday, and then, somewhat mournfully, that he had 'mixed feelings' about the past, because it reminded him that time was 'volatile' and 'transient'.

302 'He was taken to Müllheim Hospital . . .' Will Meisel was buried in the Wilmersdorf cemetery, in West Berlin, and a memorial service was held in Neukölln, in the south-east of the city. Once his will was read, it became clear that the business, including his songs from the 1930s and 1940s, would remain in the family, and would be owned equally by Peter and Thomas Meisel. In September 1967, close to what would have been his seventieth birthday, an exhibition of Meisel's work, including photographs, films and songs, was held at the Wilmersdorf town hall.

303 'Yet their father's death did not dampen his sons' drive . . .' On 22 January 1977, *Billboard* – the top-selling American music weekly – included a thirty-one-page promotional feature celebrating the fiftieth anniversary of Edition Meisel. This included a short biography of Will Meisel, a history of his company, and interviews with his sons. This *Billboard* special also featured over fifty adverts bearing congratulations and good wishes from music publishers and studios around the world, including EMI, CBS and Warner (WEA). Many of the personal messages came from Jewish music executives – such as industry legends Don Kirshner and Morris 'Mo' Levy. One of these adverts was paid for by Aaron Schroeder, a Jewish publisher who had written seventeen of Elvis's songs, including five that went to number one. In his full-page spread, Schroeder wrote: 'Dear Peter and Trudi, Meisel-tov!'

305 'Her [Cordula] father and uncle had advised . . .' On 21 October 1995, Klaus Munk (Cordula's uncle) wrote to Frank Harding (Elsie's son). In this letter, Klaus Munk makes it clear that, as far as he is concerned, the lake house still belonged to the Alexanders, describing it as 'your house'. Yet despite his appeal for an 'exchange of information' and an appeal

to learn the 'view' of their former neighbours, Klaus Munk never heard back from the Alexanders. Believing that they were attempting to repossess the house, Klaus Munk assumed that the family was busy fighting with the German legal system and did not have time to respond to him.

310 'One of Kaminski's first acts . . .' The Groß Glienicke council first decided that the area near the lake should be a public area on 20 June 1990. It took some time for this decision to become part of the local plan.

Chapter 29

311 'She was accompanied by six of her grandchildren . . .' There were eight of us on the Berlin trip: my cousins James, Alexandra and Deborah, my sisters Amanda and Kate, my fiancée Debora, myself and Elsie. I recorded the visit on a video camera, but lost the tape on my return. Twenty years later, while researching this story, I found it.

312 'she had soon returned to work . . .' Elsie's customers were sent over by Globetrotters, a Hamburg-based travel agency. That they were mostly elderly Germans gave her great satisfaction, partly because she had power over them, partly because she was making money off them, and partly because she could spend endless hours telling them how proud she was of her adopted country, of Britain's religious and cultural tolerance, of their long respect for democracy, and how they had generously given her and her family refuge from Nazi Germany. When asked how it was that she spoke such wonderful German, Elsie would tell them, 'I went to school in Berlin.' When they invariably asked, 'Aren't you homesick?' she would say, 'You can only throw me out once.' About halfway between London and Edinburgh, Elsie liked to stop off at Coventry Cathedral – where the locals called her the 'Rabbi of Coventry' – and lecture her German audience on the terrible bombings that had destroyed this city, and of the stoicism its people had showed in rebuilding their lives. Whenever one of the Germans made the point that the British

had laid similar waste to Dresden and Berlin, Elsie would pounce, reminding them of the tyranny of the Nazi state and the millions who had been murdered in the Holocaust. Another perk of the job, given that her customers were typically elderly men and women, was that by talking incessantly into the microphone at the front of the coach, Elsie was able to delay the passengers' toilet breaks. In this small way, she wreaked revenge on the German tourists.

316 'The end to the British rule at Gatow was marked on 27 May 1994 . . .' On 27 May 1994, *The Times* ran a feature under the headline PRINCE'S BERLIN PARADE MARKS BRITISH RETREAT. According to the article, the British had taken over Gatow when Berlin was 'still a labyrinth of bombed streets', and for the British soldiers now leaving, 'the withdrawal is no great tragedy'. But the closure of the base was significant, the article concluded, because 'some vital connection between Britain and Berlin is being severed. The old names and buildings were the hallmark not only of an occupying but also a protecting power, most apparent during the Berlin airlift of the Cold War years.'

317 'Over the next few years, the NVA barracks . . .' Established in 1992, the *Panzerhalle* became a haven for artists, sculptors and illustrators. The studio comprised five hundred square metres of floor space, a vaulted ceiling that was two storeys high, and enormous doors which could accommodate even the largest artwork. In 2008, the tearing down of the artists' squat provoked considerable protests and attracted wide coverage from local and national media. A smaller artists' studio and exhibition space now exists, situated in one of the brick buildings at the former barracks. In 2015, it was announced that some of the remaining barracks would be used to house refugees from Syria.

Chapter 30

320 'Inge Kühne decided to move out . . .' In August 2014, Sylvia Fiedler, a long-time resident of Groß Glienicke and local journalist, sent me an

email arguing that the local residents should be forgiven for not taking better care of their properties and pointed out that life was in some ways better before reunification. 'In DDR we could not buy building materials, pipes, pins, planks, taps and so on in a shop,' she wrote. Despite the problems, 'most houses and properties looked good until 1990'. After reunification, the villagers found it hard to maintain their homes, given that many of them lost their jobs overnight. 'Certainly it was not the deliberate will of the former residents of the lake house to destroy the house.' She added that to many, the DDR offered real benefits that West Germany did not have, including free childcare and healthcare, cheap food and full employment.

324 'One favourite was "Dark Place" by Böhse Onkelz . . .' The rock group Böhse Onkelz drew considerable controversy, particularly in their early years. Founded in 1980, they were associated with the skinhead culture and accused of promoting violence and nationalism. During the 1990s, they were banned by the large German retail stores, Media Markt and Saturn. By the end of the decade, the group repaired their image by repeatedly denouncing extremism. To date they have produced over twenty gold- and nine platinum-selling songs.

Chapter 31

335 'Someone drew a hammer and sickle and the letters YPA . . .' The Yugoslav People's Army was the military services of the Socialist Federal Republic of Yugoslavia, founded in 1945 and disbanded in 1992 with the break-up of Yugoslavia.

Chapter 32

339 'When he had mastered the loop, Chris . . .' Chris Grunert continues to participate in motocross championships. He hopes to compete professionally some day.

344 'It was around this time that a few of the original lakeside homeowners
. . .' On 15 July 1996, members of the expanded Bundestag passed the
Mauergrundstücksgesetz, or the Wall Land Law, enabling owners to
purchase the land that had been taken from them at 25 per cent of the
market value. Some Groß Glienicke landowners chose to purchase the
land back. Many did not even know that they could. Some of those
who had lived at the lake the longest now complained that they had
purchased the land twice, once in the 1930s and again in 1996.

344 'A few took more aggressive action . . .' One such resident was Peter
Daniel, a professor of medicine who lived two hundred metres south
of the lake house. A few days after he blocked the lakeshore path that
ran behind his house, a group of protesters gathered outside waving
placards, with slogans that read 'Blocking the way is violence' and 'Free
the shore at Groß Glienicke Lake'. Daniel was nervous enough to call a
security company who stationed a couple of guards by his fence next
to the trail. The following week, on Easter Monday 2010, over three
hundred protesters gathered outside the Daniels' house. This time there
was a police presence to witness a local politician shouting 'With the
lake we have a pearl' through his megaphone. Peter Daniel then came
out to speak to the protesters. It's unclear what happened next, although
Daniel believes he was struck on the head with a hard object, perhaps
a bottle. Injured, he was taken to hospital where the doctors diagnosed
concussion. The suspect, whom the police had arrested, was cleared of
charges by a local court. After that incident, the protests became less
intense as the issue moved from the lakeshore to the courts. Daniel
removed his barrier, although he would continue to tell those walking
or cycling by that they were trespassing.

BIBLIOGRAPHY

Agee, Joel. *Twelve Years.* American-born writer describes living in Groß Glienicke from 1948 to 1953.

Alexander, John. *A Brief Measure of Time.* A self-published history of the Alexander family.

Anonymous. *Woman in Berlin.* Brutal description of life during Soviet occupation.

Applebaum, Anne. *Iron Curtain.* A landmark work detailing the history of Eastern Europe from 1944 to 1956.

Ash, Timothy Garton. *The File.* A powerful personal investigation focusing on the author's own Stasi file.

Biddiscombe, Perry. *The Denazification of Germany: A History 1945–1950.* Overview of denazification process by American, French, Soviet and British powers.

Clare, George. *Berlin Days, 1946–1947.* Memoir that covers post-war Berlin and includes a passage on Clare's time working for the British denazification commission on Schlüterstrasse.

Clark, Christopher. *The Sleepwalkers: How Europe Went to War in 1914.* Ground-breaking history of the lead-up to the First World War.

Fallada, Hans. *Alone in Berlin*. Brilliant fictional account of life in Berlin during the Second World War.

Fesel, Anke, and Keller, Chris. *Berlin Wonderland*. Pictures of Berlin after the fall of the Wall, from 1990 to 1996.

Fontane, Theodor. *Wanderungen Durch die Mark Brandenburg*. Classic recollections of travels through Brandenburg by one of Germany's best-loved writers. The third volume describes his visit to Groß Glienicke.

Fulbrook, Mary. *The People's State: East German Society from Hitler to Honecker*. A useful introduction to life in the DDR.

Funder, Anna. *Stasiland: Stories from Behind the Berlin Wall*. Introduction to world of East Germany's security service through the eyes of an outsider.

Gerber, Rolf. *Recollections and Reflections*. Self-published memoir by a friend of Elsie Harding.

Gilbert, Martin. *Churchill: A Life*.

———. *Kristallnacht: Prelude to Destruction*. What took place on 9/10 November 1938 in Germany.

Groß Glienicker *Kreis. Jüdische Familien in Groß Glienicke. Eine Spurensuche*. History of Jewish families in Groß Glienicke researched by residents of the village. Booklet available from Groß Glienicker *Kreis*.

Hass, Michael. *Forbidden Music*. Review of Jewish composers during the Nazi period.

Haupt, Michael. *Villencolonie Alsen am Großen Wannsee*. An introduction to various houses and villas close to the Wannsee; includes interesting photographs.

Kalesse, Andreas, and Duncker, Ines. *Der Gutspark von Groß Glienicke*. History of the Groß Glienicke estate, booklet published by the city of Potsdam.

von Kalm, Harold. *Das preußische Heroldsamt*.

Kempe, Frederick. *Berlin 1961*. One year at the heart of the Cold War.

Kershaw, Ian. *The End: Germany 1944–1945*. Details the story of the war's end.

Ladd, Brian. *The Ghosts of Berlin*. Review of changing architecture of modern Berlin.

Laude, Ernst and Annelies. *Groß Glienicke – Geschichte und Geschichten*. History of the village by former editors of the *Chronik*. Booklet available from Groß Glienicker *Kreis*.

Lehmberg, Otto, and Toreck, Renate. *Groß Glienicke im Wandel der Zeit*. A history of Groß Glienicke through the ages. Booklet available from Groß Glienicker *Kreis*.

Leo, Maxim. *Red Love: The Story of an East German Family*. Provides insight into ordinary life behind the Wall.

Naimark, Norman. *The Russians in Germany*. A history of Germany during Soviet occupation, 1945–1949.

Nooteboom, Cees. *Road to Berlin*. Memoir of Dutch journalist's return to Berlin.

Peukert, Detlev. *The Weimar Republic*. A history of Germany, from 1918 to 1933.

Richie, Alexandra. *Faust's Metropolis: A History of Berlin*. Definitive account of Germany's capital city.

Schmidt, Bernhard. *Ein Interesse weckt nur noch das Altarbild*. History of church in Groß Glienicke by its pastor.

Schrader, Helena. *The Blockade Breakers*. Introduction to the Berlin Blockade and Gatow airfield.

Schroeder, Rudi. *100 Years of Will Meisel*. Self-published history of Will Meisel and Edition Meisel, includes CDs with composer's music.

Taylor, Frederick. *The Berlin Wall*. Introduction to life before, during and after the Wall.

——. *Exorcising Hitler*. Description of denazification process, including post-war tribunals.

Walters, Guy. *Berlin Games: How Hitler Stole the Olympic Dream*. Useful review of the Berlin summer Olympics and its background.

Woodhead, Leslie. *My Life as a Spy*. Memoir by documentary film-maker includes his time as an intelligence gatherer in Gatow.

von Wysocki, Gisela. *Wir machen Musik: Geschichte einer Suggestion*. Daughter of music producer Georg von Wysocki provides insight into living in Groß Glienicke from 1940 to 1948.

ACKNOWLEDGEMENTS

My research really started with the villagers of Groß Glienicke, and one person in particular, Sonja Richter. It was Sonja who first told me that the house was in poor condition. It was Sonja who helped me find the Gestapo's files on Dr Alexander which were buried in the Potsdam archives. And it was Sonja who introduced me to the initial village contact that led to a chain of interviews. First, there was Burkhard Radtke who lived behind the lake house, who in turn set up a meeting with Bernd Kühne. From Bernd, I found his mother, brother and sisters, and Roland Schmidt. Through Sonja, I also met the village pastor, who in turn made the phone calls to Wilhelm Stintzing, the hundred-year-old priest who had worked for decades in the village, along with Günther Wittich, the man who remembered playing in the schloss in the 1930s and the day the Canadian parachutist fell near the lake during the war. The chain went on: the village mayor, the president and volunteers of the *Kreis*, the current editors of the *Chronik*, the farmer whose house was bombed during the war. The network of contacts and interviewees grew, but none of it would have happened without Sonja.

Enormous thanks are due to Moritz Gröning. I first met Moritz at his family's house in Groß Glienicke, which Moritz and his family have beautifully restored and which itself has Denkmal status. Since that time, Moritz has petitioned politicians, architects and members of the community to help protect the house, as well as helping to restore the house himself. Moritz and his wife Friederike, along with their children Ferdinand, Helene and Johann, have welcomed me into their home on too many occasions to count, and have made me feel like I was part of the community. The lake house would not have been saved without Moritz.

It wasn't easy to find members of the Wollank family. People in the village questioned whether there were even any living descendants. To track them down, I hired a researcher. After some time he discovered a distant cousin who had compiled a family history. It was from this source that I was able to locate Helmut von Wollank, the son of Horst and grandson of Otto von Wollank. Now residing in Kirschroth, a small town in western Germany, Helmut lives alone since his wife died in 2014. In a series of telephone calls, though disinclined to talk about the past, Helmut shared his story.

A few days later, I met Helmut von Wollank's son Markus in a small cafe on the northern edge of Berlin's Tiergarten park. A celebrity reporter, who socialises with the likes of Kylie Minogue, Uma Thurman and Paris Hilton, Markus told me that his family had not returned to Groß Glienicke for decades. 'Going back there would bring waves of happiness and sadness,' he said between sips of mint tea. 'It would make me melancholic.' Instead, he prefers to live in the present. Despite his own hesitancies about the village, Markus said that he would like to see the lake house restored.

It was far simpler to make contact with the Meisels. The family business, Edition Meisel, is still going, and the contact information is readily available from their website. Following a series of emails, I met up with the grandson of Will Meisel, Sven Meisel, who is now running the company, from the headquarters in Berlin. From this and other conversations, I was able to construct a family history. Eliza Meisel died two years after her husband, on 8 July 1969. They are both buried in the Wilmesdorf cemetery in Berlin. Their sons continued to run the family music business until their deaths: Peter in 2010 and Thomas in 2014. Sven is Thomas Meisel's son. Though he has no memories of the house himself, Sven accompanied me on a visit to the lake house with his wife, daughter and dog. He was surprised by its size. 'It is much bigger than it looks from the outside,' he said. He and his family are supportive of the restoration of the house.

Once I learned that Hanns Hartmann had worked for West German Broadcasting, I was able to make contact with the broadcaster, and from there was quickly put in touch with the archivist who manages Hartmann's personal papers. From those, it was possible to reconstruct his life story. The archivist was extremely helpful, sending me a copy of Hanns Hartmann's short unpublished memoir, as well as letters he had exchanged with Will Meisel.

Lothar and Sieglinde Fuhrmann still live a mere two hundred metres from the house. After the Wall came down, Lothar worked as a caretaker in a local children's home and Sieglinde in the post office. Now retired, they spend their days pottering around their garden or visiting their grandchildren. While they worry about the cost of renovation, they would like to see the lake house restored to its former glory.

I first met Bernd Kühne in the courtyard of the Drei Linden (now called the Hofgarten Hotel). He still lives in Groß Glienicke with his wife. When I spoke to him about the house, he cried, remembering the wonderful childhood he'd had by the lake. He does not wish to return to the house until it is fully repaired, but he supports its renovation and the idea of the house becoming a cultural centre for the community.

I met his mother, Irene Kühne, now Irene Walters, in her Potsdam apartment. Unlike the untidy state of the lake house when Inge Kühne lived there, Irene's home was impeccably neat and well organised. Since her second husband, Klaus Walter, passed away, Irene has lived by herself. She is not ready to visit the lake house, worried that it will be too upsetting. Once it is renovated, she told me, she would be willing to visit. It had been her home for over a quarter of a century.

Inge Kühne is now living in a home for the elderly in Potsdam. She suffers from Alzheimer's and it is sadly impossible to have a conversation with her. Roland 'Sammy' Schmidt still lives in the village. Now in his thirties, he has no consistent job, though he sometimes works in construction. According to his Facebook page he likes to play poker, supports Manchester United and his favourite movies include *Rambo*, *Rocky* and *Transporter*. He still plays football for the village team, SG Rot-Weiß, for whom he regularly scores. Roland introduced me to Marcel Adam, who had lived with him at the house for over a year from 1999 to 2000. I met Marcel at a coffee shop in Potsdam. He told me that he had known Roland since fifth grade, when he was ten years old. Marcel now works repairing boats for competitive rowers at the Potsdam Boat Club. When asked about the freewheeling lifestyle of his late teens, Marcel told me that this was 'the best period of my life, I would like to do it again, but maybe for not as long'. In April 2015, Marcel took part in the second Clean-up Day at the house, spending hours clearing bushes and weeds from the pond which Wolfgang Kühne had installed decades before.

To my great relief, I was able to make contact with the Munk family early on. From an old letter written in the 1990s, I found the telephone number for Professor Fritz Munk's son, Klaus, and made the call. A woman answered the phone. It was Klaus's widow. When I explained who I was, she said that she knew all about the Alexanders and recommended I speak to her daughter, Bettina Munk, who still lived at the lake. A few weeks later I was eating dinner with Bettina and her cousin Cordula, who have separate houses on the parcel next to the lake house. I was struck by how easily we fell into familiarity, that despite an absence of seventy years, and the span of two generations, they both felt like neighbours. It was from Cordula and Bettina that I found out about the history of the Munk family. It was also through the Munks that I met Chris Partsch, a formidable Berlin lawyer, who helped unearth Wolfgang's Stasi files and set up the Alexander Haus charity for us.

From the start, my family has been very generous with their mementos and artefacts. My grandmother's diary, the photographs of the house, the audio recordings with my great-aunts and -uncles, Dr Alfred Alexander's memoir, Erich's uncle Max's memoir, letters between Bella and Harold, Elsie and Erich, as well as items from the house itself, all of these have been invaluable in helping piece together this story. There are too many family members to mention, but I wish to extend my heartfelt thanks to my entire family, for trusting me with this project and for their continuing support.

Elsie died in 2004, at home in her bed in north London. I was sitting next to her at the time, the only person in the room. Right at the very end I told her, in a whisper, 'I love you, Granny, I love you.' She squeezed my hand before letting out her last breath. Elsie left her grandchildren certain items in her will. I was given an envelope containing two olive-green passports, and a scrap of fabric embroidered with the letter 'J'.

I would like to thank all those who helped me in the many archives in which I researched, including: Zeitungsabteilung der Staatsbibliothek in Berlin, Stadtarchiv Potsdam, Grundbuchamt Potsdam, Brandenburgisches Landeshauptarchiv in Potsdam, Landesarchiv Berlin, Geheimes Staatsarchiv Preußischer Kulturbesitz in Berlin, Potsdam Planning Department and Monument Authority archives, Bundesarchiv Berlin, National Archives in London. Hauptstaatsarchiv in Dresden, Historisches Archiv des Westdeutschen Rundfunks in Cologne, the Stasi archives held by the Der Bundesbeauftragte für die Unterlagen des Staatssicherheitsdienstes der ehemaligen Deutschen Demokratischen Republik in Berlin, Militär Historisches Museum Flugplatz in Gatow, the Deutsche Kinemathek – Museum für Film und Fernsehen in Berlin, Yad Vashem in Jerusalem and the Imperial War Museum in London. I also made use of the private Alexander family, Edition Meisel and Wollank family archives.

I would like to thank my hard-working research assistants, Johanna Biedermann, Julia Boehlke, Daniel Bussenius and Maren Richter. Thanks to Dabney Chapman, Catherine Dring, Sheridan Marshall and Kirsten Ackermann-Piëch for their help with translations. I am also grateful to the many others who helped me, including: Joel Agee, John Alexander, Patrick Bade, Peter Benjamin, Birgit Bernard, Captain Jan Behrendt, Bettina Biedermann, Dieter Dargies, Alexandra and Robert Datnow, Heribert Dieter, Albrecht Dümling, Sophie D. Fleisch, Dr Thomas Gayda, Marion Godfrey, Peter and Michael Goldberger, Michael Haas, Martin Luchterhandt, Astrid Möser, Mareike Notarp, Julia Riedel, Kate Weinberg, Chris Weitz, Rose Wild and Raymond Wolff.

Thanks also to the interviewees not already mentioned: Hans Joachim Bartel, Hans Dieter Behrendt, Peter Daniel, Peter Kaminski, Sylvia Fiedler, Suzanne and Volker Grunert, Frank Harding, Professor Christoph and Dorothea Kleßmann, Annelies Laude, Vivien Lewis, Peter Munk, Andreas Potthoff, Betty Rajak, Dr Bernhard Schmidt, Professor Helga and Rochus Schütz, Malte Spohr, Wilhelm Stintzing, Winfried Sträter, Peter Sussmann, Günther and Heinz Wittich, and Dr Gisela von Wysocki.

My gratitude also to the city of Potsdam and the state of

Brandenburg, for their belief in our efforts to save the Alexander Haus, to transform it into a place of remembrance and reconciliation. In particular, my thanks to Jann Jakobs, Matthias Klipp, Frank Scheffler, Saskia Hueneke, Birgit Morgenroth, Klara Geywitz and Pete Heuer. Also to Andreas Kalesse, and his team at the city of Potsdam's historic monument department, Jörg Limberg, Sabine Ambrosius and Matthias Kartz.

To my readers, thanks as ever: Lucy and Zam Baring, Rupert Levy, Angela and Michael Harding, Amanda Harding, James Harding, Jane Hill, Dominic Valentine and Amelia Wooldridge.

Having been published, I realise that it is truly a team effort. So first, a shout out to those who are rarely acknowledged: the book-sellers, sales execs, designers, accountants, administrators, and all the others who have helped get this book into the hands of the readers. Next, a truly enormous 'thank you' to my editor, the always good-humoured and tirelessly working Tom Avery (William Heinemann), who was nobly helped by Anna-Sophia Watts. To Anna DeVries (Picador USA), who offered sound advice on the manuscript, and Andrea Woerle (DTV Germany), for all her enthusiastic assistance. To Glenn O'Neill for his superb cover, Emma Finnigan for her publicity brilliance, Darren Bennett for the maps, Neil Cunning for the illustrations, and for their much-appreciated support, Tom Weldon and Gail Rebuck. Thanks especially to my incredible agent, Patrick Walsh, and his superb team of international agents. I really did see a badger running along the border patrol footpath.

Finally, to my daughter Sam, it was a joy to see how much you loved spending time in Berlin, and my wife Debora, for her continued support, brilliant editorial contributions and, most importantly, for her love.

INDEX

Page numbers in *italics* refer to illustrations.

INDEX

INDEX

INDEX

ABOUT THE AUTHOR

THOMAS HARDING is an author and journalist who has written for the *Financial Times, The Sunday Times, The Washington Post,* and *The Guardian,* among other publications. His #1 internationally bestselling book *Hanns and Rudolf* won the 2015 Jewish Quarterly-Wingate Prize, was shortlisted for the 2013 Costa Book Award Biography prize, and is being translated into more than twenty languages.